DISCORD IN ZION

DISCORD IN ZION

CONFLICT BETWEEN ASHKENAZI & SEPHARDI JEWS IN ISRAEL

G. N. GILADI

SCORPION PUBLISHING LONDON

© G N Giladi 1990

Based on the Arabic edition first published in Egypt under
the title *Isra'il nahwa al-infijar al-dakhili* by Dar Al-Bayadir, Cairo,
1988, and the English translation by R Harris,
revised and updated by the author.

First published in 1990 by Scorpion Publishing Ltd,
Victoria House, Buckhurst Hill, Essex, England.

ISBN 0 905906 87 X

Editor: Leonard Harrow
Typeset by Nuts and Muttons Typesetting Limited,
Linton, Cambridgeshire, in Linotype Bembo
Printed on Astolat 80gsm
Printed and bound in England by Biddles, Guildford

Contents

Foreword

I am a Sephardi Israeli whose family has lived in the Middle East from time immemorial. In my youth I belonged to the most 'pioneering' section of the Jewish community and lived on various kibbutzim which were the power base of the Israeli Labour Party. Although I suffered occasional racial discrimination, I was led to believe that we were gradually building a just and caring society based on human and Jewish brotherhood. I even neglected my Arabic language and Middle Eastern culture for the sake of 'unity' and in the desire to be 'accepted' or 'included'. I was wrong.

My first doubts started in 1948 when I witnessed the mass expulsion of Palestinians, men, women and children, most of whom did not take part in the fighting. I also saw the last living inhabitants of Deir Yasin, paraded along Jaffa Street in Jerusalem, before they were shot.

The next shock occurred in the early 1950s when Israel reduced hundreds of thousands of Sephardim from neighbouring countries to utter destitution in terrible camp conditions, while Ashkenazi immigrants from Europe were given comfortable accommodation and jobs.

As a student of Arabic studies of the Hebrew University, Jerusalem, I was appointed special correspondent on the daily Hebrew newspaper *Al-Hamishmar* and the Arabic weekly *Al-Mirsad*. This work enabled me to talk to many Palestinians, citizens of Israel, who were ruined by the laws which confiscated most of their property and put them under military rule.

Continual research since then and the collection of a large number of documents have propelled me to the conclusion that Sephardi

Jews and Palestinians share not only the same language, culture and background, but also the fate of being wronged by the Zionist settlement of Palestine.

Israeli propaganda repeatedly harps upon the acquisition of consumer goods by Sephardim and Ashkenazim (and Palestinians) in Israel but forgets to note that Ashkenazim from poverty stricken eastern European ghettoes have fared far better in relative terms and that the material gap between previously comfortably off natives and the incoming settlers is widening constantly. There is never a positive reference to the world we have lost.

This study will show that the preferential treatment which the Russian immigrants are now (1990) receiving in housing and employment at the material level, and an instant acceptance of their outlook and values on the cultural plane is nothing new: it has been institutionalised since the beginning of Zionist activities in Palestine in the last quarter of the nineteenth century and always at the expense of Sephardim and Palestinians. Its complement is the systematic denigration and degradation of the local peoples and this book attempts to provide a record of this.

Gideon N Giladi
London, 1990

Introduction

The Jews of Israel can be divided into two ethnic groups. The first is the Ashkenazi community, made up of the Zionist colonist minority who emigrated to Palestine mainly from Eastern Europe, and also from Central and Western Europe and America. This community represents the summit of the Zionist ruling establishment's hierarchy, the overwhelming majority in the Cabinet, Parliament, the top civil service and the upper echelons of the trade unions, private and public capital, the Jewish Agency, the military establishment, the cultural elite, the leadership of the police and secret services, the media etc. As a society, this community may be seen to be arrogant, believing in its qualitative and cultural superiority to the Palestinian Arab people and the Arab Islamic Community, including those Jews who came from the Arab countries. Even the 'progressives' who oppose racism can be characterised by their paternalistic attitude towards the inhabitants of the area. The second community is that of the Arab and Islamic Jews or 'Sephardim', representing the majority of Israelis. Some of them are the original inhabitants of Palestine. Religion apart, this community forms an integral part of the Arab nation in its culture and language, ethics, literary models, traditions, homeland and history. Members of this community had lived since antiquity in the region which was to become Dar al-Islam[1] for hundreds of years before the Muslim conquests which liberated them from the burden of the Sasanid and Byzantine empires. In the Arabian Peninsula, and particularly the Yemen, Jews had lived with Arabs since the dawn of history, becoming Arabised.

This community had evolved a highly developed and prosperous

3

urban social structure consisting of powerful merchants, professionals, traders and a large stratum of artisans. The Ashkenazi settlers reduced the bulk of this community to a pool of cheap labour. Subsequently the lot of their children and grandchildren, who were born in Israel, has worsened economically and culturally. The ruling establishment has managed to destroy the social cohesion and ethical values of this community, having already eliminated Arab/Islamic culture and the use of classical Arabic. This was effected by means of a policy seen as built on racism, malevolance, hypocrisy and exploitation of religious sensitivities. Since this community has no homeland except the Islamic homeland, its fate is inexorably tied to the fate of the Islamic community.

Thousands of books have been written about the Palestinian problem and Zionist oppression but the world knows little about the policy of racial discrimination against the Sephardim in Israel because of Zionism's pervading influence. The establishment knew that the dissemination of the facts of the case would damage its reputation in liberal, humanist circles in the West and would block the flow of contributions from Sephardi Jews now living in the West, of whom there are 300,000 in France alone. Zionist spokesmen created the image that the Jews of the Arab world emigrated to Israel because of Arab 'anti-semitism', and that the state now spends billions on 'educating and civilising' since they lived in 'savage and primitive countries.'

The Arab countries generally overlook the problem since they are largely unaware of the cultural differences between the Arab Jews and the Ashkenazis. Sectarian Arabs say 'they are all Jews, and they are all enemies', thereby thinking to have dealt with the problem. At a time when Israel spends millions on intelligence operations to study the sectarian contradictions in the Middle East so that she may exploit them at will, as happened for example in Lebanon and in northern Iraq, the Arab intelligence agencies do not pay much attention to what is happening in Israeli society. Perhaps this is due to a lack of acknowledgement that the majority of the Jews of Israel are not 'foreign settlers', but from the Islamic world. It is my belief that understanding of Israel's sectarian conflict, acknowledgement of the existence of these wronged neighbours and the support of their struggle can bring only credit to the Palestinian people and the Arab nation.

The main subject of this study is the racial discrimination which Sephardim suffer in their employment, housing, education, parliamentary representation, health and social services etc, which has led to popular uprisings and to growing identification with the Palestinian struggle for self-determination.

One of the first problems is what to call this Jewish society which lived, and still lives, in the Islamic world. Israel and its media call it 'the oriental sects' (note the plural). Israel does not recognise the unity of culture of these Jews any more than it recognises the unity of the 'Arab Nation' or the 'Islamic *Umma*'.[2] They also use the term 'oriental' to imply their 'Western' 'superiority', although most of them originated from Eastern Europe. We have used a term familiar in the Arab countries, 'Arab Jews', even though there are many Jews who immigrated from Islamic countries which are not Arab, such as Iran and Turkey. There are others who came from Arab Spain after the fall of the Arab state (1492) when they were expelled along with their Muslim brethren. The Ottoman state took them in and settled them in the Balkans and Turkey (and in Palestine and Syria). These Spanish Jews from the Balkans no longer spoke Arabic, but their culture remained Arab. Therefore, we prefer to term all the Jews from the Arab, Islamic and Balkan countries 'the Jews of Islam'. There is another major reason: starting with the founding of the first Islamic state in Madina and the promulgation of the 'Community Covenant'[3] by the Prophet himself and up until the fall of the Ottoman state, these communities were considered part and parcel of the Islamic *Umma* (see chapter one). In Israel most of the Arab Jews called themselves 'Sephardim', i.e. Spanish Jews, for the Spanish Jewish community in Palestine before the Zionist immigration represented the strongest community of the Arab Jews. The Europeans used the same term to describe them since the Spanish Jews were the main Jewish group to have contact with Europeans during the Middle Ages.

The second problem is that of the exact proportion of Sephardim. Worldwide they are approximately 20 percent of Jews.[4] In Palestine, according to documents used by Eliahu Eliachar, one of the leaders of the community, they represented the majority of the Jews in Palestine before the Ashkenazi Zionist immigration, but in the face of Askhenazi immigration from 1881 on, they dropped to 30 percent by the end of the British Mandate in 1948.[5] However, immigration of Jews from the Arab and Islamic countries since 1948 increased their number to 65 percent of the Jewish population in the 1970s.[6] This statistic accords with that published in Sartre's magazine, *Les Temps Modernes*.[7]

Since the seventies Sephardim numbers have increased to the point where they are now 70 percent. This is supported by two factors. Firstly their rate of natural increase is two and a half times greater than that of the Ashkenazis, and secondly the rate of emigration of Ashkenazis from Israel to the West and particularly to the United States. The number of 'descenders', as those who emigrate are called in Israel, is one of the security secrets of the state. However, Jewish Agency sources and the Israeli press have estimated them to number at least half a million since 1948, and Yasser Arafat has estimated there to be 800,000 of them in America alone – compared with a population of 3.5 million Israeli Jews.[8]

Israel recognises that the Sephardim form the majority, but they do not disseminate the exact official numbers for 'security' reasons, due to the fact that the figure 70 percent might encourage these people to assert their rights. For this reason government statisticians have presented a picture which is deceptive and confusing. They have divided Jews as follows:
1. Those born in Israel to a father born in Israel. In 1985 these were 18.5 percent of the total Jewish population. This group contains both Ashkenazim and Sephardim.
2. Those born in Asia (that is the Arab and Islamic countries of Asia) and their children – 21.3 percent.
3. Those born in Africa (countries of the Maghreb and Egypt) and their children – 22 percent.
4. Those born in Europe and America and their children (this group contains Ashkenazim, Sephardim from the Balkans and Ashkenazi Jews from South Africa) – 38.2 percent.[9]

The official statistics estimate that in the academic year 1969-70, the percentage of Sephardi pupils in elementary school was 61 percent, that of those with a father born in Palestine was 11.9 percent. This latter group is a mix of both communities.[10] If we take into account that a section of the Sephardi pupils generally truanted (see chapter seven), Ashkenazi emigration from Israel and the natural rate of increase of the Sephardim, we can conclude that they may well exceed 70 percent of the total Jewish population. If we add together the numbers of Palestinians in the territories incorporated in 1948, which is 17 percent, the inhabitants of the West Bank, the Gaza Strip, the Golan, occupied Arab Jerusalem and south Lebanon, the percentage of Ashkenazi settlers and their children who were born in Palestine is similar to the percentage of white settlers in South Africa. This means that the overwhelming majority is Arab in culture.

Official policy has claimed that it is transforming the hotch-potch of Jews into one society, racially and culturally. However, the practice continues to strengthen the European settlers at the expense of the Palestinians and the native Jews and is epitomized by the suppression of Arab culture and the extirpation of the Classical Arabic language. In addition, the Ashkenazi community as a whole has opposed integration, believing in their racial and cultural superiority, and 80 percent reject mixed marriages. This has led to a polarisation of the two communities. The Jews from Russia, Poland and Hungary etc. have fused together to form one community, and the Jews who immigrated from Iran in the east to Morocco in the west form the other community – as they did in the era of the Islamic Empires. Despite the fact that the generation which has studied in Zionist schools cannot read or write Arabic (see chapter seven), colloquial Arabic is still alive, especially in the home. To summarise this point, integration can only take place between groups who have equal rights and duties, thereby allowing mutual respect and tolerance to prevail. This integration formerly existed in the Islamic world.

Finally there is an obvious parallel between the cultural and economic schisms. The prevailing colour in the capitalist class is that of the white European, whereas the prevailing colour in the working and poorer classes is that of the dark Arab. The combination of the ethnic and economic gaps leads to increasing polarisation from one generation to the next and pushes Israel towards disintegration and a social explosion.

This study is divided into ten chapters, the first one comprising a summary of the amicable relations between the Arab nation and the Sephardim, *Ahl al-Dhimmah*,[11] since the era of the Prophet, apart from some anomalous events. The creative cultural, economic, social, political and even military cooperation are emphasised. We also allude to the influence of Islamic civilisation and religion on Judaism and Hebrew literature in the lands of Islam. We try to refute the Zionist claims about 'oppression' of the Jews which have been nothing short of character assassination of Arabs and Muslims, and also disprove extremist sectarian Arab charges that the Jews in the Arab world are 'a foreign Zionist enemy group'. The second chapter covers the first clash between Palestinian Jews and the Ashkenazi settlers (1881-1918), with particular reference to the isolation of these settlers from the rest of Palestinian Jewish society, and how their monopolisation of Jewish financial resources for Zionist colonisation led to a deterioration of the economic situation in the community of local Jews. Additionally the matter of the immigration and exploitation of the Jewish Yemenis and the contempt with which they were treated by the settlers is considered. The third chapter summarises the founding of Zionist autonomy with the aid of the British Mandate and how this autonomy prevailed over the native Jews in Palestine. We have tried to analyse the reasons for the failure of the traditional leadership of the Palestinian Jews. In the fourth chapter Jewish resistance to the Zionist Movement in the Arab countries and participation in liberation movements is examined. Factors which led to mass emigration are analysed. We have summarised the sectarian troubles which have facilitated immigration into Israel. These have been exploited to shift the balance of forces in the Middle East in favour of the Zionist entity. Mention is made in this connection of the methods the Israelis used, such as smuggling, terrorism, bribery, deceit and imposture etc. We describe the catastrophic conditions in the displaced persons camps in Aden, Marseilles and Morocco. Chapter five, one of the larger chapters, takes up the tragic conditions of the immigrants in Israeli camps, 'development towns', *moshavim* [cooperative villages] and the 'black belt' – that is in the slum neighbourhoods of the cities – which has led to their being transformed into a 'working class', and manpower for the army. The sixth chapter tackles the absence of representation for the Sephardi Jews in parliament, the cabinet, the upper echelons of government and trade union, economic and military establishments. This chapter makes clear that the few members of parliament and ministers that this community boasts have been appointed by Ashkenazi settlers and do not represent their community. Chapter seven analyses the policy of de-education and de-skilling, and the extirpation of this community's Arab culture. The eighth chapter looks at the racist viewpoints which are hostile to the Sephardi Jews, considering them 'a primitive, savage and base group'. These opinions find their origin in the blind hatred of anything Arab or Islamic. It also discusses the opinion of the extreme left and the communists in the Ashkenazi settler community. Chapter nine describes the speedy economic development in Israel, founded on the exploitation of these immigrants and the confiscation of Palestinian property. It also deals with the socio-economic polarisation between the settlers and the native Jews (and the Palestinian people). Finally, chapter ten details the popular uprisings and the bloody clashes between the native Jews and the Israeli forces of repression, and the appearance of consciousness groups who are joining the Arab Palestinian people and the Palestine Liberation Organization in support of its rights, particularly that of self-determination and the setting up of an independent state. They call for a joint struggle in a common cause.

Some British documents have been used, but we have depended especially on Zionist documentation, Zionist books in Hebrew, Israeli periodicals, mentioned either in this work or its bibliography, and last but not least, we have made use of personal experience and that of friends and relatives.

NOTES
1 The term generally used for those lands where Islam is the preponderant religion, literally meaning 'the abode of Islam'.
2 The *Umma* is the supra-national concept of the spiritual unity of the community of believers.
3 A social contract setting down the forms for human relations.
4 Smooha, 1978, 281.
5 Eliachar, 1980, 291 and *Les Temps Modernes* (Arabic translation 1981), Albaz, 192.
6 Eliachar, 1980, 460.
7 S. Trigano, 10.
8 *Haaretz*, 3 July 1987.
9 *Statistical Abstract of Israel*, Central Bureau of Statistics, 1986, 65.
10 *Statistical Abstract of Israel*, Central Bureau of Statistics, 1980, 595.
11 People of the covenant or obligation, a term first applied only to *Ahl al-Kitab*, i.e. the Jews, Christians and Sabians, and later interpreted to include Zoroastrians and others.

CHAPTER ONE

Historical Harmony Between Jews And Muslims

In the political struggle between Zionism and Arabs, the former exploit the Prophet's quarrel with some of the Jewish tribes of Madina as well as some of the grievances of the Jews in certain parts of the Arab world. Thus we must begin this study with a brief review of the history of Jews within the Islamic community.

Harmony and good-neighbourliness had prevailed in the relations between Muslims and Jews (and Christians) in the Islamic world ever since the Islamic conquests. If there were sectarian grievances, they only occurred on the fringes of the Arab world. It is impossible to appreciate the tolerance of Islam toward the 'people of the book' (the Jews and Christians) unless one contrasts the lot of the Jews under the aegis of Islam to that of the Ashkenazi Jews under the Christian states from the Middle Ages until the fall of Nazi Germany. Despite Ashkenazi Jews' pride in being Europeans, Christian Europe dealt harshly with them, oppressed them, drove them from one country to another and finally built death camps for them. This animosity was not just religious but racial, for the Nazis even killed Jews who had embraced Christianity.

THE PROPHET MUHAMMAD AND THE JEWS

In spite of its religious overtones, the quarrel between the Jews of Madina and the Prophet was political and economic, and was local rather than universal; it only concerned the Jews of Madina. It was of a temporary nature and ended with the defeat of the Jewish tribe Banu Qurayza and the exile of the Jewish tribes of Banu Nadir and al-Qaynuqa' from Madina. The Jewish leadership in Madina was quite affluent, owning fertile land suitable for wheat, barley, vegetables and date palms. In addition, it had great political sway in the balance of power between the two squabbling tribes of Madina, the Aws and the Khazraj. Since most of the Jews had fought on their side, the Aws had previously defeated the Khazraj. Thus, when the Prophet reached Madina surrounded by the poor Emigrants (orphans and widows), the Jewish leadership feared for its wealth and power. This was the basis of the quarrel which ended in victory for the Prophet.

In 628 the Prophet conquered Khaybar, made peace with the Jews there and offered them security. Thereafter no dispute occurred between them. He also offered security to the Jews of Wadi al-Qura and Tayma. They joined the Islamic community with equal rights and obligations according to the Community Covenant, *'Ahd al-Umma*. The historian al-Maqdisi who visited this area in the tenth century tells us that most of its inhabitants were still Jews.

In October 630 the Muslims advanced towards Tabuk to confront the Byzantines. As the conquering Muslim forces passed by Wadi al-Qura, they were greeted by the Jews and provided with water and provisions. Subsequently the Prophet expressed his gratitude to them and offered them special privileges, including a yearly stipend. When he reached Tabuk the Prophet concluded various treaties with the Jewish and Christians inhabitants of al-Jawf, some of whom embraced Islam. The Prophet offered security to Yuhanna, the Christian King of Aylah, and to three Jewish villages, al-Jarba, Adhruh (in eastern Jordan) and Maqna on the Red Sea coast. Then he sent letters to the Yemen and Oman granting security to the Jews and he advised his messengers not to force Islam upon them.

There was no religious dispute in principle, for the Quran recognises the sanctity of the Torah, and equality between Muslims and the People of the Book, since they all believe in God, do good works and receive their recompense from Him. It recognises the right of the protected communities to security: 'Lo! those who believe (in that which is revealed unto thee, Muhammad), and those who are Jews and Christians and Sabaeans – whosoever believeth in Allah and the Last Day and doeth right – surely their reward is with their Lord, and there shall no fear come upon them neither shall they grieve' (*sura* II, 62 and V, 69). This verse was revealed twice in almost identical terms because of its importance in the cause of tolerance towards the revealed religions and the rejection of blind sectarianism. For this reason the Prophet and the caliphs did not compel the Jews and Christians to embrace Islam.

It is true that most of the Jews in the realms of Islam did not embrace Islam, but they did apparently recognise the mission of the Prophet. Among the intellectuals who supported this mission was Abu 'Isa al-Isfahani, who was known in Hebrew as Yitzhak Ben Ya'akov. He lived in the time of Caliph 'Abd al-Malik ibn Marwan. Abu 'Isa said that Muhammad and Jesus were the true prophets and he urged the Jews to study the Quran and the Gospels. Rabbi Shim'on Bar Yohai, who lived at the end of the Umayyad Caliphate said 'Muhammad is the true prophet of God. He was sent out of pity for the Arabs.' The same position was taken by Arab Jewish philosophers such as Ibn Kammuna and Natan'el ibn al-Fayyumi.

The Qaraites (who rejected the Talmud) wrote all their studies in Arabic and their ideas and expression were influenced by Islam. All Jewish philosophy written in the Islamic world was in Arabic, and it constitutes an inseparable part of Islamic philosophy.

The graves of Jewish holy men and prophets are still sacred to both Muslims and Arab Jews. In Morocco it is commonplace to find native Jews visiting the graves of Muslim saints and asking them for favours, and vice versa. In Iraq, ships make a stop out of respect at the grave of Ezra in the south.

It was the Prophet himself who laid the foundation stone of the economic and political relations in the 'Community Covenant', which became a basic law in all Islamic states. According to Ibn Hisham's *Biography of the Prophet*,[1] where he quotes the text of the Covenant from Muhammad Ibn Ishaq's *Biography of the Prophet*, the Jews and the Muslims and their followers constitute one community, each section of which is free to practise its own religion and enjoy protection of life and property. Criminals were excepted from this.

Thus the Islamic state whose basis, from its inception, was not purely religious but also political, encompassed all monotheistic believers. It offered them physical and economic security as well as religious freedom, a form of tolerance that did not occur in Christian European states until the nineteenth century. Catholicism in the Middle Ages believed that Hell was the lot of those who did not grow up in the Church, and for this reason the Christian states did not grant civil rights to members of other religions. In some parts of Europe this state of affairs last until this century.

It should be noted that the Community Covenant does not compel the assimilation of the Muslim and Jewish tribes, but allows each tribe to preserve its essence, leadership, organizations and administration. In this way the Islamic state up to 1918 was decentralised, offering autonomy to all its communities but internally united against crime, murder and plunder and against anti-Islamic hostility from the outside. While Jews were not obliged to join Holy Wars (*jihad*), Islam did impose the *jizya*, or community tax, to cover some of the expenses of security. Arab Jews refused to refute this tax since it gave them rights of safety.

The Quran says that the Jews broke the contract. Some Muslims assume this contract to be the Community Covenant. Others say that it was a contract concluded between God and the Jews of yore. We have already seen that all the agreements completed between the Prophet and the Jews of various towns were based on the principle of the Community Covenant and no Muslim sources claim that Jews (outside Madina) broke it. This applied to the Jews of Iraq, Syria, Palestine, Egypt, North Africa and Spain. All the Jews of these areas welcomed the Islamic revolution which liberated them from Sasanid, Byzantine oppression and that of the Visigoths of Spain.

THE JEWS AND THE ISLAMIC CONQUESTS

In Iraq the large Jewish community represented a spiritual centre for all the Jews of the world for many centuries until the fall of Baghdad to Hulagu[2] in 1258. This community helped the conquering Islamic armies. After the conquest, Islamic rule abolished all the burdens imposed by the Sasanids on the Jews. The exilarch at the time was named al-Bustani. Yazdagird III, the Sasanid king, removed him from office and sentenced him to death, but he was rescued by Islamic troops and restored. His grandchildren stayed in power until the position was finally abolished four hundred years later. As a result of the conquest, Jewish seminaries such as those of Sura and Pumbeditha were reopened. Sura lay to the north of Babylon and Pumbeditha to the south-west of contemporary Baghdad, near the Euphrates. They constituted the most important religious and educational centres for the Jews of the world. The position of *gaon*, the spiritual leader of world Jewry, was also strengthened. He exerted his authority over Jews of the world by means of *responsa*,[3] whereby the Jewish communities would send him questions about various religious, social and educational problems and he would write a long response which in itself became a whole literature. These *responsa* were generally written in Arabic after the accession of Islam. The exilarch was the head of the autonomous administration granted to the Jews in Iraq and the Islamic world in general. His authority increased after Baghdad became the capital of the Islamic empire and the two seminaries were transferred to Baghdad, the capital of the Jewish religion in the Islamic world.

It is indeed strange that not a word came out of this great spiritual centre about the quarrel between the Prophet and the Jews of Madina, all material about which has come to us from Islamic sources. It is probable that Jewish intellectuals in the Fertile Crescent did not accord it any significance. Towards the end of the nineteenth century, a *geniza*, a hidden storeroom, was uncovered in the synagogue in Fustat (Cairo) which contained thousands of Jewish documents, mostly in Arabic. From these emerged some stories about the Prophet, including 'The Prophet's Covenant of Protection' in which the Prophet said that the Jews were his relatives since he was their son-in-law. The Prophet did marry a beautiful Jewish woman from Khaybar called Safiya. Hence, according to the story, 'the Jews fight alongside the Prophet'.

The *Geniza* documents show that the Jews of Syria and Palestine welcomed the Muslim conquerors. At Hims in Syria they helped the Islamic army openly and after the liberation of Jerusalem 70 Jewish families were moved there from Tiberias, then the centre of the Palestinian Jews. For the first time in five hundred years, there were Jews in Jerusalem. The same sources say that 'Umar ibn al-Khattab, the second caliph, visited Jerusalem accompanied by some Rabbis. The position of Jews in Palestine improved immediately after the conquest. Rabbi Yehudai recounted that 'when the Ishmaelites [i.e. the Muslims] came, they allowed the Jews to study the Torah.'[4] The popular Jewish holy man, Rabbi Shim'on Bar Yohai, in his *Nistaroth* observed that "Umar ibn al-Khattab loved the Jews. The angel Metatron reassured him saying "Fear not, O son of Adam, for God Almighty has established the state of Ishmael (i.e. of Islam) to aid you against the sinners."'[5] The same source quotes *Pirqe de Rabbi Eliezer* that 'Bar Yohai confirms the similarity of Jewish and Muslim belief in God and from amongst the seventy peoples that God Almighty has created, He has set his name on two and they are the children of Israel and Ishmael' [i.e. both names end in *el* which means 'God' in Hebrew]. There are other Jewish stories which praise 'Umar ibn al-Khattab in spite of the fact that non-Jewish sources inform us that he exiled the Jews of Khaybar. We have already mentioned that Jews remained in Khaybar until the tenth century. In any case, 'Umar ibn al-Khattab settled some Jews of Khaybar in Kufa, to further the development of trade in this new military town.[6]

In Spain the Jews had suffered such miseries under Visigoth rule that they emigrated to North Africa. Thus they cooperated with Tariq ibn Ziyad.[7] The Spanish writer, F.T.B. de Quiros (p. 17), comments that Tariq ibn Ziyad was a Muslim of Jewish origin, and that many Jews returned to Spain after the Muslim conquest. Cooperation between Arab Jews and Muslims reached its zenith in Andalusia where Jews were prominent in the highest public offices, in poetry, philosophy and trade. They paid the price for this after the fall of the Muslim state in Spain when church, state oppression and torture caused them to leave finally with their Muslim brethren in 1492 and to take refuge in the Ottoman Muslim Empire (especially the Balkans) and North Africa.

In the first century after Mohammad, when northern Syria was exposed to attacks by the Byzantine fleet, the caliphs transferred many Jews from Palestine to Syria and settled them there, depending on the Jews' loyalty against their Byzantine enemies.

When the city of Qayrawan was founded in Tunisia in 670, the ruler of Egypt was ordered to send one thousand Jewish and Christian families in the hope of stimulating its economic development.

When Jerusalem fell at the hands of the Crusaders in 1099, its Jewish and Muslim inhabitants were slaughtered. Geniza sources say that Saladin had an entourage of Jewish advisors with him when he conquered Jerusalem and that he ordered the synagogues of the city to be rebuilt at his expense. They also claim that Richard the Lionheart asked Musa ibn Maymun (Maimonides), who was Saladin's personal physician, to go with him to England as his doctor. Maimonides turned down the offer.

During Ottoman times, the authorities would transfer Jews, particularly those exiles from Spain, to the Christian cities of the Balkans as they conquered them, hoping to use the Jews in their government.

In this fashion, the Arab Jews joined their fate politically to that of the Islam, and thus they flourished, declined and perished together – as was the case in Spain.

In addition to persecution, before Islam, Jews had suffered from political, cultural and economic disruption. After the conquest, the Islamic state united economically and culturally all these countries

15

thereby enabling their Jewish communities to unite and to form one community, that of the 'Jews of Islam', now termed 'Sephardim'.

JEWISH AUTONOMY

Jews in the realms of Islam were granted autonomy in religious, community, cultural and legal affairs as well as the setting and collection of tax. The exilarch in Baghdad represented his people at court, appointed community officials, set taxes and appointed judges. He executed the judgements of the courts against transgressors and criminals, received a weekly stipend which came out of the taxes levied on the markets as well as from Jewish communities inside and outside Iraq. When Imam 'Ali ibn Abi Talib welcomed the *gaon*, Rab Ishaq, in 655, this latter spiritual leader was at the head of a procession of 90,000 Jews who had come to greet the Imam.[8] The office of *gaon* existed from 589 until 1038 when the exilarch made it part of his office. The rise and fall of this Jewish spiritual centre was synchronous with the rise and fall of the 'Abbasid Caliphate.

In 1168, Benjamin of Tudela visited Baghdad and witnessed that the Jewish population of Baghdad had reached 40,000 and that they led secure and prosperous lives under the rule of the great caliph, al-Mustanjid. The Muslims called the exilarch Daniel 'Our Master Ibn Da'ud' (the son of King David). He had been appointed by the caliph as the head of all the Jewish communities.[9] The 'Abbasid caliphate favoured the exilarch over Christian notables, and the caliph set up a special office for him at his court. In his book, *Travels of Rabbi Benjamin* (1173), this Spanish traveller describes how the caliph would receive the exilarch. 'The procession of the exilarch wound its way through the festive streets of Baghdad. 'The community leader wore embroidered silk clothing, with a white jewel-encrusted turban. He had an entourage of horsemen and at a front of the procession was a crier shouting "Clear a path for the master, son of David." When the procession reached the court, the caliph would be standing to receive the exilarch, and would seat him on a throne in front of the caliphal throne. The princes would remain standing in his honour.'

Every Islamic province had its head of Jewish communal affairs, the *nagid*, or prince, just as every Jewish congregation was headed by a *muqaddam*. During the Crusades Arab Jews collected donations to help refugees from Palestine and Syria who had lost everything. Jewish charitable foundations in the Islamic world were organized across the empire, along the lines of Islamic charities.

PARTICIPATION IN GOVERNMENT

Jews were active in the Islamic government apparatus, especially in the financial, commercial and diplomatic departments and, in Spain, also in the military leadership. One of the advantages of Islamic power and government was that the conquering Muslims neither destroyed cultures nor the administration and social apparatus in the countries they conquered, but absorbed them and fashioned them in accordance with their own culture and establishments. Thus Islamic culture flourished. The caliphs allowed Christian and Jewish to continue their work using their own languages such as Greek, and only gradually was the bureaucracy Arabised. Such tolerance was not however purely religious in nature, but represented great political foresight, since the Muslim rulers still formed a minority at that stage.

In his book, *Jews in the Economic and Political Life of Islam in the Middle Ages*,[10] Fischel writes that one caliph in the tenth century changed his vizier fifteen times, but kept the same Jewish treasurer throughout his reign. At that time, most of the bankers in Syria and Egypt were Arab Jews. One of the most important Jewish ministers was Hasdai ibn Shaprut who worked in Andalusia as a physician and general inspector of customs in the service of 'Abd al-Rahman III (912-961) and al-Hakam II (961-976). He also carried out secret diplomatic negotiations for the caliph, then became director of customs in Cordova, foreign minister and special advisor to the caliph. The Andalusian Jewish poet, Ibn Nagrila (or Samuel Hanagid) (993-1056), was also famous. He started off as a keeper of a spice stall in Malaga in Andalusia and used to write the letters of the vizier's slave-girl. The vizier was impressed by his style and appointed him his secretary. Prior to his death he recommended that Ibn Nagrila succeed him, and thus Ibn Nagrela governed Grenada and led its army in numerous wars. He was later termed in Hebrew *nagid*, that is 'prince', and worked as the head of the Jewish educational institute because of his religious and secular knowledge. He was one of the greatest Jewish poets in Andalusia. He carried out important correspondence with the leading personages in Iraq, Syria, Egypt and Morocco.

Jews were able to exert influence over the government through their doctors who worked in the palaces of the caliphs, viziers and sultans. Ottoman rule was kind to native Jews, granting them diplomatic posts by reason of their knowledge of European languages. The Ottoman government trusted the Jews and settled them in Constantinople, Salonika, Cyprus and Rhodes for economic and security reasons.

In 1733 the Jews defended Baghdad against an Iranian siege. In 1775 they defended Basra when it was besieged for 13 months. The banker, Jacob ibn Harun Gabbai, helped the Ottoman government to fund this defensive war, becoming later the head (*nasi*) of the Jewish community of Basra.

In 1900, the Ottoman government changed the jizya tax to one 'in lieu of military service', but this was abolished in 1909 and military service was imposed on the Jews. In the First World War thousands of native Jews fell with their Muslim brethren. The Ottoman authorities strengthened Jewish autonomy in Constantinople under the aegis of the chief rabbi. Jewish deputies were appointed to Parliament (1876, 1908) and to the courts. Jews were granted the right to open French Alliance Israélite schools in all parts of the empire to teach a contemporary curriculum and foreign languages, which helped the Jews to gain government employment and to participate in the economic developments.

IN THE SERVICE OF THE ISLAMIC ECONOMY

Jews provided a very important service for the economy. The Prophet and the first Muslims lived by commerce, and thus it was one of the 'respected' occupations. The Islamic state encouraged trade in word and deed, through the abolition of arbitrary strictures, control over organization and security and an active fight against crime – especially through political and economic union of all the Islamic provinces.

The integrity of the Islamic empire at its height helped the Jews to participate actively in the bourgeois mercantile revolution which blossomed in the realm of Islam. Thus they helped reinforce the economic base of the Islamic state and of Islamic civilisation, and their caravans from Andalusia to India carried the imports and exports of the Muslim world as the wealth of the state and the living standard therein increased. The Geniza documents indicate that the commercial activities of the Sephardim were helped on by the safety of the highways, the freedom of movement and the reinforcement of the religious, cultural and family ties between the Jews of the various provinces. In every Muslim city Jewish traders had an agent, responsible for the safety of their caravans, who represented their interests to the local authorities and who concerned himself with receiving, warehousing and marketing their goods. Among his principal duties, he was also a money-changer and responsible for the post. Such empire-wide security led to the development of commercial banks whereby a merchant could draw a cheque in Baghdad and get his money in the furthest reaches of the Arab West. It also helped to disseminate learning, and intellectuals were in the habit of moving from one province to another in search of learning. The Jews adopted this practice too, causing the Jewish seminaries in Baghdad to flourish. This economic success emphasized the deepening of the economic gulf between East and West, for the former had an industrial, bourgeois economy whereas that of Europe was feudal-agricultural.

The result of economic affluence can be seen in the report of the Jewish traveller Menahem Hayyim of Volterra. When he visited Damascus in 1481, he found 400 Jewish families, all of them were wealthy and respectable merchants and the head of the community was a physician.[11] Fifty years later, the traveller Obadiah Bertinoro visited Damascus and wrote about the beautiful Jewish houses and gardens there.[12] The aforementioned Benjamin of Tudela described the Great Synagogue of Baghdad as follows: 'In the Synagogue there are columns of variegated marble encrusted with gold and silver, upon which are written in golden letters verses from the Book of Psalms. In front of the ark (where the Torah is kept) are ten marble steps, above which is the throne of the exilarch and seats for the princes of the House of David (that is, his sons).'[13]

During the Ottoman era, the Sephardim became known for their trade between Europe, the Ottoman Empire, India and China. They were prominent in fabric manufacture, collection of taxes and import duties, banking and armaments. Jewish banks helped to fund the state apparatus, as well as providing the army with weapons.

During the Ottoman period Khoja Jacob and Adon Abd Alla became known in Basra as the two chief bankers and advisers to the government. Sasson Ibn Salih, head of the Sasson family lately of India, prospered in Baghdad as did the bankers Ishaq and Menahem Eini.

This Jewish activity should be emphasised, for some Arab leaders, such as Nuri Said, were not aware of the significance of Jews in the Arab economy when they cooperated with the Zionists to transfer them to Israel after 1948 (see chapter four).

THE ARABISATION OF JEWS UNDER ISLAM

Whereas the Jews of the Fertile Crescent and North Africa had spoken various languages before the Islamic conquest, particularly Aramaic and Greek, they became arabised along with the rest of the population after the conquest. They used Arabic in their speech, writings and even for religious matters. Generally they wrote Arabic in Hebrew letters. They adopted Islamic culture in an area which had known the Babylonian, Persian, Hellenistic and Roman civilisations amongst others. The influence of Islam upon Judaism was apparent in philosophy, linguistics, medicine and mathematics, astrology, popular mythology and religious studies.

The Jews of the Middle East had also categorically rejected Hellenism and Hellenistic philosophy. Many of them had been martyred resisting Hellenism. After the Islamic conquest, however, they started to study the new culture assiduously with Muslim teachers. The reason for this change of stance can only be attributed to the tolerance of Islam, which also led many Jews and Christians to embrace it.

The pioneer of Jewish intellectuals in this field was Sa'adia Gaon or Sa'id Yusuf al-Fayyumi (882-942). He was born in Egypt, emigrated to Iraq and became the head of the Academy of Sura. Sa'adia wrote a number of books in Arabic, such as *Responsa to Anan* (who had founded the Qaraite sect), *The Book of Discernment, The Book of Inheritance Trusts*, and *The Book of Documents and Deeds*. He translated the Bible into Arabic as well as writing an extensive commentary, and compiled an Arabic-Hebrew dictionary called *Ha-Agron*. But his most famous book is *The Book of Beliefs and Convictions* in which he enumerated the virtues of intellect with reference to memory and prediction, how to master animals, the powers of nature, the construction of buildings, clothes-making, cookery, the organization of military camps, political rule and organization, culture and astrology. Sa'adia opposed the hypothesis that the scientific renaissance would lead to godlessness. His philosophy is seated in the Quran, Mu'tazila [rationalist] and Hellenistic philosophy.[14]

Sherira Gaon, the head of the academy of Pumbeditha from 968-

998, wrote the extensive *Epistle of Rabbi Sherira* about the history of Jewish Halakha (Law) after the Bible. He was succeeded by his son, Rabbi Hai Gaon, who wrote a number of books in Arabic, such as *The Book of Law and Sale, The Book of Faith, The Book of the Magician* and *The Treatise on Judicial Judgements*. Rabbi Hai neither believed in legends and miracles, nor in jinnis, being under the influence of the rational philosophy developed by the philosophers of Islam. In Malaga, in Andalusia, one of the outstanding Jewish philosophers and poets was Sulaiman ibn Gabirol (1022-1070). He composed a book of proverbs called *The Choice Jewels*, and philosophical works called *The Improvement of Moral Qualities*, and *The Book of the Source of Life*. He was influenced by al-Mutanabbi and Abu al-'Ala' al-Ma'arri.

Samu'el Ben-Hofni lived at the beginning of the eleventh century and became the head of the academy of Sura. His whole output, including *Introduction to the Talmud, The Book of Precepts*, and *The Book of Abrogation of Law, the Sources and Branches of Religion* was in Arabic. He believed in the intellect, rejected irrational accretions and carried out research in fields as varied as commerce, heredity and rivers, as well as religion. Professor Assaf, in one of his lectures at Jerusalem University, said that Ben-Hofni's output was greater and more multifarious than that of any other Jewish intellectual.

Maimonides (Musa ibn Maymun) (1135-1204) was the most brilliant of the Arab Jewish philosophers. He was born in Cordova, but emigrated to Egypt where he became the physician of Saladin. His works in medicine were translated and studied until the end of the sixteenth century. He wrote his famous philosophical work, *The Guide to the Perplexed*, in which he was influenced by Aristotle and Ibn Sina (Avicenna), in Arabic. Thus he created the intellectual foundation of Judaism. One of his teachings was that a Jew ought to accept death rather than embrace Christianity, but that he could embrace Islam rather than death.

Ibn Kammuna (thirteenth century) was also an excellent philosopher who composed a study on Islam, Christianity and Judaism, as was Abu al-Barakat ibn Malka (twelfth century), Ibn Gabirol al-Andalusi, and Bahye ben Paquda, who wrote *Duties of the Heart* in Arabic. This book represents the first work on Islamic asceticism to enter Judaism (1070). Abraham Ben Maymun (Maimonides' son), head of the Jewish community in Egypt, composed an important work entitled *A Comprehensive Guide to the Worship of God*, which was translated into English by Professor Samuel Rosenblatt as *Highways of Perfection*.[15] The author observed that the Muslim Sufis (mystics) had preserved the ideas of the prophets better than the Jews themselves. He then attempted to introduce some Muslim practices into Jewish worship, such as prostration, but failed. However, on Yom Kippur Iraqi Jews do prostrate in prayer. Thus we see that Sufism, as a comprehensive philosophical and ethical system, influenced Jewish philosophers and poets, just as the Hellenistic sciences and modes of thought had seeped into Jewish intellectual life via the Muslim teachers who developed methodical scientific thought. Professor Goitein, Head of the Oriental Studies Department at Jerusalem University, notes that the 'vice' of homosexuality among the Sufis 'sometimes penetrated into Oriental Jewish circles.'[16] This is only one of the anti-Sephardi and anti-Arab comments one may hear from Zionist professors.

Hebrew poetry did not exist before Islam, except for the Bible and some non-metrical religious poetry in Palestine. Hence, metrical Hebrew poetry composed in the Middle Ages was part of Arabic poetry in its contents and stylistics. No one who studies the Hebrew and Arabic poetry of this period can fail to see that the Hebrew imitated the Arabic. Jewish poets spoke Arabic, studied Arabic literature, their culture was Arabic, they versified in Arabic, and admired Arabic poetry to the extent that they wanted to capture its beauty in Hebrew. They started to versify in Biblical Hebrew, translating verbatim many Arabic terms and expressions. They borrowed Arabic rhetoric and stylistics such as the simile, metaphor, allusion, analogy etc. They also used the metres and subject matter of Arabic verse such as the love poetry of the *ghazal*, eulogy and Sufi poetry. When the poet's emotions ran away with him, he would often add verses in Arabic. There were scores of Arab Jewish poets, the most famous being Sulaiman ibn Gabirol, Musa ibn Ezra, Yehuda Halevi, Samu'el ibn Nagrila, Ibrahim ibn Ezra, and Yehuda al-Harizi who used the form established by the great Arab writer, al-Hariri's *Maqamat*, in his book *Tahkemoni*.

The poet Donash was the first to introduce Arabic poetic metres into Hebrew verse in the tenth century. Yehuda Halevi (Abu al-Hasan), who was born in 1086, lived in Toledo and is counted amongst the greatest poets of Andalusia who versified in both Hebrew and Arabic. He was a physician and a philosopher. His most important book on religious philosophy is *The Book of Khazari* which was written in Arabic in the form of questions and answers. Of the poets who embraced Islam, the best known is Ibrahim ibn Sahl al-Ishbili (d.1260) who studied the Quran and composed a famous collection of poems.

In the Arabian peninsula in the pre-Islamic period, the Jews had always used Arabic as their chief language, and recited poetry like their Arab brethren. In this connection we should mention al-Samawal ibn 'Adia' (d.560) who owned a famous fortress, al-Ablaq. Here he set an example of good faith; he chose his own son's death, when his son was taken hostage by Umru al-Qays' enemies, rather than betray the trust that Umru al-Qays had placed in him when he went to Syria. The opening verse of one of his famous odes begins:

'If a man's honour be not soiled by baseness which befalls him then any garment he wears is beautiful.'

Before the rise of Islam, Jewish intellectuals did not study linguistics. However, when they started to study Arabic after the rise of Islam they learnt grammar and rhetoric. Then they started to study linguistics with regard to Hebrew, applying the methods they had learnt from their teachers, the Arabic grammarians. Da'ud ibn Ibrahim al-Fasi compiled a dictionary of Biblical Hebrew in the tenth century. In the thirteenth century, Tanhum Yerushalmi also wrote a Hebrew dictionary of post-Biblical Hebrew sources. Ibn Jinah discovered that Hebrew words (as in Arabic) were derived from three-letter roots. Throughout the tenth to thirteenth centuries, Hebrew grammarians together with their Muslim counterparts continued to study the grammar of Arabic, Hebrew and Aramean, considering that these three languages were originally a single language.

Muslim, Jewish and Christian intellectuals began in the Umayyad era to undertake a far-reaching cultural endeavour: the translation the Hellenistic corpus of knowledge from Greek or Syriac. Amongst these translators was a Jew who lived in Basra in the time of 'Umar II called Masarjawaih, who translated books on medicine from the Syriac, although the most famous translator was the Christian Hunain ibn Ishaq (809-877).

In the thirteenth century a large group of Spanish Jewish scholars, particularly those settled in Provence, undertook the translation of Islamic philosophy and sciences from Arabic to Hebrew, and then into Latin thereby enabling the diffusion of the Islamic cultural heritage throughout Europe where it became part of the basis of Western civilisation. Outstanding amongst these translators were the families of Tivon and Qimhi.

Before we turn to popular culture, it is apposite to give a brief account of the curriculum in Jewish educational institutions in the

Islamic world in the twelfth century based on the book *Medicine of Souls* by Yusuf ibn Yehuda Aqnin. In addition to the Torah and the Talmud, Arab Jews studied poetry, philosophy, mathematics, engineering, logic, optics, astrology, the natural sciences, music, religious and abstract philosophy and mechanics. In the thirteenth century Yehuda ibn Samu'el ibn 'Abbas said that the first part of the curriculum mentioned in the *Medicine of Souls* included translation of the Torah into Arabic, the historical sections of the Bible, the rules of Hebrew grammar, Talmud and ethics. In the second part of the curriculum, the student would study medicine, arithmetic and music. In the third part they would study Aristotle and Averroıs (Ibn Rushd), then finally the natural sciences and abstract philosophy.[17] It appears that, apart from the Jewish subjects, this curriculum was based upon that of the Islamic schools.

Popular culture, meaning here popular myths and stories, in the Islamic world was common to Muslim, Christian and Jewish communities. Out of the four hundred stories in *The Thousand and One Nights*, forty-five are Jewish stories. In the eleventh century, Nissim Ibn Ya'qub ibn Shahin collected Arab-Jewish tales which had been generally written down in colloquial Arabic in Hebrew characters. At weddings and parties, Jewish singers would sing Arabic poetry, some of which would be made up of alternating Hebrew and Arabic verses. At weddings in Israel currently, singers omit the verses in classical Arabic, since the new generation does not understand this language due to its cultural suppression, but the music of the Arab Jews is completely Arabic, even in the synagogue. In the Islamic world there is no difference between Jewish and Islamic arts of goldsmithing and calligraphy or any of the other handicrafts. In March 1987 at the National Film Theatre in London there was a Zionist film about Yemenite popular art, which Zionists described as 'Jewish-Yemenite', and acknowledged that this art has disappeared among Yemenite Jews since their immigration to Israel.

Thus, the Jewish cultural heritage since the Arab conquest was an integral part of Islamic civilisation, mostly written in Arabic under Islamic hegemony. Ashkenazi culture, on the other hand, did not come into prominence until the eighteenth century in Germany and later in Eastern Europe. Whereas Arab Jews represented the majority of world Jewry in the Islamic period, they are now 20 percent, but 70 percent of the Jewish population of Israel.

ISLAMIC TOLERANCE

This cultural interaction between the conquering Muslims and the Jews and Christians took place in an atmosphere of tolerance and good-neighbourliness. Jewish sources recount that 'Abd al-Malik ibn Marwan (reg. 685-705) appointed a Jew to clean the Temple Mount in Jerusalem, and also to make the lanterns and light them. The Jews of Jerusalem at that time believed that this was the beginning of salvation. Prior to that time, Mu'awiyah (reg. 661-680) had built a synagogue in Jerusalem.

Arab Jews did not confront the option of Jews in Christian Europe, of conversion or death, for the Quran advises 'There is no compulsion in religion', and also 'Ye have your religion and I have mine.' Moreover the attitude of Islam towards the Jews cannot be characterised, as hatred, fear and racism which existed and is still prevalent in Europe. In the minds of the Christian Europeans the Jew, Satan and all non-Christians were part aspects of the anti-Christ. This was a real fear, and provided the basis for modern-day anti-semitism and racism. However, if a Jew embraced Islam, all differences crumbled away and he became like any other Muslim. In this manner, Islam absorbed the peoples of the Fertile Crescent, Africa and Asia.

Generally, Islam imposed no hindrances on Jews and Christians as to their type of work or place of residence. All citizens were free to live wherever they so desired and to work at whatever craft they chose. Islam did not grant privileges to a particular class of people, as happened in feudal Europe, or within the caste system in India.

In Europe in the Middle Ages, the Church eliminated all those who transgressed against Christianity. Islam, on the other hand, allowed repentance for those of the People of the Book who committed a crime such as slander against Islam and the Prophet, as well as allowing them to defend their religion orally and in writing.

The Jews welcomed the *jizya* tax, since it provided them with the right to Islamic protection. When the 'Abbasid caliph, al-Mu'atadid (*reg.* 892-902), wished to abolish the *jizya*, his Jewish treasurer opposed him.[18] Landshut writes[19] that during the Umayyad (661-750) and the 'Abbasid (750-1258) eras there is no recorded Jewish complaint of oppression or maltreatment.

The Islamic state opened up all sources of support to Jews and Christians, even land-ownership which was banned to Jews in Europe. The Fatimid caliphs of North Africa and Egypt (909-1171), for example, contributed financial support to the Jewish academy in Jerusalem. In 1020 the caliph, al-Hakim, saved the lives of 200 Jews from Muslim fanatics who wanted to kill them. Historians believe that this caliph's subsequent oppression of the 'People of the Book' was a result of mental illness.

The vizier, al-Khaqani, wrote to the 'Abbasid caliph, al-Mu'atadid, that he was employing Jews and Christians in the state apparatus, as their loyalty to the 'Abbasid caliphate was greater than that of the Muslims themselves. This exaggeration shows how much the People of the Book were trusted. Two renowned Jewish bankers of the time, Harun ibn 'Umran and Yusuf ibn Pinhas, provided loans to equip the Islamic armies.

The firman which the Ottoman sultan, Muhammad III, issued in March 1602 states that protection of the *dhimmi* (the non-Muslim citizen) was an obligation for all Muslims, their kings and governors. Islam respected Judaism and disapproved of laxity in religious observance. The aforementioned *gaon*, Hai, wrote in the eleventh century that the Islamic courts would not accept the evidence of a Jew or a Christian unless he was 'a peer', that is someone who fulfilled his religious obligations.[20]

The attitude of Islamic clerics and laity towards Arab Jews was moderate and positive, as related in *The Book of Preparation* by al-Baqillani in Baghdad in the tenth century. Intellectual, Sufi and bourgeois circles all had an empathy with Jews. Sa'd al-Andalusi, for example, eulogises Arab Jews for their assiduous studies in the divine law and the lives of the prophets. Ibn Sa'd lists in his *Classes of the Nations* the names of the nations who have helped disseminate knowledge in the world: the Indians, Iranians, Chaldeans, Greeks, Byzantines, Egyptians, Arabs and Jews. Ibn Sa'd stated that Judaism was the cradle of prophecy, and that most of the prophets were Jews. The author then discusses the history of Jewish scholars in the Islamic world, an area also covered by Rashid al-Din (1247-1318) and Ibn Khaldun (1332-1406). There is also a single rare hostile study by Ibn Hazm (994-1064) which resulted from his hostility to the Jew, Ibn Nagrila, who had reached the summit of the government pyramid in Andalusia.

When the Ottoman sultan, Sulaiman al-Qanuni decided to build the Sulaimaniya Mosque, his plan was hampered by a Jew who refused to sell a piece of his land. The sultan's advisors suggested that he confiscate the land or buy it compulsorily. The sultan, however, rejected this suggestion on the basis that it contradicted Islamic law.

There are similar stories about the second caliph, 'Umar ibn al-Khattab, and the fourth 'Ali ibn Abi Talib, the first Imam of the Shi'ah. The twelfth century Atabeg prince, 'Imad al-Din Zangi, who governed Iraq and northern Syria stated that even if the wronged party is a Jew and the accused is the son of the prince himself, justice must be done.

Just as Sephardi Judaism was affected by tolerance in the realms of Islam, so its Ashkenazi counterpart was affected by the fanaticism which prevailed in the Europe of the Middle Ages. This is seen by those who have come up against Ashkenazi religious fanatics in Israel such as the American Rabbi Kahane and Rabbi Levinger, members of the terrorist gang who carried out hostilities against the heads of the municipalities on the West Bank, and members of Gush Emunim and other settlers on the West Bank and in the Gaza Strip. Even those Ashkenazi Israelis who have neglected their religion and become secular, or more specifically atheists, have generally been affected by European nationalist fanaticism, such as Ariel Sharon, Raphael Eytan, Menahem Begin, Yitzhak Shamir, David Ben Gurion, Golda Meir, Yigal Allon and Yigal Yadin. Ashkenazi leaders, whether they be of the Labour Party on the left or of the Likud on the right, have been affected.

However, there is a similarity between the Sunni Muslim and Jewish cleric. Neither of them believes that priests may act as intermediaries between God Almighty and man, as is the case in Catholicism. There exist in Judaism and Islam no sacramental rites, nor are there any occupations which the cleric may fulfil but which are forbidden to the rest of the believers. The Muslim and Jewish cleric both achieve their ranks through deep religious study and social acceptance. The certificate of *semikha* for a rabbi is similar to the *ijazah* awarded to the Muslim cleric by his teacher. There is also a similarity between the Muslim *shari'ah* law and the Jewish *halakha* – both words meaning 'path'. In both religions the basis is in the Bible or the Quran and the Hadith (Traditions). The Talmud, which was compiled in Iraq (in 500 AD) is the Jewish equivalent of the *sunna* (custom of the Prophet) or Hadith of Muslims.

Jewish jurisprudence was affected by Islam in its subdivisions, formation and terminology. There is a similarity between the Islamic *fatwa* (religious decree) and the Responsa literature which arose in Iraq under Islamic rule and was recorded by the heads of the Iraqi Jewish community. Islam also affected Jewish laws of marriage, the construction of places of worship, discussion and precision in the holy texts, the text of the prayers, religious philosophy, and dietary restrictions (the ban on pork, for example). We should note that Sunni Islam allows the Muslim to eat kosher meat. Muslims did not consider the Jewish religion to be dangerous to Islam, since Jews did not constitute a political state. They were a small minority, whereas Christianity was the religion of powerful states which had fought against Arab and Muslim states ever since the Islamic conquests. Christianity had expelled Islam from Andalusia, from southern Italy and most of the Balkans, and finally dismantled the last Islamic empire in 1918.[21] All this shows that the present hostility between Jews and Arabs does not have its roots in the history of Islam, but that it arose as a result of Zionism.

This analysis does not mean that there were never grievances, acts of violence or arbitrary restrictions on Jews, for example, in clothing, or the construction of synagogues and homes. Zionist historians disseminate the details of these events, although they were unusual in the Islamic world. In the central Sunni regions, the Jewish community flourished. Any discriminatory regulations of the Muslims were often theoretical and not applied. Conflicts between Muslim sects were much worse than those between Jews and Muslims.

MODERN TIMES

Morocco

Although the general harmony of Jews in Islam is well established, Israeli schools continue to incite pupils against the Arab and Islamic world. Zionist teachers claim that Jews in the Arab countries suffered from oppression, poverty and contagious diseases, that residence in special ghettoes was obligatory and that their children were deprived of general education. Due to political oppression they had no opportunity to be economically active; they were forced to walk barefoot and whenever they met a Muslim they had to step aside and bow to him and Muslims exposed them to scorn and beatings.[22] Zionists who portray the conditions of Arab Jews in the Islamic world in this way are all Ashkenazi settlers who immigrated from Europe and America. The Sephardim are not allowed to speak about themselves since they have no access to the media.

In an article in the newspaper, *Yedi'ot Aharonot* (23 July 1976), the progressive journalist, Barukh Nadel, replied to these fallacious claims. 'Every Jewish community in Morocco', he wrote, 'had its own Jewish leadership consisting of its cultural and executive elite. Often Jews carried out services for the state, as counsellors, physicians, interpreters, scribes, diplomats and bankers. In Morocco, Jews worked in the shipping administration, and produced excellent poets. Muslims worked in Jewish establishments and vice versa. Massacres of Jews were almost unheard of. Jews were responsible for the mint. Mistra Musa was renowned as the king's private physician, and was succeeded by Yosef Valensa. Shmuel Halash was a signatory to the first treaty concluded between Morocco and a Christian state – Holland – and was appointed Moroccan ambassador to Amsterdam (1610). Halash was a minister of external affairs and privy counsellor to four sultans. Sultan Rashid appointed a Jew as his counsellor and minister of finance. Sultan Sidi ibn 'Abd Allah preferred to have Jewish participation in every commercial transaction and in all negotiations with Europe.'

From 1610 until 1828 Jews served as ambassadors in various European capitals. From the time of Moulai 'Abd al-Rahman (1822–1859) Jews in Morocco became more active in the economy and the field of diplomacy. The families of al-Teras, Ibn Khaymul and Ibn Sur became well-known. Some of the Western states granted nationality to a section of the Jews, hoping to be gain entrée into domestic affairs of Muslim states. This policy led to hostilities against the Jews, such as the massacre of 30 March 1912 in Fez when sixty Jews were killed and fifty others were wounded.[23]

On 23 July 1986, the *Financial Times* wrote that 'the Moroccan Jewish community has for many centuries played an important role in the political, economic and cultural life of the country. To this day, King Hassan's eldest son, Sidi Mohammed, pays a visit to the Rabat synagogue on the eve of the Yom Kippur festival. The protection traditionally afforded to the King's Jewish subjects was upheld during the Second World War when Sultan MohammedV, King Hassan's father, told the French governor-general that he would never allow the Vichy colonial authorities to force the Jews to wear the yellow Star of David but provide census lists.' The newspaper added that 'the Jewish community has today dwindled from 300,000 when Morocco became independent in 1957, to around 10,000, but many of its members still play a prominent role. The head of the community, Mr David Ammar, once an illiterate young man from the small town of Bereshid now runs Omnium Nord Africain, one of the kingdom's largest companies, which he jointly owns with the monarch. Mr Ammar, like other Moroccan

Jews who are now prominent in business in France, Canada and the US, has played a wider role. He has been dispatched to the US to lobby among Jewish congressmen and other groups to try to reduce Jewish opposition to US arms sales to some Arab countries.'

The publication of these facts had a great significance for Moroccan Jews, who suffer most from discrimination under Ashkenazi Zionist rule.

Tunisia

The American Consul, M. Noah, wrote in 1814 that 'with all the apparent oppression, the Jews are the leading men; they are in Barbary the principal mechanics, they are at the head of the customshouse, they farm the revenues; the exportation of various articles, and the monopoly of various merchandise, are secured to them by purchase; they control the mint and regulate the coinage of money; they keep the Bey's jewels and valuable articles, and are his treasurers, secretaries and interpreters; the little known of arts, science and medicine is confined to the Jews . . . they are ever in the presence of the Bey, every minister has two or three Jewish agents . . . '[24] In 1855 Mohammed Pasha abolished all theoretical impediments imposed on the Jews and granted them complete equality.

Algeria

Even though Jews in the Western and socialist countries enjoy complete equality, they do not enjoy the autonomy which Islam granted to them, as we have previously mentioned. Within this autonomy, the Jews of Algeria preserved their identity from the time of the Islamic conquests until the establishment of French colonial rule between 1834–1851. French language and culture were imposed upon them, against the wishes of their leaders. Only the Jews of Constantine and the southern oases have remained true to their Jewishness. A number of families migrated to Tunis in order not to lose their identity. Young people who stayed behind started to be ashamed of their background. This did not happen under Islamic rule.[25] During times of unrest, the Jews of Algeria would flee to the mosques for protection. In 1902, the Algerian people rejected anti-Jewish agitation and the agitators were defeated.[26]

French colonialism finally managed to separate Algerian Jews from their homeland and people and when it bestowed independence on Algeria and Algerian Jews chose to move to France. They did not immigrate to Israel, however, disdaining to be 'third class' citizens. During the Second World War, the Nazis knew that the Arabs would not tolerate the mass extermination of their own neighbours, and the North African Jews were almost the only Jews who lived under German occupation without being sent to the gas chambers. Their children in Israel hang on their walls the pictures of King Hassan II of Morocco and his father in gratitude.

Iraq

Baruch Nadel wrote in his previously mentioned article that 'when this community lived in Iraq, the proportion of doctors was four times higher than among the pre-1948 Ashkenazi Jews in Palestine. 36 percent of Iraqi Jews were involved in the liberal professions. They were a part of the governmental economic administration, directors of the railways and banks, merchants, lawyers and accountants. There were also the poor, but they were a smaller proportion than the Ashkenazi poor in Poland. The general standard of education at Iraqi Jewish schools was outstanding, with Jews studying English and French in their secondary schools, such as the French Alliance schools. Jews excelled at contemporary Arabic poetry, and the Arabic novel.' Arabic was the language of instruction. The school taught an Iraqi national curriculum, but in the religious education lessons, pupils read the Torah and translated it into Arabic.

In his book *The Jews of the Middle East*,[27] H.J. Cohen writes that the number of Jewish schools in Baghdad increased from eight in 1920 to twenty by 1948. The head of the Organization of Iraqis in Israel adds that the community abandoned thirty-seven educational institutes in Baghdad alone.[28] In addition to regular schools, the Jews had special institutions for the blind and orphans, a conservatoire for music and vocation schools, even though many Jewish students were enrolled in the free government (secondary schools). After completing their secondary school education, Jewish students would enrol in state higher education institutions, or European and Arab universities. Ishaqi stated that half of the students who studied abroad on Iraqi government stipends were Jews. In the first half of this century, 1,000 Iraqi Jewish students

31

completed higher education, studying primarily law and medicine, followed by pharmacology, engineering and economics. A number also studied at the Teacher Training College.[29]

As already mentioned, Iraqi Jews enjoyed autonomy which was embodied in two assemblies: the lay assembly and the spiritual assembly which regulated religious life. The former looked after educational, health, charitable and financial affairs. The administration of the community levied various taxes, such as a tax on meat, to fund its activities. Jews were active in the fields of literature and journalism, anti-Zionism, music, art and all aspects of Iraqi cultural life together with their Muslim and Christian brethren (see chapter four). The Shohet Report (1910) presented to the British Consul in Baghdad stated that the Jews monopolised domestic commerce and that Muslims and Christians were unable to compete with them.[30] It divides the Jewish community as follows:
5 percent wealthy merchants and bankers
30 percent middle class – petty traders
60 percent poor (i.e. artisans)
5 percent beggars

Following the economic and educational developments which occurred under the British Mandate, the number of wealthy merchants in 1938-1939 in the Baghdad Chamber of Commerce reached 39, amongst whom were 10 Jewish members rising later to be 43 percent of the total. Moreover, Jews were employed by the Mandate government in all its offices, particularly the ministry of finance. They were the majority in the railways administration, the port of Basra and the Iraq Petroleum Company. The best-known of these was Sasson Hezkiel, the first minister of finance in the first Iraqi government (1921). The main reasons for such advancement were the standard of Jewish education, their knowledge of foreign languages, family ties with other countries, the fact that they were concentrated in the metropolitan areas such as Baghdad, Basra and Mosul, their energy and enthusiasm, their traditional commercial skills, and, last but not least, the fraternal relations which prevailed with the Muslim community on both official and popular levels. This situation led to the development of a new class of Muslim merchants and an intelligentsia which started in the thirties to compete with the Jews in all fields. This competition was one of the reasons for subsequent sectarianism and emigration in addition to more significant factors: Zionism, Nazi propaganda and Western intervention (see chapter four). The appearance of this competition did not mean that the volume of

Jewish trade decreased, rather, during the thirties and forties, the number of Jewish merchants increased.[31] They continued to have a proportionally large presence in trading activities, until they were displaced in 1950-1 (see chapters four and five).

ANTI-ARAB PROPAGANDA

Despite the evidence of historical facts, Zionist propaganda in the domestic and foreign media continues to nourish the legend of Muslim oppression of Jews in the Islamic world. The aims of this bizarre attempt are as follows:

1. the Israeli people is a divided people. Behind the curtain of 'Jewish National Unity', the slums and the so-called 'development towns' are in a state of permanent ferment by reason of the grievous conditions arising from sectarian exploitation. The ruling establishment has directed these grievances against the Arab and Islamic peoples, telling the Sephardim 'You should be grateful. We have saved you from Islamic oppression.' Some Sephardim believe this fiction, having been born in Palestine and not having lived in any other Arab country.

2. an unsuccessful attempt to disrupt the progressive current of thought which calls for a common effort between the Palestinian people and native Jews against Zionism.

3. to incite all Israelis and prepare them for wars of expansion.

4. as many Sephardim long to return to their countries of origin, Zionism tries to convince them of the principle of 'no return to Arab or Islamic countries'. Moreover, Israeli law bans travel to the Arab countries, except Egypt and except for spying and terrorism. When Israel conspired over Jewish emigration with Iraq under Nuri Sa'id, for example, it tried to have their Iraqi nationality withdrawn before they left to prevent them ever returning to their homeland.

5. To justify the crimes that Zionism committed against these Jews in the process of immigration and 'absorption' (see chapters four and five).

6. To bring the Arab nation and the Islamic world into disrepute in the eyes of the Western world. In this respect, Zionist historians and journalists have acted energetically.

7. The Palestinian cause is not only a political, nationalist cause, it is a cause of people who have lost everything, their homes and lands, indeed everything down to their clothing. Hence the Zionist establishment tries to justify its pillage of the Palestinians by

inventing stories of the spoliation of Jews in Arab countries. The freezing of the assets of Iraqi Jews who left their country only occurred with the collusion of Israel, for the clique of Nuri Sa'id which governed Iraq at the time was pro-Western and could not have frozen Jewish assets without Western permission. This freezing of assets provided Israel with a pretext to pursue its long-standing policy of confiscation of Arab property and land.

NOTES
1 Ibn Hisham, *Sirah*, 119-123.
2 Grandson of Chingiz Khan (Ghengis Khan).
3 The Latin term usually used to describe a literature genre which means 'Questions and Answers'.
4 Rejwan, 121.
5 Baron, 93.
6 Rejwan, 81-84.
7 Berber freedman of Musa ibn Nusayr, governor of North Africa under the Umayyads. His first landing in Spain was near the mighty rock was has since immortalized his name, Jabal (mount of) Tariq (Gibraltar). Hitti, *History of the Arabs*, 493.
8 Letter of Sherira Gaon.
9 Adler, 39-42.
10 London, 1937.
11 *The Jewish Encylopaedia*, New York 1925, vol 4, 417-418.
12 ibid.
13 *Travels of Benjamin of Tudela*.
14 *Encyclopaedia Brittanica*.
15 Baltimore, 1927 and 1938.
16 *Jews and Arabs*, 153-154.
17 Rejwan, 144.
18 Rejwan, 88-89.
19 P. 8.
20 Sassoon, Daud, 7-15.
21 Lewis, 79-86.
22 See Kirschenbaum, S, *Jewish History in Modern Times*, used in Israeli secondary schools.
23 Chouraqui, 173.
24 Noah, M, 306.
25 *Les Temps Modernes de Sartre*, Richard Ayoun, 67-71.
26 Chouraqui, 152-153.
27 Cohen, H.J., *The Jews of the Middle East, 1860-1972*, 1973, 123.
28 Twena, A.H.,(ed), *Dispersion & Liberation*, vol. 5, *Jewish Education in Baghdad*, Geoula Synagogue Committee, Ramlai, 1975, 173.
29 Cohen, op. cit., 124-125.
30 Kedourie, Elie, 'The Jews of Baghdad in 1910', *Middle Eastern Studies*, vol. 7, no. 3, October 1971, 355-361.
31 Shiblak, 23-36.

CHAPTER TWO

The First Clash Between Zionism And Jewish Palestinians 1881-1918

THE STATE OF THE COMMUNITIES BEFORE ZIONISM

After the liberation of Jerusalem at the hands of Saladin and the subsequent defeat of the Crusaders, Jews living in the lands of Islam returned to Palestine and Jerusalem in particular. This Jewish community developed gradually to the point where it became a Palestinian community, Jewish in religion, and Arab/Islamic in language and culture. After the fall of the Arab/Muslim state in Andalusia, the Spanish Jews were driven out and emigrated to the countries of the Arab Maghrib (west) and provinces of the Ottoman Empire. Some of them reached Palestine where they mixed with the Palestinian Jews. Jewish groups in 'Dar al-Islam'[1] sent financial contributions to the Palestinian Jewish community which used them to support religious and cultural institutions and the poor.[2] In spite of the emigration of some religious Ashkenazi Jews from Eastern Europe, the Sephardim remained the majority.[3] As the migration of the religious Ashkenazis continued, the proportion of Arab Jews declined by 1875 to 60 percent of the Jewish population. However, the autonomy granted to the Jews in Palestine remained in the hands of the native Jews since they held Ottoman nationality. The Ashkenazi Jews were of various European nationalities and thus they were protected under the Capitulations by foreign consuls, especially those of Britain and France. Jewish autonomy was under the leadership of the Sephardi chief rabbi who was chosen by the other rabbis and who was recognised by the sultan in a special firman (decree), and 'crowned' in a special ceremony in Jerusalem.

This rabbi had a special position in the religious affairs of world Jewry. The Palestinian Jews formed a special committee called 'Knesset Yisrael' to run the affairs of the community and the Ottoman authorities granted it the right to mint coins for the community. There is a Jewish legend which relates that when God called a sultan to Him, the gates of Jerusalem were shut in mourning for the spirit of the deceased. The keys were then sent to the chief rabbi to be blessed, indicating that the new sultan was to enjoy the support of the Jewish community. This story shows the spirit of brotherhood and amity which obtained in the relations between the Palestinian Jews and the Ottoman Islamic authorities. The former were occupied in manual labour, such as goldsmithing, carpentry, food manufacture and as barbers etc. Some were merchants, doctors and tax collectors, and some became renowned men of science, politicians, writers and officers in the armed forces. Some native Jews acquired higher scientific learning, among them Nissim Behar who founded and directed the Alliance School in Jerusalem, and Yoseph Seby, who studied in France, Professor Ariel Ben Siyoon who emigrated to Germany and wrote on Jewish religion in the East, Professor Ibrahim Salem Yehuda a specialist in Arab affairs and a famed linguist, Daoud (David) Yellin, Yoseph Barein Meyuhaas, and Ishaq Hesqiel Yehuda, who wrote a book on Arab proverbs, Yaqub ben Attar, Avraham Almaliah, and Yehuda Burla. The community founded the Misgav Laddakh foundlings' shelter on the Jaffa Road in Jerusalem, and an old age home. It also elected members to the council which ran their affairs, and the Ottoman authorities tried to strengthen the two communities, the Jewish and the Islamic, fearful of European Christian penetration. These Ottoman or Palestinian Jews assisted Ottoman armies, participating in various wars as soldiers and doctors and furnishing the military units with provisions and ammunition.

The Andalusian (Sephardi) Jews who had settled in Jerusalem, Hebron, Tiberias and Safad set up religious high schools. Their greatest intellectual was Yosef Caro who wrote the *Shulhan Arukh* (one of the most revered religious texts after the Talmud), and Yisrael Najjara. The Palestinian Jews thus opened schools, built law courts and appointed judges, collected taxes and elected their religious and temporal leaders.

However, the Ashkenazi immigrants rejected autonomous Palestinian 'authority' and set about dismantling it. The Ashkenazi rabbi, Menahem Mendel Mishkleff, was the first to set up an isolationist community (1816) which started collecting donations from abroad for its aims. This secession lead to the economic weakening of the Palestinian Jewish community.[4] The Ashkenazis kept themselves apart from the Palestinian Arabs and the Jews, setting up for themselves ghettoes similar to those they had left in Eastern Europe, with special schools for their children, moreover they refused to use Arabic or Turkish as a means of communication.

Whilst Askhenazi Jews were dissociating themselves from secular studies, Palestinian Jewish clerics were helping to found modern schools such as the Lemel School in Jerusalem. Since 1860, the French Alliance Israélite Society had been founding new schools for Jews in the Middle East and North Africa, and with tuition in these schools being free, or at very reduced rates, the Jews could acquire a level of education superior to that of the Ashkenazis in Eastern Europe.[5] Furthermore, additional native schools were set up in the Arab countries. After the First World War, Arabs and Jews started to send their children to the free state schools in the Arab countries as well but not in Palestine, (see discussion in chapter four).

Relations between Palestinian Jews and Arabs were good. Jews participated in the local councils with Muslims and Christians. Ishaq 'Abadi observes in his article on Jerusalem, 'I do not remember any incident of incitement against the Jews on the Temple Mount during the Turkish period.'[6] It was common for a Jewish woman to enter her Muslim or Christian neighbour's house to borrow some little item, and vice versa. There were amicable intercommunal family meetings. Jewish children would play with Muslim and Christian children in the street, and the Jews spoke Arabic. Prior to the first Zionist Aliya (1881)[7] some of the religious Ashkenazim would marry Arab Jews. In economic life there was harmony and cooperation among all groups, including the religious Ashkenazis. Native Jews would offer necessary loans to Arab villages, and then distribute the harvest. Some Muslim students, such as the children of the Khalidi family, enrolled in Jewish schools (the Lemel or Alliance School).

Eliahu Eliachar, one of the leaders of the Jewish Palestinians, says in his Hebrew book, *Life with the Jews*, that when Raphael Eliachar died at an early age, his partner, Abdul Dajani, cared for his widow and her children. One of the children, later Colonel Y.R. Eliachar of New York, returned the favour by helping Dajani's grandchildren with their studies in America. Local Jews wore Arab clothing and one could hardly distinguish them from a Muslim or Christian. At Passover, the Muslims would send around trays with bread, and ghee and honey as a present for their Jewish neighbours, and the Jews would then place on the same trays jam, matzah and other presents in return. Speaking of his military service, Eliachar says that he was appointed as a military doctor (*küçük zabit*) during the First World War and was posted to Nazareth where he was billeted in the house of Nasir Musa al-Hakim. He worked there in the Russian Hospital (the Moskobiya), and had excellent relations with the inhabitants. He remembers one of his friends, Tawfiq al-Husseini, who was a cavalry officer. There were commercial relations between Eliahu's father and Tewfiq's uncle, who was a regular visitor to Eliahu's house in Jerusalem. After the war Tawfiq became a high-ranking official in the government immigration office. Warm relations with the Eliachar family lasted up to the foundation of the state of Israel. Eliachar remembers that although he suffered poverty and hunger when the British occupied Jerusalem, his Arab landlord refused to take any rent and gave him food and drink. This friendship lasted until the end of his life.

All of this happened either before the arrival of Askhenazi Zionism or outside its domain. We shall see how the Zionists poisoned the atmosphere of Palestine and the Middle East with their divisive sectarianism.[8]

ASHKENAZI SEPARATISM

In 1882 the first Ashkenazi Zionists arrived from Russia, calling themselves *Biluim*,[9] or 'the First Aliya', as if no one had ever immigrated to Palestine before them. This stems from the fact that the Zionists disregard the history of the Jews and Palestine from the period of the destruction of the second temple in 70 AD until their pioneers reached Palestine to build the 'Ashkenazi National Home'. In 1904 more waves arrived in what was termed the 'Second Aliya', followed by more nationalist groups. The First Aliya owed its origins to the Hovevei Tsion Movement, the first Zionist organization and the forerunner of the World Zionist Organization which was founded towards the end of the century. Its first act in Palestine was the creation of a sectarian isolationist unit called Hayishuv Hehadash (the New Settlement) in contradistinction to the indigenous Jewish population which they termed the Old Settlement. The difference between the two communities – in their opinion – was not just temporary, but qualitative for they had emigrated to Palestine to set up the agricultural production which would help build the Zionist national entity economically and politically, whereas the Old Settlement lived by 'begging', that is by donations from world Jewry. In fact Palestinian Jews lived by manual crafts and commerce etc, and such financial help as reached Palestine was spent by them on charitable works. The Ashkenazi Zionist pioneers, however, built their settlements with cheap Arab, and then cheap Jewish Yemeni labour and with financial support which they received from world Jewry through their Zionist organizations. This indicates the isolationist mentality which prevailed from the beginning, not only with regard to the Palestinian Arab population, but also to the indigenous Jews and even extending to the non-Zionist Ashkenazis. The roots of this isolationism go back to the ghettoes in Eastern Europe, and even the kibbutz might be considered a sort of regenerated 'Ashkenazi ghetto' in that it often only accepts Jews, particularly Ashkenazis. This sectarianism combined with extremist nationalist views borrowed from the nationalist movements which flourished in Europe in the nineteenth century. None of these perspectives have any connection with the Jewish religion, for the overwhelming majority of Zionists were and still are non-practising and non-believing Jews.[10]

The Sephardim received their first financial shock when religious Ashkenazis seceded from the community (in 1816) and a second shock when the Zionists set up their own society collecting funds to build settlements and to cement political, cultural and economic control in their own hands. This led to the drying up of sources of income of local Jews who were obliged to give up collecting funds from abroad. This was the most important reason for the economic, political, organisational and cultural evanescence of the Palestinian and other Arab Jews who had joined.

During the First World War, hunger, poverty and contagious diseases were widespread within the Old Settlement whereas the Ashkenazi settlements were receiving financial support via Germany, Turkey's ally. They then distributed this aid amongst their own in settlements loyal to the World Zionist Organization. We shall see that the tragedy of the Palestinian Arab people paralleled the destruction and dispersal of Arab Jews at the hands of Zionists and their supporters.

Relations between Zionists and Palestinians were bad as the settlers were buying up land from absentee landowners who lived in the large cities in Syria, Lebanon and Palestine. The peasants were driven off the land and colonies were set up. The newcomers used these peasants as agricultural workers, subjecting them to rough treatment. The Russian Jewish writer, Ahad Ha'am, saw this treatment and criticized it in his essay, 'The Truth from the Land of Israel' (1891). 'Really, we could have learnt from our past and present history that we should not arouse the anger of the natives of the country through atrocious deeds. We must also be wary in our dealings with the foreign people among whose ranks we have started to renew our life. We must forge relations with them based on love, honour, correctness and justice. But what are our brethren doing in the Land of Israel? The complete opposite. They were slaves in exile and suddenly they have found themselves living a life of absolute freedom, the barbarous freedom that could only exist in the Ottoman Empire. This sudden change gave birth in them to the tendency to tyranny which is what happens usually with the slave who becomes king. They deal with the Arabs with an unjustified excess of harshness and hatred. They beat them and despise them for no reason whatsoever, and are, moreover, proud of it. There is no one to challenge these base and dangerous tendencies . . . and if [the Palestinian people] remain silent and patient for long it is because their anger is bricked up in their hearts for they are a people characterised by revenge – more than any other people.' Ahad Ha'am believed in spiritual, not political, Zionism, and his essays, except for this one, are studied in Israeli schools.

Zionist historians disregard these facts, and describe the Arabs as 'gangs of primitive murderers' and claim that Palestine was an arid desert or swampland. Zionist historians also disregard any modern economic developments by the Arabs which took place in Palestine before Zionist immigration, such as the development of trade and the new ports in Jaffa and Haifa. The same goes for the building of new commercial quarters in the cities, and new residential districts outside the old cities. For the Zionists saw themselves as the harbingers of innovation particularly in agriculture and Hebrew labour. They also discount the participation of Palestinian Jews with their Muslim and Christian brethren in the cultural, trade, and economic developments which took place prior to their arrival. Y.Bartel remarks that the majority of English tourists who visited Palestine in the Ottoman era praised the Palestinian Jews, describing them in a positive light and preferring them to the Ashkenazis by dint of their customs and tolerance of cultural changes.[11]

THE EXPLOITATION OF YEMENITE LABOUR

Sephardim then received a third shock when Zionist policy started to transform them into cheap labour due to the Zionist collectives' aversion to Arab labour. This policy was highly successful not only in relation to the Palestinian Jews, but to those from the Yemen and other Middle Eastern countries who were dislodged within Dar al-Islam and brought to Palestine, both prior to and after the foundation of the state of Israel. However, developments in the Israeli economy after the war of 1967 necessitated the proletarianization of the bulk of the inhabitants of the West Bank and the Gaza Strip as well.

From its very inception Zionism has faced a paradox: firstly, the principle of an improved standard of living. Herzl (the founder of the Zionist movement) promised poor European immigrants that they would experience an amelioration of their social situation in Palestine. Zionist emissaries promised the Jews a life of abundance in the 'Promised Land'. Most of the immigrants after 1881, having a Zionist outlook, managed to improve their standard of living in Palestine by means of the exploitation of cheap Arab labour and subsidies from overseas.

Secondly, the principle of 'Hebrew labour' which says that the Zionists would not be able to occupy Palestine as long as agricultural and manufacturing labour remained in the hands of the 'foreigner', that is the Palestinian, for 'he who ploughs the earth is its owner and master.' The Zionist socialist immigrants who arrived after 1904, in what was termed the Second Aliya, believed in this principle. They were the first Zionists to found agricultural cooperatives, and they started to found kibbutzim and labour unions, and after the First World War they set up the Histadrut. What was immediately apparent from the application of this principle was that young immigrants knew little about agricultural labour and that they were much inferior to Arab labourers who were also the former landholders. This led the Zionist movement to bring in Yemenites as a cheap workforce to replace Arabs. Thus, on the one hand the Ashkenazi agronomist could continue making a profit, and on the other hand the Zionist Left would be happy since the land was still in Jewish Ashkenazi hands, as long as the Yemenis did not show too much initiative.

Like Jews elsewhere in Islam, the Yemenites enjoyed self-rule. Their economic situation was good enough for them to own their own houses, and they lived through their handiwork as goldsmiths, metalworkers, and armourers etc.

After the foundation of Hovevei Tsion in Russia in 1882 news spread to the Yemen that rich Russian Jews had bought Palestine from the Turkish sultan and that the long-awaited Jewish Messiah had come to set up His divine world state centred in Jerusalem. Seven Yemenite families emigrated as a result, but when they reached Jerusalem they were surprised that the Jews there neither rejoiced to see them nor welcomed them since they would now have to distribute their funds amongst more people. They suffered severe hunger and disease and one of the families was forced to return to the Yemen via Cairo, from where the head of the family, Ibrahim al Sheikh, sent a letter warning the Yemenites that they would find neither help nor succour in Jerusalem and that the Yemen was a thousand times better than Palestine. This had a negative effect on the flow of emigration from San'a'.

In 1882 the Yemeni rabbi, Yoseph ben Shlomo Mas'ud, placed a notice in the Havatselet newspaper describing the wretched conditions of the immigrants in Jerusalem and asking for donations. The rabbi said that two hundred Jews of San'a' who had lately emigrated were living rough in the streets, and that none of their fellow Jews were showing as much pity as to give them shelter. They were reduced to begging for bread.[12] The press of the time was replete with the hardships of the Yemenites, and the lack of help offered by the Ashkenazis, and even that offered by the Palestinian Jews did not keep them from hunger. The Ashkenazi press could have called upon the Jews of the world to help. It was up to Israel Frumkin, who had set up a society called Ezrat Nidahim to combat Christian missionaries, to help set up the first Yemenite village at Kufr Silwan. A Yemenite elder described their condition thus: they were living without any shelter, suffering from the heat of the sun by day and from the cold by night, begging bread from passers-by to no avail. They were sleeping under trees and dying of hunger and disease among the garbage heaps of Jerusalem. Then some Christians from the American Colony found them, heard their story and started to help them with food and housing, to the disgruntlement of Jewish religious circles who accused the Americans of attempted proselytizing. The head of the Americans was Horatio Spafford whose daughter, Bertha, wrote about this in her book, *Our Jerusalem* (1951). The accusations were unfounded and amicable relations between the Yemenites and the Americans lasted until 1948. Jewish sources indicate that many Yemenites lived as beggars in the large cities such as Jerusalem, Safad and Tiberias.

In 1883 the Yemenite community in Jerusalem sent back to the Yemen two emissaries – Salim Hamdi and Yoseph Naddaf – to collect monies, but the community there refused to contribute since Rabbi Sulaiman al-Qara, the head of the community and judge of the religious court in San'a', withheld his consent to emigration for reasons both economic and religious. The Jewish Messiah had not yet come and the economic situation in Jerusalem did not allow for the absorption of immigrants. The religious authorities of the Arab Jews in Jerusalem and Alexandria had recommended the Yemenites not to emigrate, and thus Sulaiman al-Qara refused to make any donation and requested the emissaries to return whence they came. The rabbi had another reason, which was that the economic situation in San'a' had deteriorated as a result of the emigration while the amount of *jizya* tax which was payable to the Ottoman sultan had not diminished, meaning that each Jewish family had to pay more. A portion of the emigrants had to return to the Yemen between 1882 and 1895, while the rest joined the Sephardi community in Palestine.

Living six to a room, in insanitary conditions with a meagre diet, disease spread among the emigrants. The child mortality rate went up with some families losing all their children. But the Ashkenazi Zionist community, the New Yishuv, refused to help the Yemenites, considering them part of the dwindling Old Yishuv.

In 1895 thirteen Yemeni families attempted to set up a moshav at Bani Samu'il near Jerusalem. They bought a 600 *dunam* plot of land helped by a Jewish society in Poland and the afore-mentioned Frumkin. Arab peasants came to help them, and together they sewed 150 *dunams* of wheat and planted 7,000 seedlings while living in caves. Conditions obliged them to turn to the Zionist organisation, Hovevei Tsion, for help, but they were turned down. Subsequently a quarrel between the Yemenites and their Arab neighbours resulted in the abandonment of Bani Samu'il.

The Yemenites made various attempts at agricultural self-sufficiency through smallholdings. In 1904 they tried to set up an agricultural village in the Jordan Valley, then at Har Tuv, but all their attempts failed. We shall see that prior to 1948, almost all Palestinian and Arab Jews' attempts in this domain failed since all Jewish funds were being spent on founding Ashkenazi Zionist settlements which were considered to be 'pioneer work' and kept 'pure' Ashkenazi with national, security and economic significance. They thus had a monopoly over the foundation of kibbutzim and moshavim and the role set aside for the Arab Jews was that of cheap hired labour. However, the number of Yemenite immigrants was only 1000 between 1882-1904 while the number of Ashkenazi immigrants was 24,000.[13]

The second chapter in the Yemenis' sad history – their immigration and employment (more specifically their exploitation) in Palestine – happened during 1910-14 and was orchestrated by the secular Zionist movement. In this period the number of Yemenite immigrants reached 2,000 (opposed to 38,000 Ashkenazi immigrants). In 1908 Dr Ya'akov Thon, a specialist with the Zionist organization in Palestine, declared the necessity of creating a Jewish workforce able to compete with the Arab labourers on Jewish settlements. Thon suggested using the Arab Jews, particularly the Yemenites and the Iranians, since their 'cultural level', according to him, was that of the Arab peasants. He suggested employing the wives and daughters in the homes of the Ashkenazi farmowners in place of Arab women. He got over the problem of accommodation for the Yemenite workers on the settlements by demanding that they return to their families at the end of their seasonal employment, and during their employment they could sleep on the ground in the fields! Thon divided the workers into two – the Ashkenazis from Russia were the 'elite' and the Arab Jews the 'rabble', adding that the Russian Jews being culturally more refined than the Yemenites could not take the place of the Arab workers. Alex Bein, who quoted these facts in his book, *Return to the Land* (pp. 97-101), remarked further that the eastern Jews had few needs and could therefore compete with the Arabs, and if the Yemenite Jews who had already been employed on the settlement were to be kept there permanently they would not lack work.

In the same year (1908), a veteran settler wrote an article in the newspaper *Hatsvi* in which he mentioned that although the Ashkenazi Jews had fought for equality in Russia, they were suppressing the rights of others and that he opposed the concept of 'Hebrew work' on principle.

The party of Hapo'el Hatza'ir (later named Mapai and then the Labour Party) was the first Zionist organization to have the Yemenites work on Ashkenazi settlements. In its 1908 conference, this *socialist* party passed a resolution stating the necessity for Jewish employers to exploit the Jews from Islamic countries to do the work of the 'foreigners' (i.e. Palestinians).[14] The resolution also speaks of the need for an active propaganda effort to get these Jews to immigrate to Palestine and of the necessity for 'the conquest of labour'.[15] In 1910 the Yemenite worker started competing with the Ashkenazi, leading one of the leaders of Hapo'el Hatza'ir, Yosef Aharonovitch, to warn that 'we have created a competitor more dangerous than the Arab worker, who will make the life of the Ashkenazi youth impossible.' He added, 'in spite of all that, we can in no way fight him, but at the same time we shall commit a crime against the Yemenite by leaving him in his degenerate state of physical and intellectual development to be cheap enough labour to compete with similar servants . . .'[16]

Thus the Zionists dealt with the problem. They used Yemenite workers against Arab workers and when the Yemenites started to compete with them, they said 'How wrong we were to exploit the Yemenite and use him for such work' (which meant his dismissal!). In spite of this, and in accordance with Thon's resolution, the Zionist organization in Palestine decided to import more Yemenites by sending to the Yemen a member of the (socialist!) Hapo'el Hatza'ir party, Samuel Yavni'eli, né Warshavsky. Once there he took on the name of Eliezer ben Yoseph, making out that he was a great rabbi sent by the sages of Jerusalem, and carrying with him forged documents to that effect. The Zionist agent spoke and acted like a Yemenite whilst he informed them of the imminent coming of the Messiah and the Day of Resurrection. He told them that the time had come to emigrate to the Promised Land and furthermore promised them a life of luxury in the land of milk and honey – but not everyone could go. He chose 1,500 able-bodied people and started to transport them. However in April 1912 the Zionist organization sent him a telegram demanding him to cease because the Ashkenazi workers feared the competition. Yavni'eli tried to stop the transports, but the Yemenites objected, fearing that a delay would keep them in the Yemen on the Day of Resurrection. 500 of them emigrated to Palestine without his permission.[17] In his book,[18] the Zionist emissary recounted how his conscience troubled him as he demanded that the Yemenites leave their property, comforts and decent economic and social conditions in order to be labourers for the settlements. Upon reaching Palestine, they were not granted accommodation and were obliged to live in the streets and the fields, constructing huts from branches. With the arrival of the rains and the cold of winter, they called on their Ashkenazi 'brethren' and asked for mercy. One of the settlers allowed three families to live in a cowshed. Then every family tried to find a stable or a cowshed for the winter months. This was the situation in Rehovoth, Hadera, Zichron Ya'akov and Petah Tikvah among

others. These conditions worsened during the First World War.[19]
The child mortality rate increased in these insanitary living
conditions. In her thesis on this subject, Nitsa Druian states 'The
prevailing belief during those days was that the Yemenite child
born in Palestine would die, and if he arrived in Palestine under
three years old, he was not expected to survive.'

Moreover, the settlers treated their Yemenite workers so
despicably that one of the Yemenites, who returned home described
the life of those in Palestine as 'exile upon exile'. The contempt
directed towards them was worse than that of some of the Muslim
extremists in the Yemen. The Ashkenazis would inflict beatings
upon them and refer to them as 'donkey, son of donkey',[20] 'dirty
Arab', 'barbarian' and 'lousy Yemenite', and were taken aback when
a Yemenite tried to defend himself. In Rehovoth, for example,
some Yemenite women were collecting dry twigs from the ground
in one of the orchards when the Ashkenazi owner pounced upon
them and beat them viciously, tied them to the tail of his donkey
and rode back to the settlement with the donkey dragging the
women along the ground behind it. This event, called the Makov
Incident after the name of the brutal Yonatan Makov, was the cause
of much complaint in the Yemenite community. A similar incident
happened in Petah Tikvah where Hayyim Kossovsky fell upon a
Yemenite Woman, beating her about the ribs and arms even as the
woman screamed and begged for mercy. In Haderah the guard of
a settlement savagely attacked Yemenite workers as they slept. The
case was taken up by the Ashkenazi administration of the settlement,
but Zionist justice was denied the victims. Berl Katznelson, one of
the leaders of the Zionist Labour Movement disapproved of this
and criticized the exploitative and disdainful treatment meted out,
calling for a curb on these barbaric impulses.

Katznelson warned against forcing the Yemenites to believe that
there was no hope of justice in the Zionist community.[21] He
remarked that the settlers treated the Yemenites like slaves. They
were forced to leave the settlement of Milhamiya because of harsh
treatment, and generally ended up moving from one settlement to
another in search of work. They were expelled from Migdal because
their employer claimed they were not employable. They were,
however, allowed to stay permanently on settlements in the south,
on condition that they erected their quarters outside the settlements.
The principle of 'Hebrew Labour' was failing, since the settlers
could not do without skilled, cheap Arab labour. In 1913 another
30 families returned to the Yemen and letters from the Yemenites

sent from Palestine hardly encouraged their relatives to emigrate.

Even the humanist, Ahad Ha'am, in an essay published in 1912, said that 'Yemenite immigration affects the nature of the Zionist settlement by dint of their different culture and mentality'.[22] This outlook remains deeply entrenched and is a major factor in the crusade to bring in Russian Jews today, so that they may 'ameliorate' the make-up of Israeli society and dilute the majority of 'native Jews' (see chapter four).

Haim Arlozoroff, one of the leaders of the Zionist Labour Movement, wrote 'It appears that the case of labour in South Africa is almost the only situation which has a bearing on the conditions here.'[23] Katznelson avers that he saw 'innocent souls being beaten for no crime, the corruption of justice which was the lot of those beaten by the elected officials of the 'chosen people' in the chosen land'.[24] The Yemenites then started to struggle for an end to the discrimination, injustice and contempt heaped upon them. In 1913 they issued a communiqué condemning the policy of discrimination directed against them, and the duplicity which had been employed in bringing them to Palestine. Addressed to the Ashkenazis, the communiqué, inter alia, stated 'In your opinion we are insignificant and filthy dogs . . . We are despised by all for our poverty, but as God is our witness we only came from the Yemen on your advice.'[25]

The newspaper *Ahdut*, which appeared between 1913–14, informs us that the wages earned by the Yemenites were less than those of the Palestinians labourers. The same newspaper published a letter written by a Yemenite labourer, condemning the low wages and the scorn of the Ashkenazis who called the Yemenites 'gentile dogs'.

Unable to change jobs without their employer's permission, Yemenites were scarcely even 'free' labour. Forbidden to live inside settlements, they constructed their own poor quarters outside. Some of these, Mahaneh Yehuda, near Petah Tikvah, for instance, still exist. By 1918 there were 5,000 Yemenites, 10 percent of the Jewish population of Palestine.[26] Mikhael Albaz, a Sephardi intellectual, writes that researchers ascribe the exploitation and oppression of the Yemenite immigrants to rich Jewish farmers rather than to the socialist settlements. In fact, he maintains, the latter were more to blame since it was they who sent the emissary Yavni'eli to bring them, who went to great lengths to limit their ownership of land and who deliberately established their low living standards.[27]

In 1944 the veterans from the Ashkenazi settlements gathered at a graveside to commemorate the anniversary of the death of Berl Katznelson, the Zionist socialist intellectual. One of the 'comrades' eulogized 'If we had to study history through commemorative monuments, there would be no better one than this grave for the study of the history of that period, particularly the security situation and the health and social conditions, the life of the masses and the ethical level of the individual.' This woman, Aliza Shidlovsky, digressed to mention 'In this cemetery there is a special corner for graves of the Yemenites who came to Palestine following the mission of S. Yavni'eli. Family after family succumbed to malaria and other diseases. They went down like flies. There are no monuments on their graves, except for that of the rabbi's family which was completely wiped out.[28] This 'comrade' made no mention of how her 'socialist' comrades treated the Yemenites.

During this period (1881-1918) the conditions of all the Sephardim in Palestine deteriorated owing to the Zionists' monopoly of all Jewish financial resources. They made use of the Arab Jews, including the Yemenites, for hard physical labour such as quarrying, road building and household service. Even today Ashkenazi women are not to be found as servants. In this manner most of the Arab Jews were transformed into an exploited working class, like their Palestinian Arab Muslim and Christian brothers. We shall see how this era determined the role of the Sephardim during the British Mandate and after the founding of the state of Israel in 1948 when Zionist crimes against the Yemenites reached the zenith.

NOTES

1 The term generally used for those lands where Islam is the preponderant religion, literally meaning 'the realm of Islam'.
2 *Shevet va'am*, 1954.
3 Smooha, 1978, 281.
4 Eliachar, *Shevet va'am*, 1970.
5 Eliachar, *Life with the Jews*, 1980.
6 *Shevet va'am*, 1970, 34.
7 The Zionist term for immigration to the Holy Land, meaning literally 'ascent'.
8 Eliahu Eliachar's memoirs reminded me of the story of the Muslim 'Pasha' who was a friend of my father, and owned tracts of land with herds of sheep and cattle. Every spring he would present us with a sheep, saying: take this as a present for the New Year and the Day of Atonement and when you go to the synagogue pray God to grant me forgiveness. We would raise the sheep through the summer, feeding and washing it, and playing with it until it became one of the family. On the Day of Atonement, my father entreated God to forgive the sins of his friend. God would be entreated to pardon the Pasha and we would eat kebab throughout the successive festivals – Rosh Hashana, Yom Kippur and Sukkot. This went on year after year until that lifestyle was destroyed and we were scattered around the world. May God have mercy upon the Pasha.
9 An acronym from the initial letters of the Hebrew for Isaiah II, 5 ('O house of Jacob, come ye, and let us walk in the light of the Lord').
10 I have lived on six different secular kibbutzim which are the majority and have not seen a single member who believed in God (except for some parents of the members). As for the 'religious' minority, except for Neturei Karta who are

anti-Zionist, they exploit religion for political and colonialist purposes distancing themselves from Judaism since the Torah says: 'Thou shalt love the stranger, for thou wast a stranger in Egypt . . . '

11 *Cathedra*, November 1976.
12 Nini, 1977, 34.
13 Smooha, 281.
14 *Proceedings of Hapo'el Hatza'ir*, 226.
15 Kibbush ha'avodah – the Zionist term implies the exclusion of Arabs from the employment market.
16 *Hapo'el hatza'ir*, no. 4, quoted by Nini, 1977.
17 Nahum Menahem, 108.
18 *Journey to the Yemen*, 1952.
19 Nini, 1977, 78.
20 The 'son of' formula is typical of an Arabic curse.
21 Nini, *Cathedra*, 1977.
22 *Collected Works*, 1947, 426.
23 A. Muharib, *Palestinian Affairs*, August 1973.
24 Ibid.
25 Ibid.
26 N. Menahem, 109–110.
27 *Les Temps Modernes* (Arabic translation 1981), Albaz, 103.
28 Hayyim Hannegbi, *Bamerhav*, 20 May 1986 – *Ha'aretz*, 20 May 1986.

CHAPTER THREE

Under Zionist Autonomy
1918–1948

After the British gained control of Palestine in the First World War, they helped the Zionist organization create an autonomy and rule over the native Jews of Palestine. Simultaneously the British Mandate, having little sympathy with Palestinian Jewish leaders, and considering them a part of the enemy Ottoman system, kept them out of government, and weakened the influence of their chief rabbi by appointing an Ashkenazi chief rabbi as well as a rabbinical committee made up of equal numbers of Ashkenazi and native Jews. This policy led to:

1. Closer cooperation between foreign rule and the settlers.
2. The implementation of the Balfour Declaration and the eventual formation of a 'homeland' state for Ashkenazi Jews at the expense of the Palestinian population Christian, Muslim and Jewish. Native Jews were placed under the aegis of the Zionists since they had no representation in the world Zionist establishment. Clearly Ashkenazi Zionist domination did not start in 1948 with the founding of the state of Israel but began with the British Mandate. It is worth mentioning that Ashkenazi anti-Zionist religious establishments were placed outside this autonomy.

The most important institutions of the autonomy were:
1. The World Zionist Organization. In 1929 the Jewish Agency was founded to represent world Zionism in Palestine and to constitute its executive arm under article IV of the Mandate which called for the government of Palestine to recognise a 'Jewish Agency' and also an elected body to cooperate in the economic and social administration of Palestine, and, inter alia, to pave the way for self-determination.

2. The National Council (Hava'ad Haleumi), which resembled a cabinet.

3. The Jewish National Fund (Keren Kayyemet Leyisrael), whose purpose was to buy up Arab lands and settle Zionists on them, provided that the lands were never to be sold nor worked by non-Jews.

4. The Assembly of Deputies

5. The Foundation Fund (Keren Hayesod), which funded and equipped the settlements with agricultural machinery and livestock etc.

6. The Hagana, the secret army run by the Jewish Agency. The British pretended to know nothing about this army. In the Second World War the Hagana set up special commando units, called *Palmach (Palmah)*, made up mainly of left-wing settlers and kibbutz members, particularly those belonging to the Ahdut Ha'avoda party, which later joined the Labour Party. *Palmach* also had members from the Labour Party, Mapam and some city-dwellers. In addition the Hagana set up Shay, or the Intelligence Service, which after the foundation of the state became the Shin Bet[1] domestic intelligence service, and Mossad which specialised in foreign intelligence and spy operations.

7. The Histadrut (General Trade Union) and its components; the settlement organizations (kibbutzim and moshavim), marketing and banking organizations, the Sick Fund (Kuppat Holim) and the socialist schools, factories etc. The Histadrut is an empire with its most important economic posts in the hands of 'Socialist' Ashkenazi Zionists.

During the British Mandate this governing apparatus was termed 'Establishments of the Settler Community' (*Mosdot Hayishuv*), or the 'State-to-be' (*Ha-medina Badderekh*). In 1948 this very apparatus took on the name 'the State of Israel' and the head of the Jewish Agency, David Ben Gurion, became the Prime Minister of the Government of Israel. The Hagana became the Israeli Defence Force. The National Council became the Government of Israel and the Assembly of Deputies became the Knesset, i.e. the Parliament, and so on.

In addition to setting up this governing apparatus, the British Mandate appointed some British Jews to high government posts in Palestine, such as Norman Bentwich as attorney-general and chief legislator of Palestine law,, Ralph Harari as Director of the Office of Trade and Industry, Max Nuruck as first secretary at the main secretariat, Albert M. Hyamson as Director of the Office of

Immigration, etc. Nor must we overlook the fact that the British Government appointed the British Zionist, Herbert Samuel, as High Commissioner.[2]

This apparatus received financial and political support from the World Zionist Organization, enabling it to control the Sephardi Jews in Palestine and to transform them into second class citizens, (as it did to the Arabs in 1948) using the following methods.

PARTY LISTS

These were imposed in 1944 as opposed to voting for individuals. Under this system, the elector votes for this or that party, then the leaders of the party appoint the 'delegates'. However, all the parties in Palestine, before and after the founding of the state, are Ashkenazi parties, generally founded, and still in existence, abroad. They are funded by world Zionism and no Sephardi grouping has managed to obtain enough parliamentary power to represent their own interests or numerical power. Consequently Sephardim boycotted the election of 1945 (see chapter six). In addition, all the newspapers and organs of propaganda remain under Ashkenazi control and the governing apparatus has continuously fought off any attempt at political organization by Sephardim. Those who struggle for their oppressed community have been accused of treason, sectarianism, opportunism and exploitation of their community's plight and have lost their jobs. In spite of greatly increased Ashkenazi immigration during the Mandate, Sephardim constituted one third of the Jewish community in Palestine in 1948. However, if we take the Jewish Agency which wielded greater power, we note that its leaders were appointed by the World Zionist Organization which included no Sephardim on its higher bodies.

Even municipal elections took place along party list lines with the result that the interests of native Jews in the slum neighbourhoods were ignored, especially with regard to education, employment, housing, delinquency etc. In Jerusalem in 1938, for example, the 'Sephardi Community Council' won four out of a total of forty seats in spite of the fact that the majority of Jews in Jerusalem were Sephardim. For this reason the leaders of the Sephardi Community Council boycotted the elections and demanded individual elections along the British model so that a Sephardi could vote for his representative directly. The Ashkenazis, however, rejected this suggestion and this situation continued until

1945 when the two sides made a compromise. The party list system would remain on condition that Ashkenazi and native Jewish candidates alternated, leading Sephardim to achieve an overwhelming majority – 19 out of 30 seats. Panic started to spread amongst the ranks of the Ashkenazi settlers and the National Council (i.e. the Ashkenazi 'government') decided to annul the elections as one of their parties (the religious Hapo'el Hamizrahi) rigged the results. They then abolished the principal of alternation, and by means of various stratagems and ploys they managed to fragment the unity of Sephardi Jews and have the municipality abolished in 1948. David Ben Gurion then appointed a known opponent of the Sephardim, Dov Joseph, military governor of Jerusalem (see chapter seven).

FINANCE AND SETTLEMENTS

Contributions from world Jewry were monopolized and diverted for the benefit of Ashkenazi Zionist colonisation. We have already mentioned this point in the previous chapter, but the changes during the mandate period were qualitative not quantitive and led to the widening of the economic and educational gap between Ashkenazim and Sephardim. Having previously been a small minority in Jewish communities, the Zionists were now gaining ground, especially after Nazi Germany started to oppress the Jews. Inside Nazi Germany the Zionist Party was the only political movement, except for the National Socialists, allowed to carry out political activity. The Zionists set up trade relations with Nazi Germany and brought out some of the German Jews' capital in the form of goods.[3] At the same time, Sephardim were not allowed to collect donations for their community in Palestine. Funds accumulating in Zionist banks were used to ship Ashkenazi immigrants to Palestine and settle them there. These immigrants founded many of the kibbutzim and moshavim which became a political and military pillar of Zionist colonisation. They also made arms purchases, set up the Palmach or offensive units of the Hagana and established marine units (*Palyam*). They distributed funds to Ashkenazi parties under the guise of 'Zionist Education' and published Zionist newspapers and books etc. The interests of local Jews in the cities were ignored to such an extent that their neighbourhoods became deplorable slums. Most of the Sephardim who came to Israel after 1948 did not realise that the cultural and economic gulf did not only occur after 1948 but has been entrenched since the start of Zionist colonisation. Some

Arab Jews tried to settle some of the poor in rural areas to live off the land like their Palestinian neighbours, but the Zionist leadership insisted that agriculture remain in the hands of the Ashkenazi settlers and that native Jews be hired labourers. Out of the eighty settlements set up prior to 1926, not one was for local Jews, except Har-Tuv, which was founded in 1895 and financed by the Sephardim in Bulgaria; the Zionist establishment refused thereafter to extend any financial help to this village. Eliachar[4] observed that all Sephardi attempts in this domain failed. The advertisement placed by the office of Zionist agricultural settlement is most instructive on this subject. Regarding Yemenite Jews it was stated 'We are pleased to inform you that we have work for some families in the areas of water-transport, laundry and other domestic jobs.'[5]

At the fifteenth Zionist Congress in 1927, Eliahu Eliachar raised this matter. The head of the American Delegation, Steven Wise, expressed his interest in it to the anger of Chaim Weizmann, Chairman of the World Zionist Federation. Addressing Eliachar, he advised him not to arouse dangerous resentment amongst the various Jewish groups. He then ordered him to 'Go back to your city, and I will clarify the problem.'[6] If a leader of Sephardi Jews was treated so contemptuously, we can surmise just how the rest of the community or the Palestinians were treated. Eliachar states that even though Chaim Weizmann encouraged Sephardim to set up their own world organization, he exploited their leaders to secure his own position and did nothing solve the ethnic problem which was starting to get out of control. Weizmann expressed annoyance whenever the subject was raised. Celebrations for the founding of the Hebrew University in Jerusalem in 1925 were attended by Hajj Amin al-Husseini, considered at that time a moderate nationalist. Weizmann was asked to greet the Hajj and shake his hand – he refused. On 24 June 1919, Musa Kasim Pasha, the Mayor of Jerusalem, welcomed the Zionist leader, Menahem Ussishkin, upon his arrival in Jerusalem. The latter started criticising the municipality and intimidating the Arabs with talk of the 'Jews' strength and their arms'. (For details of the conversation see Nahum Menahem, 349-354.)

In 1925 native Jews attempted to lease a piece of government land in the Jericho area and to settle 500 families there. The British government agreed, but the Zionist establishment under the leadership of Menahem Ussishkin thwarted the plan on the pretext that government land leases were the prerogative of the Zionist Organization alone. The role of Sephardi Jews was to be that of servants, hired labourers in the settlements and quarries, newsvendors and shoe-blacks, not that of farmers mingling with the Palestinian Arab people near Jericho. The Yemenite tragedy played on throughout the Mandate (and still does), and the 'humanist' Zionist Moshe Smilansky published an essay in *Ha'aretz* (6 January 1927) in which he wrote that the Yemenite Question was a stain on the conscience of the Zionist Organization, and that 300 Yemenite families still lived in harsh conditions next to Ashkenazi colonies. Despite the fact that they included skilled farmers, the Zionist Organization gave them promise after promise, but no concrete help. Eventually some Sephardi Jews managed to set up the village of Hittin near Tiberias in 1944 with the help of Sephardim abroad. Hittin suffered from a shortage of water and a paucity of funds and housing. The agricultural lands they received were poor and most of the inhabitants lived, not from the land, but from their work outside the settlement.

At the same time as the Zionist Organization refused to help Sephardim, it was sending its emissaries to Arab and Islamic countries to exploit the Jews' religious feelings and to collect money for its Ashkenazi Zionist settlers. Those Jews who contributed, thought it was for 'the Holy Land'. Between 1920–1925, for example, 4,060 dinars (the equivalent of the same amount in sterling) were collected from Jews in Iraq for the Foundation Fund in addition to the contributions of Hezkiel Sasson, the minister of finance of Iraq. During 1920–1922 a total of 32,187 dinars was raised for the Jewish National Fund, and in 1921 Hezkiel Sasson donated 36,500 dinars. In 1920 Elie Kedourie of Shanghai gave 10,000 dinars to found a National Library on Har Hatzofim in Jerusalem, as well as donating a sum to found the Kedourie Arab and Kedourie Zionist Schools, at which latter school all the pupils were Ashkenazi. Donations from Iraq were, relatively, double those from the Jews of Poland. In 1920–1923 the Zionist Organization used the Iraqi donations to buy 76,000 *dunams* in Marj Ibn 'Amir (Emeq Yizra'el) between 'Afula and Beisan where they set up a number of settlements which count amongst the richest kibbutzim, such as Geva, 'Ein Harod, Tel Yoseph, Beit Hashitta and Kfar Yehesqel. In 1923 the Zionists managed to gain control over most of the lands adjoining the Haifa-Damascus and Haifa-Nazareth roads. Zionist documentation shows that contributions from the Jews of Egypt surpassed pro rata those of the Jews of Eastern and Western Europe. In 1921 alone the Zionists managed to collect 67,800 Italian lira from Tripoli (Libya). During the French Mandate in Syria and

Lebanon, the Zionist Organization set up Jewish youth organizations such as the scouts and the sports association (Makkabi HeHalutz), and sent the children out to collect donations for the Jewish National Fund. On 8 July 1926 they sent 1,200 collection boxes out and ordered the community to collect £200 annually. In the twenties the contributions of Syrian and Lebanese Jews reached £6,000,[7] which was spent on land purchases. The Zionist Organization demanded that the Jews of Marrakesh increase their donations, and the Zionist emissary, Tortus, wrote in an article that 'we don't just want American gold but Marrakesh gold too.' This comment aroused strong resentment from Moroccan Jews who started to feel that the Zionists wished to exploit them economically.[8] In the meantime, native Jews in Palestine were writing to their kin in Arab countries warning them not to give to Ashkenazi Zionists and detailing Ashkenazi arrogance and discrimination, but the Zionist Organization was stronger. How could the writers hope to defeat Zionist hegemony when the security apparatus and governments of Arab and Islamic countries failed to prevent funds pouring into Zionist settlement? At a time when children in the Islamic world were dying, year after year, from poverty and disease, Arab funds were being used to build kibbutzim whose members and children ran the Zionist military, economic and political establishment in the Zionist entity. Part of Arab Jewry was rich, and the state of Jews in general was better than that of the Muslims. Most Jews in the Islamic world in general, and in Palestine in particular, were poor and these funds should have been used to ameliorate the conditions of all citizens in the Arab world, not for Zionist colonists. The Zionists continue to employ deceitful methods against the Arab world: there is an Arab boycott of Israeli goods, but even so Israeli goods reach Arab countries with the place of origin concealed.

Even though the settlements in Emeq Yizra'el were built with Iraqi Jewish funds, Iraqis owned only the name of the Ashkenazi settlement 'Kefar Yehesqel' (called after the Iraqi Jewish minister mentioned above). For example, 'Na'im', who grew up in Iraq and Palestine, was surprised because he had not heard about it. 'At the start of the forties,' Naim said, 'I went to kibbutz Geva in Emeq Yizra'el to study agriculture. There were only 150 Ashkenazim on the kibbutz including women and children. The percentage of those in high positions in the Zionist establishment was very large, as in the rest of the kibbutzim.' Then he started to name the members and their jobs in the Zionist establishment:

Yehudit Simhoni: head of the Woman's Organization in the Histradrut. Her son lived on the next kibbutz and was an senior army commander during the Sinai War in 1956.

Yosef Efrati: one of the heads of the Agricultural Bureau of the Zionist Organization and a minister after the founding of the state.

Yosef Gurion: chairman of Tenuva, the marketing company of the Histradut.

Moshe Hofman: a leading member of the Hever Hakvutzot, the main coordinating organisation of Mapai kibbutzim.

Shaul Rosenfeld: head of the Armed Youth Detachments (Gadna').

Nahman Rezhik (now Nahman Raz): a leading member of the Workers Youth Organization, Hano'ar H'oved, in the Histradrut. In the 1980s he was chairman of the Educational and Cultural Committee in parliament.

Mikha – son of the aforementioned Efrati – became in the 1980s one of the heads of the Kibbutz League and the National Bank of Israel.

Since the forties, the number of members who have reached the top has doubled through cheap Arab and Sephardi labour. 'I went to that kibbutz,' Na'im continued, 'to study applied agriculture but they started to use me for the arduous and unskilled jobs. I told them "I want to learn about agricultural machinery." When I complained, Nahman Rezhik who was in charge of my squad said, "You just want to ride the tractor", and then "You work for your food" (meaning – you don't work for nothing). Of course we received no wages from the kibbutz, but the kibbutz members were paid, with education for them and their children, with comfortable apartments, and so on. They lodged us on top of the cowshed and when the bugs bit us then gave us a tent to live in – three of us to one small tent. In this way the kibbutz exploited many groups of youths who came from the cities for a two-year stint.' I asked Na'im whether he had finally learnt anything about agricultural machinery. 'Nothing,' he replied. 'After two years they finally told me, "Look, we won't teach you that." They didn't give any reasons but a friend said to me "Your origin is the reason." The kibbutz member, Nahman Rezhik, who as Nahman Raz became head of the Educational and Cultural Affairs Committee in the Israeli parliament said "Their treatment was disgusting", but he didn't help me. When they gave me their final "no", I was very ill for a few weeks and then I left. My back still gives me trouble. I have read lately that one of their children, Amnon Yadin, who became one of the heads of the Kibbutz Organization and who spent millions buying shares for the "Socialist" kibbutzim, committed suicide when the market crashed and that the kibbutzim lost huge amounts of money. They are building on sand. As children of the Arab world, we know that Arab sands are fickle.' The Iraqi Na'im did not benefit from the Iraqi funds which were used for Nahman Raz and other Russian settlers.

SEPHARDI PORTERS

Discrimination against the immigrants from the Arab and Islamic countries was rife. Apart from a few thousand Sephardim, the Zionist movement did not concern itself with bringing in Arab Jews until it became clear that most of the Jews of Europe had been slaughtered at the hands of the Nazis. We have already mentioned the 2,000 Jews who had been brought over from the Yemen in 1911-1912 to compete with Arab labour. During the British Mandate a few thousand Jews were brought over from Kurdistan and Iran to work in the quarries and do other menial jobs. Additionally, a limited number of Arab Jews immigrated to Palestine during this period. They became 10 percent of the immigrant total and they came for religious reasons. We should mention that thousands of Arab Jews had immigrated to Palestine during the eras of the Islamic Caliphate and the Ottoman Empire and that no one objected to them – precisely because they had come for religious reasons.[9] While the Zionist autonomy during the Mandate absorbed 382,000 Ashkenazi Jews,[10] and spent millions to get them there and to employ and house them, they completely overlooked the Sephardi religious immigrants. These latter joined what is known as the 'Black Belt', the slum areas around the large towns, which only deepened the gulf between the Ashkenazi and native Jewish community. Amongst the Jews who immigrated after the First World War were some Sephardim from Salonika (a community which originated in Arab Andalusia). They were skilled merchants and sailors and wished to use their talents in Palestine. Maurice Raphael and the Sarfati family attempted to found a marine engineering company, but the Zionist establishment decided that the role these Jews were to play was not that of merchants, but that of unskilled port workers. It transformed them into dockers and porters and the Ashkenazi community nicknamed them 'Horanim', meaning 'riff-raff' in Hebrew. 'Salonikan' came to mean 'porter',[11] and 'Kurd' came to mean 'quarry-worker'. 'Yemenite woman' meant 'servant' and 'shvartse' ('black' in Yiddish) meant 'Sephardi Jew' or 'Arab'. One of the Yemenite leaders at the Eighteenth Zionist Congress in 1933 declared that his brethren were considered third class citizens, like the non-Aryans in Germany.[12]

EDUCATION

Native Jews were stultified. After the foundation of Zionist autonomy, education in the Jewish community in Palestine fell under the authority of the ruling Zionist establishment. All the Jewish philanthropic societies which funded and ran educational programmes in Arab countries before the First World War had ceased their activities in Palestine. These societies told the Zionist establishment that, while they had to help with education in Arab countries since the Jews there were receiving no funding from world Jewry, the Zionist authorities ought to use some of their Jewish funds to finance Jewish schools in Palestine. The governing Zionist establishment in Palestine decided to pay no attention to native Jews and moreover hinder them in getting an education by imposing school fees. Since most Palestinian Jews were impecunious, they were compelled to leave school. Additionally many children had to go out to work to help their large families, joining the large army of newspaper-vendors, matchsellers and shoe-blacks, or the army of maids in Ashkenazi homes. Ignorance was prevalent in the streets of the 'Black Belt' and it begot poverty, crime, debauchery and drug-abuse. The Zionist Professor R. Backi admitted in a study he made in 1943 that 67 percent of native Jews did not even earn £2 a month, the wage of an Sephardi Jew was less than that of an Ashkenazi and that most of the Arab Jews were menial workers.[13] Naturally they could not afford their children's school fees and after three years 25 percent of children had already dropped out in the large town. A mere 11 percent of Sephardim completed their elementary schooling. Consequently more than 95 percent of university students were Ashkenazi. Many members of the community sent their children to religious schools which were more like prison camps.

On 21 November 1945, the magazine *Hed Hamizrah* sent a detailed report to the British Committee of Enquiry which was studying Jewish education in Palestine. The manifesto contained the aforementioned facts, and the magazine demanded Sephardi participation on governmental education committees.[14] On the other hand, in Arab countries, Jewish children were studying free at Alliance, parochial or government schools. When these Jews reached Israel after 1948, the superiority of their education was apparent.[15]

After a monumental struggle by the Sephardi leaders, the Jewish Agency decided in 1948 to establish a bureau of Sephardi affairs, headed (of course) by an Ashkenazi Jew, Y. Zerubabel. In an article entitled 'Observations on Political and Social Problems with regard to the Eastern Communities',[16] the Ashkenazi Professor Eisenstadt demanded the establishment of organizations to enable Sephardim to assimilate Ashkenazi values, on condition that they enjoyed autonomy in these organizations. The professor warned against eliminating the spirit of self-confidence and enterprise in Sephardi society. This sociologist from Jerusalem University did not see the contradiction in his opinion. How could native Jews recover their self-confidence and spirit of enterprise when they were being told to abandon their culture? The outcome for Sephardim was cultural nihilism (see chapter seven).

Na'im was asked how he got to university. He replied, 'When it became obvious to me that the kibbutz would not allow me to study agriculture, I left. I started work as a labourer raising cattle. It was really tough work, starting at two in the morning and finishing in the evening. After a year I found some light work elsewhere and I studied day and night preparing for university entrance examinations.'

THE WEAKNESS OF THE PALESTINIAN JEWS

How did the native Jewish community face up to this challenge? Did they fight, comply or surrender?

Due to the fact that the clash took place between two unequal forces, the reaction of the majority was a mixture of discord and adjustment. The confrontation ended with Zionist victory in 1948, as happened to the Palestinian Arab people despite the help they received from the peoples of the Arab and Islamic world. The Palestinians were united, and Muslims and Christians fought as one. They had a firm economic base in the land and agriculture, a developed national bourgeoisie and a common language and culture. They had lived on this land, not for hundreds but thousands of years. In 1918 they constituted the overwhelming majority – over 95 percent. In spite of these factors, the Zionists won in 1948, destroyed hundreds of Arab villages and put most of the Arab inhabitants to flight. If the Palestinian people failed, then how could the small weak Sephardi community succeed?

The Ashkenazi settlers adopted the policy of divide and rule towards the Sephardi Community Council of Jerusalem. As a result, a number of leaders of the organization split away and formed sectarian groups based on their Arab roots. Even those leaders who stayed with the organization were divided into two groups. The first, headed by Abu al-'Afia, supported the Zionist party list elections and demanded that only Spanish Jews be allowed to join this organization – a view always supported by the Zionist Movement which stated that Spanish Jews were 'Europeans'. Nevertheless, Arab Jews who had lived in the realms of Islam from Central Asia to Spain considered themselves a single community brought together by a common culture. The Zionists were the first to divide them into what was termed 'the Eastern communities', and the Andalusians (Sephardim). The second group was headed by Eliahu Eliachar and supported the conventional view that the Jews of Islam were one community. This section supported the adoption of the British electoral system rather than the party lists approach. They boycotted the Zionist elections. In 1946 the Committee decided to remove David Abu al-'Afia from his post, and Eliahu Eliachar was elected as his replacement on 20 February 1947. Finances were bad, as the Committees debts reached £3,000. Eliachar started to improve the economic situation. He paid off the debts and renewed relations with Sephardi Jews throughout the world via the World Organization of Arab Jewry, and convened a World Conference of Sephardim. The Zionist establishment opposed this Conference being convened in Jerusalem, lest facts about racial discrimination be revealed to delegations from all over the world. David Ben Gurion called Eliahu Eliachar 'Enemy Number One' for encouraging Arab Jews to defend their rights, and argued that, if he succeeded, the Mapai Party[17] would lose many votes in that constituency. Ben Gurion also said that if an organization arose to bring together all the individuals of that community, he and his associates would need that organization's endorsement. He added that the Sephardi community would not be able to take on responsibility concomitant with their electoral power.[18] (See chapter eight for Ben Gurion's views on Sephardim.) As a result of this Zionist pressure, Eliachar handed his administrative duties over to Meir Moshe Levi and David Sitton.

After the British occupied Jerusalem in 1917, Sephardim set up the Organization of Sephardi Youth, which soon became the Organization of Eastern Pioneers. It looked after economic and cultural affairs in the community, but suffered through lack of financial resources, being the only Jewish organization without financial help from the ruling Zionist establishment and consequently it ended its activity in 1929.

The native Jewish leadership tried asking for help from Sephardim throughout the world and to this end they convened a world conference in Vienna in 1925. They demanded the participation of native Jews in the cultural and economic development of Palestine. Delegations from around the world, except Arab and Islamic countries, attended the conference. The conference resolved to found a world organization for Sephardi Jewry, and we shall see how the Zionists later took it over. After this conference, the Fourteenth World Zionist Conference also took place in Vienna (1925). Eliahu Eliachar, Rabbi Uzi'el, and Zekharia Gluska all attended to demand rights for Sephardi Jews in Palestine. Eliachar commented that help offered by the organs of the Zionist movement to the Sephardi Organization had been minimal. 'Zionist leaders such as Weizmann and Ussishkin have praised Sephardi delegates and encouraged them to organize, but in reality they have helped very little. Sometimes we found them opposing this community's organization, after having made promises to it.'[19]

Zionist leaders claimed that Sephardi unity would cause the fragmentation of the Jewish community in Palestine. These claims were supported by some native Jewish opportunists who had left their community to join the Ashkenazi party organizations. The truth is that the Jewish community in Palestine was, and still is, divided. They feared the political organization of Sephardi Jewry, since this threatened Zionist Ashkenazi domination.

Even in the Histadrut, the General Federation of Labour, discrimination was rife. Whenever Arab or native Jews asked for work, Histadrut officials would palm them off with one excuse after another. Palestinian Jews thus decided to found their own trade union, 'The Union of Sephardi Workers', in Jerusalem in 1941. Amongst the founder members were Ishaq al-Iskandari, Secretary of the World Organization of Sephardi Jewry, Ya'qob El'Azar, Ya'qob Mizrahi, Yehuda Habshush, Y. Yafe, and Nahum Chucha. After protracted negotiations between the union and the Histradrut, the latter agreed to grant 16 percent of jobs to Sephardim despite their being the majority of Jews in Jerusalem. Another workers union was later formed in Tel Aviv.

Subsequently the Histadrut decided to destroy the Sephardi Union by paying to some of its leading members 'bursaries' (i.e. bribes) which totalled £1,775. Some were offered positions in the Histadrut (such as Ya'qob El'Azar, Ya'qob Mizrahi and Ishaq al-Iskandari). Moreover, anyone who tried to extricate himself from Ashkenazi patronage was subjected to intimidation and job loss. These Sephardi unions thus died away[20] and Sephardi workers were left with no union representation. In June 1948 Hanukka Mizrahi from Petah Tikvah sent a letter to the newspaper Kol Ha'am describing the Histadrut's policy of racial discrimination practised against Arab Jewish workers. He said that throughout his life he had felt that he was a second class citizen, that the Histadrut only gave him menial and low paid work. When he started to do night-work in a factory the Histadrut gave him no help in obtaining the proper pay and the factory owner actually lowered his wages. The Histadrut acceded to this and the union subscription was still taken out of his wages at the higher rate. His family's access to Histadrut health services was limited. After he was badly burned at work, he received payments for only four months although he needed medical treatment for a whole year. His doctor recommended that he do light work, but he remained unemployed and without Histadrut unemployment support. No longer able to afford his Histadrut dues, his medical treatment stopped and he was expelled from the union. Mizrahi added that Ashkenazi officials looked after their own and rejected work applications from the so-called 'Orientals'.

When the Labour Exchange Offices were formed, workers were promised equality, but they quickly became centres of discrimination which ignored the rights of Sephardi workers. Many from this community left the Histadrut unions, but others stayed in them since they needed the medical service which was, and still is, a part of the Histadrut. There is no equivalent of a National Health Service. Forty years after the appearance of that letter, the newspaper *Zu Haderekh* republished it on 25 June 1987. The Histadrut's policy alienated many Sephardi Jews from the Zionist 'Left'. The Zionist right exploited 'Socialist' discrimination, hoping to gain the votes of this down-trodden group. Arguably this laid the foundations of the rise of the Zionist Right.

In the field of journalism, the Hassolel Group arose in Jerusalem and published a weekly Arabic magazine called 'The Daily Post' (*Barid Al-Yawm*) which appealed for fraternal relations with the Palestinian Arab people. Sephardi leaders demanded Arabic language, history and culture to be taught at Jewish but the Ashkenazi Zionist leadership thwarted this. In 1942 Moshe Levi Nahum published the magazine *Al-Sharq* with Eliahu Eliachar as editor. They produced thirteen issues until Eliachar managed to publish *Hed Hamizrah* as its official editor on 15 January 1943. The magazine continued to appear until 9 August 1946, then ceased publication until 12 November 1948 when it restarted. In 1950 it folded due to lack of funds. David Sitton and Abraham al-Malih were also on the editorial board. David Sitton then became editor of the magazine *Bama'arakha* which was the organ of the Sephardi community. These Sephardi magazines covered Sephardi Arab culture and community problems on the principle of intercommunal harmony and cultural cooperation. The rest of the daily, weekly and monthly newspapers, the radio (and television later) were, and still are, controlled by a handful of Ashkenazi settlers and funded by World Zionism.

As we have seen, the leadership of the native Jews failed in its struggle for equality during the Mandate period. The causes of this failure can divided into two main categories.

a. Ashkenazi Zionist Strength

1. The help given by the British Mandate which enabled Ashkenazi Zionists to gain control over all Jews in Palestine (followed by American support after the founding of the state).
2. The efficiency of the World Zionist Organization, the fact that it was Ashkenazi, and its status in Jewish society in Europe and America which is overwhelmingly Ashkenazi.
3. the success of the Zionist establishment in monopolising the contributions of world Jewry, including those from the Arab world.
4. The strength of the Ashkenazi community which developed as a result of centuries-long European oppression.
5. The strength of Ashkenazi party organization which developed before the immigrations to Palestine and the Labour Party's control, both before and after the founding of the state, over the government, the Histadrut and the Jewish Agency. This party fought any independent Sephardi identity and organisation.
6. Despite the native Jews having formed a majority of the Jews in Palestine in the nineteenth century, they dwindled to 30 percent by 1948 due to increased Ashkenazi immigration during the Mandate.
7. Some Ashkenazi settlers formed a wealthy bourgeois class which used its money for its own ascendancy during the Mandate.

8. The use of bribery based on the principle of divide and rule to destroy the unity of native Jews and those Arab Jews who joined with them, and the use of the secret services to crush any Sephardi opposition after the founding of the state.

b. The Weakness of Sephardi Jews

1. Party political organization was more or less non-existent in the Arab world. Thus Sephardi Jews did not have sufficient political experience to found political parties to defend their interests. At the same time Zionism managed to divide them up according their countries of origin and bribe some of their leaders.
2. The paucity of financial resources for political work. The overwhelming majority of Arab Jews lived below the poverty level, and the racist employment policy aggravated this situation. One of the reasons for the success of the Palestinian revolution since 1965 has been the abundance of funds for revolutionary work.

The bourgeois class of native Jews in Palestine was very weak, and the wealthy class very small and not too concerned at the fate of the toiling masses. A large part of this class emigrated to the countries of Europe and South America as did some wealthy Jews from Arab countries, preferring Europe and America over Israel.
3. Due to the curtailment of free education, ignorance was widespread amongst this community and no new educated generation grew up to defend its interests and those of the community.
4. The political naïveté of Arab Jews. They believed in the religious unity of all Jews, not realising that the majority of Ashkenazis were non-religious. The liberal democratic principles common in Western Europe were almost non-existent amongst the Ashkenazi settlers, especially toward the native populations, be they Muslim, Christian or Jewish, since the Ashkenazi settlers had been born and educated in the shadow of authoritarian states such as Czarist Russia, Poland and Nazi Germany and other authoritarian Eastern European régimes. Most Zionist leaders had neither secondary nor university education, but still reached the top through party channels. Consequently their political vision was, and still is, necessarily short-sighted. Arab Jews had lived in peace for centuries with their Muslim and Christian brethren and all three denominations, as is the case with the Palestinians, were predisposed towards tolerance. Thus they were not on their guard and could

not prepare themselves quickly enough to confront the colonialist challenge.

Sephardi leaders did not mobilise the masses. They held discussions on the situation in the framework of their Jewish and humanist values. These means had worked in the Arab world for hundreds of years enabling Jewish leaders to safeguard their honoured position up until the twentieth century. However, the Ashkenazi Zionist establishment was not moved by these diplomatic methods and considered those who employed them to be naive and weak. In addition, most of the Sephardi leaders were from traditional wealthy and aristocratic families and mass struggle did not form part of their class mentality.

Sephardi Jews, along with Islamic society, including Muslims, Christians and Jews, had no notion of the racist nature of Ashkenazi Zionist nationalism, since racist opinions and nationalist ideas were alien to their way of thinking. This made it easier for Zionism to dupe Sephardi Jews, exploit their religious feelings over Jerusalem and the Holy Land and dominate them.

NOTES

1 This stands for the two initial letters of the Hebrew words *sherut bitahon* – security service.
2 *Shevet va'am*, 1970.
3 Lenny Brenner, *Zionism in the Age of the Dictators*.
4 *Life with the Jews*, 179.
5 Gluska, 454.
6 *Life with the Jews*, 184.
7 Menahem, 114–121.
8 See M. Abu Tbul, 'Zionism in North Africa', *Pe'amim Magazine*, 1979, 65-91; quoted by Nahum Menahem.
9 Smooha, 281.
10 Ibid.
11 Eliachar, 1980, 204.
12 Laqueur, *History of Zionism*, 1972.
13 Eliachar, 1980, 493.
14 *Hed Hamizrah*, 7 December 1946, Eliachar, 1980, 492-501.
15 In 1951 a large number of Iraqi Jews joined the Hebrew University in Jerusalem. The government felt these students might change the ethnic composition of the elite. Therefore most of them were immediately conscripted. (Personal communication, 1952, from Dr Yitzhak Shamush of the Hebrew University.)
16 Appeared in *Yalkut*, February 1949.
17 Labour Party.
18 Eliachar, 1980, 125–126.
19 Eliachar, 1980, 146.
20 Eliachar, 1980, 273–275.

CHAPTER FOUR

The Jewish Exodus From The World Of Islam

SEPHARDIM REJECT ZIONISM AND COLONIALISM

The Zionist movement claims that it is the 'National Liberation Movement of the Jewish People', but in reality it is an Ashkenazi nationalist movement which has attempted to solve the Jewish problem in Europe through the colonisation of Palestine.

The non-participation of Sephardim in the Zionist Organization can be ascribed to many reasons, the most important of which are as follows:

1. Sephardim did not suffer racist oppression, except for some isolated incidents in the long history of the Islamic world (see chapter one).

2. the nationalist and racist ideologies widespread in Europe in the nineteenth century were and still are alien to people living in Dar al-Islam, including the Jews, as we have previously explained. Even though the concept of nationalism was exported to the Arab world in the last century, this cannot belie the fact that the roots of Islam are much deeper than those of Arab nationalism, and we do not mean Islam from the purely religious point of view, but its totality as a way of life which unites all those living under it regardless of religion or race. On the other hand, Zionists always refer to Saladin as 'the Kurdish leader', reflecting their own nationalist extremism and their exploitation of the Kurdish movement in Iraq. Saladin however, did not see himself as a Kurdish, but rather an Islamic leader. He did not fight for Kurdish nationalism, but for the glory of the whole Islamic community. Jews in the Islamic empire saw

themselves as a religious and a cultural community, a part of the Islamic community, and they had preserved their religious feelings for Jerusalem, which was to be the centre of the heavenly kingdom on the Day of Judgement. Justice, truth and peace would reign there amongst all peoples, great and small. None of this applies to the Israeli state which has destroyed the Palestinian people and attacked Egypt, Syria and Lebanon amongst others.

3. the Zionist movement is an overwhelmingly non-religious organization. There are indeed some small religious parties, representing 15 percent of the population, but they exploit religion for political ends. Since 1967 groups of American Jews have been arriving in Israel such as Rabbi Martin Kahane and the Ashkenazi terrorist bands on the West Bank and the Gaza Strip. They have been influenced by the born-again Christian religious movements, which have recently appeared in the United States, and encouraged by the Zionist establishment to vindicate its occupation of the West Bank which was the centre of the Jewish state millennia ago. Israeli leaders' display of religion, particularly when they go to the West to collect donations from religious Jews, is good for business. Moreover, since the founding of the state no party has ever been able to form a government without having the religious minority tip the balance (in spite of all this, Arabs in general emphasise the religious character of Zionism and Israel). The irreverence of the Zionists who eat pork and have discarded all their Jewish traditions has, since the inception of the Zionist movement, been alienating Sephardim who, like the rest of the Muslims and Christians in the Middle East, are a traditional society.

4. the Zionist movement believes in the emigration of all or most Jews to Palestine as a political solution to the Jewish problem. Mass emigration is not a concept alien to the Ashkenazim, since the history of European Jewry is replete with oppression and dispersal, as they were displaced from one country to another. These migrations caused Europeans to see Ashkenazi Jews as rootless foreigners. Finally a great number of them emigrated to America. Many Ashkenazi Jews also lived in ghettoes, cut off from the surrounding population and ignorant of their language and customs. They did not dress like their neighbours or eat the same food. This situation continued into the nineteenth century, and in some areas until the twentieth. On the other hand, the concept of mass emigration was alien to Sephardim, since they had not been expelled from any Arab or Islamic state (except by the Christians after the fall of Muslim Spain). They did not live in ghettoes, but sometimes

in homogeneous or sometimes in mixed quarters. They spoke the same language and shared the culture of the Islamic community, following the same traditions and wearing the same clothing. They ate the same type of food and shared the same values. My father refused to change his traditional Arab clothing. He refused to wear a European suit and carried on wearing a tarbush in summer and a kaffiya in winter. He refused to trim his long moustache and used to say 'A man's moustache is a sign of his honour and manhood.' He was proud to go out wearing his silver-embroidered *abaya*[1] and derided the younger generation which aped the Europeans. He absolutely refused to speak Hebrew and steadfastly spoke Arabic until the day he died.

Sephardi Jews' roots go very deep in the land of Islam, and when they did move around it was always to another Islamic country. Sephardim were treated as fellow citizens by Muslims. Jews in the Arabian Peninsula, and particularly in the Yemen, became Arabised over time. Thus Jews had lived securely in the Arab world since the dawn of history, that is, until they were transported to Israel after 1948. The native Jew felt that he was one of the oldest inhabitants of the region and very often would look upon the country-folk who came to the cities, where he generally lived, as outsiders. Sephardim, specifically those from Iraq, the Yemen and Morocco, use the classical Quranic pronunciation of the consonants even when speaking colloquial Arabic. The Spanish Jews who were expelled along with their Muslim brethren and went to Turkey, the Balkans (and North Africa), are not 'European', as Zionist historians (such as Bernard Lewis) term them, but Middle Eastern.

5. Zionism is a colonialist movement which represses the native population. Sephardim used to hear reports of arrogance and racial discrimination by Ashkenazi Zionists from their cousins, the Palestinian Jews, and from other Sephardim who had emigrated to Palestine and then went home. Sephardim had observed that all leaders of the Zionist movement were Ashkenazi. Discrimination excluded Sephardim from Zionist programmes. Moreover, those Sephardim who had insight took part in the struggle against Zionism along with Muslims and Christians. In Egypt an Ashkenazi member of Hovevei Tsion wrote a letter on 31 December 1910 to the Zionist Office in Cologne. He described Egyptian Jews' opposition to Zionist ideas. The writer said that they were the overwhelming majority of the Egyptian Jewish Community. The only pro-Zionists were the minority who had emigrated there from Europe over the previous thirty years and were unable to infiltrate

the native community. He continued that the head of the Egyptian Jewish community, Monsieur Cattani, had poured scorn on Herzl's scheme.[2] Many Jewish intellectuals, with Ya'qub Sanuwa' (or Abu-Nadarah) at the forefront, joined the popular struggle against foreign rule. Sanuwa' was a playwright and journalist who set up the first Egyptian theatre in 1870. Some people called him 'the Egyptian Molière'. Under the name of Abu-Nadarah, he also published the first humourous magazine in the Arab world containing cartoons in 1876. The British exiled him to Paris where he continued his writings against colonialism. He was one of the pioneers of the doctrine of 'Egypt for the Egyptians' and 'Egypt for all Egyptians', which slogan was raised at popular meetings in front of the pyramids. In Cairo the anti-Zionist party rallied around the head of the Jewish community and a Christian was appointed to run the community's schools and to stop Zionist propaganda in the schools. The Ashkenazi Zionists were determined to get funds for Palestine, but Egyptian Jews countered that this would doom them to poverty and disintegration. The Ashkenazim were a community apart from Egyptians Jews, not only because of their Zionism but also their impiety. Since political Zionism was secular, the Ashkenazi Zionists were foreign to the Egyptian Jews. In Zionist circles, talk was mainly of European Jews, as if Sephardim did not exist. 'What could Zionism, expressed in terms of Russian thinking, mean to those who were imbued with the philosophy of the East and who were only affected superficially by Western values. What were the solutions which Zionism had to offer to their problems.'[3]

In May 1938, during the Palestinian Rebellion, as some of the 'Azaris were demonstrating against 'the Jews', and the Egyptian Parliament was demanding measures against Jewish financiers, the Egyptian chief rabbi, Hayyim Nahum Effendi, called upon his community to defend their country against Zionism and urged them to contribute for the relief of Palestinian refugees.[4] This call proved the claim of Chaim Weizmann that 'Zionism does not exist in Egypt.' In the forties, many Jews were involved in the Egyptian Communist Party, or the MDLN Organization for National Liberation. The Qaraites formed their own communist organization in Cairo (the Red Star) to fight Zionism and imperialism. In spite of this, sectarian Muslim circles in Cairo accused all the Jews of being 'Zionists' and with 'helping imperialism'. After the founding of Israel, and particularly after Suez (1956), Egyptian Jews were practically forced to leave the country they had lived in for more than two thousand years. Out of the 79,000 Jews there in 1946, only 2,000 remained. Two thirds of the emigrants went to the West. The other third being too poor to go to the West had to go to Israel. Anwar Sadat knew what a mistake the Egyptian Government had made and called upon Egyptian Jews in Israel to 'return as first class citizens,' – a wry comment on their second class status in Israel.[5]

In Algeria the Zionists failed in their attempts to get Jews to go to Palestine. 150,000 Algerian Jews (99 percent) emigrated to France, and from Tunis 60 percent of the Jews went to France and other European countries.[6]

In Iraq, Jews participated in the cultural, social and political life of the country, and many were radicals. There were famous Jewish literati such as Meer Basri, the poets Anwar Shaul, Murad Mikha'il, Ya'qob Balbul, the brothers Salim and Salman Darwish, Ibrahim Ya'qob, Obeida and Salim al–Katib and Salim Qatan. Jewish writers were among the first to translate works from European languages into Arabic. They published various periodicals such as *Al-Haris* (1920), *Al-Misbah* (1924–1929), *Al-Hasd* (1929-1937), *Al-Bustan* (1929-1938) and *Al-Barid Al-Yawmi* (1948) – all of which were in Arabic – and were active on other Iraqi periodicals. From the twenties Jews had stood out in modern Iraqi theatre and particularly in the field of Arab and Iraqi music. See the list of Jewish Iraqi musicians in the work of Y. Kojman (1978).[7]

Some extreme nationalistic circles accuse Iraqi Jews of 'having cooperated with imperialism'. This accusation was based on the opposition of some Jewish notables to Iraqi independence, but this same stance was taken by some Middle Eastern Muslims and Christians as seen in the statement made by the British High Commissioner in Iraq on 11 June 1921 to the Minister for the Colonies.[8] Many Jews considered that the division of the Middle East into small states and regional governments under leaders from one community or another would be detrimental to religious minorities and would encourage sectarian and regional chauvinism. Some, however, wanted just that, and in Lebanon the results are seen. Some Jewish leaders sent telegrams to the newspapers Iraq and *Al-Nahda* on 1 September 1918, expressing their support for Arab opposition to the Balfour Declaration.[9] On 13 September 1929 Jews participated in the National Rally at the Haydar-Khana Mosque, with Ja'far Abu al–Timman and others giving speeches. The Jewish poet, Anwar Sha'ul, blamed British imperialism in Palestine and said that the Balfour Declaration was to serve colonialist aspirations,[10] and in his book, *Zionist Activity in Iraq,*

H.J. Cohen writes that the British presence was the most important factor for Zionism in Iraq. Indeed, in March 1921 the British allowed the Mesopotamian Zionist Organization to operate in Iraq. Two years later permission was withdrawn, but this did not prevent a handful of foreign Ashkenazi Jews from continuing their Zionist fund-raising and 'representing' Iraqi Jews at the World Zionist Conferences. Despite British help for the Zionist emissaries, the native Jews of Iraq were indifferent or hostile to Zionism. When the 'Zionist Council' was allowed to carry on political activity, the British High Commissioner received a delegation of Jews who expressed their opposition. The Zionists thus failed to win over any important personage except for the man known as 'Hamoré', whose real name was Harun Sasson. On the anniversary of the Balfour Declaration, Sir Arnold Wilson wrote to the Colonial Office that the Declaration had aroused no interest in Iraq. He added that he had discussed the matter with Jewish personages, but they had expressed their sense of belonging to Iraq, which they described as a paradise compared to the poverty of Palestine.[11] This too was the position of Menahem Salih Daniyal, one of the Jewish leaders of Baghdad and a large landholder. He sent a letter to the World Zionist Organisation warning of the havoc Zionism could wreak for the Jews of Iraq, and that Zionism could alienate Jews from Iraqis and damage inter-communal relations. He continued that every Arab felt Zionism infringed upon his rights and that it was thus incumbent upon him to spare no effort to fight it. 'Any sign of sympathy for Zionism', he added, 'will be taken as a betrayal of the Arab cause.' The author relates this to the sensitive situation Iraqi Jewry found itself in due to its economic power and government posts, particularly in Baghdad where Jews formed one third of the population.[12] One of the most eminent Jewish lawyers of Baghdad also found fault with Zionism. In the English-language *Iraq Times* of 5 November 1938, Yusuf al-Kabir wrote that the Balfour Declaration was a dangerous and foolhardy policy and pointed out the folly of the historic fallacy that Zionists used to link their 'rights' to a Hebrew state which disappeared two thousand years previously.

After the Second World War, the Zionist Organization sent delegations to the Arab countries to smuggle Jews to Palestine. However, native Jews challenged these attempts and the number who left Iraq, for example, between 1946-1948 was just 65.[13] Many of these immigrants relate that they were children at that time and that Zionist agents tricked them into leaving Iraq with neither the knowledge nor agreement of families. People started leaving Iraq at the beginning of the Second World War, particularly after mob violence, known as *al-Farhud*, and the Rashid 'Ali al-Gailani Movement in 1941 which encompassed Iraq, Syria, Lebanon and other countries. It was a disaster for the parents of those chidlren. Some of them went to the Iraqi Ambassador in Jerusalem and wept as they begged him to send them back home. Dan Ram, one of the Zionist emissaries, informed Yigal Allon – chief of external operations of the Hagana – in a letter dated 9 October 1945, that Zionist activity in Iraq was devoid of results and suggested that the Ashkenazi emissaries return to Palestine.[14] Enzo Sereni, head of the secret Zionist mission in Iraq, wrote a letter to the Jewish Agency in which he opined that the Zionist movement had failed 'due to native Jewish apathy'.[15] Even after the attacks and killings which occurred in the Iraqi *Farhud*, the Jews still did not evince any support for the idea of emigration. Sereni attributes this to Jewish readiness to forget what had happened and get on with their lives, and as well as to the swift economic development which resulted from the war and the compensation paid by the government to the victims.[16]

The Jewish emissary to Syria and Lebanon, Munya M. Mardor, also wrote that the native Jews were not interested in emigration, and the secret Zionist organization directed its efforts only at the youth.[17] When Ruth Klieger arrived in Egypt to organize the emigration of the Jews and collect donations from the well-to-do, Katani Pasha, head of the Jewish community, declared that he would set his dogs on her and any other Zionist emissary.[18]

When they arrived in Tunis after the Second World War, Zionist emissaries found that Tunisian Jews had no dislike of the Germans. Tunisian Jews could not believe that a holocaust had taken place in Europe, since the Muslim Pasha of Tunis had guaranteed their safety in a private meeting in his palace attended by the heads of the Jewish community and the leaders of the Muslims. The Pasha promised his Jewish citizens that he would protect them for they were *dhimmis*. When the influence of the Zionist emissaries grew after the war, the leaders of the Tunisian community demanded their expulsion. They went to the Tunisian authorities with a letter from the Jewish community objecting to their activities – and they were indeed expelled.[19]

In 1948 Iraqi Jews participated with their Muslim and Christian neighbours in the struggle against the pro-British Salih Jabr and the Portsmouth Treaty. When the Jewish activist, Shamran 'Alwan, was killed by the police, the right-wing nationalist newspaper,

Al-Yaqza, in its edition of 5 February 1948 eulogised him as a martyr of the Iraqi people in its struggle for freedom. It also published the names of Jews who contributed to the Palestinian Arab people's cause.[20]

In 1946 Iraqi Jews, Muslims and Christians had formed 'The Anti-Zionist League' to oppose Zionist plots and the smuggling of Jews to Palestine as well as to preserve their Iraqi identity. According to Ma'arakhot (1969), 'Whereas the secret Zionist meetings were attended by approximately thirty-six people in 1948, the League's newspaper (*'Usbah*) came out daily in 6,000 copies.' In October 1949 the police arrested forty-eight suspected Zionists and Cohen comments on this event that 'those arrests finished off the Zionist movement in Iraq.'[21]

The Israeli politician, Eliahu Elat, averred that 'Sephardim do not desire to transfer their allegiance to Israel,'[22] and during the Zionist propaganda onslaught, the chief rabbi, Sasson Kedourie, pronounced that 'the responsible leaders of Iraqi Jewry believe that this country is their homeland through thick and thin' and the leadership, according to the chief rabbi, believed that the difficult times would soon pass.[23] On 11 December 1949, Sasson Kedourie resigned his position as head of the Jewish Community because of the strictures imposed upon the Jews as a consequence of the Palestine war. In its issue of 30 December, 1949 the British newspaper, *The Jewish Chronicle*, commented that 'the Chief Rabbi and Iraqi Jews do not like Zionism since it has caused difficulties for them. They prefer to stay in Iraq and live under the patronage of Islam and its tolerance. They are attached to their houses and traditions, and to the graves of their prophets in Iraq. They have no desire to leave their country and live in refugee camps in Israel. They believe that people there are not too friendly towards oriental Jews.'[24] Sephardi Jews in Turkey joined in the anti-Zionist movement also. Between 1897 and 1919 they published a newspaper called *Al-Masirant* which warned all Jews against Zionism.[25]

Even though they had had French nationality and culture imposed on them, educated Jews in Algeria joined the National Resistance – especially the revolt of Jawzi Abu Al-Khair on 8 November, 1942. The revolt paved the way for the American Army to liberate the Maghreb from the Germans. When the Jews ascertained that the French had destroyed Jewish/Muslim relations, they did not emigrate to Israel, rather to France. In Syria the majority of the Jews voted with their feet! Even though there were 29,770 Jews there according to the 1943 census, 22,000 went to the United States in the middle of the forties.[26]

To sum up, the overwhelming majority of Sephardim either resisted Zionism or were just not interested in it. They naturally attempted to stay in their respective Arab-Muslim countries. The minority who cooperated with the Zionists did not grasp actually the import of Zionism until they came up against racist discrimination in the labour camps in Israel. Most looked back with regret.

ZIONISM REJECTS THE SEPHARDIM

As well as Sephardi opposition to Zionism, this reticence was mutual. The Zionist movement refused to bring these Jews over to Palestine or to let them participate in their settlement programmes. That is, except for a couple of thousand Yemenites, Kurds and Iranians, who had been shipped to Palestine to do the menial jobs which Ashkenazim did not want to do. The most important reasons for this policy were as follows:

1. The Zionist movement, being a European Ashkenazi movement, was only concerned with Ashkenazi Jews.
2. Having lived in ghettoes for hundreds of years, the Ashkenazim constituted a closed community and rejected anyone from outside.
3. Believing themselves to be the elite of the Jewish people, they considered Sephardim to be inferior and incapable of carrying out pioneer work (see chapter eight – Ashkenazi views on Sephardim). Since they had nothing but contempt for the Arabs, the Ashkenazim viewed Jews who had lived with Arabs in the same light (see Kedourie, 1970, 310-311). Moreover, their arrogance would not let them admit to an unconscious fear of Arabs and Sephardim.
4. As donations from world Jewry were divided amongst Zionist programmes and Zionist parties, the participation of Sephardim would have meant a diminution of funds for the Ashkenazim.

REASONS FOR EMIGRATION

After the foundation of the state of Israel, most Jews from Arab and Islamic countries emigrated to Israel. Historians disagree over the exact reasons for this. Zionist historians ascribe it to 'Muslim and Arab oppression of Jews', but anti-Zionist historians agree that it was a result of a Zionist plot.

After the Second World War, the Zionist establishment decided to bring over all the 'Sephardim', although this decision alone was not enough to get Jews from Arab and Islamic countries to leave and come to Israel. All the means employed by the Zionists such as deceit, terrorism, bribery and pressure on the Arab government were of no avail. For this reason the Zionists had need of another factor to push Sephardim into emigrating. This factor was the sectarianism whose seeds colonialism had sown, and which had been nurtured by the Arab-Zionist conflict and the catastrophe of the Palestinian people. One must, however, avoid generalising, since the factors involved differed from place to place and according to class and society. This also applies to the motives of Arab and Islamic governments in allowing the Jews to emigrate to Israel.

During the Second World War it became apparent to the Zionist establishment that Nazi Germany had destroyed the reservoir of Jewish immigration from Europe. Moreover, American and British Jews showed no desire to emigrate to Palestine, nor did the majority of Ashkenazim in the Soviet Union, thus the Zionist establishment changed its stance on Sephardi immigration from Arab and Islamic countries. Between 1948 and 1975, the authorities managed to bring in 819,000 Ashkenazim (especially from socialist countries), but the Zionist establishment was still not satisfied since most of them were averse to doing manual labour and some were using Israel as a half-way house for America. So it was decided to bring over Sephardim as cheap labour and for military service. Ben Gurion often declared that 'it is immigration which strengthens the security of the state more than anything else,' and that 'the fate of the country depends on immigration.' Shimon Peres, later head of the Labour Party, stated at the end of the fifties that sustained immigration would enable Israel to have a million-strong army which in turn would help Israel to impose its hegemony over the Middle East, a statement rejected by Ben Gurion, then Prime Minister, for tactical reasons. Peres, considered one of the Labour Party hawks, was Director of the Ministry of Defence, had changed his Polish name 'Persky' to the Hebrew for vulture. Israel also intended to settle all the Arab territories it had occupied and whose Palestinian inhabitants it had expelled to prevent their return and to vindicate its claims that what had happened there was simply a 'population exchange' between Israel and the Arab countries. During this period the number of 'Sephardim' who reached Israel was 751,000, or 48 percent of the total influx of 1,570,000. The catastrophe of Palestine, the Arabs and Islam is that the enormous manpower that shifted the balance of power in favour of Israel was not from enemy countries, but had come from those very Arab, Islamic, and socialist countries. This diplomatic, or nationalist, failure requires very careful study. We can gauge the economic and military developments which occurred in Israel as a consequence of this mass immigration if we bear in mind that the total number of Jews in Palestine at the time of the foundation of the state was only 630,000 , constituting a third of the population. The matter also demands a study of the economic development which occurred as a result of the importation of cheap labour into Israel (see chapter nine). In addition, we must compare this influx with the Jewish immigration which had taken place since the beginning of Zionist settlement in order to extract the proportion of the Jews of Islam.

Jewish Immigration to Palestine and the Proportion of Immigrants from the Realms of Islam (1882-1975)[27]

Aliyah (Immigration)	Date	Total number immigrants	No. from of Islamic countries	Proportion of Sephardim
First Aliyah	1882-1903	25,000	1,000	4%
Second Aliyah	1904-1914	40,000	2,000	5%
Third Aliyah	1919-1923	35,000	2,400	7%
Fourth Aliyah	1924-1931	82,000	9,800	12%
Fifth Aliyah	1932-1948	265,000	36,200	10%
Post founding of Israel	1948-1975	1,570,000	751,000	48%

Israel managed to double its population within the first three years from its founding. The 559,675 immigrants who arrived between 1948-1951 can be divided as follows:
271,188 from Eastern Europe
241,870 from Dar al-Islam
46,617 from Western Europe, America and other countries.[28]

By 1954 the number of immigrants since the founding of the state reached 725,000, divided as follows:
From Arab and Islamic states[29]

Iraq	125,000
Yemen and Aden	49,000
Morocco/Tunisia	90,000
Turkey	35,000
Iran	27,000
Total	326,000

From Eastern Europe (i.e. Ashkenazim, except for the Bulgarian Sephardim):

Bulgaria	38,000
Hungary	15,000
Rumania	122,000
Poland	107,000
Other countries	117,000
Total	725,000

By 1954 the proportion of Palestinians had gone down from 70 percent to 11 percent due to their expulsion and Jewish immigration. During the same period 50,000 Jews representing 7 percent of the total of immigrants and mostly Sephardim, left the country.[30]

In 1958 Abraham Abbas, a Syrian Jew who belonged to Ahdut Ha'avodah (the Socialist Zionist party) wrote that the number of Sephardim had immigrated since 1948 was 600,000 (out of a total of 900,000 immigrants during the same period). He broke down their countries of origin as follows:[31]

North Africa	150,000
Iraq	125,000
Yemen	50,000
Libya	40,000
Egypt	40,000
Iran	35,000
Turkey	40,000
Bulgaria	40,000
Greece and Yugoslavia	10,000
India	10,000
Other countries	60,000
Total	600,000

The story of Jewish immigration from Arab and Islamic states to Israel after 1948 is a bizarre tale. It highlights not only the Zionist establishment's devious activities but also the backwardness of the political structure of Arab and Islamic world and the naïveté and weakness of the Jews of Islam in confronting Zionism and Western influence. Arabs or Muslims reading the facts about anti-Sephardi discrimination in Israel may not be too sympathetic and they might well say that it is their own fault for going to live there in the first place. Undoubtedly the major factor in this catastrophe is Zionist intrigue, but this alone could not have succeeded if the soil in which it was planted in had not been fertilised by colonialism and the Palestinian tragedy of 1948.

Arab nationalist sources state that the British and French favoured Jews in the Arab countries and helped them into high government posts as well as encouraging their financial and commercial endeavours. If this is true for the twentieth century, it still does not adequately reveal how ever deepening Western involvement in the Arab and Islamic world had been damaging the position of the Jews since the eighteenth century.

We have described above how the Islamic state preferred Jews to Christians in matters of the state and economy. However, the European states tried, from the eighteenth century, to strengthen their influence in the Ottoman Empire by interfering in internal affairs and protecting 'the interests of Christians' by means of the Capitulations. Christians also enjoyed the protection of the Church and European Christian missions and they received help from European traders. We should also mention that trade was monopolised by the British in one half of the Ottoman Empire and by the French in the other. It was a British trading firm, the Levant Company, which banned the use of Jewish translators in Greater Syria. Arab Christians started sending their children to Europe for their education and when they came back they would get the government jobs which previously went to Jews. Simultaneously, European anti-semites (diplomats and clerics) exported the myth that the Jews killed Christian children to use their blood for the baking of matzah. In Europe this fuelled anti-Jewish pogroms over hundreds of years. There had not been any such accusations of ritual murder in the Islamic world until the nineteenth century. The best known case in the Middle East was the disappearance of Father Tomaso in Damascus in 1840 when the French Consul, Ratti Menton, whipped up anti-Jewish sentiment. Anti-semitism was thus imported into the Middle East, and particularly into Christian circles, by European colonialists who exploited the competition between the communities in trade and government employment to further sectarian chauvinism.

Inside the Muslim community, from the eighteenth century on, the realm of Islam had been subjected to fierce encroachments on the economic, military and cultural fronts which reached their peak in 1918 with their complete subjugation to European control. During this period of defeat Muslims started to voice their grievances over non-Muslim communities, particularly the Christians. Notwithstanding the protection granted to Jews by the authorities, their position weakened with respect to their compatriots. This was not a financial deterioration, since after the First World War they participated in economic developments and became affluent, but this was paralleled by deterioration in community relations caused by the following factors:

1. The British and French authorities after 1918 favoured non-Muslims in their political and economic systems in the Arab countries. There were various reasons for this, such as the policy of sectarian differentiation, the imperialists' suspicion of Islam, and the professional qualifications which the minorities were gaining in their modern schools (see chapter one). All of this led to the growth of intercommunal envy.

2. The upsetting of the intercommunal equilibrium as a result of the establishment of regional Arab states.

3. Anti-Jewish Nazi propaganda in the thirties and during the Second World War, including Yunis Bahri's Arabic programme 'This is Berlin'.

4. Ashkenazi Zionist settlement at the expense of the Palestinian peasantry, the founding of the state of Israel, the destruction of hundreds of Palestinian towns and villages, the expulsion of most native Palestinians and the expropriation of their property and lands, martial law after 1948 for all those Palestinians remaining inside the Zionist entity, the appropriation of more than 80 percent of the lands of this minority in addition to the refugees' lands.

In addition to all this there was the blood – the blood which flowed between Zionism and Arabism, the bloodshed of Deir Yassin, Kafr Qasim and Eyn Zeitun amongst others. Then came the Tripartite War against Egypt in 1956.

5. Zionist anti-Arab propaganda in Europe and America which exploited the Sephardim's predicament in order to get them to immigrate to Israel.

There is no doubt that the Jews benefitted from the modern political and economic systems which had been set up in Arab countries after the Great War. They opened many schools and educational institutes, developed their commerce and accepted government positions. The British High Commissioner to Iraq stated in 1918, for example, that the Jewish community in Baghdad was to be encouraged.[32] The progress of the Jews was not due to the British or the French alone, but due to other historical reasons:

1. The majority of Jews were city-dwellers whereas the majority of Muslims lived in the country.

2. Since the Jews were not part of the military or political elite in Dar al-Islam, they had for some hundreds of years concentrated on commercial and financial activity. Their relations with world Jewry helped them in this and when the doors to progress were opened they were quicker off the mark than their Muslim brethren.

In the thirties there arose a new class of Muslim employees and intellectuals which found that the proportion of Jews in the upper and middle classes was relatively greater than that of Muslims. This paradox had also occurred in Europe, America and previously in the Islamic state. In Germany, the Nazi party exploited this to come to power and reinforce its influence both in Germany and later in all the countries it occupied.

In the Western capitalist and socialist countries, the ruling elites decided to exploit Jewish industry to prop up capitalist and communist rule respectively, just as in the past the Islamic state had made use of Jewish activity to reinforce Islam, especially in Muslim Spain.

In the modern Arab states traditional circles, as well as clerics and the democratic nationalist leaderships, tried to preserve equality, tolerance and just competition amongst the communities. All the left wing groups, such as that of Ja'far Abu al-Timman in Iraq, proclaimed the necessity of non-denominational national unity to confront imperialism and reaction. However, extreme rightist circles were influenced by Nazi propaganda and believed in the principle of 'my enemy's enemy is my friend', hoping to rid themselves of British and French imperialism with the help of Nazi Germany. These groups did not realise that Nazi German imperialism was much worse than the British variety. They were also influenced by Nazi anti-Semitism. Despite the slight support that these groups received amongst the upper and middle classes, they gained a large popular following by exploiting popular hostility to colonialism and mass sympathy with the Palestinian rebellion in the thirties.[33] Some Syrian and Palestinian exiles tagged along, inciting their Muslim brethren in Arab countries against their Jewish compatriots.[34]

The root cause of this problem is that extremist sectarian circles could not differentiate between the foreign Zionist and the local Jews who had, for millennia, been an intrinsic part of Dar al-Islam. Besides, it was much easier to turn against one's weak Jewish compatriot than to go off and liberate Palestine by force. This was the greatest mistake that nationalist Arabs made in the twentieth century. The tragedy of Palestine in 1948 was enormous, but the emigration of the Jews of Islam to Israel was even greater, not just for the Jews involved but for Palestine and the whole Islamic community. It tilted the balance of power in Israel's favour.

The Islamic, and even the Ottoman state, had preserved intercommunal equilibrium throughout its provinces while they remained united under a single government. After the division of the Islamic state into a number of statelets, there were endless bloody intercommunal feuds.

The other factor which undermined the position of Jews in Islamic society was the setting up of armed secret Zionist cells inside Arab countries. In spite of the fact that these organisations were established by Ashkenazi spies sent from Palestine and that they failed completely to get a large number of Jews to emigrate, they did manage to sow doubts and suspicions in the minds of Muslims about the loyalty of their Jewish compatriots.

Furthermore, Zionist anti-Arab propaganda in America and Europe, together with the demonstrations organised by Israeli agents, castigated Arabs and Muslims over Jews in Arab countries. These Zionist activities abroad only worsened the situation of Jews in Dar al-Islam.[35]

The Iraqi government ultimately had another reason for supporting the Exodus of Jews: to get rid of Jewish Radicals and communists. The Shah of Iran also encouraged 3,000 Jewish communists to emigrate to Israel.

The prevailing belief in the Middle East is that the Western nations advised Arab governments to ease Jewish emigration in exchange for resettling Palestinian refugees. Those who hold that opinion point out that the leaders of the Arab states at that time were extremely pro-Western and that the confiscation of Jewish property by some Arab states was a part of a conspiracy aimed at 'justifying' the expropriation of Palestinian property in Israel. This opinion is backed up by a memorandum from the British Foreign Office on 5 September 1949 about the resettlement of 100,000 Palestinian refugees in Iraq in exchange for the export of 100,000 Iraqi Jews to Israel.[36] After the Iraqi government declared in March 1951 that it was freezing the assets of Jews who had chosen to renounce their citizenship and emigrate to Israel, Lord Samuel, the British Zionist, proposed to King Abdallah of Jordan the expulsion of Iraqi Jews and confiscation of their property as a quid pro quo for what happened to the Palestinians. This view was supported in the Iraqi Senate by Muzahim al-Pachachi on the basis of a suggestion by an American Zionist writer.[37] At the same time it was reported in *The*

Scribe, London, June 1990, that the Israeli foreign minister, Moshe Sharett, made it clear that in any future settlement of Palestinian frozen property a set-off will be made of frozen Jewish assets in Iraq.

Israeli diplomats were already active in Washington, Paris and London trying to arrange the emigration of Jews from Morocco, Tunisia, Egypt, Iraq, Iran and the Yemen, which entailed the Western powers putting pressure on the governments of Arab and Islamic states. Of course, the theory of 'population exchange' was baseless since the populations involved, Jews and Palestinians, had not agreed to such an exchange. The Palestinians did not receive Jewish assets, nor vice versa, but both groups lost everything. The British Consulate in Jerusalem commented that Israel would welcome the immigrants who would form a cheap workforce and that Israel would demand that Iraq absorb the Palestinian refugees to take the place of the Jews who had left.[38] The Israeli historian Segev says that 'Israel was in urgent need of these immigrants,' and *Ha'aretz* wrote on 13 April 1949 that 'many saw them as cannon fodder'.[39] Israel and the World Zionist Organisation used all types of pressure and propaganda to force Arab governments to squeeze out their Jewish populations. In March 1949 Zionist propaganda claimed that Iraq had hanged seven Jews for Zionist activity. The truth is that these seven had already fled Iraq before their trial. Israel went to great lengths to try and prevent the World Bank from granting a loan to Iraq, organising demonstrations in front of Iraqi embassies around the world and harassing the Iraqi ambassador to the United Nations whenever he went into the building or came out. Israel turned to the United Nations and to Eleanor Roosevelt with its threats to crack down on Arabs inside Israel and to organise a secret movement against Nuri Said inside Iraq.[40]

With regard to the Jews of the Yemen, the British authorities, at the outbreak of the Palestine War of 1948, prevented Jews from leaving Aden. The Zionist Organization used diplomatic pressures to get this ban rescinded. A representative of the World Jewish Congress, Leon Kobovitsky, met Muhammad Jibli, a representative of the Imam, to discuss the question of Jewish emigration from the Yemen and the areas under British protection. Jibli agreed to persuade the Imam. After the Egyptians signed an armistice with Israel, the Imam agreed to the emigration programme.[41] An emissary of the Jewish Agency, Yosef Tsadok, actually met the Imam and an emissary of the Ministry of Immigration, Ovadiah Tuviah, met Sultan al-'Awadhli.[42] They managed to transfer 50,000 Jews from the Yemen and Aden in operation 'Magic Carpet', in addition to the 35,000 Yemenites who had previously immigrated to Palestine, but these Jews paid the price in property and dignity as we shall see later.

SECTARIAN HARASSMENT

The six factors we have discussed created an anti-Jewish atmosphere in Arab countries and there were some instances of anti-Jewish disturbances, attacks and killings which helped Israel to transfer most of the Jews to Israel. The rest emigrated to Western countries (the number of Jews still living in Arab countries is 63,000, mostly in Morocco. Researchers at a symposium at Baghdad University estimated there to be 21,000).[43] The following is a précis of those disastrous events.

Iraq

In September 1934 the Minister of the Economy and Communications sacked scores of non-Muslim employees. After protests from the Jewish community, some were reinstated. A year later the Minister of Information sent secret instructions to secondary schools and institutes of higher education calling for a *numerus clausus* and ordering the Jewish schools to cease teaching Hebrew as a language, except for religious purposes. In September 1936 the 'Committee for the Defence of Palestine' accused Iraqi Jews of supporting Zionism. Then some unknown assailants opened fire on two Jews and killed them. The following day, unknown assailants again attacked two Jews, killing one and seriously wounding the other. On 27 September 1936 a grenade was thrown at a synagogue, but did not explode. It was only too apparent that the attackers did not know the difference between their Jewish compatriots and the Ashkenazi Zionist settlers who were emigrating from Europe. The head of the community, Sasson Khedourie, and the community leadership therefore declared their abhorrence of Zionism. A school headmaster and famous writer, Ezra Haddad, wrote in an article in the newspaper *Al-Bilad* that 'we are Arabs first, Jews second'. Ya'qob Balbul stated in *Al-Akhbar* of 21 July 1938, that 'Jewish youth see in Zionism nothing more than colonialism and domination.' In July 1937 two Jews were killed in a demonstration against the government of Hikmat Suleiman, and, during demonstrations resulting from the Palestinian uprising, street attacks on Jewish citizens continued. In August 1938 thirty-three Iraqi Jewish leaders sent a telegram to the Colonial Office in London and to the League of Nations expressing their opposition to Zionism and their devotion to their true homeland. At the same time Jewish writers and journalists were expressing their loathing of Zionist operations and settlement designs in Palestine. In October of 1938 the Iraqi government undertook various measures intended to quell any further sectarian agitation.

In May 1941, during the Iraqi–British War which followed the coup d'état of Rashid 'Ali al-Gailani, some hostile incidents were directed by sectarian nationalists against Jews in the streets. They charged that the Jews had distributed pro-British pamphlets or simply read the pamphlets which British aircraft had dropped on Baghdad. Jews were also accused of using mirrors to send secret signals to the aircraft as well as other fraudulent charges. Thirteen Jews were killed, ten of whom were from the northern village of Sandur. German military support was insufficient to beat the British, and Iraq lost the war. At the beginning of June 1941, after al-Gailani's government fell and he fled to Iran, mob violence was unleashed. Many Jewish homes and shops were looted, a large number were injured and 170-180 Jews were killed. A greater number of Muslims were killed, some of them rioters and some who had been protecting their innocent Jewish compatriots. Had the Jews not been protected by their Muslims neighbours, the number of victims would have been many thousands. We should mention here the leader of the Shi'ites in Baghdad, Abu al-Hasan al-Musawi, who refused to issue a *fatwa* against the Jews and ordered the Shi'ites not to take part in the massacre. The British forces which reached the vicinity of Baghdad refused to intervene to stop the bloodshed, fearing to undermine the new pro-British government. The British role in these events seems suspect, particularly since the British have decided to seal one of their documents until 1992,[44] and another until 2017.[45] David Kimche, the director of the Israeli Foreign Ministry, said that British units (Gurkhas and Assyrians) participated in the anti-Jewish riots in May 1941.[46]

These events, manipulated by the German ambassador, Dr Fritz Grobba, and his wife, had a profound effect on Iraqi Jews. Their confidence was shaken by the killings and they were worried about their future in Iraq.[47] After the Second World War, constraints were placed on foreign trade and the number of Jews in state secondary schools and institutions of higher education was reduced. The Ministry of Information imposed Muslim teachers on Jewish schools to teach various subjects. The number of Jewish teachers in higher education was reduced, and the School of Law had only nine Jewish students out of a student body of three hundred. These steps were taken by a pro-British government to satisfy sectarian nationalists and to prove its nationalistic credentials. Meanwhile, the Zionist movement started its secret activities and succeeded in poisoning the atmosphere against Jews, particularly in right-wing circles. The director of the Foreign Ministry, Dr Muhammad Fadil al-Jamali, admitted this in his testimony before the Anglo-American Delegation in Cairo (March 1946). He described the difficulties faced by his government in trying to keep peace between the Jews and the Muslims. Two years later al-Jamali said that 'the fate of the Jews in Islamic countries depends on developments in Palestine.' Nuri Said in turn stated that 'the Jews of Islam are "hostages" of the Islamic states.' And thus the Arabs fell into the Zionist trap.

In 1948 Jews took part in the riots against the pro-British Portsmouth Treaty, trying to prove their nationalism and loyalty to Iraq, but this aroused the ire of the British and their clients in the Iraqi régime. On 27 April 1948 the government was finished off by the Battle of Jisr in which a large number of police and demonstrators were killed. The demonstrators took over the streets and rioting spread to Suleimaniya, Arbil, Kirkuk and Mosul. Nuri Said disappeared, Salih Jabr fled to Cairo, and Fadil al-Jamali did not leave his house – the three of them licked their wounds and started plotting to come back to power. Later on many were taken to court and thrown into prison. Others, including Jews, were hanged. Doubtless one of the reasons for the mass emigration was the elimination of radical Jews.

When the United Nations voted for the partition of Palestine on 29 November 1947, the head of the Jewish community declared his rejection of Zionism and his support for the rights of the Palestinian people. In spite of this demonstrators took up the slogan of 'Death to the Jews' after the killing of 'Abd al-Qadir al-Husaini in the Battle of Castel, near Jerusalem. On 27 April 1948 one of the synagogues in Baghdad was burnt down. Jews then became actively involved in the anti-Zionist League which organised demonstrations against imperialism and Zionism. After the founding of Israel a state of emergency was imposed, and Muzahim al-Pachachi declared that 'the harsh measures being taken are directed solely against the Jews.' The government dismissed a large number of its Jewish employees, including Ibrahim al-Kabir, director of the Ministry of Finance. The sackings reached their peak in October 1948 when almost all Jewish employees were fired and Jewish banks were banned from dealing with foreign banks. The government arrested many innocent Jews, Christians and Muslims.

The Iraqi army had been packed off to save Palestine, but it hardly took part in any battles and did not occupy a single Zionist settlement. When the Iraqi army withdrew, the Umm al-Fahm Triangle was handed over to Israel under the Rhodes Agreement between Israel and Jordan. In Iraq, the anti-Jewish trials continued with fines of twenty million dinars (dinar = £ sterling) being imposed to be paid to the Ministry of Defence to cover the expenses of the 'fierce battles' fought to 'liberate' Palestine. The most notorious of these trials was that of Shafiq Adas, a Jewish businessman from Basra, who in 1946 had sold British war matériel to the Italians, matériel which later turned up in the hands of the Zionists. Even though the court could not prove any connection, he was sentenced to death and his fortune of 5,000,000 dinars was confiscated. His Muslim partners were not sentenced. Adas was hanged in public on 27 September 1948. In July 1948 forty of the most eminent Jewish merchants were tried by a military court on charges of trading with the Soviet Union. Although their deals had been concluded in accordance with the Iraqi-Soviet trade agreement, they were each fined 10,000 dinars. No Muslim who carried on business with the Soviet Union was tried. In September Ezra Menahem Daniyal gave a speech in the senate in which he drew attention to the historic ties between Iraq and its Jewish citizens and called for an end to harassment. The government promised him that it would safeguard the rights of his co-religionists and indeed their situation showed some improvement until October of that year when the government confiscated the assets of Iraqi Jews abroad if they had not returned by a specific date. Then the Ministry of Health refused to certify any new Jewish doctors and would not renew the licences of practising Jewish doctors. At the beginning of the academic year 1948/49 the headmasters of state schools informed their Jewish pupils that they could not guarantee their safety in the face of Muslim students' hostility. During this campaign aimed at the 'Salvation of Palestine', the group of Salih Jabr redoubled its activities and paved the way for Nuri Said to form a new government in January 1949. In the summer of the same year the police arrested some Zionists, but the leaders of the underground managed to flee to Iran. Disturbances broke out again and there were renewed arrests of innocent victims. Israeli agents accused the head of the community, the anti-Zionist Sasson Khedurie, of cowardice. They forced his resignation and by devious means managed to get Hesqel Shemtov appointed, and began using him for their interests. Thus the anti-Jewish measures helped the Zionist clique to dictate its rule both directly and indirectly. When the state of emergency was lifted they started smuggling Jews to Palestine via Iran. On 2 March 1950 Salih Jabr presented a bill which would allow Iraqi Jews to emigrate, provided they renounced their nationality. The bill was passed by a majority. In March 1951, after an overwhelming majority of Jews had given up their nationality, Nuri Said's government froze Jewish assets.[48]

Morocco

Even though the authorities in Marrakesh refused to implement the Vichy government's policy of racial discrimination and saved its Jewish citizens from destruction, the establishment of the state of Israel aroused the anger of Muslims in Auja where, on 7 June 1948, they attacked the Jewish district killing five people, wounding thirty-seven and destroyed a number of houses and shops. On the same night disturbances broke out in Jarada where thirty-nine Jews were killed. When the authorities finally managed to restore order they arrested some of the rioters, tried them and two were sentenced to death.[49]

Aden

On 2 December 1947, Muslim nationalists announced a three-day general strike in protest at the Resolution to partition Palestine. They attacked their Jewish compatriots, killing one and wounding 20. There were subsequent bloody strikes during which 122 people were killed and a large number wounded. Many homes and stores were looted. The security forces, which were under British leadership, participated in the disturbances in which eighty-two Jews and thirty-eight Muslims were killed.[50] The unanswered question is just why the British authorities allowed the security forces to take part in this carnage.

Syria

On 18 November 1945 sectarians in the city of Aleppo carried out an attack on the Grand Synagogue. They smashed the *menorahs* (candelabras) and assaulted the old men during their prayers. Sectarian provocation spread, leading to the killing of Jack Franco, deputy headmaster of the Alliance school in Damascus. After the Resolution to partition Palestine, sectarians burned down 18 synagogues in Aleppo on 2 December 1947, destroyed 150 houses and killed a number of Jews. Following the declaration of the state of Israel on 15 May 1948 all relations between Syrian Jews and the world outside were cut and Jewish foreign trade ceased. On 5 August 1949 a grenade was thrown into a synagogue in Damascus killing 12 Jews and wounding 26 others. President Husni al-Za'im ordered the execution of those accused, but a few days later the coup of Colonel Sami Hinnawi took place and al-Za'im himself was executed.[51]

Egypt

On 2 November 1945 members of *Misr al-Fatat*[51] carried out anti-Jewish riots in Cairo which resulted in the burning of a synagogue, the destruction of a hospital, a home for the elderly and a number of Jewish shops. After the foundation of Israel a state of emergency was declared, and the government confiscated the assets of scores of mostly Jewish individuals and companies. The police also arrested a number of Jews. Between June and November 1948 a number of anti-Jewish riots took place with some Jews being injured and killed. In 1949 scores of detainees were set free, their assets returned to them and they were allowed to leave Egypt. Some Jews were accused of Zionism even though it was legal. When the Wafd came to power at the beginning of 1950, the rest of the detainees (except the Communists) were released. During the Tripartite Aggression against Egypt in 1956 all but 2,000 Egyptian Jews were expelled or 'encouraged' to leave.

The latest Arab mistake in this respect was when the Muslim 'Organisation of the Oppressed on Earth' tortured and then killed several poor Lebanese Jews,[53] in 1989.

THE UPROOTING OF THE JEWS OF ISLAM

When Israel saw that neither diplomatic manoeuvres in Western capitals, nor anti-Jewish harassment had succeeded in uprooting these Jewish communities, it started to use other methods: (anti-Jewish) terrorism, bribery, smuggling, cheating and deception.
1. Israeli terrorism: Yitzhak Menahem, one of the Israeli agents abroad, wrote that 'far reaching emigration will only occur due to extreme hardship. This is the bitter truth, unpalatable as it may be. We must study the possibility of manufacturing this hardship ourselves. We must give the impetus and be the catalyst in the various Jewish diasporas . . . for the Jews need to be pushed involuntarily into leaving their places of residence. We must give them a shock and rouse them from their indolence as the poet [Hayyim Nahman Bialik] wrote:

It (the Jewish people) will not wake unless
woken by the whip
It will not stir unless
stirred up by attack.'[54]

The chairman of the executive committee of the Zionist Organisation, Berl Locker, said at one of the committee's meetings on the Jews of the Yemen that 'even the Jews who do not want to emigrate will have to.'[55] Yitzhak Rafael, head of the Immigration Department of the Jewish Agency, indicated that, with regard to the Jews of the Yemen, Zionist agents had hired Arabs to 'speed up' the departure of the remaining Yemenite Jews, but he did not clarify exactly how this took place. Yemenite Jews have stated in this respect that Arab hirelings used to attack them and beat them up as well as harassing them in their day to day work. Moreover, the emissary of the Jewish Agency in Aden, Shlomo Schmidt, demanded that he be allowed to petition the government of the Yemen to issue a proclamation expelling the remaining Jews from the Yemen.[56]

When the Iraqi government announced in March 1950 that Jews were free to emigrate the offer was taken up by just 4,000 out of a total of 130,000. Israeli agents started employing terror to arouse hysteria amongst the Jews. On 8 April 1950 a bomb exploded in the Dar al-Baida' Cafe which was full of Jews, wounding four – Akram Ezra, Murad Khedouri, Sha'ul and Elias Yosef. The police arrested three suspects, but the Jews were afraid that the Muslims would attempt to kill them as had happened in the rioting of 1941 and they started applying to emigrate. When the flow of emigrants ebbed another bomb went off on 14 January 1951 in the Mas'uda Shemtov Synagogue, killing four including a child and wounding twenty. On 14 March 1951 another bomb was detonated in the American Cultural Centre in Baghdad wounding some of the Jewish intellectuals who were using the library. On 10 May 1951 bombs went off at the Jewish car company, Beit Lawi. On 5 June a bomb exploded at the Jewish Stanley Shasha Trading Company. Following this terror, all except 5,000 Jews applied to emigrate. Then the government decided to confiscate their assets and arrested some of the Zionists who had been involved in these terrorist operations. Two were executed. But Israel succeeded in transfering this whole community and lashing it to the wheel of Zionist colonialism since they were forced to go to Israel and Israel alone. The British government had ordered its embassy in Baghdad not to grant any visas for Britain.[57] In 1951, as the Israeli spies set off their bombs in Baghdad, pamphlets were distributed calling upon the Jews to send their children to Israel.[58]

2. Bribery: in addition to terror, Israeli agents used bribery to 'purchase' Jews from various states. They paid $50 for each Bulgarian Jew, 100 dollars for each youth and $300 for each Zionist detainee in Bulgaria. The Israeli emissary, Ephraim Shilo, handed over a down-payment three million dollars to the Bulgarian authorities, to be followed by more payments by other emissaries. They managed to persuade the socialist countries that immigration into Palestine and arms purchases would help the struggle against British imperialism, since Israel was fighting pro-British Arab states.[59] The Lebanese Chief of Police accepted 25-30 Lebanese liras for each Jew provided that between 150-200 Jews were smuggled out each week.[60] Shlomo Zalman Shragay stated that Moroccan ministers were paid off via Swiss bank accounts. According to a report in The Guardian on 29 December 1988, '$500,000 [was paid] to Moroccan police and security officials, who agreed to turn a blind eye to the Israeli networks . . . [and] the assistance of the fascist regime in Madrid had allowed Mossad agents to smuggle 76,000 Moroccan Jews into the Spanish enclaves of Ceuta and Melilla, and then to mainland Spain and France on their way to Israel.' The Yemeni authorities demanded to be paid cash. Emigration from Iraq was to the benefit of the Iraqi Prime Minister, Tawfiq al-Suweidi, who was also the director of the Iraq Tours travel company. The bribe paid to the rulers of the Yemen included the

property of Yemenite Jews, as well as 'protection fees', removal tax, a poll tax, the usual bribe and various presents.[61]

Bribes were paid, and not just to the Imam, but also to the local rulers. Yosef Tsadok said that 'when we parted, I offered Sultan al-'Awadhli presents of blankets and carpets which made a great impression on him!'[62] In this way certain Arab rulers sold off the Sephardim and Palestine at the same time.

3. Smuggling: the Zionist establishment set up a special organisation called *Mossad La'aliyah* or 'the foundation for the immigration and smuggling of Jews into Palestine'. Zionists smuggled Jews from Morocco to Algeria, from Libya to Malta, from the Yemen to Aden, from Iraq to the Shah's Iran, from Hungary to Austria, and from the Soviet sector in Vienna to the American and thence to Palestine. In March 1949, by means of a secret agreement between Israel and the Lebanese Chief of Police, extensive smuggling operations took place in Syria and Lebanon – via Beirut and then by car to the mountainous border regions, then on foot to kibbutz Kfar Giladi. According to informants, smuggling operations from Syria and Lebanon had already started at the beginning of the Second World War. The agents in each country had a code name, such as Maxi for Egypt, Berman for Iraq, Goldman for Iran and Barukh for Bulgaria. They had wireless sets and sometimes received their instructions from the Hebrew songs on the *Listeners' Requests* programme of Radio Israel. The Zionist emissaries paid off customers inspectors, border police, the secret police, officers, the consuls of foreign countries and even ministers. They had meetings with Nuri Said, the Shah of Iran and Rakoczi, the Jewish Communist leader in Hungary. In July 1949, Jack Gershoni, a representative of the Jewish Agency reached an agreement with the French Governor in Rabat about the quiet and orderly departure of Jews from Marrakesh to Marseilles.[63] Iraqis who fled via Syria and Lebanon told me 'the Zionists relied upon Syrians and Lebanese who made a living from smuggling'.[64] But it was the Jewish fugitives who had to come up with the money to pay them off.

4. Cheating and deception: Zionist propaganda methods included cheating, deception, intimidation and provocation. Jews were warned of the danger of mass extermination and they were promised luxury and happiness in Israel. Any letters describing the hardships of the transit camps inside Israel were intercepted. The Immigration Mosad spent untold millions and an inspector at the Jewish Agency pointed out that prior to the establishment of the state no proper books were kept, and even after the foundation of the state this

'Mosad' avoided proper control over its books. In 1948 it set up a shipping company to transport the immigrants, and with the forty dollars paid for each one by the American Joint Distribution Committee, the Immigration Mosad amassed millions. Among those who benefitted from these stolen funds were the Zionist parties inside Israel. The controller of the Jewish Agency accused this foundation of exploiting the immigrants and making exorbitant profits from overcrowding and inhuman conditions on board the ships. The Mosad doubled the number of immigrants in each ship in order to double its profits.[65] Before the Yemenites boarded the planes, all their valuables, including ancient Hebrew bibles, religious artifacts, jewelry, embroideries, gold and silver objects, old books and manuscripts were taken by the Mosad and the immigrants were assured that these belongings would be sent on by ship, but a large part was stolen en route, and another part reached tourist trinket shops.[66] A string of Israeli investigations uncovered many such cases.[67] Later, hundreds of the immigrants' babies were stolen and sold on the black market. The Zionists later stole ancient books and historic artifacts from the the Jews of Ethiopia, the Falashas.[68] When the immigrants reached Israel, they were shared out amongst the Ashkenazi political parties even though they had no knowledge or understanding of their theories or manifestos. The parties then cut deals to get the immigrants' votes and to win over their rabbis and notables. In one of the files of the Ashkenazi religious party, Hamizrahi, there is a note sent by Y. Weinstein to Shlomo Schmidt, in which he wrote the following, 'Please give Rabbi Badihi a small amount of pocket money each month.'[69] In Marrakesh, for example, this party made the emigrants pay an amount equivalent to 20,000 francs for an exit permit, 50,000 francs for a passport with an exit permit, and 100,000 francs to emigrate directly to Palestine without having to pass through a transit camp in Marseilles.[70] Tsvi Hermon of the Absorption Office of the Zionist Executive Council said on 21 March 1949 that 'Immigration Mosad is sending to Israel inferior elements.' On 6 October 1949 he said that there was no messianic movement in Tunis, and so they organised one. Yosef Tsadok had letters distributed amongst Yemenite Jewish notables proclaiming the Day of Judgement and urging them to go to Aden.[71]

Due to the friendly relations between Israel, the Shah's Iran and America, 50,000 Iranian Jews were transferred in the 1950s. Between 1960 and 1975 Israel transferred 70,000. However the new immigrants refused to be cheap labour like the Iranians who had arrived previously, and many of them went on to the West. Shortly before the Islamic Revolution, secret agents distributed leaflets, which they signed 'Muslim Revolutionaries', threatening Iranian Jews with death if they stayed in Iran. This caused between 30,000 and 50,000 Iranian Jews to emigrate. *Ha'aretz* on 4 April 1980 estimated this number to be 30,000, of whom only 6,000 stayed on in Israel. *Ha'aretz'* weekly supplement on 9 April 1982 estimated the number to have reached 50,000 by 1979 of whom only 15,000 remained in Israel waiting to return to Iran or to go to the West. The other 35,000 returned to Iran or went on to Europe and America. The majority refused to stay in Israel for two reasons: firstly, the efforts of the PLO in Tehran to encourage Iranian Jews to return home, creating an atmosphere which favoured their return; secondly, the catastrophic state of those Iranian Jews who immigrated in the fifties. The newcomers could not believe the poverty and degredation they saw in the black belt and the development towns where Iranian Jews lived with their Sephardi cousins. Turkish Jews were similarly shocked when they saw how their relatives were living and promptly returned to Turkey. Moreover, these short-term Iranian immigrants, who lived in hotels, complained about the way the Israeli authorities and Israeli society treated them with regard to work and housing. Ashkenazi Jews called them 'Khomeinists', 'Primitives', 'Persians' and 'Levantines'. This group of Iranians was mostly made up of the affluent, merchants, professionals and intellectuals. Approximately 500 of them entered Israeli universities. Following discussions between representatives of the PLO and the Iranian authorities in Teheran, relatives among the 50,000 Jews who had stayed in Iran started to telephone and advise them to return to Iran where they would be warmly received. As a result, a large number did go back to Iran, and most of the others chose to go to the West for economic reasons.[72]

In the seventies Israel managed to dupe Sephardim in the Caucasus in the southern Soviet Union into immigrating in their thousands. Israel then settled them in the development towns with other Sephardim where they suffered racial prejudice in employment and housing and were the butt of a newspaper campaign which termed them 'drunken criminals'. Gideon Eilon wrote in *Ha'aretz* on 15 February 1980 that fifty Georgian families out of a total of 33,000 had left Israel, and that Ben Tsiyon Yakovshvili, one of their leaders, had stated 'We shall never come back to Israel.' It is worth pointing out that 20 percent of these immigrants were professionals in the

USSR and 70 percent were skilled workers. Once in Israel, they could not afford to leave for the West. When the Soviet Union refused to repatriate them, Georgian Jews who arrived in Vienna staged rowdy demonstrations. Hanna Kalderon, correspondent for *Ha'aretz*, wrote on 17 October 1986 that the Caucasian Jews had led traditional lives. In Israel they had been settled in Pardes Hanna, Or Yehuda and Or Akiva where they were left to their own devices. The environment was hostile towards them and various factors, such as low wages and poor housing, turned Georgian youths in just a short time into thieves and robbers. They were generally subjected to derision such as 'dirty Georgian', or 'thieving Caucasian', and hence they preferred not to assimilate. They started to watch Soviet rather than Israeli television programmes and the young people preferred the education they received at home over that in Israeli schools. 'It's chaos here. There everyone had a house. Everyone was the equivalent of a mayor here.'

TRANSIT CAMPS ABROAD

The Zionist establishment realised that the Jews of Islam would not accept the low status assigned them in Israeli society. Hence, they had to be degraded and their identity and dignity destroyed to make them so desperate for work that they would be grateful to the establishment for giving them menial jobs. Transitional 'laboratories' were set up for them and the Sephardim would enter them as merchants or professionals or craftsmen and come out a few years later as highly mobile cheap labour for the capitalist and 'socialist' labour market.

These laboratories were the immigration camps outside and inside Israel, then the *ma'barot*, the harsher forms of transit camps in Israel. When the immigrants had been refashioned they were placed in 'development towns', 'cooperatives' and in the 'black belt'. This was generally how the Sephardi immigrants were absorbed, but in the case of the Iraqi Jews, for example, they were sent directly to *ma'barot*. Zionist historians and their allies blatantly lie by claiming that Ashkenazim suffered the same hardships. Only a small number of them entered these camps and they were granted many privileges. Moreover, their stay in the camps was very short indeed, and they were then placed in the large towns or on Ashkenazi settlements where they were given jobs commensurate with their qualifications as well as comfortable dwellings. They assimilated quickly into

Ashkenazi Zionist colonist society. The establishment, however, continued to refer to the Sephardim and even their children and grandchildren as 'immigrants', or by the euphemisms 'distressed populations', 'development town dwellers', 'inhabitants of the neighbourhoods' (i.e. the slum neighbourhoods) or the 'second Israel'. Their children were referred to as 'in need of care' meaning 'remedial' or 'backward'. Actually, for many years the adjective 'backward' used to be attached to peoples of the third world in the Israeli media. The Zionist establishment thus divided the Jews into two inimical factions, and the gap between them widens and deepens from one generation to another.

The common denominator in all of these camps is the crudest living conditions which deprive the inmates of the simplest rights and dignity. The transit camps which were established abroad for the North Africans and Yemenites can be summed up thus: in February 1949 the Jewish Agency sent Iris Lewis to the transit camp in Algeria. After she returned she wrote in her report that 'people are living like animals in overcrowded conditions in a narrow street behind the buildings of the Alliance school . . . they are subsisting without food, dying from disease, reproducing and dying . . . men and women, young and old. More than 50 live in one room whose area measures between four and five square metres.'[73] Heda Grossman, a Zionist youth leader, wrote that 'all the children came from large families, and immigration caused the breakdown of family ties. Tenderness and passion for their families as well as anguish over their fate continually upset these children, and, at the beginning, caused hysteria, crying and screaming throughout the night. The youth from the town of Jabas were generally calmer and more under control. Although relationships between children of the same sex are generally physical, there were also cases when these relationships were abnormal. Naturally this problem will cause complications. For example, in the group in question there was not a single girl.'[74] The Immigration Mosad preferred to transfer boys to Israel so they could go straight into the army. H. Artzieli, the emissary of the Jewish Agency in Libya, described Moroccan Jews as if he were a horse trader. 'Their bodies are slender and their appearance is handsome, but I have difficulty distinguishing them from an outstanding Arab type.'[75] One of the doctors in the transit camp in Marseilles wrote to the Immigration Department in Israel that 'the North African immigrants reach Marseilles in a state of deprivation . . . they have almost no clothes and have had nothing to eat during the three-day journey by ship.

Conditions on board are horrific. They sleep on the ground with the barest of covering to protect them from the elements. On 23 September 1948 a child died on board ship and the French authorities ruled that it had died of hypothermia and hunger. I demand that the appropriate authorities be contacted to correct this situation... There is a great lack of blankets in the two camps in Marseilles. The immigrants sleep on military beds with not a shred of covering in huts with wooden roofs. As a result of the dreadful living conditions and the deterioration in the standard of nourishment lately, twelve children have died . . . There is also a lack of soap and clothing . . . I fail to understand why clothing is distributed to all European immigrants, whereas nothing goes to the North Africans?'[76] At one of the sessions of the Jewish Agency's Executive Council, Dr Yisrael Goldstein warned of discrimination in the camps against the Jews of North Africa.[77] On 31 July 1949, at a session of the Zionist Executive Council, Eliahu Dubkin admitted that there existed the 'phenomenon of a lack of desire to travel'. Elie Peleg said in his report on 24 July 1949 that 'these people had to be taken by force to board the ship.'[78] The Zionist establishment destroyed the unity of the Moroccan families by choosing the strong and the young and taking them to Israel while leaving the old and infirm to die slowly in the transit camps in France. The Zionists used the same methods regarding the Falashas, the Jews of Ethiopia, in 1974 and 1975. This also happened in Morocco before they even left for France. Zionist emissaries pressurised Moroccan Jews from the countryside. They forced them to abandon their houses and work and go to Casablanca, where they were ignored. For a long while they waited there, suffering from hunger and disease while Zionist emissaries were busy sifting out the 'sound ones' for emigration.

In one of the files of the Immigration Department there is an undated document, written by a doctor who worked for about a year and half in a transit camp for Moroccans in Marseilles. 'The immigrants from North Africa,' he wrote, 'will provide Israel with cheap and unskilled labour in place of the Arab workers who used to do this type of work before the war of independence [sic]. The standard of living of the North Africans is no higher than that of the Arabs, and they will be better off than ever in Israel even if they do not achieve the European standard of living which the Ashkenazim enjoy. The North African immigrants will have no difficulties adapting to this situation...'[79]

In October 1948 Berl Locker said to the wealthy American Jewish politician Henry Morgenthau that 'it is our view that the Sephardim and the Yemenites will have to play a large part in building the country.'[80]

During that period many immigrants from Islamic countries, particularly those with higher academic qualifications, were marginalised socially or forced to emigrate to France, America and Britain. Selim Ruben, for example, lived in the Kfar Ana camp near Tel Aviv. He had worked in the upper echelons of the Iraqi Railways Administration, having been the director of the main stations in Baghdad, Kirkuk, Mosul and Khaniqin. When he came to Israel, the authorities refused to employ him in his profession and he remained unemployed, cursing Israel from his poverty. In 1962 a Moroccan leader commended on this phenomenon that 'there are more Moroccan professors at the Sorbonne than Moroccan students at Jerusalem university.' Notwithstanding these facts, the progressive historian, Tom Segev, states that the Sephardim 'were marginalised because they did not bring with them the requisite skills to be able to compete freely for status in Israeli society . . . or because they cannot speak Hebrew well enough.'[81] (It is important to note that the Ashkenazi immigrants did not know Hebrew. If this was the stance of a progressive historian, we can imagine how it was seen by a reactionary – see chapter eight.)

In spite of the secret agreement between the Zionists and the Imam of the Yemen, the transfer operation was not overt, out of fear of Arab public opinion, and it was decided to send the Jews first to Aden. There they had to sit it out in a sandy waste called 'Redemption Camp' until planes were ready to take them to Israel. Dr Yosef Meir described the arrival of the Yemenites at this camp as follows: 'Fifteen trucks arrived, carrying 313 naked or semi-naked bodies. Whether it was due to the summer heat, or it was their custom, or due to a lack of clothing, they were sitting packed together, filthy, their bodies covered with sores, their faces staring out and silent. Even after they were greeted it was difficult to talk with them. It might have been shyness; it was said that they had been walking for the last fifteen days, or it could have been unconcern, or distress, or fear of what they were about to embark upon. Some of them asked us "Are you English?" even though we spoke Hebrew and were trying to establish a rapport with them. They started getting out of the trucks, one by one, very slowly and calmly. There was hardly the sound of a baby crying. The image is that of a flock of sheep being led from a field at evening, one head following the other's tail, until they reach the shady field where they can all huddle together. The first night they get bread, water and dates. This first night is a historic meeting between an ancient Hebrew group and Jewish groups from Europe and the Middle East. Their faces showed no signs of happiness, emotion or any indication that they were aware of salvation and an end to their trials. I will say it bluntly, they have quite animal features although we know that they have a very high level of intelligence and intellectual capacity . . . '[82]

This camp was set up to process five hundred Yemenites, but the total number there reached twelve thousand. There were no tents – they simply lay down to sleep on the sand at night. They defecated in the sand inside the camp perimeters or nearby. Sometimes sandstorms would blow over the camp, or torrential rains would almost drown the refugees and carry off their belongings.[83] Dr Meir added that 'no one knew how many sick there were in the camp, or where they were. Some managed to make it to the clinic to get bandages or a penicillin injection. Others were breathing their last wherever they lay, particularly the old men and women.' Women were giving birth on the sand, and the nurse would only get to them in time to cut the umbilical cord. When the women came to the clinic or the sick room, they would slump onto the ground with their children nearby showing no sign of joy or excitement. The dead were buried in the sand unaccompanied by sounds of weeping (according to the report of Dr Meir). When the Yemenites arrived at the camp, all their clothes were taken from them and burnt and they were given European clothes instead – a first stage in the destruction of their identity. The women felt naked as they put on modern dresses, since they had been used to wearing baggy trousers down to their ankles underneath their dresses. Yemenites had new Hebrew names imposed on them to replace their traditional Arab or Muslim names. In the files of the Jewish Agency there are many complaints about the beatings, derision and brutality to which Agency officials subjected the Yemenites.

In Israel there was discussion about the transfer of the Yemenites. Yitzhak Greenbaum, Minister of the Interior asked 'why are we trying to make the community in Yemen disappear and to bring here people who are more harmful than beneficial for us? When we transfer 70 percent of the sick, we are hurting both ourselves and them . . .' Yitzhak Rafael, head of the Immigration Department, tried to placate his colleagues in the Agency's Executive Council by stating on 5 June 1949 that 'there are not many sick amongst the

Yemenites,' intimating that the sick would die en route. He then added that 'there is no need to fear the chronically sick, for they have to walk about two weeks [to get to the camp]. Those who are dangerously ill do not even start out on the trip.' On 28 September 1949 Ben Gurion wrote in his diary that 'the [Yemenite] children are dropping like flies. We must save them. It is true that the death rate is high here too, but we also have more efficacious medicine.' A few weeks later he wrote 'if it is written that they have to die, then it is better for them to die here.'[84]

It appears that the harsh conditions the Yemenites had to undergo to get to Aden, as well as the health and food situation in 'Salvation Camp' only served to get rid of the weak, sick and aged. This way only the hale and hearty had to be absorbed in Israel, that is those who could serve the Israeli economy or in the armed forces. One could pose the question here as to how Great Britain could allow such inhumane acts to be carried out in Aden. Between 1948-1975, Israel brought over 719,000 Ashkenazim from Europe, but it did not treat them the same way. Surely this difference in treatment constitutes a heavy indictment of Israel's practice of racial discrimination.

NOTES

1 A long Arab cloak.
2 Landau.
3 Bat Ye'or in *Les Temps Modernes*, 85.
4 Schechtman, 1961, 190.
5 See also Iskandarani, *Khamsin*, No. 5, 30-34; cf Shiblak.
6 A. Chouraqui, 1968, and Schechtman, 1961.
7 Shiblak, 28 and *'Alam al-Yahud fi 'l-'Iraq*, Jerusalem, 1983, by M. Basri.
8 (CO-730/2/34955).
9 'Abd al-Muhsin, 1983, 253-340.
10 Ibid
11 Shiblak, 42-43.
12 Nissim Rejwan, 207-209.
13 Kimchi, 1976, 60-62 and Cohen, 1969, 109-112.
14 Cohen, 1969, 159.
15 Ibid, 156.
16 Woolfson, 146-147.
17 Ibid, 143.
18 Ibid, 144.
19 Ibid, 148-149.
20 See editions of *Al-Yaqza*, 12, 13, 16, and 17 February and 7 and 28 March 1948
21 1969, 178.
22 2 November 1949. From Washington to the British Foreign Minister. Telegram number 5182, Foreign Office 371/75187
23 Berger,1955, 30
24 On the Jews of Iraq, see the valuable study written in English by the Palestinian 'Abbas Shiblak.
25 H.J. Cohen, 1969, 38-47.

26 Landshut, 1950.
27 Smooha, 281.
28 Twenty Third Zionist Congress, 178 ff.
29 Y.N. Shay, *Shevet Va'am,* 1954.
30 Ibid.
31 *Shevet Va'am,* 1958.
32 Batatu, 1978, 311.
33 I still remember the rabble who used to threaten us with 'Just wait a bit, Hitler'll do you in!'
34 The Palestine Liberation Organisation was the first Arab/Islamic organisation to correct this error, demanding that the Arab and Islamic states take back Sephardim from Israel. After the Islamic revolution in Iran, the PLO succeeded in stopping Jews leaving Iran for Israel, and discussions in Teheran led to many Jews being encouraged to leave Israel and return to Iran.
35 See *The Jewish Chronicle* of 29 October, 1949.
36 FO 371/75152 E9114/ 1105/ 93.
37 Jerusalem – British Foreign Office 24/3/51, FO 371/91690, EQ 1571/45.
38 Jerusalem – to the British Foreign office on 14 February, 1949 – FO 371/75182/ 024566.
39 Segev, p. 110 of Arabic translation.
40 Ibid, 176.
41 See letter from Kobovitsky to the Jewish Congress dated April 24, 1949, in the files of the Ministry of Immigration, Israel Army Archive 14/49.
42 Ibid. See letter from Tuviah to the Ministry dated 14 May, 1949.
43 *Ha'aretz,* 29 May 1987.
44 Pro/FO E 4209/1/93.
45 Pro/FO E 4154/1/93.
46 *Voice of the Arab World,* January, 1983.
47 See FO 371 23202, Confidential, No 251, British Consultate, Damascus to FO, London 14.4.1939, and FO 624/24/448, Nazi Propaganda in Iraq, undated, and FO 37/2302, No. 150, British Embassy to FO 11.4.39.
48 See Nissim Rejwan's book.
49 Chouraqui, 181 and 182, and *Encyclopaedia Judaica,* vol 12, 344.
50 British Royal Commission of Enquiry, 22 September, 1948. Published in *The Economist* on 9 October, 1948 and *The New York Times* of 6 December, 1947.
51 Wolfson, 174–176.
52 The 'Young Egypt' Party, also known as the Green Shirts.
53 Julie Flint, *The Guardian,* 2 August 1989.
54 Ben Menahem, 179.
55 Committee Minutes, 22 April, 1949.
56 Rafael to Locker, 22 January, 1951, Central Zionist Archive.
57 See Foreign Office correspondence with the its embassy in Baghdad on 29 September, 1952 – FO 371/98767, Eq 1571/24.
58 See the magazine, *Ha'olam Hazeh,* 20 April 1966 and 1 June 1966, Kedourie, 1970, pp. 313–315 and Marion Woolfson, *Prophets in Babylon,* 1980.
59 Segev, 109–110.
60 State Archives, Ministry of Foreign Affairs, 2451/11.
61 Segev, 115 and 176.
62 Tsadok to the Zionist Office in Aden, 20 December, 1949. Central Zionist Archive, L27, 4th file. See also Tsadok's memoirs and letters.
63 Rafael to the Zionist Executive Council, 9 September 1949. Central Zionist Archive, Immigration – S41/256/11.
64 See Shlomo Hillel's book, *Operation Babylon,* 1989.
65 Minutes of the Zionist Executive, 21 March 1949 and 29 April 1949.
66 Ben Tsvi's Report, 18 December, 1949 – Central Archive for the History of the Jewish People: Archive of Nahum Levin.
67 Menahem Ben Yosef to Ephraim Hadar, 9 October, 1949 – Central Zionist Archives, Office of Middle Eastern Jews S/20/600, also S/20/109 and S/20/547 II.
68 See *Ha'aretz,* 11 January 1985.
69 Central Zionist Archive in Aden, L27.

70 Israeli Army Archives – 14/5/A.
71 31 December, 1949, Central Zionist Archive, L27.
72 Ibid.
73 Central Zionist Archive, S20/5501.
74 Files of the Immigration Deparment, Bundle 61, File 393 – Original numbering 2421/73, undated.
75 9 August 1949, Central Zionist Archive, S20/555.
76 Dr Goldman to Dr Kornblitt, 31 December 1948, Central Zionist Archive, S20/550 I.
77 Zionist Executive Council, 18.7.49.
78 Central Zionist Archives, S20/562.
79 Files of the Immigration Department, Bundle 61, File 393, original numbering 2421/73.
80 Zionist Executive Council, 24 October 1948
81 Segev, 180 and 181, Arabic translation.
82 Ministry of Health, September 1949, State Archives, Ministry of Foreign Affairs, 2397/15 – quoted by Segev.
83 Yosef Tsadoq to Menahem, 21 July 1949, Central Zionist Archive, S20/457 II.
84 Knesset Minutes, Volume 3, 128, 21 November 1949.

CHAPTER FIVE

Absorption Or Destruction Since 1948?

This chapter deals with the absorption of the immigrants in Israel, although 'absorption' is too kind a word to describe what we believe actually happened. 'Destruction' better reflects what actually happened in the Zionist camps which were set up for the immigrants and where they lost their human rights. The proletarianisation of the Sephardim began in the transit camps abroad, as we have mentioned in the previous chapter. It then continued in the 'Immigrant' and 'Transit Camps' inside Israel, and then in their final destination which was either the development towns, the 'cooperatives' or the 'Black Belt' of the large towns.

THE IMMIGRANT CAMPS

Widad told me about her emigration from Baghdad. 'We were wearing our Sabbath clothing. We thought as the plane landed that Israel would welcome us warmly. But, goodness, how wrong we were! When the plane had landed at Lod airport, a worker approached us and sprayed us all over with DDT, as if we were lice-infested. What sort of welcome was that? We felt that they were spitting in our faces. When we disembarked from the plane, they herded us into a train, which was so crowded that we were stepping on each other and our fine clothes were dirtied. My husband was crying and so was I. Then the children started crying and our sobs went up to heaven and cast a pall over the train. Since it was a freight carriage it had no electric light, but as it sped along we thought of the death trains which had taken European Jews to the Nazi camps. Finally we reached the "Sha'ar Ha'aliya" camp and we were taken in with other families, then they wrote down our names and "gave" us new Hebrew names. "Said" became "Hayyim", "Su'ad" became "Tamar" and I was renamed "Ahuva" and so on. Then we had to wait in long food queues, as if we were beggars. We had no idea what was to become of us.' She looked towards me with wet eyes and asked 'Is this the Israel they told us about?'

'Sha'ar Ha'aliya Camp had been a British army detention centre before it became an immigration camp. The Israeli security authorities had reinforced the camp's security by doubling the height of barbed wire around it and installing a direct telephone link to the Israeli police in Haifa port. There was a police force of sixty constables, four sergeants and an officer to supervise the immigrants, who were housed in tents or tin-roofed barracks, which had previously been ammunition warehouses and which did not have tiled floors. As I wandered amongst these tents an elderly Iraqi waylaid me. "I have just got one question," he said. "Are we immigrants or prisoners of war?" My tongue was tied and I could not reply. The old man spat on the ground and cursed Israel and everything to do with Israel. I also observed that the sanitary conditions in the camp were very primitive. The toilets were overflowing. There was almost no separation of the sexes, and due to the lack of washing facilities people started to smell.'

The immigrants were taken from this 'Gate of Immigration' Camp to other camps where the accommodation was no different. In 1948 there were 90,000 immigrants, that is a third of the total, in camps. Ashkenazi immigrants, on the other hand, were allotted the good homes of Palestinians who had been driven out. Yehuda Burginsky, an official of the Department of Absorption, warned that food supplies were running low, and that 10 percent of camp dwellers would suffer hunger.[1] The following month the camp-dwellers received bread and milk for their children only, and vegetable rations were reduced by two-thirds. The immigrants in Pardes Hanna Camp organised an angry demonstration.[2] The sanitary conditions together with a shortage of doctors, medicine and food, caused a deterioration in the health of the immigrants, the spread of contagious diseases and a rise in the death rate. Dr Moshe Sneh, a Mapam member of the Knesset, reported that out of the 370 children in Ra'anana Camp 200 were sick, and that the hospitals would only take 25 percent of the cases which local doctors sent.[3] Yakov Gil, MP, reported that he had seen new camps with hundreds of immigrant families where there was no permanent doctor or suitable clinic.[4] He also saw hundreds of people with contagious diseases who were still living amongst their families, since the hospitals would not accept them. In the village of Brandeis, near Hadera, he saw a child with tuberculosis sleeping in a bed used by two other families.[5] Tsvi Hermon, an official from the Department of Absorption, said that 'conditions in the immigrant camps are intolerable. It is no exaggeration to say that conditions were better in the Nazi camps after the Second World War.'[6]

In September 1949 Ruth Cleager, an official of the Immigration Mosad, wrote in her report, 'In the camps Jews keep other Jews down. It seems that they have not learnt anything from the tragedy of the past.'[7] She added that 'these immigrants feel as if they are second class people.' There was absolutely no education in the camps. There were no schools, nor activities for the children and most of the adults were without work. We should mention that the person directly responsible for these conditions, Geora Yosephtal, was a Jew who had fled Nazi Germany before the war and then become director of the absorption department of the Jewish Agency. Files in the Prime Minister's office include a number of reports about the hardships faced by the immigrants. In the Central Zionist Archives there are reports of corruption in food distribution.[8] Yehuda Burginsky told members of the Zionist Executive Council that 'we have prepared for them [the Yemenite immigrants] neither camps nor accommodation. What should I do now? I am having wire pens built and keeping them there like animals in a state of optical illusion.'[9] Even hardhearted Ben Gurion declared when he visited the Yemenite children in Tel Hashomer hospital 'This is the worst thing I have ever seen in my life.' In his speech to the Knesset he added that those children 'looked more like skeletons than living creatures . . . they were too weak even to cry, and some of them were too weak to be able to swallow food.'[10]

In April 1949 the secretary of the ruling Mapai (Labour) Party declared that 'the bureaucracy is almost criminal' with regard to the absorption of immigrants. Yosephtal informed his party that the camps under his supervision were supposed to process 40,000 immigrants, but they in fact held between 50,000 and 60,000, half of whom were living in tents. Pinhas Lavon, Secretary of the Histadrut, expected a 'great explosion'. Ben Gurion, the Prime Minister and party leader, opposed that thesis, saying that the state was spoiling the immigrants. 'I cannot accept this pampering . . .

these people can quite well live in tents for a number of years. Whoever does not want to live in one should not come here.'[11] A year later, I went to Saqiya Camp to visit my relatives. The camp consisted of tents packed close together. Ben Gurion gave a speech there in which he stated 'Moses kept you in tents for forty years in the wilderness of Sinai. I shall only keep you in tents for a few years.'

Golda Meir was responsible for the construction of immigrant accommodation in her position as Minister of Labour. She first ordered huts to be built of tin or wood and then of cement. The hut was no more than a single room and was constructed by a machine with horizontal pipes, nicknamed 'Golda's Cannon'. 27,000 of these huts were built in 1948, of which 18,000 were built of wood and were to house those living in tents.[12] Hermon, the official in charge of absorption, said on 29 March, 1949, at a session of the Zionist Executive Council, that 'we are moving towards erecting slums and chronic overcrowding.' That is exactly what happened with regard to these camps, the development towns and the 'cooperatives'. They have all become slum districts just like the 'Black Belts' in the large towns. An American journalist, Ruth Gruber, wrote to Ben Gurion that 'the mass apathy is shocking. Zionist society fought throughout the British Mandate for the right to immigrate and won it, but now no one pays any attention to the camp dwellers, and the few who feel guilty say: It was hard for us when we first came, so let them suffer too.'[13] The military authorities, who immediately enlisted the young immigrants and sent them to the front, refused to shelter the aged and the young during the serious floods in Lod. Yehuda Burginsky demanded that the army put the airport at Kfar Sirkin at the disposal of the Department of Absorption. The army refused, but did offer the Tel Nof Camp which was next to a parachutists' camp which informed Burginsky that they would plant mines to prevent the tent-dwellers living near them.[14] Kibbutz Misgav Am refused to shelter immigrants smuggled in from Lebanon and they had to continue another two hours by foot. When they reached Kibbutz Manara they were told that if their upkeep was not paid for the Kibbutz would not accept any more immigrants in the future.[15]

Na'im related 'the way the Sephardim were treated by the Zionists who smuggled them in is not new. I remember how they treated me and my Iraqi friends at the beginning of the Second World War. Zionist agents smuggled us to Beirut, then they sent us down toward the Palestine border with a Lebanese guide – a Muslim as far as I remember. The car stopped in a mountainous region and we started walking behind the guide for some hours. When torrential rain started falling the guide said "Keep on toward that electric light – that's the kibbutz." Then he left us and went back to Beirut. We walked through the night through sheets of rain and biting cold. The electric light was absolutely miles away. By the time we reached the kibbutz our clothing was drenched and filthy. Some of us had lost our shoes in the mud. The guard took us to the dining room and they gave us cups of tea and bread and margarine. Then they took us to the library, and sat us down there even though we were shivering with the cold and our clothing was still wet. In the morning they took us to the hay-loft and we slept there as if we were cattle. It was an illuminating lesson in Ashkenazi hospitality. This was kibbutz Kfar Giladi. Then we were split up and I was sent to Kibbutz Hulata near Lake Hula. There they shoved me into a small wooden hut, infested with lice and bedbugs, which lay right at the edge of the settlement and which was specifically for Sephardim. It was just like a cowshed. Even though I was a boy, slight of build and pallid, I was made to do physical work from morning to night. At night one of the kibbutz members would teach me Hebrew for half an hour. The work was very hard. I thought that my back was going to break from the pain and fatigue. The head of the labour gang was a German girl called Gerda who kept on yelling at me and who humiliated me the whole day long. I didn't know why, because at that time I tried my best, but Gerda would still oppress me throughout the day and my dreams would oppress me through the night. Add to that the fact that I was attacked constantly by the bugs and lice in the hut. In my sleep I could see my father looking for me in the mountains and valleys, with hatred in his eyes because the Zionists took me without my parents' knowledge. I would think about Hitler and Gerda without knowing what was going on around me. Hitler oppressed Gerda, then Gerda came to Palestine, and now Gerda oppresses me! In the end I ran away from vegetables and agriculture, and from Gerda . . . I didn't care about anything. I started running towards the mountains, crying as I ran away from the settlement. Suddenly I came across Musa, who was brown-skinned, had sparkling blackish eyes and spoke Arabic. He and the other Musa, the cobbler, were the only Sephardi members on the kibbutz. The first Musa was a native Palestinian Jew, I believe of Yemenite origin, and the second was from Syria. He asked me, "What's the matter, Na'im? Why are you crying?" When I told him the way Gerda had been treating me he became angry and rebuked her harshly. "Stay with me," he said, "and we'll work together with this wheelbarrow." This Musa was the first person to treat me humanely in the Zionist community. I would often go to the workshop of Musa the cobbler from Damascus, and I would feel an indescribable delight as we spoke in Arabic. I now know the reason – it is the language of conversation, the language of my parents and grandparents. I could not understand why Gerda treated me the way she did until an incident occurred which clarified to me my position in Ashkenazi society. In Kibbutz Hulata there was a member called Yisrael, as far as I recall, but the people on the kibbutz used to call him "Stalin". I didn't know why. This Stalin made use of a group of Arab fisherman on Lake Hula. One day I saw him standing on the bank of the lake with his Arab labourers. He was shouting at them and cursing them, then he grabbed hold of one of them and started beating and kicking him ferociously. The Arab did not defend himself. His mates remained silent and did not move. I was very surprised since, in my whole life, I had never seen a Jew treat a Muslim like that. Here was a German or Polish Jew, a foreigner, beating a human being, who happened to be a native Arab. Here was Gerda too, treating me harshly. From that moment on I was aware of my debased position, as well as those of my Palestinian Arab brethren. I was not surprised when my father and my family were brought over in the early fifties and crammed into Pardes Hanna and then Saqia and Petah Tikvah Camps where my father died after surviving for ten years in a wooden hut where the camp doctor refused to come and treat him. The doctor had said to my mother "Have him come and see me", but my father was too ill to walk. He stayed in his bed until he died a few weeks later. They then took him to Abu Kebir Hospital to ascertain the cause of his death. My mother said, "That's what the Nazis did to them."' That was all Na'im could say.

In spite of the tragic conditions in these camps, Ben Gurion, the Prime Minister and leader of the Mapai (Labour) Party, begrudged the Sephardim every morsel of bread they ate. At the Eighth Conference of Moshavim, the leader said that '100,000 Jews are living in immigrant camps and the food they eat is provided as charity.'[16] Just a few weeks later Ben Gurion demanded that the immigrants be organised into 'work battalions' along military or semi-military lines and used as forced labour in construction and road building, for the public welfare with no special remuneration. Ben Gurion thought that these work parties should include men between 18 and 45 years of age who would receive enough for their own and their family's needs, as well as the same amount of money as a military conscript. A committee was formed to look into the suggestion. Its members included Yehuda Almog, Hayyim Gevati, Hillel Dan, Gershon Zak, Geora Yosephtal and Shalom Hacohen. The committee suggested setting up the first camp for 3,000 conscripted immigrants in the vicinity of Beer Sheba. However, the programme failed due to opposition from the Ministry of Labour which did not have enough financial resources to back the programme, nor could it relinquish jobs that it had already promised for other immigrants.[17] The idea of 'work battalions' cropped up later in the form of emergency work and emergency wages, which we shall examine later.

When the Jewish population of Palestine reached the one million mark, the Executive Council of the Jewish Agency organised a celebration in Tel Aviv, but only 15 people accepted the invitation.[18] This shows that mass immigration was rejected by the immigrants, and also by the Zionist Yishuv which was now a demographic minority and which started grumbling about the 'composition of society'. The Foreign Ministry prepared a communiqué which it distributed to Israel's representatives abroad and in which it drew attention to the fact that most immigrants were now arriving from Arab Islamic countries, and that the proportion of Sephardim would continue to rise. The Ministry warned that this fact 'would make an impression on all fields of life in the state', which meant that in order to preserve the 'cultural standards' of the Yishuv they would need abundant numbers of Western immigrants and not just 'Orientals.'[19] Shoshana Persitz, MP, said of the Sephardim that 'we have no common language with them, just as our stage of development does not match theirs. They are still living in the Middle Ages.'[20] Simultaneously the Israeli media, all of which were under Ashkenazi control, carried out a racist campaign against these native Jews and their 'inferior' Arab culture to justify discrimination against them (see chapter eight).

The Yemenite member of the Knesset, Zekharia Gluska, protested about discrimination directed against members of his poor community in the field of housing, religious services, the civil service, child benefit and even radio programmes. He said that even Yemeni radio programmes were prepared by 'Ashkenazi experts'.

Though the Yemenites were fastidious about cleanliness to a greater extent than any other community I have seen, a representative of the Jewish Agency claimed that 'there is a type of resident whom it is very difficult to instruct in sanitary matters.'

The Agency promised that it would 'persevere in building toilets near the dwellings in order to house-train 'these people' (i.e. the Yemenites) to use them.'[21] Moreover, Ashkenazi party workers actively tried to change the life-style of the Yemenites to destroy the influence of the father and the teacher.

THE DISAPPEARANCE OF YEMENITE CHILDREN

Since April 1950 the Yemenite Organisation has been sending letters to the Minister of Police about the disappearance of hundreds of Yemenite children after they were transferred to hospitals.[22] The Minister has not replied to any of these letters. 18 years later the military authorities sent out orders for the conscription of these lost children, and this appalling problem came out into the open. Sephardi sources in Palestine say that Ashkenazim who were 'taking care' of Yemenite affairs stole the children and sold them to adoptive parents both inside and outside the country. The government committee of enquiry which was formed in 1968 put the disappearances down to the state of disorder in the camps but admitted that the problem had been shocking. The committee looked into 342 complaints, mostly from Yemenites with the remainder being from other Sephardim from Arab countries. It only found four children and came up with no results about the others. It did, however, indicate that its information warranted a police investigation at home and abroad, and sent a report to this effect to the Ministers of Police and Justice, but the authorities shelved it.[23] In July 1986 Sephardi Jews staged a mass meeting at Yad Eliahu near Tel Aviv and called upon the authorities to carry out the necessary investigations to find the 559 children who were stolen in the early fifties.[24]

Oppression directed against the Yemenites was undeniably worse than that suffered by any of the other Sephardim. Perhaps it was because the Yemenites were completely Arabised and until very recently had been untouched by European culture. I shall never forget the winter of 1944 when the Jewish Agency brought over hundreds of Yemenites and settled them in a camp near Kiryat Shmuel in the district of Haifa. They were sent by the labour union of the Histadrut to Motzkin Camp and it was there that I saw them walking around in bare feet wearing rags, and shivering from the cold. Their tents overlooked the sea and were exposed to cold winds and torrential rains. The Mapai Party and the religious Hapo'el Hamizrahi Party were only worried about getting these wretches' votes. In summer the Yemenite camp turned into a hell because of the overcrowding and piles of filth. Eventually they rose up and occupied the uncompleted houses the authorities had been building. Ashkenazi municipal leaders responded by not putting in doors or windows and turning off the water supply in the hope of evicting the Yemenites. At the same time Ashkenazi immigrants were being housed in finished dwellings in Kiryat Hayyim. When Yemenites complained they were asked sarcastically 'Were you better off in Yemen?' and they answered 'Yes, by God.'

After the state of Israel was founded, discrimination became an overt policy. Ashkenazi immigrants were granted the best houses of the Palestinian refugees, or were given new houses free of charge. After 1950, when it was declared that immigrants had to pay for their housing, the Jewish Agency, the Histadrut and the local municipalities started building houses for the Ashkenazim and giving them 30-year mortgages. Simultaneously, the Zionist establishment was cramming hundreds of thousands of Sephardim into the camps which were not finally closed down until 1980.

The following Minutes of the Zionist Executive Council show how all the Zionist parties, from the extreme right to the extreme left, decided to favour Ashkenazim from Poland at the expense of the Sephardim.

Date: 9 October 1949
Eliahu Dobkin (Mapai-Labour): We must grant these immigrants privileges, and I am not afraid of that word.
Levi Eshkol (Mapai): . . . if we set up camps with a hundred thousand people in them and then suddenly give the Ashkenazim privileges, it is not hard to imagine the outcry . . . 'nothing is spared for the Ashkenazim!'
Tsvi Hermon (Mapam-Zionist far left): . . . if it is a question of granting privileges during absorption, I am afraid that we won't get through this alive . . . can't you see what it would mean if twenty thousand people got special measures?
It was unanimously decided to form a committee to study the matter.

Date: 26 December 1949
Y. Greenbaum (Independent): . . . There will be a need to prepare a hotel for approximately 800 people who will be the first arrivals

from Poland at the end of November. We have got to hurry so that we won't be taken by surprise, and so that respectable people will not be forced to go to the camps. There are people of rank amongst the immigrants and it will be a disaster if we are forced to send them to the camps.

E. Dobkin (Mapai): We need to make an extraordinary effort to ease the absorption of these people. I see no harm in the committee hiring a hotel to put them up . . . Immigration from Poland depends upon how these first immigrants are absorbed. If we fail, the others will not come.. and that will be a blow to the whole Zionist movement.

M. Grossman (Revisionist-Right): I believe that we must do everything that is within our capability to help absorb the Polish immigrants, but I object to the undertaking being officially in the hands of the Executive Committee [of the Agency]. With all due respect to the Jews of Poland, the affair will not be understood. Why should these Jews suddenly be treated cared for differently from others? The matter is published and a special member of the Executive Committee is being appointed. What about the Jews of Germany, Marrakesh, Tunis, Tripoli and the rest of the Jews? I am with opinion that says that we should decide here in the committee whatever we decide, but the Executive Committee must not co-opt Mr Greenbaum. He is an important personality and accepted by the Polish Jews and will accomplish whatever he is charged to do, and we will all help him. I do not want the whole world to know that we have taken on the responsibility of taking care of this matter . . . A public committee could be set up for the Jews from Poland, provided Mr Greenbaum is in it, but not as a appointee of the Executive Council. I can already imagine the newspaper headlines. I am ready to earmark funds for this project, but without any publicity – for publicity will be detrimental and I see no need for it.

B. Locker (Mapai): Truly we all support this project, but the question is 'Do we need a formal mandate from the Executive Council or not?'

Y. Greenbaum (Independent and Home Secretary): With regard to publicity, you can depend on me . . .

The Council then resolved to set up a public committee to deal with the absorption of Jews from Poland with the participation of Mr. Greenbaum. It will be shown that he was not representing the Executive Committee but was acting as one of the leaders of Polish Jewry.

A week later (2 January 1950), the Council met to discuss setting up a special camp for the immigrants from Poland where each family would have its own room, as opposed to the multi-family dormitories elsewhere. The Department of Absorption undertook to accommodate 2,000 Polish immigrants under these conditions. Y. Greenbaum (who was Polish) requested that these facilities be extended to cover all the Polish immigrants, but this was turned down.

Y. Greenbaum: That means that from February there will be a need to put Polish immigrants into huts with 20 to 30 beds close to each other and that whole families will sleep together . . . if news of this gets around it will cause a very bad impression.
Y. Rafael (Hapoel Hamizrahi – a religious Labour party): The Polish immigrants are not like immigrants from other countries. Immigrants from other countries are here because we demanded. For a long time they did not want to immigrate and put it off. For that reason we have no obligation toward them whereas Polish Jews could not immigrate – they did not have the opportunity to do so. If we exempt them from the camps and give them priority in housing, they will settle down much more quickly than the Orientals in the camps for there are amongst them professionals who are much in need in the country. It will be beneficial for the economy as a whole and therefore I suggest giving them priority in housing. The Jews of Poland come from a comfortable background and thus camp life would be more difficult for them than for the Yemenite Jews who consider the camps a rescue operation. So I think that there are sufficient grounds for favouring the Jews of Poland, and this must happened in two ways. First, they must be granted priority in housing and second, if that is impossible – then I support the suggestion of Mr Greenbaum that we provide them with better conditions in the camps . . . We can set up a special mortgage fund, financed with help from their relatives and the money they bring with them. This group of immigrants is not like the Yemenite immigrants. When a Polish Jew gets a loan, he knows he has to pay it back.
Y. Burginsky (Mapam-Zionist/Marxist): There is a possibility that we will only have one camp, which is Atlit Camp where there are at present Yemenites. We'll shove them somewhere else and then we'll be able to cram in between three to four thousand (even though it will not be as luxurious as Greenbaum is demanding), like in the other camps . . . as a precautionary measure we have rented between

two and three hundred flats at 200 Israeli pounds each. We shall take the houses that have been allotted to the North Africans and Yemenites and hand them over to the Polish Jews. For this we shall need not two hundred but three hundred pounds. The problem is whether we can collect such a sum?

E. Dobkin (Mapai, or Labour): We have resolved correctly to give preferential treatment to the Jews of Poland. [But] priority should be given to those who arrive first. This does not have to continue throughout, but our aim is that the first to come should communicate to the others in Poland that the situation is not too bad here. We don't have to treat all the ten thousand like this. There is no harm in letting those who follow on later live like the rest of the refugees.

Y. Greenbaum: Instead of cramming the Polish Jews together like this, I believe it would be preferable to treat the Turkish and Libyan Jews that way. That would not be unfair. You ought to know that those [Polish] Jews are the élite. Every family had three or four rooms – a German house with German furniture and the latest German conveniences. There will be doctors from Poland. You just put one of them in Beit Leed or Pardes Hanna camps and see what he'll think then and how he'll feel.

Levi Eshkol, Yitzhak Greenbaum and an appointee from the Department of Immigration were delegated to look into ways of housing the Polish Jews 'in the spirit of the suggestions raised at the session'.[25]

Most of the decisions which were inhumane or against international law were not taken officially. The decision to expel the Arabs from Lydda and Ramleh is an example of that. Yitzhak Rabin, says that when he, as an army officer, went to Ben Gurion, the Minister of Defence and Prime Minister, to ask about the fate of the inhabitants of those two towns, Ben Gurion did not reply but made a gesture which meant 'Get rid of them'. It was later denied Ben Gurion had ordered the expulsion of the inhabitants of Lydda and Ramleh. In 1956 when an officer asked what would happen when peasants who did not know about the curfew which had been imposed after they had gone out to the fields, came home in the evening to their village of Kafr Qasem, the ranking officer replied with the Arabic phrase 'God have mercy upon them', which in army jargon means 'slaughter them', and this they did. In Lebanon the Christian Phalanges were ordered to enter Sabra and Shatila, which order could only mean a massacre of the Palestinian refugees. When David Levi, an Israeli minister of Moroccan origin, warned that this entry of the 'Keta'ib' meant a massacre, he was completely ignored.

THE TRANSIT CAMPS (MA'BAROT)

In the previous section we mentioned how Ben Gurion begrudged the meagre rations which were given to the immigrants and how he wanted to draft them into special unpaid work groups. The plan was then dropped due to various difficulties, but the principle was applied starting in 1950 in a different way. Either the immigrants' camps were transformed into transit camps, or the immigrants were forcibly removed to new camps, and thus most Sephardim ended up in transit camps. The Zionist establishment stopped providing the immigrants with food and they were told that they had to find work and earn a living. The aim of the establishment was to reduce the cost of the vastly increased immigration and to force Sephardim to do physical labour for much reduced wages. When some of the immigrants refused to go to the new camps, the establishment pressurised them by stopping all social services.[26]

These transit camps were erected next to the comfortable Ashkenazi settlements or the large cities, to provide them with cheap labour. The living conditions in the camps were uniform: tents and huts of wood and tin. Perhaps conditions in these camps were worse than before, for the ruling establishment was not responsible for ensuring food supplies to the inhabitants. There was no 'welfare state', and if a person was without a job, he received no financial help from the government. Whereas some of the inhabitants of the older camps received free houses or flats, the inhabitants of the transit camps had to buy their dwellings from a government company. The authorities, particularly the ruling Mapai party, used unemployment to debilitate the Sephardim and the search for work, any work (and it was usually unskilled labour), became a matter of life or death for someone with a large family. The Sephardim were used to develop the Israeli economy and to increase the profitability of businesses without gaining any benefit. They were paid low wages, could lose their jobs at any moment and were victims of every economic crisis the country underwent. In 1952 the unemployment rate in the camps oscillated between 40-50 percent, whereas the general unemployment rate in the country was only 6-10 percent. Even when unemployment went down throughout the country, the rate in the camps stayed high although some camps were not troubled by unemployment – where the inhabitants worked in construction, road building, afforestation, or in the settlements of the Jordan Valley and Ginossar. Everyone with a job worked a four-day week and earned two Israeli pounds a day.

After the residents of Kiryat Shemona camp had finished draining Lake Hula, Ashkenazi kibbutzim received 40,000 *dunums*[27] and four large new plantations were set for cotton and other products to be used in industry. The workers from Kiryat Shemona camp were not even allotted the smallest piece of reclaimed land. The army also used many of the residents for engineering works. Others worked on the 'Malha' project which was run by the Mekorot [Water] Company. A large proportion of the camp inhabitants did seasonal agricultural work such as fruit picking. A resolution of the local council in Migdal on 8 June 1951 stated that 80 percent of the residents of Migdal and the camp were unemployed at the end of the vegetable season.

The bosses were not content just to pay niggardly wages, they also received financial support from the authorities to encourage them to employ the immigrants. In chapter nine we shall see in detail how their profits helped the Israeli economy to develop. The government, moreover, invented a new way to reduce wages, which was to employ the immigrants in 'emergency work', whereby they would receive 'emergency wages' which were much less than the previously mentioned wages. The government claimed that 'emergency work' was not vital, and that its purpose was to prevent the spread of unemployment. Research has shown that this work was indeed included in the development budget. Emergency work in 1953-1954 consisted of the following examples: landscaping, increasing productivity of vegetable plots, nature preservation, afforestation, government land and forest reclamation, cultivation of National Fund lands, citrus cultivation, landscaping of school and hospital gardens, rubble clearing, development projects and public works, irrigation projects and road-surfacing. The development budget covered similar projects and the government in fact had no right to call this 'emergency work'. The average daily wage at the time in the large cities was five or six Israeli pounds a day (about one pound sterling). The camp inhabitants were paid only one Israeli pound or at most a pound and a half. One must also bear in mind that this was hard labour for the Sephardi immigrants who had previously been merchants, writers or artisans. Widad's family, whom I met in the

Sha'ar Ha'aliya Camp, were sent to the Megiddo transit camp, then to Tel Mond and then on to Salama C. Her husband, a small businessman called Abu Salih, had owned buses in Baghdad and had worked as a coach driver in his own enterprise. Though he had done this for thirty years, he was refused a driving licence in Israel and as a middle-aged man he was forced to do heavy physical labour. After ten years of this he developed a heart disease. His doctor at the time told him he could not work anymore. The author told Widad 'If he keeps on doing the same work it will kill him.' She replied 'What is worse? That we should die of hunger? We have seven children! The government did not help them.' Abu Salih carried on working and a few weeks later he died. Widad took up sewing and doing housework to raise her seven children.

In addition to low wages, recognised workers' rights were not granted to these immigrants. Wages were paid late. While some immigrants worked five-day weeks, some had just four- or even two-day weeks, and lines would stretch outside labour offices from midnight until the end of the day. Community or party patronage played a part in getting a job, but as often as not the immigrants would go back home jobless. Quarrels and fights would break out as the immigrants shouted at the labour exchange office 'You have tricked us into coming here, to these camps. May God take His revenge upon you! Go and rot in Hell!' The officials would then shout back 'Go back to Iraq!' There was a very popular song in the camps in those days:

> Look what you've done to us, Ben Gurion,
> You smuggled us out,
> because of the past,
> we have renounced our (Iraqi) citizenship
> and come to Israel.
> If only we had come by donkey
> we never would have made it!
> What a wretched time!
> What a wretched plane that brought us here!

The Iraqi immigrants believed that their emigration had taken place after a secret agreement had been signed by Nuri Said and Ben Gurion. They composed a folk song about that:

> They sold us there!
> They bought us there!
> Then they brought us here!

On some occasions, labour offices were stormed. The police would arrive quickly, clear them out and close them down. On other occasions wages were not paid for weeks or months. The Histadrut actually allowed emergency wages to be reduced by one third and in 1954 the Histadrut Council refused to listen to camp representatives. The camp-dwellers then demonstrated noisily outside the Histadrut building and again the police had to rush in to defend Council members.

The ruling party (Mapai-Labour) exploited the immigrants' ordeal to cement its authority. Mapai headed the government, the Histadrut, the Jewish Agency, the Ashkenazi agricultural settlement, and Histadrut plants, banks, marketing companies and other things. In the camps jobs were often handed out exclusively to members of Mapai and the small religious parties who were in the government coalition. The job hierarchy in the camps was as follows: camp director, head of the labour office, party secretary, sanitation workers, intelligence officer (the Shin Bet) and his spies. All these positions, except for those in sanitation, were held by Ashkenazim. The ruling party used bribes, usually in the form of jobs, intimidation and violence, and cultivated gangs to terrorize anyone who criticised the government. Progressive democratic circles which had participated in the struggle for national and social liberation in Arab countries were destroyed. The secret police used hysteria to cover up its tyranny and to keep Mapai in power. Anyone who dared open his mouth to stand up for his people's rights was called a communist, and terror was sown with threats of dismissal from work. This state of affairs lasted until the right-wing Likud party came to power in the election of 1977. Previously the ruling Labour party had an overwhelming majority of the votes in the camps in Parliamentary elections due to economic pressure, whereas it only won a third in the large towns.

The camp dwellers were unrepresented on the local councils to which their camps belonged because 'the election had already taken place before the camps joined the councils.' The Ministry of the Interior issued a decree limiting the authority of the local councils which the camps set up themselves, and in some of the camps the Jewish Agency appointed a committee which could intermediate between the camp residents and the administration. The Ministry of the Interior had not recognized any appointed or elected committee in the camps.

Quite often the party secretary's clique and that of the intelligence officer were the same. The party and the secret police (Shin Bet) relied upon criminal elements to frighten the camp residents. The official role of the secret police was to guard state security against spying by Arab countries, but in fact there was none and no one was ever accused of doing so. The Shin Bet was simply a political secret police force which worked to shore up the ruling party. S.M. told me that he had been given a small post in return for supplying information to the Shin Bet about people who were criticizing the state or the system. He added that he felt guilty because his information had destroyed those peoples' families, since they were fired from their jobs and had no means of sustenance. He pointed out that most of those people had not been enemies of the ruling party at all, but his Shin Bet had pressured him into supplying more names of 'suspects' and he had been obliged to give them the names of people who were apolitical, or even supporters of the ruling party. On one occasion I met Zekharia, one of my friends from school days, and he started complaining about the Mapai Party. 'They used me to control the Yemenite camp and then they threw me out.' Zekharia (who was Yemenite) carried on, 'I was appointed as an agricultural trainer on that camp, but my real job was to help Mapai. On the day of the parliamentary elections representatives of other parties came to the camp to lobby the residents. We decided to impose a curfew on the camp, "for security reasons" – we told the residents, and we kept them in their tents until the politicos had left. By these methods Mapai managed to win 90 percent of the Yemenite camp vote.'

The government and the Jewish Agency decided not to supply any social services to the camps. The local councils in whose jurisdiction the camps lay were supposed to supply them, but being Ashkenazi councils they had little contact with the camps. They also opposed the construction of new camps in their neighbourhood since camp dwellers could not pay local taxes. There were other racist reasons too, for example, when the Herzeliya municipality refused to have any camps in the area because of the large tourist hotels, and visible masses of dark-skinned poor would be detrimental both to the hotels and to Israel, which had spread far and wide the myth of its social justice and true democracy. Thus in 1953 in spite of the law, there were twenty-six camps (with 30 percent of the total camp inhabitants) outside any municipality and the rest were part of poor municipalities. Twelve camps were forced to set up local councils and to supply their residents with services, but due to the overwhelming poverty of the camps, the necessary services could not be provided and the government decided to place them under the authority of the Ministry of the Interior – which then did nothing. The municipalities which did accept the camps did not provide them with services, because again the camp dwellers could not pay local taxes. When the local councils requested more government help they received nothing. In 1952/3 and 1953/4 government help to local councils actually went down, causing a reduction in the level of whatever services existed. In some cases the number of camp inhabitants was much greater than the number of residents in the neighbouring municipality. In Nahalat Yehuda it was four times more. Tel Aviv, with 254,000 inhabitants, accepted 2,700 immigrants from the neighbouring camps and then only after intense pressure. Camps in the countryside actually belonged to the Ashkenazi Kibbutz and Moshav councils, who would accept no representatives from them. However, the Ashkenazi settlements did make use of the camp dwellers as cheap labour and consequently their profitability doubled and their standard of living rose dramatically compared to the period before the mass immigration.

Between twenty and thirty percent of the camps were set up in remote and border districts. They suffered from the following economic hardships:

1. Unemployment. Private and Histadrut bosses who received financial support to absorb the immigrants, preferred to use these funds in the central regions where the profits were greater.

2. The Histadrut preferred to build dwellings in the central regions, since profits were greater than in the border areas. The government then agreed to build dwellings in the outlying areas, but these flats were much smaller. Building work proceeded very slowly causing the inhabitants to live in tents for a number of years.

3. Scarcity of supplies. The Histadrut allowed its marketing company (Hamashbir Hamerkazi) to open many shops to sell food and clothing in the central regions, causing a shortage of supplies and higher prices in the remote camps. In short, the government decided to distribute the population around the country without forcing the authorities which had received government funding to use it in all regions of the country.

The Histadrut's neglect of its duties toward the Sephardim in the camps will be seen in sharper relief when it is realised that the camps had in fact enhanced the Histadrut. 76 percent of the camp inhabitants were forced to belong to it (in order to obtain work and medical treatment), whereas the average membership throughout the country was between 40 to 50 percent of the population (1950-1954). 78 percent of camp children went to Histadrut 'Socialist' schools, as opposed to the national average of 43 percent. The ruling party obtained between 40 and 50 percent, or in some camps between 80 and 90 percent, of the vote, as opposed to 32 percent of the general vote. If we add to the camps the development towns, the cooperatives and the people who lived in the 'Black Belt', we see that it was Sephardi immigration, in addition to economic exploitation, which kept the Mapai (Labour) Party in power for 29 years. Israel's spokesmen abroad claimed that the Israeli system was the most firmly established democracy in the region, but anyone who has lived in Israel knows that government control over the individual is unbelievably tight.

Sephardi Jews suffered from harsh health conditions in the camps with each family, usually with many children, living in one tent whose area was smaller than a normal room. In 1950/1 the winter was unusually harsh, with snow falls everywhere. The tents and the huts had no heat, and since there were only a few standpipes in every camp people had to stand in long queues for their water ration. In rural areas, priority was given to the Ashkenazi farmers and the camps had their water cut off. Often the water was muddy and unfit for drinking which led to an increase in complaints and violent demonstrations against the authorities which were put down with a steel hand. There was one shower, with cold water naturally, for every 16 people, but it was rare to find a shower which worked regularly. The toilets consisted of a small pit measuring one metre square, and there was one of these for every four families. The queues to use them were long and sometime there was only one per hundred people. After heavy rainfall, the contents of the pits would overflow and in summer they gave off a foul stink and nourished armies of stinging insects. The government did not bother about rubbish removal, and, since the camps had no gutters, mounds of rubbish piled up. Since some of the camps lay on the Lod-Tel Aviv highway, Ashkenazi journalists wrote that these camps were jeopardizing Israel's image since they could be seen by foreign tourists and it would be better to move them away from the highway. The establishment thus started building cement huts a few kilometres away and demanded that the camp inhabitants buy them and move into them. The Sephardim, however, spurned the offer because there was no asphalt road from the new location to the highway, but the Ashkenazi newspapers picked this up and reported 'these Sephardim refuse to live in buildings because they are used to living in tents like the Bedouin.'

The government did not link the camps to the regional electricity grid and the residents had to use paraffin lamps. Outside the tents it was pitch-black. There was no surfaced road inside the camps and the ground was so full of puddles and mud that it was difficult to get from tent to tent. Frequently communications between the camps and the neighbouring towns were very difficult due to the bad roads and the scarcity of transport, as a result of which the geographic and social isolation of the camps was heightened.

The only relations between Sephardim and Ashkenazi settler society was that of ruler and ruled. Contacts between the recent Sephardi immigrants and the native Palestinian Jews were difficult, since the latter lived in the large towns, but this isolation had one advantage in that the Sephardi camp dwellers kept their traditions alive. They continued to speak Arabic, to listen to Arabic music and to preserve their identity. This was of great use in the seventies and the eighties when there was a revival of Arabic culture amongst Sephardim. On the other hand the establishment split their families up amongst a number of camps, which weakened their struggle against the authorities. In spite of all this, Sephardi Jews did fuse into one society, mainly Arabic-speaking and united by their common cultural heritage. Simultaneously the Russian, Polish, Hungarian and other Ashkenazi Jews intermingled to form a single Ashkenazi society, united in their arrogance toward Jews from the Arab world and the Arabs living in it.

The geographical isolation of the camps led to goods being scarce and expensive. The government imposed austerity measures and issued ration cards. A black market thus grew up and Ashkenazi families in the cities could buy their provisions on the black market, which caused shortages. Most of the camp inhabitants, however, could not even afford to pay for the rations they were allowed to buy. The unemployed and heads of large families would sell their food rations to the Ashkenazim. Moreover, the food shops in the remote camps were also short of basics.

Health services were provided by the Sick Fund which belonged to the Histadrut, as well as by the Ministry of Health and the army. The health services suffered from a shortage of doctors and clinics. The government tried to conscript doctors to work in the camps, but it failed and had to appoint doctors from amongst the immigrants themselves. During visits to Saqiya, Pardes Hanna, Petah Tikvah and Tel-Mond camps, amongst others, it became clear there were deaths, mainly of the aged, which people were unaware of until the dead bodies started to smell. The child mortality rate was very high in comparison to that in the large cities and the Ashkenazi settlements. Indisputably the high death rate was due to the food shortage and the health and living conditions in the camps.

Sephardim in the camps took part in a number of demonstrations, and they sent numerous petitions to the authorities complaining about their living conditions. This is one of them:

March 28 1954

To the Prime Minister
Jerusalem

We the undersigned, residents of Camp Bet and Camp Gimmel near the town of Ramleh, respectfully present to you our vital requests as follows:

We are living in shocking economic, cultural and material circumstances – to which we are unaccustomed. The overwhelming majority of residents are unemployed or partially employed and receive emergency wages, that is three and a half Israeli pounds per day for a maximum of twelve days a month. We have lived in these dreadful conditions for more than three years with no interest or help from government or municipal establishments. There are 8-10 people per hut and we are living amidst mounds of filth, which are causing diseases and epidemics since the germs and bacteria have the most conducive of situations for their growth. A large percentage of our children is not sent to school due to a shortage of financial resources. We have one doctor and one nurse for 5,000 people. We have no paved road connecting the camp to the town, which causes transport difficulties and forces our women, including the pregnant and the old, to go to town and back on foot. This is also the situation for the men who work in the town and who have to walk long distances after a long day's work. Most of the inhabitants of the camp have been unable to pay their rent and municipal taxes for the last two years or more, and the Amidar company and the Ramleh municipality have taken people to court over this. Recently municipal taxes have gone up 20 percent and income tax has gone up 7.5 percent in an attempt to pay off our debts to the municipality. The Social Welfare Office gives the needy £4-8 Israeli a month, but this small sum is not enough to solve the problem since it is nowhere near enough to support a family of 6–8 members [then the petition demands the supply of electricity and telephones to the camps as well as the provision of an ambulance] . . .

This situation was a violent psychological shock for the Sephardim, since most of them had lived in the finest districts of Baghdad, Cairo, Alexandria and Beirut. Their despair deepened together with their sense of indifference, but sometimes acts of violence were carried out against the Zionist establishment.

Deborah Burnstein wrote in her detailed study, *The Transit Camps in the Fifties*, that official documents do not mention anything about the psychological problems in the camps. However, some of the residents did write about these problems in short stories such as the Iraqi Shimon Balas who wrote the best novel in Hebrew about the transit camps – *Hama'bara*. Sami Mikhael, another Iraqi author, wrote the well-known novel *Equal and More Equal*. The hero of this story, David, who is sixteen years old, and who lives in one of the transit camps (Ma'barat Khairiya, near Tel Aviv), says:

My father wept! I listened, stunned, to sounds I couldn't believe. Abu-Shaul was crying! After a moment, Mother shook him by the shoulders. 'Ya'qub,' she whispered. 'Enough! Ya'qub. Let's not dwell over what has happened. But I knew that father would never stop dwelling over his shattered dream. Was he not standing at the door of his new love affair? He had entered quite happily and shut the door behind him only to find that he was in the company of an indifferent monster . . . Perhaps Mother couldn't understand, but I did. Father's body was still alive but his spirit was dying inside him. He was a new immigrant from Iraq, this old man, burdened with a family, short of money and transplanted amongst a group of people with no hope of supporting his family honourably. All of this formed the base of another revelation which was many times worse: it transpired that he belonged to an inferior race . . . and he could not get over this burning humiliation.[28]

One half of Khairiya Camp has turned into a huge rubbish dump which daily absorbed all Tel Aviv's rubbish. As far as I'm concerned it is a living memorial to what was going on there. As far back as I can remember, I knew that all of us residents had been thrown into that human rubbish dump by those anonymous pale-faced men from the big city.[29]

We thought that our arrival in Israel would be like a

homecoming. Jews among Jews. One nation. But it wasn't like that. Someone has split us up into two nations. I remember the troubles we went through in Iraq – but we were never inferior! They don't persecute Jews here, thank God, but before we arrived they had decided to make us second class people.[30]

Tsiporah, the Ashkenazi official responsible for sanitation in the camp, believed it was not just the toilets and showers that needed to be cleaned out, but the inhabitants as well.[31]

When David was late for work washing bottles, Goldenburg, his boss, told him 'Laziness is a despicable Arab characteristic . . . ' When David tried to explain that all the buses had been full, Mr Goldenberg sighed. 'Ah, David, David! You've got to leave all that Arab stuff behind you for ever. You cannot get by here on lies and excuses.'[32]

David feels that the solidarity between the Ashkenazi soldiers and the Sephardim is purely transient and that when they come back from the Six Day War they will have to return to their former place in society, that of the 'dark' community. The Ashkenazi will return to his white bedsheets and the Sephardi to his slums. Then he adds that he was forced to go to war and that he will defend himself. He dislikes Israel . . . but he does not know a single Egyptian. Then he wonders how he can hate a person he has never seen.[33]

During the Parliamentary elections, Ashkenazi landlords offered the camp residents ten Israeli pounds cash for every vote.[34]

'It's the same there (on the kibbutz) also. The 'blacks'[35] are second-class citizens. They watched over me all the time, as if I were a time-bomb – or a stink-bomb.'[36]

Tzipora (the Ashkenazi) said to David, the Iraqi, 'Keep away from my daughter, do you hear? Margalit is not for a dirty black like you . . . '[37]

David said, 'Look at the schools and particularly the universities. How many "Orientals" do you find there, even though we are the majority. There is discrimination at every level. North Tel Aviv versus Ma'abarat Khairiya and the Hatikva slum district, Ashkenazim versus Sephardim. Even at the window of the labour office, there is Tzipora on the one hand and me on the other.'[38]

In the armoured car, the soldier David thinks about the Ashkenazi soldiers around him, but cannot see any link between himself and them. There is no friendship, no empathy, no brotherhood of arms ' . . . I am a foreign body amongst them.'[39]

Then the author describes the biggest gangster in the camp – Abu

Halawa: 'He feared no one. All the political parties tried to please him. The camp secretary licked his arse and the police were blind to his deeds.'[40]

A favourite joke of the Ashkenazim was:[41] 'There are two things which I hate with all my might, and they are firstly sectarian discrimination, and secondly Franks.'[42]

The story has a happy ending with the hero receiving a medal for bravery in the 1967 war and with it a sense of arrival and acceptance in Israeli society. This conclusion is so far at odds with the central themes of the book that it is evident that it was tacked on to make it publishable.

The policy of de-education in the camps was reaching its zenith. A large part of the children received no education whatsoever, in spite of the law stipulating that elementary education was obligatory. The only educational establishments in the camps were primary schools and kindergartens, which suffered from a shortage of building, qualified teachers, books and equipment. Children between 6 and 12 represented 75 percent of the pupil body in the country, but in the camps they were only 50 percent and the remainder received no education. The standard of education was much lower than that in schools in the rest of the country. A Sephardi of Syrian origin who was a member of the Zionist left-wing Ahdut Ha'avodah party, Abraham 'Abbas, wrote that 50 percent of camp pupils in the Beer Sheva region could not read or write. The educational level of these primary schools did not go beyond that of the third grade of regular schools (elementary schools in Israel have eight grades). He added that a third of all children between the age of 6 and 13 did not go to school in spite of the compulsory education law, and that 90 percent left school at the end of the fourth grade. 'Abbas observed the breakdown of values and emphasises that the real reason for this phenomenon was the atrocious educational situation, not just in the area of Beer Sheba but in all the camps, Sephardi cooperative villages and the 'Black Belt'. 'Abbas stated that school fees effectively prevented children from getting a primary education, which is the reason why there are so few Sephardim at university. The World Organization of Sephardi Jewry had put immense pressure on the government and the Jewish Agency which resulted in the appropriation of 145,000 Israeli pounds to help students from this community. 90 percent of Sephardi immigrants were unaccustomed to doing physical labour, having been involved in commerce and the civil service. 90 percent of the unemployed were Sephardim, in addition to those employed in emergency work and receiving emergency wages. Abbas added, quoting Dr Smilansky, that forty thousand children between the ages of 14 and 18 were not in any educational establishment, one third of those who were not at school were unemployed, another third did casual jobs, and the other third lived by dubious means. The proportion of Sephardim in secondary schools was almost zero – out of 1,300 secondary school pupils in Tel Aviv, for example, there were just 13 Sephardi children[43] (see chapter seven).

By 1954 the number of camp dwellers had reached 200,000, with 80 percent being Sephardim, (although according to Central Zionist Archive S84/77 they were more than 90 percent in 1953). However, the few Ashkenazim in the camps only stayed for a few days or weeks, whereas the Sephardim were there for years. In 1954 Yitzhak Rafael, head of the Immigration Department of the Jewish Agency, suggested to the Knesset that they look into anti-Sephardi discrimination, but he was defeated by an overwhelming majority.[44]

In his speech in 1954 to the World Conference of Sephardi Jews which was convened in Jerusalem, Avraham al-Maliah, a community leader, described the tragic conditions in the camps, the diminished educational level of the new generation, and the inability of the fathers to pay secondary school and university fees. He mentioned how students had to leave school to help their families out, and spoke of unemployment, the bitterness of their lives, hunger and discrimination. Al-Maliah also observed that many Sephardim wanted to go back home. He accused Ashkenazi officials of tyranny and of not understanding the psychology of their victims due to the cultural divide between them and the Sephardim. Instead of solving their problems, these officials keep putting the immigrants off, behaving arrogantly with them and sending them from one official to another until the immigrant is driven mad with frustration. Even though they brought them to Palestine, they scream at them 'Who asked you to come to this country? Who asked you to have so many children?' and so forth. Al-Maliah criticised the Zionist emissaries who wasted the money they collected from contributions on luxurious living instead of spending it on the poor immigrants. He accused them of disseminating a spirit of hatred amongst family members and of snatching children from their parents, and of dividing them out amongst the parties, as if they were sharing out cattle.[45]

Owing to the fact that welfare aid for the unemployed, and widows and orphans was almost non-existent, I have seen mothers abandon their children in the offices of the Ministry of Social Affairs and run off. The police would then track down the mothers and arrest them, to make them take back their children. One can just imagine the trauma these children underwent. Doubtless most of the women involved in vice or in prison today (1990) were born and brought up in those terrible camps. I asked an employee of the Ministry of Social Affairs 'Do you not feel guilty when you see those children screaming and crying hysterically?' 'No,' he replied. 'For Israel needs street sweepers and workers to do the menial jobs, and these children will do that . . . '

In her study, Deborah Bernstein says that by the end of 1951 there were 127 transit camps containing 250,000 inhabitants.[46] She adds that usually the immigrants could not choose which camp they would live in.

I saw the hardships which befell the family of the Abu Salih when they moved from Megiddo Camp to Tel Mond Camp, without permission, since Abu Salih's brother and sister were there.

After several years, the dwellers of the transit camps were moved into ugly cement huts nearby and the camp name was changed. This is what happened to the Saqiya and Khairiya camps which were merged and renamed Or Yehuda ('The Light of Judah'!). Others were transferred to 'cooperative work villages' and 'development towns'. A portion moved to the slum areas of the large towns and the 'Black Belt' sprawled further. In spite of the fact that these camps were called 'transit camps', there were 30,000 people still living in them in 1980[47] – in the camps of Jesse Cohen, Nof-Yam, Holon and Bat-Yam. Israeli newspapers have published much material about the living conditions in the camps and the violence and stormy demonstrations against the establishment staged in them. The demonstrators called upon the United Nations to intervene on their behalf and to look after them as they looked after refugees in other places in the world. These wretches stayed in the camps for more than 30 years.[48] Nahum Goldman, the head of the World Jewish Congress in 1959, admitted that the flats which had been built to house the Sephardim were, at the eleventh hour, handed over to Ashkenazim – which caused the uprising of Wadi al-Salib in Haifa.[49] Prof. Kedourie (1970) sums up the tragedy of the Iraqi Jews: 'In Israeli immigrant camps, tricked and dissatisfied, their livelihood and homes taken away from them, their coherent community destroyed and themselves forcibly brought to the service of an ideal which they neither understand nor share' (p. 313); he goes on to accuse the Zionist and Arab rulers for the fact that 'the Jews of Iraq were uprooted, dispossessed and scattered in the space of a year' (pp. 314-315). (For further illustrative material, see Appendix I.)

THE DEVELOPMENT TOWNS, OR CHEAP LABOUR CAMPS

In 1952 the Zionist establishment changed its policy on the absorption of Sephardi immigrants, particularly the Moroccans. Instead of sending them to the afore-mentioned transit camps, it started to erect what were called 'development towns' and also stopped bringing over to Israel the aged and infirm or indeed anyone who could not do heavy physical labour. This wave of immigration was termed 'select immigration' and did not apply to Ashkenazim. The immigrants were forcibly taken from the ship straight to the Negev desert, the Lebanese border or other remote districts. When they saw the arid desert and the lack of housing, and refused to disembark from the trucks, they were unceremoniously tipped out. They were then forced to put up their tents and to work for the neighbouring Ashkenazi settlements or on other capital projects. This was a much cheaper method of absorption than transit camps since it was direct and permanent. Between 1954-1956 42 percent of immigrants were taken to the Negev, 42 percent to the Galilee, 8 percent to the Jerusalem area and 8 percent to the coastal district.[50]

Hayya Zuckerman-Brali wrote in her article, 'Reasons for Leaving a Development Town', that according to official government pronouncements, these towns were set up for 'economic, security and settlement reasons'.[51] This can be interpreted to refer to the supply to Ashkenazi settlements and private capital of cheap seasonal labour, the settlement of empty districts to prevent the return of the Arab inhabitants and the construction of a human wall to protect Ashkenazi settlements from Palestinian guerilla activity.

By 1984 there were twenty-nine such towns, and by 1985 there were half a million people living in them – constituting 15 percent of the total Jewish population of Israel within the 'green line'.[52] There are twelve towns which resemble development towns in their poverty and economic under-development, but which the government refuses to classify as development towns. If they were included, the number of inhabitants of 'the third Israel' would be 750,000,[53] or 25 percent of the Jewish population. If we take into account economic, cultural and living conditions, we will find no difference between the development towns and the slum districts of the large cities and the cooperative villages where the Sephardi immigrants live, both recent arrivals and long-time inhabitants.

By the seventies, the number of workers in the development towns had reached 150,000, 45 percent of whom worked in industry, 12 percent in construction, and the remainder in agriculture and the service industries. The industries which receive the greatest government support were textiles, clothing and food, which do not require huge amounts of capital but which need cheap unskilled labour. In Dimona the two textile mills employ 96 percent of the industrial work-force, or 50 percent of the total work-force of the town. In Kiryat Shemona 71 percent of the work-force is also employed in textiles. In Yeroham 92 percent are employed in the chemical works and the quarries. If the town factory closes, most of the town's inhabitants are left unemployed. Due to this economic structure, the blue collar workers in the development towns constitute 78 percent of the total work force, as opposed to 51 percent in the large towns. White collar workers are only 22 percent, as opposed to 46 percent nationwide. The white collar workers are Ashkenazim whereas the blue collar workers are Sephardim. Class and racial discrimination is thus twofold.[54] The class of business owners in the development towns is made up of two sub-divisions, Ashkenazi capitalists and 'Socialist' kibbutz members – also Ashkenazim. Government support to business owners has included grants of nearly free land, loans and other government funds.

Swirski and Shushan write that wages and conditions on the shop floor in these factories are much worse than those in the same industries in the large towns, and, moreover, the differential between wages in the development towns and in the large towns grows larger from year to year.[55]

The census of 1983 proves that there is a huge gulf between the development towns and other regions of the country in the areas of unemployment, housing and the standard of living. In development towns 30 percent of families need government benefits, whereas the nationwide average is 20 percent. Based on data from government employment offices in 1985, unemployment in development towns is 28 percent of total unemployment, whereas the residents of development towns only make up 15 percent of the population, and this percentage rises from year to year.[56] If we examine each town individually we will find that unemployment is worse than that. In Shderot, for example, there were 1080 unemployed out of a population of 2700, meaning that the unemployment rate was 40 percent whereas the national rate was just 7 percent.[57] If we examine unemployment conditions nationwide, we find that almost all the unemployed are Sephardim. In the Ashkenazi settlements the unemployment rate is zero, and this cannot be sheer luck.[58] There are Ashkenazi settlers in the lands occupied after 1967 who have two jobs – one on the settlement and the other in Jerusalem or one of the Jewish cities in Israel. They have two homes, one in Israel and one in the occupied territories, at the expense of the state.

All the social services in the development towns are second-rate compared to the rest of the country, and third-rate when compared to the social services provided to the Ashkenazi settlers. Most of the development towns are far from the large hospitals and the clinics in the towns lack specialists and new equipment. The proportion of clinics in the large towns is 2.35 times greater than in the development towns, and there are three times as many doctors in the large towns even though there are only twice as many inhabitants. This is one of the reasons for the infant mortality rate in the development towns being two and a half times greater than in the Ashkenazi settlements.

This gulf carries through into the field of education also. Sephardi children receive a third-rate education due to the lower quality of schools, equipment, books, teaching qualifications and teaching itself. The drop-out rate is therefore greatest in the development towns. The following table shows up the difference between the achievements of Sephardi school children in the development towns and the achievements of Ashkenazi schoolchildren in the wealthy Ashkenazi settlements:[59]

Town	no. of inhabitants (15 yrs +)	Percentage gaining Secondary Certificate	Percentage gaining University Degree
Sephardi Development Towns			
Ofakim	8,185	33.4%	1.2%
Beit She'an	8,145	30.0%	1.9%
Hatzor (Galilee)	3,605	32.4%	1.1%
Yeroham	3,845	33.5%	2.1%
Shderot	5,715	30.8%	1.9%
Shlomi	1,400	30.1%	1.1%

Ashkenazi Settlements

Giv' atayim	36,575	58.3%	10.9%
Herzeliya	43,550	57.6%	13.2%
Savyon	1,820	74.5%	25.8%
Omer	2,780	76.3%	36.0%
Kiryat Uno	15,320	61.1%	15.4%
Kiryat Tivon	7,835	56.0%	13.1%

The reality was in fact worse that these figures show, for two reasons: most of the students from the development towns who gained either secondary school certificates or university degrees were members of those towns' Ashkenazi business or administrative elite; and secondly, the exclusion of many Sephardi workers and servants who lived on Ashkenazi settlements distorted the percentages. (See chapter seven.)

The wretched economic and educational conditions, and particularly unemployment, helped to drive more people out of the development towns than were moving to them, as the following figures for the period 1978–1984 show:[60]

Town	Shderot	Bet She'an	Migdal Ha'emek	Netivot	Neroham	Average (all Development Towns)
Departure Rate	32%	26%	28%	36%	41%	37%
Arrival Rate	13%	2%	13%	13%	0.5%	13%

The departure of the elite is weakening these communities and subjecting them to further exploitation and domination.

At the end of 1985, the leaders of Histadrut workers' councils in the development towns of Shderot, Kiryat Shemoneh, Yeroham and Bet She'an, convened a press conference with members of the Histadrut. They declared that the development towns were quickly heading towards decline, with 90 percent of their youth leaving because of unemployment, having lost 25 percent of their inhabitants between 1979 and 1984.[61]

REASONS FOR THE DECLINE OF THE DEVELOPMENT TOWNS, UNEMPLOYMENT AND THE DEPARTURE OF RESIDENTS

1. These towns lack an economic base. They need funding to be able to carry out their economic programmes. From their very

inception, these towns were not planned with their residents in mind, but rather for the interests of Ashkenazi settlers and the expansionist policy and security needs of the ruling establishment. It must be observed that the construction of one factory employing the locals, does not constitute an economic base upon which a town can grow up.

2. The residents were not allowed to participate in administration of projects or technical matters, but simply provided menial labour. They were provided no means of vocational advancement and were subordinate to the Ashkenazim who received development funds from the government.

3. The policy of belligerency against Arab states swallowed most of the state's resources at the expense of the development towns, the 'Black Belt' and other Sephardi villages.

4. Since 1967 the government has granted priority to the Ashkenazi settlements in the occupied territories and has left the development towns to lurch towards economic and social disintegration. This cannot be explained simply by the expansionist policy, since the government would not have ignored the development towns had they been populated by Polish or American Jews. By 1984 the amounts spent on Ashkenazi settlements in the occupied territories were 7.2 times those spent on development towns.[62] On 23 November 1979, *Ha'aretz* wrote that the government intended to spend $4.7 billion on building new settlements, which represented 40 percent of the state budget or four times as much as would be needed to rehouse slum dwellers in the large towns. *The Times* of London wrote on 4 March 1980 that the state was going to spend £100 million sterling on settlement during that year. Ezer Weizmann, a moderate Zionist, believes that the settlements do not enhance Israel's security as the rulers claim.[63] Charlie Biton, the leader of the Black Panthers, declared in the Knesset on 19 November 1980 that settlements in the occupied territories were classed as Grade A or A+ development areas, whereas the Sephardi development towns were classed as Grade B, which is why 80 percent of the construction budget was spent on rural Ashkenazi settlements in the occupied territories. This discrimination, he continued, extended into education also, with gross overcrowding in the schools, whereas Ashkenazi schools in the settlements had only a small number of pupils per class. The government budgeted 413 million Israeli pounds for school construction nationwide, of which 76 millions were spent to build one school in the West Bank settlement of Ma'aleh Adumim.

The government paid enormous reparations to the 350 families who had settled in the Sinai. Each family received £190,000 sterling, even though the lands that they were vacating did not belong to them but were Egyptian property and that most of the money invested in the settlements had come from the state. On 21 November 1980, *Ha'aretz* called these settlers 'peace-brokers'. In addition to these sums paid out by the state, similar amounts were paid to residents of Yamit in Sinai. As a result of these hand-outs the government had to reduce the education budget by 7.5 percent, and the social support budget by 3.3 percent, after the education budget had already been reduced 23 percent the previous year, and school construction by 50 percent.[64] Ezer Weizmann said that he was afraid to meet the development town residents who had voted for Likud in 1977, since Likud was doing nothing to improve their conditions.[65]

On 5 February 1982 *Ha'aretz* published a statement issued by the Congress of Development Town Mayors in Hertzeliya. The mayors attacked the government policy which favoured the settlements in the occupied territories. The mayor of Netivot said that the government was only constructing thirty-six flats that year in his town which had 9,000 inhabitants, and that two thirds of the newly-weds were homeless and forced to live with their families. The mayor of Bet Shemesh added that housing was provided for almost nothing in the settlements on the West Bank and in the Gaza Strip. On 26 November 1979, the newspaper *Yedi'ot Aharonot* reported that 85 percent of Ashkenazi settlers owned two homes – one in Israel and one in the occupied territories. The Conference proved to the mayors that there was a clash of interests between the Sephardi residents of development towns and the Ashkenazi settlers. The state spends 75 percent of its budget on security, which includes Ashkenazi settlements in the occupied territories and the consolidation of the occupation at the expense of social services in Israel. On 17 January 1986 *Ha'aretz* reported that the mayors were camped out in the Prime Minister's office to emphasise their demands.

On 7 March 1986 *Ha'aretz* published a table which demonstrated how Ashkenazi settlements were favoured over development towns. The table was based on official government figures, and can be split up into four schedules.

The first table deals with government encouragement of trade and industry. The government divided the development towns into three categories – A+, A and B, but the settlements in the occupied territories were only divided into A+ and A.

1. Poor development towns like Bet Shemesh and Kiryat Malachi amongst others were placed in the third category, whereas all the affluent settlements, such as Ariel, were placed in the first or second preferential categories.

2. Development towns such as Dimona, Shderot, Netivot, Ofakim and others, which suffer from unemployment and hunger are classed in the second category.[66]

Development Towns and 'Growth Areas' (mainly Sephardim)			Settlers in the Occupied Territories (mainly Ashkenazim)	
A+	A	B	A+	A
Kiryat	Karmiel	Yokna'am	Ma'aleh	Other existing
Shemonah	(Ashkenazim)		Efraim	and future
Shlomi	Safad	'Akko	Ofra	settlements
Ma'alot	Tiberias	Bet Shemesh	Kdummim	
Hatsor	Rosh Pinah	Kiryat	Bet El	
(Galilee)		Malachai		
Bet She'an	Afula	Kiryat Gad	Ariel	
Katsirin	Gush Segev	Beer Sheba	Snor	
Metulla	Nahariya	Ashkelon	Tekoa	
Migdal	Migdal		Neveh Tsof	
		Ha'emek		
Yavni'el	Ofakim		Shiloh	
Benei Yehuda	Netivot		Karnei Shomron	
Merkaz	Shderot		Elon Morehı	
Hasbit				
Yeroham	Dimonah		Ma'aleh Shomron	
Mitzpeh	Arad		Dotan	
Ramon	(Ashkenazi)			
Élat	Ramat Hovev		Rimmonim	

The second table shows the racial discrimination in the way house mortgages are granted.

1. Much larger mortgages are granted to Ashkenazi settlers in the occupied territories than to poor residents of the development towns.

2. The percentage of loans, not linked to the dollar, which are granted to the Ashkenazim is greater than in the Sephardi development towns. This means that inflation will gradually lessen the amount of Ashkenazi borrowings. This is an important point which has caused the bankruptcy of many poor families who have received dollar-linked loans to buy houses. As inflation goes up, mortgage repayments increase, but many borrowers fall into arrears and their debts pile up to the point where the whole family's income is spent on servicing their debts. Sephardi Jews have thus become hostages to the greed of both the private and public sector banks

which are run by Ashkenazim.

Loan Distribution	House Mortgages in Development Towns to families with:			House Mortgages in Settlements in the Territories to families with:		
	3 children	4–5 children	6 children and more	3 children	4–5 children	6 children and more
New Shekel	26,000	23,700	40,400	38,900	43,200	48,300
Non-dollar linked	15%	27%	34%	15%	31%	38%
Dollar linked	85%	73%	66%	85%	69%	62%

(2.5 New Shekels = £1 sterling)[67]

The third table published explains the reason for the relative expense of housing in development towns compared to settlements in the occupied territories. On the West Bank, for example, the cost of land plots for housing is only 5 percent of the official cost in order to encourage the settlers. Plots in development towns vary between 12 and 60 percent of the official cost.[68]

The fourth table in the newspaper shows that residents of the settlements on the West Bank enjoy another privilege, that of a reduction of 7 percent in the income tax they pay, whereas the poorest Israelis in the development towns get a rebate of between 3–10 percent.[69]

We can thus sum up the privileges which Ashkenazim in the settlements in the occupied territories enjoy as follows:
1. Grants to encourage industry and trade.
2. Long-term mortgages
3. Cut-price land for housing
4. A reduction in income tax
5. High-quality schools with small classes

THE PRIVILEGES OF THE OLD KIBBUTZIM

These privileges have not just been granted since 1967, but since the start of Zionist colonisation, as we have mentioned in chapters two and three. We shall in the following pages discuss discrimination against development towns compared to the Ashkenazi settlements in pre-1967 Israel.

Whereas the Ashkenazi kibbutzim and moshavim are built on a firm economic foundation by reason of their geographical location, the amount and quality of the land attached to them, and their funding, development towns own neither land, nor factories nor working funds. They merely provide labour for the Zionist establishment and for private capital, or the 'socialist' kibbutzim. They are located far from the economic centres, in the Negev desert or on the borders, for security purposes, with no regard to the interests of their inhabitants, apart from the fact that funding for jobs was much less than that available in Ashkenazi settlements. Health and education services in the development towns are much inferior to those in neighbouring kibbutzim. Consequently, the gap in the standard of living is very wide.

This has caused the destruction of the socialist foundation of the kibbutzim which have exploited the cheap labour pool and made such inordinate profits that they have now started to speculate on the stock exchange. On 18 March 1983 *Ha'aretz* reported that the Amalgamated Kibbutz Movement had decided to invest fifty million dollars abroad. Its current investments are as follows: $72 million in the financial markets, $8 million in property and $60 million in stocks. The kibbutz organisation also bought 25 percent of the shares of KayMed in the United States.

The establishment of industries in kibbutzim was the turning point for their economies. Their income went up 39 percent, and the proportion of members working in industry and services went up to 50 percent.[70]

On 10 January 1986 *Ha'aretz* stated that the sixth formers (17-18 years old) from Kibbutz Yiftah had published an open letter to the kibbutz members demanding a return to the principle of equality. They protested that some of the members had bought private cars, video machines and flats in the towns, and opened private bank accounts etc.

We should point out that until 1948 all kibbutzim refused to hire non-member workers, whether they were Jews or Arabs, since they were opposed to making profits from other people's labour. Profits signified 'capitalist exploitation' and that went against the most important ideological precept of the kibbutz movement. During the Mandate, the kibbutzim would not allow their members to have private radios or electric kettles, since it was in the nature of consumer durables to arouse 'capitalist impulses, greed and individualism'. After 1948, when the kibbutzim received grants to open factories with the aim of employing Sephardim, for the 'nationalist' reasons supported by David Ben Gurion himself, profits started to accumulate and people started to succumb to materialist greed. The socialist foundation of the kibbutz movement was destroyed, and as far as the hired workers were concerned they were capitalist establishments. Their standard of living rose and the ideals of socialist austerity and equality fell by the wayside. The members who worked with the labourers always got the 'clean' jobs. Alcoholism and drug abuse spread and more often than not the exploitation of Sephardim was worse than that of the regular private factories. The Sephardim who worked for the kibbutzim concluded that their enemies were the kibbutz members and not the capitalists in the Likud block under Menahem Begin. This phenomenon (together with the Labour government's policies toward Sephardi immigrants) was one of the most important reasons why the Sephardim started voting for Likud and Begin in 1977.

The kibbutz can fire a worker when he reaches the age of forty or fifty. Workers are not allowed to eat in the settlement cafeteria, or to use the swimming pool or library. Kibbutz members treat the Sephardi workers badly and scorn them for their ethnic background and their dark skin. Sephardi workers do the menial jobs with no hope of advancement or vocational training. Gadi Elat, a member of Kibbutz Beit Alfa, tried to improve relations between the kibbutz and the workers but he failed and resigned from his position. His successor, Dan Sa'ar also failed, and told *Ha'aretz* on 22 October 1982 that the leadership of the Labour Party and the kibbutzim had not given the reconciliation process any support.

Yitzhak Navon, a native Palestinian Jew and former President of the State, said that 'when a worker from Migdal Ha'emek [a development town] who works for Kibbutz Alonim is not allowed to use its olympic-size swimming pool this reflects the disappearance of basic pioneer aspirations.'[71] The director of the Ministry of Employment said that in 1984 40 percent of the unemployed nationwide were in the development towns, even though they only contained 15 percent of the total population. Thus unemployment in the developments is almost 3.3 times greater than anywhere else. In 1984 the nationwide unemployment rate was 7 percent but it was 30 percent in the development towns.[72] The mayors spend most of their time dealing with the problem of unemployment, and because of economic weakness 75 percent of municipalities' income comes from the government.[73]

In a letter to *Ha'aretz* on 25 September 1981, Professor Ezra Zohar pointed out that Sephardim who grow up in development towns and slum areas are not offered any educational opportunities. It was in practice forbidden to leave the development towns, since one lost one's place on the housing list. Professor Zohar confirmed that Sephardi intellectuals in Israel do not have the same social standing they had in the Arab countries. He claimed that the state had destroyed the Middle-Eastern family unit but had not replaced it with anything, and that Sephardim could not integrate into Ashkenazi settler society due to bureaucracy and favouritism.

The journalist, Ze'ev Yefet, made a comparison between government policy in development towns and its policy in the occupied territories, and came to the following conclusion:
1. The government deems the Ashkenazi settlements in the occupied territories 'development regions' to justify pouring funds into them.
2. Land for construction in the development towns is ten times more expensive than that in the occupied territories. An Ashkenazi settler pays only 5 percent of the price of the land, or receives it free. The price of a half *dunum* in the occupied territories is only 3,000 shekels, whereas it varies between 120,000 and 246,000 shekels in the development towns in the pre-1967 areas.
3. The government is constructing new factories in the settlements in the occupied territories, whereas residents of the development towns suffer from unemployment due to lack of investment in their economy.[74]

As for cultural life – arts, music, drama, etc. – the central government imposes Ashkenazi culture on these communities through its company 'Metnasim'. The mayors, too, have not been residents of the towns but imposed by the Ashkenazi parties. Now they are local people but controlled by those parties. Thus the Zionist establishment controls every aspect of life in these communities.

Kiryat Shemonah

The journalist Amos Elon estimated the population of this town on the Lebanese border to be almost 14,000 and compared it to the neighbouring kibbutzim, such as Kibbutz Dan, Kibbutz Dafna, Kibbutz Kfar Gil'adi and Kibbutz Manarah. Elon stated that young people were leaving the town due to unemployment and the lack of skilled jobs. 50 percent of the children are classified as 'remedial'. People live in box-like apartments like those in the shanty-towns in South Africa. The neighbouring kibbutzim are classed as border settlements and thus receive government reparations for the losses they suffer as a result of guerilla operations. Kiryat Shemonah does not, however, receive any reparations. For the same reasons, the Ashkenazi kibbutzim do not pay state taxes, but Kiryat Shemonah has to pay in full. There are doctors living on the kibbutzim, but none live in Kiryat Shemonah. The town started off as a transit camp, but has lately turned into a slum neighbourhood surrounded by rich Ashkenazi kibbutzim which draw their cheap labour needs from it.

The journalist then compared the town to Ashkenazi Kiryat Arba, near Hebron. He wrote that in Kiryat Arba' every house has a telephone. A flat in Kiryat Shemonah costs I£20,000 more than a comparable one in Kiryat Arba'. There are 400 empty apartments in Kiryat Shemonah awaiting new settlers, whereas there are 90 young families who are homeless. Prices are higher than in the large cities by 3–10 percent, and building materials are 25 percent more expensive. He writes that the same conditions prevail in other development towns such as Bet She'an, Karmiel and Ma'alot.[75]

To make matters worse, the ruling establishment sends Ashkenazi volunteers to the development towns, to 'help the residents and propagate the settler spirit'. Tsvi Tsameret, the headmaster of the town's school, criticises these youngsters for their racial arrogance and ignorance. David Oren describes the prevailing conditions in the development town of Yeroham in the Negev and wonders 'why does the government not spend its money on helping these towns rather than spending it on these arrogant volunteers?'[76]

During the election campaign of 1981, Likud workers published a popular cartoon with the heading 'The Kibbutz Mafia'. It had a picture of a monster on whose chest was written 'The Kibbutz Movement', on his belly 'The Labour Alliance', his forearms were inscribed with 'incitement' and 'intimidation', while he brandished a hammer labelled 'threats'. The monster led a great pack of savage animals, representing the various kibbutzim surrounding the town. The cartoon had a subtitle which read 'Hush! They are coming'. In the foreground are the buildings of Kiryat Shemonah.

Israel Shahak, head of the League of Human Rights, wrote that the reason for intercommunal hatred is the exploitation and gulf between their respective standards of living. He continued that the kibbutzim have threatened to impose the communal punishment of an economic boycott on Kiryat Shemonah because of its resistance. In addition to economic tyranny, kibbutz members also dominate the town politically.[77]

According to reports in *Ha'aretz* on 24 July 1981, most of the

17,000 residents of the town fled from the guerilla bombardments, leaving behind only 3,000 to 4,000, because the authorities had not provided the town with properly equipped shelters, as they had in the kibbutzim. The few shelters in the town are in a lamentable state, full of rubbish, filthy water and foul smells. These shelters have neither drinking water, electricity nor telephones.

Shimon Peres, the leader of the Labour Party, acknowledged that the town has just 0.4 sq. metres of shelter space per person.[78] *Zu Haderekh* reported on 29 July 1981 that 95 percent of the inhabitants had fled the town because of guerilla bombardments and the local authorities refused to hold open their jobs for them, which aroused much resentment amongst the population. There were no occurrences of this type on the Ashkenazi kibbutzim since the government had supplied them with comfortable and well-equipped shelters.

Rafi Peretz, who worked in the quarries of Kibbutz Kfar Gil'adi, stated that kibbutz members did not work in the quarries and that the kibbutz objected to the establishment of a joint school for its children and children from Kiryat Shemonah. He added that kibbutz members 'screw us', and that they 'are only friendly to us during election periods. They are amassing riches at our expense. They buy colour televisions and come into town in their private cars.'[79]

Amnon Shamush[80] attacked the arrogance of the kibbutzim. He contrasted the situation of Moroccan Jews in Israel with that of their brethren in France and emphasised that France treats its Moroccan Jewish immigrants with respect. They lived in dignity.[81]

Another journalist, Yoram Hamizrahi, wrote in an article in *Ha'aretz* on 25 December 1981, that the poor of Kiryat Shemonah lived on bread, margarine and jam. One of the older residents told him, 'Tell them that we are suffering from hypothermia and that we have no money to buy paraffin.' A grocer told him, 'People only buy bread, milk and margarine and my business cannot survive on that.' Hamizrahi ascertained that residents had abandoned the town, and that some of them had emigrated. Unemployment was widespread. The director of the 'Ramim' factory, Shmuel Ohna, told him that he needed at least 70 million shekels in investment, but that the government had only come up with 13 million. Correspondents of *Ha'aretz* added that all the Sephardi towns in Galilee were in a recession. The village of Margaliot cut back its peach trees fearing the income tax they would have to pay, and Yardenah was threatening to go on a general strike and shut down the schools. The police and courts were swamped with cases of

141

unpaid debts. The monthly wage of a worker in Kiryat Shemonah was 11,000 Israeli pounds, whereas the wage of a youth working in a garage in Tel Aviv was 18,000 Israeli pounds. The residents of the town had been the ones who had drained Lake Hula but it was the Ashkenazi kibbutzim who had snatched up the 40,000 *dunums* which had been reclaimed and who used the town residents to grow their cotton and industrial crops. The kibbutz members controlled all aspects of life in the town since they were the bosses, factory owners and union leaders and held all the official posts in the Jewish Agency, the local government through the ruling Labour Party.[82]

The writer, Dan Shavit, of Kibbutz Kfar Sold in Galilee, loathed the tyranny of the kibbutzim over the Sephardim in the development towns. In an article in *Ha'aretz* on 20 May 1983 he characterised the stance of the kibbutzim toward Sephardi Jews as 'paternalistic, authoritarian and elitist'. Shavit wondered 'How could I be happy when someone from another community comes to me and interferes in my life, saying "I know what is good for you and I'll help you on."' He added that he could understand the resentment of the Sephardim, for no one wants to live with an official stamp that says 'inferior – he knows less than others, understands less and is less skilled.' The author then expressed his support for Menahem Begin who had censured the kibbutzniks and called them 'arrogant millionaires'. Shavit concluded by condemning the greed and egotism of the kibbutzim.

For further material on Kiryat Shemonah, see Appendix II. A detailed examination of other development towns reveals similar patterns. See Appendix III.

THE MOSHAVIM (COOPERATIVE VILLAGES)

The fourth way of absorbing the immigrants from the Arab world was to settle them in the moshavim which were set up in remote areas, particularly the hilly regions of Galilee, Jerusalem and the Negev. Aryeh Nehemkin, the Minister of Agriculture in 1986, ascribes the founding of these moshavim to security and political reasons. The problem of earning a living was of less importance.[83] The Israeli military leadership desired moshavim (and development towns) in the border areas to fortify the rich Ashkenazi settlements by using Sephardi settlements as a buffer against Palestinian guerilla attacks. The aim of the political establishment was to distribute the population evenly, but particularly in the areas which had been inhabited by Palestinians before they were driven out in 1948, in order to force the Arabs to accept a demographic *fait accompli* and to make it impossible for the Palestinian refugees to return to their villages. The Minister of Agriculture admitted that the common denominator among the moshavim was the lack of any economic base. He added that no one in the beginning thought of making these villages into moshavim, which is why they were first called 'afforestation villages' since the ruling establishment wanted to employ their inhabitants in their afforestation programme for the Jewish National Fund. This work was part of the afore-mentioned 'emergency jobs', and when they came to an end it was decided to transform these villages into moshavim.

The minister did not mention the establishment's economic aim, which was to use the residents as a cheap work-force for the Ashkenazi settlements. What actually happened was that the majority of the inhabitants worked as hired labourers outside their villages. Due to a lack of any economic infrastructure, the cooperative base of the villages broke down and two hundred and fifty of them went bankrupt.

In 1983 there were 402 moshavim, of which 65 were Ashkenazi moshavim founded during the Mandate. These rich settlements have the original classical characteristics of the cooperative village known as 'Moshav', in which each member has the same amount of land, livestock etc., but they share machinery, marketing, cooperatives stores, etc. Most of the moshavim founded after 1948 were for Sephardim and, as we have mentioned, they lacked any economic base. By 1983 their debts had reached 7 billion shekels (70 shekels = £1 sterling).[84] Pinhas Moscow, deputy director of the Jewish Agency in the Negev district, added that the moshavim in the Negev owed the purchasing organisation $130-150 million in addition to the sums they owed the banks and financial institutions in the both the free market and the black market. Out of the 3,360 families in the Negev moshavim, 1,400 (a third of the families) have no hope of ever paying off their debts and are dependent upon their moshavim. Yitzhak Nehemiah, director of the purchasing organization, said that the debts of an average family had reached $50,000-100,000 , but that there were families who owed more than $200,000.[85]

Representatives of the moshavim in Galilee informed the then Prime Minister, Shimon Peres, that each family owed $100,000 (at an interest rate of 60 percent, thus making an economic revival impossible). The head of the local council in Ma'aleh Yosef declared that there were 1,200 children of moshav members who were not entitled to inherit from their fathers (only one child can inherit from his father) who were now homeless and landless[86] The police arrested 12 out of the 80 members of Kiryat Noga and the court ordered them to pay its debts, which had reached 2,000,000 shekels, to sell off the moshav's holdings or go to prison.[87]

There was also a political reason for making these moshavim members of the moshav organization. As the Labour party (Mapai) was in complete control of this organization, it could place the residents of these villages under its hegemony and win most of their votes in the elections (as happened in the transit camps and the development towns). The Sephardi inhabitants were not allowed to choose the political affiliation of their moshav and were not allowed to move to a moshav of a different political colour.

In the previous section we have mentioned the 'lack of any economic base' in purely economic terms, but this also included a string of discriminatory steps against the Sephardi inhabitants of these moshavim which can be summed up as follows:

1. When the Zionist establishment sets up a new Ashkenazi settlement, it immediately provides it with enough land for agricultural production, and with the necessary means of production such as livestock and machinery, together with annual allowances for subsistence and development. The Sephardim, however, were trucked straight from the ships to arid regions where they were tipped out like gravel and ordered to pitch tents for themselves. They were employed in the most menial jobs, and received the lowest wages – 'emergency wages'. They did not even receive the small plots of stony land which was set aside for them, for their rich neighbours, the Ashkenazi settlers, snatched up all the land on the pretext that the Sephardim did not know how to farm. The Ashkenazim are still holding on to some of these plots.

2. Discrimination in the distribution of agricultural lands. Every family in the Ashkenazi settlements received between 80 and 150 *dunums*, but in the Sephardim moshavim, even though the families were much larger, each was allocated only 18 *dunums*.

3. The quantity of water for irrigation, financial credits, and means of production given to the Ashkenazi settlements were much greater than those set aside for the Sephardi moshavim. 54 percent of all monies invested in agriculture went to the Ashkenazi kibbutzim and 37 percent to the moshavim, in spite of the fact that the kibbutzim constitute just 12 percent of nation-wide agricultural settlement, whereas the moshavim constitute 66 percent. In 1960

there were 229 kibbutzim and 366 moshavim. In addition to this discrimination in favour of the kibbutzim, there was a marked partiality in the ranks of the moshavim for the old Ashkenazi moshavim which were founded during the Mandate. A member of an old Ashkenazi moshav owned 2.3 cows and 300 chickens, whereas a member of a post-1948 moshav owned 1.2 cows and 50 chickens. An Ashkenazi moshav owned 2.5 tractors whereas a post-1948 moshav owned 0.7 tractors. In addition, Ashkenazi moshavim set up after 1948 were favoured at the expense of Sephardi moshavim.

4. Quality of the land. The lands which the Ashkenazi settlements received were much more fertile than those upon which the Sephardi moshavim were set up, which were, as we have previously stated, tracts of the Negev desert, or stony lands in Galilee and the Jerusalem area, which the Sephardim generally had to reclaim before they could farm.

5. The Ashkenazi settlements were built in the centre of the country, which helped them to market their agricultural production more easily and to increase their profits. The Sephardi moshavim were located in the remoter areas, thus making it more difficult to market their crops and reducing their profits, as well as raising the cost of communications and essential goods.

6. Government support. Even though the Ashkenazi settlements were prospering, the amount of government financial support to them was greater than that given to the inhabitants of the poorer Sephardi moshavim. Between 1948 and 1977 the moshavim were relatively well off due to financial support by the Labour government. However, when Likud came into power in 1977 it cut off all financial support and encouraged them to grow flowers promising the moshav residents that necessary loans would be provided and then failed to follow this through. In the meantime, the villages had taken out massive loans and were paying 300 percent interest, and thus their debts piled ever higher.[88] These debts are commonly greater than the whole moshav's income, which generally puts them in default and pushes the moshav into marketing its agricultural produce outside the Zionist marketing organization. These practices constitute one of the causes of the breakdown of the fundamentals of cooperativism.

7. The development of industry on the kibbutzim. Prior to 1948 the standard of living on the Ashkenazi kibbutzim was not at all high. However, after 1948 the government invested huge amounts in the kibbutzim to develop industries which would employ

Sephardim and increase their income and standard of living. This did not occur on the moshavim. The government did not invest any funds to develop industry in the moshavim, nor did their narrow agricultural base furnish them with enough to support a Sephardi family. Moshav residents thus started to earn their living as hired workers outside the moshavim (61 percent of them work as hired labour for kibbutzim. In Kiryat Elyakim, for example, only 5 percent of the inhabitants work in agriculture, 30 percent are unemployed and 65 percent work as hired labour on Ashkenazi kibbutzim).

8. Ashkenazi kibbutzim and central government. As agricultural settlement was one of the most important Zionist aims from the very start, Ashkenazi settlers were the most important group in the world Zionist hierarchy and the local leadership, that is in the government, the Jewish Agency and the agricultural settlement organizations. *Ha'aretz* wrote on 5 August 1983 that the Labour Party government included four ministers from settler communities and that they, and their top civil servants, were therefore in a position to give economic, political and commercial advice to the settlements. They defended the interests of the settlements and kept them up to date on the government's future plans. This 'inside information' enabled the settlements to plan more successfully. The Sephardi moshavim were not so 'efficient' since they had no members at the top of the hierarchy, and no one to represent their interests to the various authorities. Moreover, economic planning for moshavim was in the hands of Ashkenazi 'leaders' from the neighbouring settlements who tailored it to their own interests. In addition, the Ashkenazi settlements, and particularly the neighbouring kibbutzim, have complete control over the moshavim (and the development towns) via the Labour Party, the Histadrut and the local councils. Ashkenazi settlers, members of the rich pre-1948 moshavim, such as Nahalal (Moshe Dayan's home), also control the Organization of Moshavim, which in turn controls the Sephardi moshavim.[89] Whereas kibbutz children can stay with their families on the kibbutzim, the lack of any means of earning a livelihood on the moshavim forces the children to leave, splitting up families.

Against this background one can understand why some Sephardim wrote the following slogan on the walls of the agricultural union building in Tel Aviv: 'The kibbutzim suck the blood of the moshavim. Long live the Sephardi revolution!' It was signed by 'Ma'atz',[90] which was the most violent of the secret organizations founded by Sephardim. It carried out many acts of arson (see chapter ten).

An aide to the director of settlement, Aryeh Eliav, MP, said of the granting of the fertile lands to the Ashkenazi settlements, that 'this was not the result of an Ashkenazi plot . . . or of bad intentions. It was just that the leaders of the settlement movement took those who were around them, and who had a similar mentality, background and outlook on life. They had nothing in common with the others. They also took into consideration that the settlers would vote for the Labour Party.'[91] Yosef Weitz of the Jewish National Fund said 'the hill areas could be reclaimed and settled with the "simple" Jews,' noting also that 'these stony lands are no good for Ashkenazi kibbutzim.'[92]

One of the obstacles of this policy was the unsuitability of agricultural work for Sephardi Jews, since in their countries of origin they had followed urban professions. The establishment imposed agricultural work on more than 70 percent of the Yemenites, and between 1948-1953 they were crammed into 57 cooperative villages of which only 39 survived. Often these villages were called 'work villages', i.e., labour camps, and the inhabitants worked at clearing stony land. A journalist wrote, 'the Yemenites work at land-clearing and planting tomatoes, for the kibbutz member has more useful work to do.' Another newspaper reported, 'the new immigrants from the Yemen work [on the kibbutz] even though they get Arab and not Jewish wages.'[93]

The Yemenite member of the Knesset, Zekharia Gluska, protested about a string of discriminatory acts in the field of housing, religious services and support for families with many children. Benefits were only paid for up to three children and one wife. The Torah does not forbid polygamy, and Sephardi Rabbis did not recognise the ban issued by the Ashkenazi rabbis in this regard.[94] One of the reports sent to the Prime Minister, Ben Gurion, stated that most of the residents in twenty-eight cooperative villages were unemployed and that there was widespread hunger. The report, written by Ami Assaf of the Agricultural Settlement Organization, continued that people could not even afford the basic subsidized food rations. Neither could they afford to buy the clothing which was sold to them for almost nothing. The writer expressed his fear that acts of despair might be committed by these people when they see hunger on the faces of their children.[95]

Most of these villages were not tied into the electricity grid, or a water or sewage system. Their shacks were far from a surfaced road. They had marketing problems – Tnuva, a Histadrut company, bought their produce at a very meagre price. They suffered a lack of health and education services.[96] Aryeh Eliav, an aide to Levi Eshkol who was head of the Department of Settlement, stated that 'these immigrants too refused to get out of the trucks. They had to be tipped out.'[97]

In 1953 Ben Gurion commissioned Zalman Aran, Yisrael Yesha'yahu and Kadish Luz to study the situation in the Yemenite villages. In their report they wrote that poverty and neglect had reached the point of disintegration due to a lack of any help from the authorities. There was a lack of work since the office of settlement, which was part of the Jewish Agency, thought this was one of the duties of the Ministry of Labour. The Ministry of Labour believed the contrary. Houses developed cracks within two years and the agricultural 'experts' were incompetent. Residents were too poor to pay taxes and so health services were cut off. The villages were devoid of any educational activity. Most young people had departed leaving only the old behind. The residents had to work by day, and be watchmen by night, which left them exhausted.[98] In 1963 the Ministry of Social Affairs described these Yemenites as 'retarded and primitive, completely powerless'. Ashkenazi 'experts' pressured the Yemenites into changing their customs, then they destroyed the authority of the father in the family. Most of the 'experts' were party emissaries.[99] When I visited the Yemenites in Rosh Haayin during the fifties, I found that tuberculosis was rampant.

A few years later the authorities forced the mountain villages to raise chickens, even though this work only took up two hours a day. When productivity rose, they were forced to decrease it. This work, however, only created half of the necessary family income and most of the residents of these villages had to continue as hired labourers which covered 60 percent of their living expenses. The villages in the hill areas near Jerusalem have ceased to be productive at all and became just residential areas which empty first thing in the morning as the inhabitants rush off to earn a living elsewhere.[100]

In the area of Lakhish in the south, thirteen of the fourteen cooperative villages have lost their cooperative base. The head of the local council described this breakdown, 'They stuffed us into an Ashkenazi frame.' Pinhas Moscow, regional deputy chairman of the Jewish Agency, commented that most of the cooperative villages would disintegrate into residential villages with nothing to do with farming. He added that in the region between Elat and

Qastina there were 76 cooperative villages (with 29,000 residents). 48 percent of them live from farming, 19 percent earn most of their livelihood outside the villages, but they work part-time in agriculture. 21 percent work outside their villages, and 12 percent live off welfare payments.[101]

We shall describe the conditions in some of these moshavim using as a basis the Zionist press, and particularly the independent newspaper *Ha'aretz*. (See Appendix IV.)

THE BLACK BELT: URBAN SLUMS

These slum areas started to arise towards the end of the nineteenth century, when the Ashkenazi Zionist establishment started channelling all Jewish resources and contributions into the Zionist plan of setting up Ashkenazi settlements, the Zionist administration, secret military preparations and the secret services. Accordingly they ignored the interests of Sephardi communities who lived in large towns. Poverty spread through the neighbourhoods of the Sephardi Jews.[102]

After the foundation of the state of Israel, hundreds of thousands of Sephardim were brought to Israel, crammed into immigration camps, transit camps, developments towns and moshavim. But because of the harsh conditions described in this chapter, many thousands fled to the poor districts of the towns in search of a living. In this manner the slums spread out, and poverty deepened. When Menahem Begin came to power in 1977 and started his programme of reviving these areas, there were 169 of them including whole development towns.

The only basic economic difference between the development towns and the slum areas is geographic. The development towns lie in the country and supply the Ashkenazi settlements with cheap labour whereas the slum areas form a belt around the large towns and supply Ashkenazi capital with cheap labour. They also provide servants for Ashkenazi women. It must be mentioned that these servants and their daughters face the worst form of oppression. They are deprived of education, and usually have none of the social guarantees which are granted to union workers. The following are the most important problems in the slum areas:

1. Housing. There is abysmal overcrowding. Children have grown up and married, but they cannot afford to buy their own dwelling, and thus most of them stay at home with their parents and in turn

their children are born there. Hence, one can find three generations living in the same small flat. The municipalities run by Ashkenazim are trying to gentrify these slum districts by razing them and building shopping centres and expensive apartment blocks. Thus the residents are not granted planning permission to enlarge their homes. Quite often Sephardi Jews build an extra room without planning permission, but the police them come along and knock them down – as happens in the Palestinian villages. This has caused bloody clashes between the Sephardim and the police, but Zionist influence over the Western news media has meant that this is rarely reported.

2. Education. There is a deep gulf between schools in the slum districts (generally Sephardi) and Ashkenazi schools. This can be seen in the quality of the buildings, the standard of education, the aptitude of the teachers, educational equipment such as laboratories and books, and also the number of children per class. Owing to these awful conditions there are problems of discipline. In order to conceal this situation, the government decided to send a number of Sephardi pupils to Ashkenazi schools in the richer areas and named them 'Comprehensive Schools'. However the two groups do not mix, since the Sephardi pupils are segregated in lower streams. The administration, the teachers and the Ashkenazi pupils all patronize 'retarded Sephardim'. At the end of the day the Sephardi pupils are bused back to their slum neighbourhoods whereas the Ashkenazi pupils stay on to take part in extra curricula activities. Sephardi pupils are also prevented from participating in school parties in the evenings. Some of these ostracized pupils try to challenge the ban and gate-crash, and this has resulted in violent clashes (see chapter seven).

3. Unemployment and the disaffection of youth. Unemployment is one of the biggest causes of poverty. In Kiryat Ata, for example, eight people who were laid off committed suicide.[103] Those with work are very badly paid, since they are generally in unskilled jobs. If we add the size of the family, which is usually double that of an Ashkenazi family or greater, the housing conditions, the lack of qualifications as a result of costly yet bad education, the difference between the standards of living of the Sephardim and the Ashkenazim are apparent. Ben Gurion's government encouraged population growth and gave a prize of 50 Israeli pounds to a mother who bore ten or more children. Poor women fell into the trap of providing the government with more children to be workers and soldiers.

There are many thousands of young people who neither work nor study and who also refuse to do military service. There are whole 'no-go' areas where the military authorities find it impossible to impose conscription. They know that if they were to try, bloody clashes would sully the reputation of the army which 'is not an offensive army'. Those who pay attention to this law of conscription are the small minority who expose themselves to the derision of their friends. The most common question posed to them is 'Why should you serve the state? What has the state done for you?' The army has started to overlook these fugitives and the state has enacted laws curtailing the rights of those who do not fulfil army service which means ostensibly Muslims, Christians and Sephardim who refuse to go into the army. Members of the Ashkenazi employer class have started to treat these fugitives as untouchables and refuse to employ them. This boycott has exacerbated the situation and there have been popular uprisings to protest against it. These groups have also cooperated with the Palestinians (see chapter ten) on the basis of a common fate and culture.

Poverty and ignorance have fostered alienation, delinquency, crime, drug abuse and prostitution amongst young people. these phenomena were unheard of in Jewish society in the Arab world.

4. Old Age: Dr Yuli Nudelman of the Rambam Hospital in Haifa stated that people in homes for the elderly in Israel look as if they came out of Nazi concentration camps at the end of the Second World War.[104] By 1986 there were 430,000 aged people (out of a Jewish population of 3.5 million). Over half of them had no pension and were living below the poverty level. 12,600 were in special establishments and most of the remainder were living without care in lamentable conditions.[105] Since it considers those who were brought up in Arab countries 'the desert generation', Israel is just waiting for them to die off.

5. Women and children in the Black Belt. A majority of the women and girls in Sephardi society have been transformed into a great army of under-paid household servants for Ashkenazi women whose relative emancipation is built on the exploitation of an ethnically differentiated underclass. Generally they stand on street corners waiting to be looked over and hired. Most of the pupils who leave primary school are girls, who do so in order to help their families. There is also a substantial number of women and girls who work in factories and in the fields as cheap seasonal labour.

Owing to poverty and ignorance as well as the destruction of the traditional family, a lamentable number of women have fallen into prostitution. The Ministry of Labour and Social Affairs published a study on prostitution[106] which stated that 97 percent of prostitutes are of Sephardi origin. Another study published by Dinah Gil[107] stated that unmarried mothers suffer from undernourishment and that 50 percent of them are of Moroccan origin. Most of the remainder are of various Sephardi origins. This phenomenon was never a part of Jewish life in the Arab world, but is a product of Israel. The governmental Bureau of Social Affairs reported[108] that 38 percent of widows live below the poverty line. 43 percent of them work as maids and 25 percent have had no schooling whatsoever. Professor Shevah Wise confirmed[109] that the position of women in Israel is much worse than that of women in the West. There are 60,000 battered wives – and the police generally do not intervene in domestic matters. Due to the cut-backs in social services, women's' shelters have been closed down. Women's' wages are 60 percent of men's', but in agriculture this goes down to 50 percent. Israel has 352 job categories, but 50 percent of women work in only 20 of these categories. Only 6 percent of higher civil servants are women while the proportion of women in local government has gone down from 4 percent in 1950 to 2 percent in 1983.

These figures include all ethnic groups and therefore may mislead the reader who does not live in Israel, for the deep gulf is not between Ashkenazi and Western women, but between Eastern (Jewish, Muslim and Christian) woman and western women. We must point out that Sephardi women represent 70 percent of all Jewish women in Israel, and we must add the Palestinian women, who represent 17 percent of all women in the country. In spite of the afore-mentioned facts, Zionist propaganda abroad still tells how liberated Israeli women are. The truth is that Sephardi women were better off and had more dignity in the Arab world.

See Appendix V.

As we have shown, the Zionist establishment succeeded in absorbing hundreds of thousands of immigrants from the Middle East and transforming them into a cheap work force. This success can be shown more clearly by reference to a study written by Nuzha Katzav about the fate of Iraqi Jews, for example, in Israel.[110] Even though this community fought to preserve its culture and skills more heroically than any other community which immigrated to Israel from the Middle East, it was doomed to failure. The following breaks down the community into the different vocations followed by Iraqi Jews prior to their departure from Iraq in 1950/51:

16 percent in the administration and office work
6 percent in the professions and engineering
27 percent in domestic trade; they also controlled external trade and a large part of the banking system.
51 percent craftsmen, goldsmiths, carpenters, etc.

After ten years under Zionist oppression, the break-down was as follows: 28 percent worked in trade, the bureaucracy and the liberal professions (generally with lower ranks than the Ashkenazim) and 72 percent had become labourers.

This shows that the proportion of merchants went down from 27 percent to 7 percent (as well as occupying a qualitatively lower status, which was more significant than the percentages). White collar workers fell from approximately 50 percent to 28 percent. Craftsmen and petty shopkeepers lost their economic independence and became hired workers, subject to unemployment and economic exploitation. There had been 490 doctors, 224 engineers and 716 teachers (these figures probably do not include those Jews who stayed on in Iraq and who later emigrated to the West). Their children and grandchildren who were born and educated in Israel did not do nearly so well. What happened to the children of these doctors, writers, engineers, lawyers, teachers and poets? That is a well-known 'security' secret. The transit camps, the development towns, the moshavim and the slum neighbourhoods did not produce what Baghdad and its Jewish community had produced. Conditions in Israel produced unskilled workers, juvenile delinquents, drug users and prostitutes inter alia. The very few who have reached the apex of the military and political hierarchy mouth the words of their Ashkenazi masters who appoint them. The fate of the Yemenites and the Moroccans and other North Africans was much, much worse, and they constitute a majority of the Sephardim in Israel. They generally faced much harsher discrimination than that directed against the Iraqis who had a more advanced political awareness and who had participated in Iraqi and Arab liberation movements before Nuri Said sold them to Ben Gurion.

NOTES
1 Minutes of the Zionist Executive, 12 August, 1949.
2 Central Zionist Archives, S 41/2471 – Yosephtal to Locker, June 9 1949.
3 Knesset Minutes, 7 June, 1949.
4 Knesset Minutes, 10 August, 1949.
5 Ibid.

6 Minutes of the Zionist Executive, 29 March, 1949.
7 State Archives, Prime Minister's Office, Section 333/0/43.
8 Absorption, S41/2471.
9 4 September, 1949.
10 Knesset Minutes, 21 November, 1949.
11 Labour Party Archives, 22 April 1949, 24/49, Second Series.
12 Office of the Prime Minister, State Archives, Immigrant Housing, 7135/5559 C.
13 Gruber, 12 August, 1949, State Archives, Office of the Prime Minister, Refugee Camps, 5588 C.
14 Zionist Executive Council, 12 October 1948, 21 March 1949 and 2 January 1950.
15 Central Zionist Archives, Middle Eastern Jews, S20/538
16 Yitzhak Koren, 56.
17 State Archives, I/160.
18 Zionist Executive Council, 18 December 1949.
19 2 October 1949, Files of the Mosad of Immigration and Army Archives, 14/372.
20 Knesset Minutes, 6 March 1950.
21 *Ha'aretz*, 18 December 1950.
22 State Archives, Prime Minister's Office, Immigrant Camps 5558C: 11 April 1950, 18 April 1950 and 8 May 1950; see also *Ma'ariv* of 1 April 1966.
23 March 1968, State Archives, 1/968/1.
24 *Zu Haderekh*, 9 July 1986.
25 Segev (Hebrew, pp 171-174). Arabic translation, pp 184-188.
26 Minutes of the Zionist Executive Council, 2 January 1950.
27 *Dunum* = approximately 900 square metres.
28 Samy Mikhael, *Shavim ve-shavim yoter*, 21-22.
29 Ibid, 10.
30 P. 25.
31 P. 30.
32 Pp. 52-53.
33 Pp. 54 and 55.
34 P. 78.
35 That is, Sephardim. Ironically, Ashkenazi Jews in Israel tend to describe all the peoples to the south of Russia proper as 'blacks' or 'schvartses'.
36 P. 81.
37 P. 94.
38 P. 112.
39 P. 121.
40 P. 127.
41 P. 216.
42 A derogatory name for Sephardim.
43 *Shevet va'am*, 1958, 1954.
44 *Shevet va'am*, 1954.
45 Ibid, 30-32.
46 P. 6.
47 *Ha'aretz*, 19 December 1980.
48 Cf the Palestinian refugees. See *Ha'aretz*, 23 May 1980, and *Zu Haderekh*, 13 February 1980 and 8 September 1980.
49 See chapter ten.
50 Swirski and Bernstein, *Mahbarot lemehkar ulevikoret*, No. 4.
51 *Riv'on le-kalkala*, September 1978.
52 I.e. pre-1967 Israel.
53 'Third Israel' is the name the Ashkenazi settlers give to these poor towns.
54 Albaz, *Les Temps Modernes*.
55 Swirski and Shushan, 1985.
56 For example, in 1984 it was 26.8 percent, in 1983 it was 24 percent.
57 Secretary of the Workers' Council in the town. *Zu Haderekh*, July 9 1986.

58 Viz. the amount of money spent per capita on the Ashkenazim, or the projects which employ them, compared to the amount spent per capita on Sephardim in the development towns or cooperative villages, or the Palestinian Arab villages.
59 Source: Official Census, *Zu Haderekh*, 16 July 1986, 6.
60 Source: Official Census, *Zu Haderekh*, 9 July 1986.
61 Ibid.
62 *Zu Haderekh*, 4 April 1984.
63 *Ha'aretz*, 7 March 1980.
64 *Ha'aretz*, 22 January 1982.
65 *The Times*, 20 November 1980.
66 Source: Ministry of Trade and Industry.
67 Source: Ministry of Housing.
68 Israel Land Administration.
69 Income Tax Bureau.
70 *Ha'aretz*, 8 January 1982
71 *New Outlook, July-August* (Special issue on Sephardim), 36.
72 *Zu Haderekh*, 14 November 1984 and 24 October 1984.
73 Swirski and Shushan, 1985.
74 *Ha'aretz*, 12 March 1982.
75 *Ha'aretz*, 23 February 1979.
76 *Ha'aretz*, 16 May 1980.
77 *Zu Haderekh*, 22 July 1981, and *Ha'aretz 5 July 1981.*
78 *Ha'aretz*, 31 July 1981.
79 *Ha'aretz*, 18 September 1981.
80 Amnon Shamush is the brother of Yitzhak Shamush, a Syrian Jew and lecturer of Modern Arabic literature at the Hebrew University, under whom I studied. I witnessed the hardships he underwent and which caused his death from a heart-attack. Even though he had close connections with the ruling establishment, Dr Shamush' sympathies lay with the Palestinian refugees, and he expected them to come marching back over the borders to challenge the Israeli military. He was also fiercely opposed to anti-Sephardi racial discrimination.
81 *Ha'aretz*, 18 September 1981.
82 See *Ha'aretz* of 3 April 1981, 5 July 1981, 24 July 1981, 23 February 1979, 28 September 1981 and 29 October 1982.
83 *Ha'aretz*, 29 August 1986.
84 *Ha'aretz*, 5 August 1983.
85 *Ha'aretz*, 5 July 1985.
86 *Zu Haderekh*, 20 August 1986.
87 *Ha'aretz*, 5 August 1983.
88 *Ha'aretz*, 5 August 1983.
89 *Mahbarot lemehkar ulevikoret*, No. 4.
90 An acronym for the Hebrew words 'Committee of Army Deserters'.
91 Interview on 20 May 1983, quoted in Segev, 182 and 183, Arabic translation.
92 His Diary, 7 July 1950, quoted by Segev, 183, Arabic translation.
93 *Ha'aretz*, 13 October 1950. Letter from the Yemenite Organisation about their exploitation, and letter from the same organisation to the work bureaus on May 8 1950. State Archives. Prime Minister's office. Immigrant Camps, 5558/C.
94 Knesset minutes, 18 July 1949, 27 April 1949, 16 November 1949 and 5 September 1949.
95 State Archives, Prime Minister's Office, Immigrants' Absorption in Agriculture, 23 January 1951. 7133/5559/C.
96 Segev, 135, Hebrew text.
97 Ibid, 134.
98 State Archives. Prime Minister's Office. 5581/224/9012.
99 Central Committee of Mapai, 4 January 1949, Labour Party Archives.
100 *Ha'aretz*, 29 August 1986.

101 *Ha'aretz*, 22 August 1986.
102 See chapters two and three.
103 *Zu Haderekh*, 25 June 1987.
104 *Ha'aretz*, 7 March 1980.
105 Findings of the American Joint Distribution Committee -Knesset Minutes, June 1987.
106 *Ha'aretz*, 18 September 1981.
107 *Ha'aretz*, 30 January 1981.
108 *Ha'aretz*, 20 March 1980.
109 *Zu Haderekh*, 24 August 1983.
110 *Shevet va'am*, 1978.

CHAPTER SIX

The Problem Of Representation

PARLIAMENTARY ELECTIONS

In spite of the fact that they constitute an overwhelming majority of the Jewish population, Sephardim are in fact under-represented in the state's institutions. This stems from three factors:
1. the method of party elections.
2. funding of the Ashkenazi parties by the Zionist establishment and the state (i.e. by taxation on the general public, including the Palestinians).
3. suppression of any political organization which fights for Sephardi interests. All national and international Sephardi organizations have been enfeebled and taken over, and their independence destroyed by a series of dubious means.

Even the tiny minority of Sephardim who have entered parliament and assumed posts in the government, the Histadrut or the army, are not representative. They stand for selfish and personal interests, and particularly for those stipulated by the Ashkenazi Zionist parties which nominate them. (This also applies to the Palestinian 'minority' in the state of Israel, particularly those on the Arab electoral lists linked to the Zionist parties.)

Thus the only form of intercommunal participation that Israel has created in its system of government and its economy is that of the division of labour between the Ashkenazi employer and ruler and the Sephardi (and Palestinian) worker.

We saw in chapter three how the British helped the Zionist establishment to gain control over the Jews of Palestine, whether they were Ashkenazi settlers, native Jews or Middle Eastern Jews who had recently immigrated to Palestine. The only democratic step which the British Mandate supported at the beginning was the system of elections to a Jewish Assembly which had been known from Roman times as 'Choria', and under which Jewish deputies were to be elected proportionately from both communities. Sephardim were thus allotted 24.7 percent of the seats.

In 1945 the Zionist establishment decided to substitute the party proportional method. Under this, the voters cannot elect a candidate whose character, qualifications and political tendencies are known to them – but only vote for a party. Since all the political parties were, and still are, Ashkenazi and funded by the Zionist establishment, they succeeded in having their leaders elected as deputies, proportionate to their share of the vote. Leaderships tried to cover up discrimination by having a tiny number of their sympathisers in the Sephardi community appointed as deputies. Generally they would choose people who had no local or national popular base so that they could be removed from office when they showed signs of independence (lately the right-wing Herut has helped some Sephardi party-members to rise in the party on account of their popular local support, which has increased Sephardi power in the party: and here we refer to the group of David Levi, the Moroccan). However, under this electoral system the MP has no local constituency, no 'surgery', no correspondence with the voters. In theory all the country is 'one constituency' and voters can write to any MP. In practice it is a waste of time. Not one of my letters has ever been acknowledged by an MP.

The Sephardim realised that this ruse was intended to reduce their numbers in the 'council of deputies' and they therefore opposed it. They suggested constituency elections as in Britain so that the voters could elect the candidate of their choice *directly*, to represent their interests and those of the slum districts. It is no wonder that the Ashkenazi Zionist leadership rejected that proposal and made party elections the rule. The elections were boycotted by Sephardim, as they were by the Zionist right for other reasons, and only 30 percent of the electorate voted. The British government almost declared the elections invalid, but the Zionist right decided to return to the Council of Deputies and the National Committee after it was given a large number of seats and high positions.

This boycott turned out badly for Sephardi Jews in the state of Israel, for these newly elected national bodies which only represented 30 percent of the Jews of Palestine, decided to establish the state of Israel in 1948 claiming to act on behalf of all the Jews of Palestine. Ben Gurion cynically observed, 'We must appoint one Sephardi minister and one woman,' to give the appearance of democracy. Accordingly the cabinet of Ben Gurion consisted of 13 ministers, all Ashkenazi except for Bekhor Shitrit, the Minister of Police. The State Council (quasi-parliament) was made up of 37 members, all of whom were Ashkenazim, except for Bekhor Shitrit, a member of the ruling Mapai (Labour) party.

Eliahu Eliachar, the Sephardi leader, met the Foreign Minister, Moshe Shertok (later Sharett), to discuss the situation of Sephardim in the Israeli government. Eliachar wrote of the meeting that 'Shertok is definitely not a friend of ours. He does not understand and nor does he try to understand our views. Moreover, since he holds the Sephardi members of his party in contempt, he rejects any solution we have reached with the leaders of his party about narrowing the economic, educational and political gap between Sephardim and Ashkenazim.'[1] The Sephardi leadership, headed by Eliachar, made desperate attempts to broaden its representation in the Cabinet and State Council, but to no avail.

Zalman Aran (Mapai-Labour) believed that the interests of the state demanded an increase in Sephardi representation in the cabinet, but his view was not accepted by the rest of the party leadership. A Mapai official said, 'If we have a Sephardi minister in the government, that will encourage this sectarian gang for decades to come. We do not need that at all.'[2] Aran warned that Sephardim would vote for Herut to avenge themselves on the ruling Mapai party and the mistakes it committed against their rights. Indeed, from 1949 Sephardi Jews in the suburbs of Tel Aviv started voting for the right-wing Herut party.[3]

In addition to positions in the cabinet and the parliament, civil service positions, particularly those with great executive power in the upper ranks, were awarded to Ashkenazi settlers. This meant the removal of all the Palestinian and Sephardi civil servants who had decent positions during the British Mandate. Even judges are appointed on a party basis, which is why a Sephardi judge was not appointed to the high court.

The sectarian Ashkenazi system thus had only token representation for Sephardim, who at that time represented 30 percent of the Jewish population of the country (they are now 70 percent of the Jewish population). In the Parliamentary Defence Committee there was only one Sephardi Jew out of 13 members. In the Administrative Council of West Jerusalem which consists of

27 members, there were two Sephardim even though they were in the majority in the city. After a fierce dispute this number was increased to three. The government has not appointed a single Sephardi to the Foreign Affairs Committee notwithstanding that the aim of this committee is to heal political relations between Israel and the Arab world. The Zionist establishment has always tried to keep Sephardim out of Arab affairs, since they would endeavour to find a peaceful solution to the dispute with the Palestinians and have opposed the imperious stance taken by Ashkenazi settlers toward Palestinians (see chapter ten).

In 1949 the government held general elections for the founding of the first parliament, using the afore-mentioned party system. The Council of the Sephardi Community had to plunge into the elections campaign even though it was not a party, had no party workers or any of the funding which was supplied to the others by the world Zionist establishment. Its electoral list comprised the Sephardi Committee in Jerusalem under Eliahu Eliachar, and the Sephardi Committee in Tel Aviv under Bekhor Shitrit who cooperated with Mapai and was Minister of Police and Minorities (i.e. the Palestinians who had remained in Israel). This list won only four seats and Mapai appointed two other Sephardi deputies, whereas the Herut party appointed another two deputies and the Yemenite list won one seat. Thus the Sephardim got 9 seats out of a total of 120, that is 7.5 percent when they constituted more than 35 percent of the Jewish population. If we bear in mind that most of these Sephardi deputies did not represent the Sephardim but their Ashkenazi masters, we can conclude that the native Jews were almost completely devoid of parliamentary representation. The Sephardi deputies in the first parliament were as follows:

Sephardi List: Eliahu Eliachar, Bekhor Shitrit, Avraham Al-Maliah, Moshe Ben Ammi
Yemenite List: Zekharia Gluska
Mapai: Eliahu Hacarmeli-lulu, Avraham Tabib
Herut: Avraham Rakanti, Hayyim Magori-Cohen

Discrimination was not restricted to parliament alone, as we have mentioned, but extended to all government and state institutions, religious establishments, Zionist settler establishments, central and local government offices, the Trade Unions and the judiciary.

At the opening session of the Knesset on 9 March 1949, Eliachar warned of the danger of poverty, de-education, disaffection, appalling living and sanitary conditions and delinquency and vowed that his list would fight for Jewish–Arab reconciliation. Forty years later Eliachar stated that not only had these matters not been treated appropriately but they had worsened.[4]

At the beginning of the fifties, the Ashkenazi parties tried so hard to break up the Sephardi electoral list by a policy of 'divide and rule' that the Sephardim later attached themselves to the General Zionist list which represented the Ashkenazi conservatives. Thus they managed to cleave the Sephardi leadership from the poor Sephardi masses in the camps who were in the hands of Mapai which controlled their every move. Thus the number of seats which the Sephardi list won in the second Knesset went down to just two. In the parliamentary elections of 1954, the Sephardi list failed altogether and the Ashkenazi parties appointed eleven of their own nominees from the Sephardi community. In the fourth parliament in 1959, the Ashkenazi parties appointed fourteen of their own 'supporters' from within the Sephardi community as deputies. Their party affiliations were as follows:

Mapai: eight deputies as opposed to thirty-nine Ashkenazi deputies.

Mapam: one deputy

Herut: two deputies

Ahdut Ha'avodah: one deputy

Religious parties: one deputy

General Zionists (= Conservative): one deputy

Progressives (liberals): none

Agudat Yisrael (non-Zionist religious party): none

Communist: none

As we have previously stated, there were in total 14 out of 120 deputies in the Knesset, and we must point out that the proportion of Sephardim had increased as a result of immigration to 65 percent of the total Jewish population. All the Sephardi lists in this election failed.[5]

In this manner the Ashkenazi Zionist establishment, which deemed itself 'the only democracy in the Middle East' managed to efface all Sephardi endeavours to achieve independent democratic parliamentary representation and to defend their own interests as a Middle Eastern community with chronic economic problems. In a letter to Bernstein, the Chairman of the General Zionists, Eliachar described the difficulties of the struggle against discrimination. 'Even though discrimination does not exist *de jure*, it exists *de facto*, and constitutes the most dangerous internal problem for the people and the state.'[6] Eliachar concluded that Sephardim were incapable of fighting the apparatus of the Ashkenazi parties which controlled all financial resources, and subsequently accused the Zionist tools within his community of selfishness.[7]

WHO FINANCES THE ZIONIST PARTIES?

Owing to their poverty Sephardim could not fund a political party able to compete with those of the Ashkenazim which receive financial support not only from world Zionism, but from the state of Israel. At the expense of the taxpayers, the government started to grant the parties annual sums proportionate to their number of deputies in the Knesset. The large parties therefore receive large amounts of financial support, which helps them to beat the smaller parties or the new parties which receive no grants. In July 1969 the Knesset decided to pay the sum of I£120,000 to each deputy to cover his party's election campaign to the seventh Knesset.

In the elections to the ninth Knesset in May 1977 every MP received I£580,300, making a total of I£69,636,000. Since 1973 the government has paid the parties in the Knesset additional sums for party expenses and to cover their activities. By 17 September 1978 each MP was receiving almost I£37,995 per month.[8]

In 1983 the government decided to pay the expenses of the Ashkenazi parties in the local election campaign as well. Since Sephardim do not have any representative parties in parliament or in the local authorities, they did not receive any financial support to take part in the campaign. Indeed, along with their Palestinian brethren, they paid for most of the expenses of the Ashkenazi parties through government taxation. It is a case of the hanged-man paying for his own rope.

Usually political parties in other countries are funded by their own members and supporters and their costs are not imposed upon the general public through government taxation. In its issue of 29 July 1983 *Ha'aretz* estimated that the amount of government support given to the parties to cover their local election expenses was almost £11,500,000 sterling.

CONTAINMENT OF THE WORLD SEPHARDI ORGANIZATION

Before we set out the data on racial discrimination in the rest of the state apparatus, the Histadrut and the international Zionist establishment, we ought to view the way the World Sephardi Organization has been contained by world Zionism.

Sephardim in Palestine sought help from their brethren who had emigrated to the West, and they founded the 'World Council of Sephardim'. In 1960 this Council consisted of 30 members, of whom 10 were from Israel and represented the Israeli administration of the organization. The leadership of the council consisted of three members: the administrative chief in London, Mr Denzil Sabbagh Montefiore, the administrative head in New York, Dr Shim'on Nissim, and the administrative head in Israel, the Minister of Police and Minorities, Bekhor Shitrit and his deputy Eliahu Eliachar.

Members of the council in Israel represent the Ashkenazi parties as follows:

Mapai: Shitrit, Avraham Khalfon, Shlomo Hillel, Ya'acov Nitzani

Mapam: Avraham 'Abbas

General Zionists: Eliahu Eliachar, David Sitton, Yitzhak Ganon, Binyamin Sasson

Herut: B. Arditi[9]

On 4 November 1951 the Sephardi World Conference was convened in Paris. The Zionist establishment with the help of its placemen in the Sephardi community tried to prevent it taking place, but they failed. The delegation from Palestine was headed by Eliahu Eliachar, Rabbi Uzziel and Bekhor Shitrit. Agents of the Zionist establishment tried to foment discord in the sessions of the conference by claiming that there was no 'Sephardi problem' in Israel, that there was no discrimination and that Eliachar and his associates were trying to stir up sectarianism amongst the ranks of 'a united people'. They opposed the setting up of any social or political organization to defend the rights of Sephardim. They succeeded in preventing the passing of a motion criticising racial discrimination in Israel, and then managed to transform the conference into an instrument of world Zionism and the state of Israel. The following are the resolutions of the conference.

1. Regardless of their ethnic origin, Jews form one nation.
2. It is a duty to help Israel carry out its lofty aims.
3. Jewish culture is to be fostered within the various communities.

4. There is to be close cooperation with Jewish organizations throughout the world.

5. A World Sephardi Organization is to be founded, provided it is not political.

6. The administration of the World Organization in Israel is to consist of 50 percent Histadrut representatives and 50 percent Sephardim from the Ashkenazi parties which are not in the Histadrut, and representatives of the committees of the various 'Sephardi' communities, – which meant total domination by the Zionist establishment.

After great effort this establishment agreed to hand over 25 percent of Sephardi donations from Britain to the World Sephardi Organization. The Zionist establishment opposed the setting up of a special fund to accept Sephardi donations from all over the world. The afore-mentioned 25 percent was not worth the paper it was written on. Eliahu Lulu-hakarmeli, who had the post of Head of the Bureau of Sephardim in the Histadrut and was a representative of Mapai, was known to be acting as a hireling during the conference, along with a number of other Histadrut workers.

There were also Ashkenazi participants at the conference, who were representatives of the state, the Jewish Agency and the Histadrut. Bekhor Shitrit, a Mapai representative, wrote that 'one of the problems which worried the delegations to the Conference was the rumour about anti-Sephardi discrimination in Israel, but delegates from outside Israel were greatly relieved when this was proved to be untrue.' On the evening of the opening of the conference, Shitrit called upon the Sephardi masses: 'uproot from your hearts any belief in or thought of intentional and malicious discrimination in the state of Israel.'[10]

At the third World Jewish Conference which was held in Geneva in 1953, Eliahu Eliachar tried to convene a special meeting for Sephardim to discuss their affairs. Asher Ben Roy, the head of the World Sephardi Organization, came from London and demanded an end to the meeting. He requested that discussion of Sephardi affairs take place in Israel and not abroad. It was clear who stood behind this intervention since the officials of the World Sephardi Organization in London had been appointed by the World Zionist Organization and received their wages from it. One of their duties was to send two thirds of the funds they received from the Jewish Agency to Jerusalem to cover the expenses of the Sephardi Organization inside Israel. However they did not send a penny.

In May 1954 the Sephardi World Conference was convened in Jerusalem. Representatives from most of the Jewish communities in the world and Israel took part. The delegations were split into two groups; one defended the rights of Sephardim in Israel against Zionist racial discrimination and another defended discrimination, that is, those who would not acknowledge its existence. These latter accused the first group of sectarianism. A Sephardi delegation met representatives of the Jewish Agency, which controlled Jewish contributions from throughout the world, and discussed the question of funding for the World Sephardi Congress. The two parties agreed as follows:

1. all Sephardi communities throughout the world will pay 25 percent of their donations to the World Sephardi Organization and the Zionist Organization will receive the remainder of the contributions.

2. the World Sephardi Organization must get the approval of the Jewish Agency for any special operations which require its participation, both in Israel and abroad.

3. the centre of the World Sephardi Organization will remain in London (and not in Israel, where the poor Sephardim live), and the Ashkenazi secretary would also keep his position in the administration of the Sephardi community in London and the administration of the World Sephardi Organization.

During this conference, all the political material and leaflets which the Sephardim had had printed, and which they had intended to distribute to the media and the conference delegations, disappeared. A few years later, Charles Khalfon, one of the members of the conference, admitted in a letter to Eliahu Eliachar that he had arranged the disappearance of these materials and also that his party, Mapai, had ordered him to do so.[11] Moshe Shertok, the former Israel Foreign Minister and Prime Minister wrote in his diary[12] that 'I am greatly relieved by the results of the conference and by the failure of Eliahu Eliachar's intrigues.'[13] Retshavi in *Hapo'el Hatsa'ir* commented on this that 'the Zionist establishment abroad and inside Israel was prepared to foil any constructive or practical steps taken by the Sephardi community, and to crush any independent action undertaken by any non-Ashkenazi community for its members.'[14]

THE ATTITUDE OF THE WORLD
JEWISH CONGRESS 1959

In 1959 the leadership of the Fourth World Jewish Congress, which was being convened in Stockholm, decided to discuss the problem of Sephardim in Israel in the aftermath of the bloody clashes with the police in Wadi al-Salib in Haifa. It did not, however, allow any Sephardi participation in the conference, which caused Eliahu Eliachar and his comrades in the World Sephardi Organization in Israel to protest in a letter published by *Ha'aretz* on 27 July 1959. They claimed that the conference was neither 'Jewish' nor 'World', but 'Ashkenazi'. Then they formed a delegation and sent it to the conference uninvited to set forward the problem of Sephardim in Israel. The Israeli Ashkenazi delegation refused to discuss this topic, claiming that it was an Israeli internal affair. They also refused to accept the Sephardim as part of their delegation. The Sephardi delegation was thus not allowed to participate in the political and cultural debates. At the last moment, the Zionists produced sympathisers from within the Sephardi community who declared to the world that the government and the Zionist establishment in Israel were expending every effort to improve the lot of the Sephardim and that the problem was not urgent.

The Sephardi delegation convened special meetings attended by members of Jewish communities abroad, journalists and foreigners and before the end of the conference the leaders of the conference were forced to let the Sephardi delegation join in. Nahum Goldman, head of the World Jewish Conference and head of the Jewish Agency, expressed his animosity to the Sephardi delegation, and then made some resounding but empty promises. Eliahu Eliachar's presence and his speech had an enormous impact on world media and there was fear amongst the ranks of the Ashkenazi Zionists. Moshe Sharett sent a telegram to the Jewish Agency in Jerusalem which read 'Kill Eliachar.' He later claimed that he had meant simply to shut him up and stop him from publishing his views. [15]

Eliachar, the head of the World Organization of Sephardim in Israel, concluded that the only way to solve this matter was to get rid of Ashkenazi tutelage . . . 'otherwise there is no alternative to what we saw in the uprising of Wadi al-Salib in Haifa, the bloody clashes with the Black Panthers and the emergence of the Ohalim movement which is a mass revolution in the making' . . . 'only the blind cannot see the dangers facing Israel as a result of these developments.' [16]

ZIONIST ASHKENAZI 'DEMOCRACY'

Ashkenazi Zionists claim that the Arab and Islamic states are 'dictatorships' and 'backward', which explains why the Jews who came from these states do not know how to found political and social organizations. This is untrue since the Jews enjoyed autonomy in Dar al-Islam and set up their own extensive social, education and religious apparatus.[17] The Zionists also claim that they learnt their democratic skills and party organization in democratic Europe, but in fact 95 percent of Ashkenazim in Israel did not come from Western countries, but from Eastern Europe, particularly Czarist Russia, Poland, Nazi Germany and other right-wing regimes. Thus, while their 'democracy' takes on the outward appearance of western parliamentary rule, its content is authoritarian.

Ashkenazim in Israel have formed 164 organizations, compared with 12 Sephardi organizations. Mati Ronen explains that Sephardim have failed to organize politically owing to hostility from the ruling establishment, and he concludes that the rulers were not really worried about the question of unity of the nation but about the real danger that they might lose power.[18]

Aryeh Eliav, the moderate Ashkenazi Knesset member, criticizes the Zionist doctrine which says that 'the Sephardim were of the lowest class when they arrived in Israel, having had no education, or leadership experience . . . ' Eliav says, 'What a shocking lie about communities which in their countries of origin produced ministers, counsellors, financiers and members of the liberal professions.' He attacks the meagre numbers of Sephardi ministers in Israel, adding, 'I am convinced that the orientals are as capable as Ashkenazim of providing any number of ministers in the government, for any of the ministries.' Of the Sephardi MPs he says, 'they flatter their party bosses hoping to see their names appear in the lists for the next elections.' Only one tenth of the ministries are given to Sephardim, which are second and third rank ministries. 'The head of the police (a Sephardi minister) and his men (most of whom are orientals) must be prepared to disperse demonstrations, which are mostly organized by orientals . . . don't some people want to see the blacks beating blacks?'[19] Then Eliav wonders, 'Why must the second oriental minister be responsible for communications? Is it not because this post is considered "junior", and those who fill it only have to lick stamps and carry post bags?'[20] Of discrimination in union affairs, Eliav says, 'the situation does not differ one iota from the Histadrut leadership to the government, except that the

167

former is supposed to represent the workers.'[21] Eliav is certain that the class of managers who run the public economy and the Histadrut economy (e.g. the Histadrut factories) is completely closed to orientals.[22] Then he adds, 'I am convinced that we can find Sephardim of sufficient aptitude to fill any administrative position in the public or private sector as well as in the political parties. Let any man who dares doubt my words say so in public.'[23]

In an article in the magazine *Shevet va'am* in 1954 B. Arditi (of Bulgarian origin and a right-winger) enumerated cases of racial discrimination against Sephardim, including mistreatment and the lack of representation in the government, as follows: 'They have one minister out of 16, 11 MPs out of 120, no representation in the Jewish Agency, and only one Sephardi on the Executive Council of the Zionist Organization. The proportion of Sephardim in the diplomatic service is negligible, as it is in the leadership of the Ashkenazi parties. There are no Sephardi mayors of municipalities and in the development towns there are two Sephardim who occupy the post of head of the local council. There are just two out of the 300 officials in the Ministry of Religion, and none in the administration of the national bank (in spite of their experience in Middle Eastern banking before they emigrated to Israel). There are only three or four Sephardi judges, and in the High Court, moreover, there are none.'

The author blames the Ashkenazi Zionist media. 'When they broadcast news on crime, the perpetrator's origin is only mentioned if he is Sephardi.' He also blames *Ha'aretz* for publishing the racist articles of Aryeh Gelblum (see chapter eight). Arditi criticizes Ashkenazi intellectuals such as Shalom Ben Horin who declared, 'Herzl said that we are one nation, but he was wrong. He did not know about the Jews of Marrakesh and Iraq. One Ashkenazi is worth 1,000 Sephardim.'

Whenever the Israeli system wanted to undertake an act of suppression against the Sephardim, it appointed one of its servants inside the community to carry out this work. In the fifties, they appointed the Minister of Police, Bekhor Shitrit, to suppress the unruly demonstrations which Sephardim were staging in the camps. In 1971 it was the Iraqi Shlomo Hillel, as Minister of Police, who crushed the protest movement known as the 'Black Panthers'. In 1987 they appointed Yitzhak Navon as Minister of Education to reduce educational facilities and to impose school fees, just as they employed Nissim as Finance Minister to reduce social services and to put masses of Sephardim out of work. In the Palestinian and

Lebanese arena, they appointed Sa'd Haddad and Anton Lahad commanders of the South Lebanese Army and used the so-called Village Leagues and some Druze to carry out brutalities against the Palestinians.

However, it is important to review the ethnic composition of the state apparatus of Israel to show that most of the doors to advancement are shut to Sephardi intellectuals. The following are the data to support this claim:[24]

The Ethnic Composition of the Cabinet

Year	1952	1958	1973	1977
Sephardim	1	1	2	3
Ashkenazim	15	15	16	16
Total	16	16	18	19
% Sephardim	6.3%	6.3%	11.1%	15.7%

It is apparent from the above table that between 1949-1959, the Sephardim had only one minister, the Minister of Police. Between 1959-1977 the number of Sephardi ministers doubled, and in 1977 when Menahem Begin came to power with the help of the Sephardi vote, he added a third minister! By 1987 there were four Sephardi ministers out of a total of 23. However the Sephardi proportion of the population had risen from 30 percent in 1948 to 70 percent currently.

One of these Sephardi ministers is David Levi, a Moroccan, about whom the Ashkenazi press used to print racist jokes. His children would come home from school every day in tears.[25] The Ashkenazim made him Minister of Housing, hoping thereby to cover up the official policy of spending millions on settling Ashkenazim in the occupied territories while not rehousing the Sephardim from the slum districts.

Yitzhak Navon, a native Palestinian Jew, who was appointed honorary president of the state and then the minister of education, came in for criticism in the Ashkenazi press and was taken to task by Moshe Dayan himself. When Navon stated that his mother liked the Egyptian singer Umm Kulthum, Moshe Dayan accused him of crawling to the Arabs. Following this, the Ashkenazi media attacked the president over his peaceful overtures to the Arabs by claiming that it did not behove the president to make any political statements.[26] When Navon became Minister of Education in 1985, he called a press conference during which he and the journalists were informed that his ministry had decided to reduce the education budget by 20 percent with neither his knowledge nor consent. Navon became angry and walked out of the conference in protest at the behaviour of his Ashkenazi aides. Clearly even if a Sephardi reaches the rank of minister, he must still dance to the tune of the Ashkenazim.

Aharon Abu Hatsera, the Moroccan, tried to preserve his independence, and for this it was decided to destroy him completely. He was tried for financial irregularities of a type which are committed all the time by most Ashkenazi politicians. He formed the Tami party and won three seats in the 1981 parliament but immediately the policy of 'divide and rule' began, with all the Ashkenazi parties trying to attract members of this party away. They succeeded in winning over most of its seats by 1984.

Proportion of Sephardi Jews amongst Ministers and Front Bench Knesset Members by rank, 1971[27]

First	Senior cabinet ministers	0%
Second	Other ministers	18.2%
Third	Speaker of the Knesset	0%
Fourth	Deputy ministers	11.1%
	Chairmen of top Knesset committees	0%
	Members of the Defence and Foreign Foreign Affairs Committee	10.5%
	Members of Constitution, Law and Justice Committees	10.5%
Fifth	Deputy speakers	33.3%
	Chairmen of other committees	33.3%

Proportion of Sephardim in the Knesset[28]

Knesset	1st 1949	2nd 1951	3rd 1955	4th 1959	5th 1961	6th 1965	7th 1969	8th 1973	9th 1977
	6.8%	6.3%	8.8%	12.4%	12.3%	18.6%	15%	16.7%	17.6%

Representation of Sephardim became wider in 1965 owing to the split in the ruling party and the formation of an opposition front – Gahal. Representation then weakened again after 1967 following improvements in employment and the channelling of anger against the Arabs in the Six Day War. It rose again in 1971 following the uprising of the 'Black Panthers'. We can conclude that the aim is not equality but the anaesthetizing of the community.

Ethnic and party composition of the Third Knesset (1955-1959)
(excluding non-communist Arab deputies)[29]

Party	Ashkenazim	Sephardim
Mapai (Labour)	35	5
Herut	13	2
General Zionists		
(Conservative)	12	1
Religious	10	1
Ahdut Ha'avodah		
(Left-Nationalist)	9	1
Mapam (Zionist-Marxist)	8	1
Agudat Yisra'el	6	0
Progressives (= Liberal)	5	0
Communist	6	0
Total	103	11

Proportion of Sephardim in the Jewish population at the time = 55%
The six communist deputies were Ashkenazim and Palestinian
Arabs.

Sephardim in the top ranks of the civil service[30]

Year	1961	1969
Ashkenazim	77	76
Sephardim	3	3
Percentage of Sephardim	3.7%	3.9%

There were fewer Sephardim in the upper ranks of the civil service
than in parliament because it was precisely these positions that
wielded more power than the deputies in parliament.

Amongst the ranks of the of the top managers, judges,
ambassadors and generals in 1955, there were a total of 1,966
Ashkenazim as against just 77 Sephardim, or 8.2 percent.[31]

Ethnic composition of the Judiciary, 1954[32]

Court	Ashkenazim	Sephardim	Total
High Court	9	0	9
Jerusalem District	5	2	7
Tel Aviv District	13	2	15
Haifa District	7	2	9
Magistrate Courts-Jerusalem	6	0	6
Magistrate Courts-Tel Aviv	20	2	22
Magistrate Courts-Haifa	13	0	13

Ethnic Composition of the High Court[33]

Year	1950	1955	1960	1965	1969	1973
Ashkenazim	7	9	8	9	8	9
Sephardim	0	0	0	1	1	1
Proportion of Sephardim	0%	0%	0%	10%	11.1%	10%

Proportion of Sephardim in the Civil Service, 1961[34]

Ministry	Proportion of Sephardim
Industry and Commerce	9.5%
Foreign Affairs	10.3%
Defence	10.1%
Education	10.9%
Agriculture	10.2%
Health	24.0%
Communications	23.6%
Justice	26.4%
Post	27.3%
Police	29.3%
Railways	35.4%

It will be noted that the reality was worse than these statistics, since they do not show which civil service rank Sephardim held. These were generally lower than those held by Ashkenazim: 40.1 percent of the lower grades, 20.6 percent of middle ranks and 6.6 percent of the higher ranks (in 1967 this was 3 percent).[35]

Number and proportion of Sephardi Mayors[36]

Year	1955	1972
Ashkenazim	85	65 (in the large towns)
Sephardim	11	33 (in poor development towns)
Proportion of Sephardim	11.5%	33.7%

Between 1955–1972 all the mayors of the large and medium–size 'veteran' towns were Ashkenazim. In the remaining 'veteran' small towns and villages, the proportion of Sephardi council chairmen vacillated between 4.4 percent, 27.3 percent and 19.4 percent.[37]

Ethnic composition of the Higher Executive Committees of Israeli parties, 1958[38]

Party	Number of Ashkenazim	Number of Sephardim
Mapai (Labour)	15	1
Ahdut Ha'avodah (nationalist left)	10	3
Mapam (Marxist Zionist)	11	0
Herut (right wing)	12	0
General Zionists (Conservative)	16	0
Religious Party	15	0
Liberal progressives	15	0

In 1973 the proportion of Sephardim in the leaderships of the five main parties was 10.8 percent. In the fifties it had been 7.7 percent.[39]

Ethnic composition of the party leaderships, 1973[40]

Party	Number of Ashkenazim	Number of Sephardim
Mapai (Labour)	16	2
Ahdut Ha'avodah	5	0
Mapam	9	0
Herut	27	4
Mafdal (Religious-Nationalist)	12	4
Liberal Party	5	0

These statistics explain why we have claimed that Israeli political parties are intrinsically Ashkenazi colonist parties.

Discrimination in the police

The Israeli government vaunts what it claims to be 'equality' amongst the various racial groups in the police and has stated that by 1961 the proportion of Sephardim had reached 42.1 percent.[41] This high figure is then mixed in with the low proportions of Sephardim in the government apparatus to increase the average.

One thing though is certain: Sephardim never had a fondness for police work, and have only joined the force due to unemployment. This has also been to the advantage of the government which uses them to suppress Sephardi demonstrations, as we have mentioned. In any case, the police are under the authority of the officers, the majority of whom are Ashkenazim. Amongst the 497 officers, there are only 35 Sephardim or 7 percent.[42]

Discrimination in the armed forces

Israel did not start building its armed forces in 1948 when it emerged as a state, but during the British Mandate when it founded the semi-official 'Haganah'. Most of the infrastructure of the Haganah, particularly the Palmach commando force, came from the kibbutzim and various Ashkenazi settlements, where most of the military men lived and the arms depots and training camps were located. Thus, since the time of the British Mandate, the Zionist military establishment has been overwhelmingly Ashkenazi. In 1948, when the state of Israel was declared, the name of the Haganah, which means 'defence' in Hebrew, was changed to the Israel Defence Force, and its Ashkenazi leadership remained intact.

One of the reasons for bringing over the Sephardi Jews was to furnish this military machine with manpower. Moreover, Sephardim in the army hold menial jobs such as kitchen workers, chauffeurs, military maintenance workers, cleaners, sappers, quartermasters, etc. In the combatant units they are infantrymen and in the armoured units they serve as back-up forces to the tanks. The Ashkenazim are the generals, officers and pilots, the men of military history, the missile and tank operators, or military intelligence officers and other technological experts in the military leadership. Consequently, military service greatly enhances the employability of many Ashkenazim after their discharge.

Aryeh Eliav, the moderate Ashkenazi deputy, witnessed this discrimination. 'They claim – and this is an old cliché – that Tsahal [the army] is a melting pot for all Jewish groups from the diaspora. But how surprised we are when we see that the military driving schools are full of orientals while the Navy's schools are completely "white" – which is a true reflection of society. I don't want to be told about the few colonels (Sephardi) and senior officers. They are the exceptions who prove the rule.'[43]

Ethnic Origin of Major Generals in the Israel Army (1951-1973)[44]

Year	1951	1955	1960	1965	1970	1973
Ashkenazim	12	6	6	12	17	21
Sephardim	0	0	0	0	0	0

Discrimination in the Histadrut (Trade Union Federation)

Avraham 'Abbas, of Syrian origin, and a member of Ahdut Ha'avodah, claimed that 'seven years ago the Histadrut decided to abolish its Sephardi Bureau, in the hope of absorbing Sephardi activists in the union. However, the number of Sephardi union officials over the last seven years has been fewer than ten despite the Histadrut's expansion due to mass immigration [of Sephardim].' Then Abbas wonders, 'What is the lot of Sephardim in the Secretariat of the Workers Councils, in the Histadrut apparatus and its commercial enterprises such as the Solel Boneh Company, the Kur Company, Tnuvah and Hamashbir Hamerkazi.' He adds that 'a year and a half ago, a Histadrut conference was convened to elect the Executive and the Administrative Committees, but has the composition of these organs changed along with the general make-up of the Histadrut membership? Mapai has nine members on the Administrative Committee, all Ashkenazim. You will not find a single Sephardi in any of the delegations which go abroad, not even to Islamic countries (such as Iran and Indonesia).' The Executive Committee of the Histadrut consists of ninety members, divided according to their party affiliation as follows:
Mapai (Labour): 55 of whom 5 are Sephardim
Ahdut Ha'avodah: 12 members, of whom 3 are Sephardim
Mapam: 12 members – all Ashkenazim. This applies to the rest of the parties.

'Abbas discounts the Ashkenazi Zionist claims that Sephardim are not qualified to hold high office. He reiterates that Sephardim are perfectly capable of carrying out any job, provided they do not come up against the policy of 'divide and rule'.[45]

Proportion of Sephardim in the Central Committee of the Histadrut (1949-1973)[46]

Year	1949	1955-59	1960-65	1966-69	1970	1973
Percentage	0%	0%	8.7%	27.8%	27.8%	25%

Proportion of Sephardim in the Executive Committee of the Histadrut (1949-1969) not including Palestinians[47]

Year	1949	1956	1960	1966	1969
Percentage	5.9%	8.8%	11.2%	16.9%	20.9%

The proportion of Sephardi Jews in the upper ranks of the Histadrut, excluding Palestinians, was 15.8 percent in 1971, or 37 Sephardim by contrast with 197 Ashkenazim).[48] Their proportion in the nationwide Histadrut trade union leadership was nil in 1973, at a time when there were 42 Ashkenazim in these positions.[49] The proportion of Sephardim Jews in management positions in the large industrial projects owned by the Histadrut was 3.6 percent in 1970 (that is five Sephardim to 134 Ashkenazi managers).[50] In the Steering Committee and the Industrial Project Secretariat of the Histadrut, the situation was as follows:

Proportion of Sephardim in the Steering Committee and Secretariat of the Histadrut Industrial Complex (Hevrat Ha'ovdim), 1973[51]

Number	Steering Committee	Secretariat
Ashkenazim	11	32
Sephardim	0	1
Percentage of Sephardim	0%	3%

Discrimination in the Jewish Agency and the Executive Committee of the Zionist movement

Avraham Abbas writes that these two establishments conspired with the Ashkenazi parties to keep Sephardim out of the higher institutions of the Zionist movement. The Executive Committee consisted of almost eighty members and had scores of delegates, almost all Ashkenazi.[52]

Ethnic composition of the Executive Committee of the Jewish Agency (1951-1973)[53]

Year	1951	1955	1960	1965	1970	1973
Ashkenazim	12	12	12	11	11	12
Sephardim	0	0	0	1	1	1
Percentage of Sephardim	0%	0%	0%	8.3%	8.3%	7.7%

Ethnic background of departmental directors in the Jewish Agency (1951-1973)[54]

Year	1951	1955	1960	1965	1970	1973
Ashkenazim	28	20	21	21	13	16
Sephardim	1	1	0	1	0	1
Percentage of Sephardim	3.4%	4.8%	0%	4.5%	0%	5.9%

It is my belief that Avraham Abbas' stance on this problem is naive and that the Zionist movement was, and still is, Ashkenazi and exploits the Sephardi's emotions, finances and religiosity.

In *Society*[55], Prof. Sammy Smooha sums up discrimination in representation as follows: resources such as income, education and work are divided amongst the Ashkenazim and the Sephardim in a ratio of approximately 2 to 1. The disparity of power is even greater. The Ashkenazim have complete control over the three power centres in the country, that is the government, the Histadrut and the Jewish Agency, in addition to the public and the private sectors of the economy. In the intermediate power echelons the gap is even wider, with an Ashkenazi/Sephardi ratio of 5 to 1. Only in local government is there proportional representation for almost all the communities, but not equality. Ashkenazim also control cultural life and the Ashkenazi elite runs society. The history books studied in schools have almost no mention of Sephardim over the last five centuries. Hebrew literature is confined to Ashkenazi works, and the music taught is European. The correct way to behave in Israel is the Ashkenazi way, and the Sephardi feels out of place there. He adds, 'Even the few who have been allowed to participate in government make many complaints about discriminatory practices.'[56]

The state of Israel is not the state of the Sephardim, which is why they have started to demand self-determination and an end of Ashkenazi Zionist domination.

NOTES

1 Eliachar, 1980, 291 and 292.
2 M. Grokhovsky, Mapai Office, 21 February 1949, Labour Party Archives.
3 Ibid.
4 Eliachar, 1980, 310.
5 *Shevet va'am*, 1960.
6 Eliachar, 1980, 340.
7 Ibid, 340 and 341.
8 Eliachar, 1980, 388.
9 Abu Shlomo, *Shevet va'am*, 1960.
10 *Shevet va'am*, 1954 and 1958.
11 Eliachar, 1980, 459–475.
12 17 May 1954.
13 Personal diary, part one, 489.
14 Eliachar, 1980, 471.
15 Eliachar, 1980, 469.
16 Ibid, 475.
17 *Shevet va'am*, 1973.
18 Ibid.
19 *Les temps modernes*, 22 and 23.
20 Ibid, 24.

21 Ibid, 24.
22 Ibid, 25.
23 Ibid, 26.
24 Smooha, 1978,310.
25 *Ha'aretz*, 24 October 1980 and 13 April 1980.
26 *Ha'aretz*, 7 November 1980.
27 Smooha 1978, 310.
28 Smoohha, 1978, 311 and the Israeli press.
29 Abraham Abbas, *Shevet va'am*, 1958.
30 Peres, 1977, 126.
31 Avraham Abbas, *Shevet va'am*, 1958.
32 Eliachar, 1980, 332 and 333.
33 Smooha, 1978, 313.
34 Prime Minister's Office, 1961.
35 Smooha, 1978, 167.
36 Smooha, 1978, 309.
37 Ibid, 314.
38 Avraham Abbas, *Shevet va'am*, 1958.
39 Smooha, 309.
40 Smooha, 1978, 321-329.
41 Israeli Police, 1962.
42 Ibid.
43 *Les temps modernes*, 29 and 30.
44 Smooha, 1978, 313.
45 *Shevet va'am*, 1958.
46 Histadrut Archives.
47 Histadrut Archives.
48 Smooha, 317.
49 Ibid, 318.
50 Ibid.
51 Smooha, 320.
52 *Shevet va'am*, 1958.
53 Israel Government Yearbook.
54 Israel Government Yearbook.
55 *Society*, 'Black Panthers: the Ethnic Dilemma', vol. 9, no. 7, May 1972, 34 and 35.
56 Smooha, 1978, 194.

CHAPTER SEVEN

De-Education And Cultural Oppression

During the last century, fierce debate broke out between conservative and liberal circles in British society over the education of working-class children. The reactionaries opposed the opening of state schools to teach the workers' children lest education keep them away from manual labour. The liberals stressed that education for the workers had been vital for the development of industry, trade and agriculture during the Industrial Revolution, and that school education had been a way of influencing and controlling society. The liberals won, and compulsory primary education was introduced in Britain in 1870.

During the British Mandate in Palestine, the 'socialist' Zionist leadership supported the stance of the afore-mentioned conservatives, with regard to education for Sephardim. However, this was not translated into action through legislation enshrining discrimination, but by imposing such high school fees as to make it difficult for poor Sephardim to send their children to school. Thus the proportion of Sephardim who managed to finish primary school in this period was just 11 percent, their percentage in secondary school was below 5 percent, and the proportion at the Hebrew University and the Technion in Haifa was almost zero (see chapter three). This came about because the Zionists' 'socialism' was, and still is, limited, that is, 'not for export' to the Sephardim or Palestinian people. In this regard the Zionist leadership, of the right and left, has remained influenced by the opinions of its birthplace and original environment – Czarist Russia/Poland.

After the founding of the state of Israel, labour leaders began to be influenced by the views of Western intellectuals, and eventually in the early fifties the Knesset decided to make elementary education compulsory and free (we should point out that the Arab states which are regarded by Israel as 'reactionary' and 'feudal', had been providing free education since the twenties for their citizens). The level of education of the Sephardim who emigrated to Israel after 1948 was much higher than that of the Sephardim who had lived in Israel during the British Mandate.

Though the Knesset's legislation with regard to elementary education was a step forward, it was in fact neither 'compulsory' nor 'free' – worse, the ruling establishment used the schools as a vehicle for conditioning and cultural oppression.

At the kindergarten level, that is up to six years old, school fees have remained high, except for 5-6 year-olds. In 1980 it cost £28 sterling per child per month,[1] which meant that most Sephardi children in this age group went without any education. At the same time the parents of these children were paying taxes to the government which used them to support university education where 90 percent of the students and 100 percent of the professors were Ashkenazim. When an Ashkenazi and a Sephardi child enter the first primary grade, at the age of six, the difference in school readiness is immediately apparent. The Ashkenazi child has already had years of kindergarten schooling, whereas the Sephardi child has spent that time in the home or been left to play in the street while his mother goes out to work cleaning the houses of Ashkenazi socialists and businessmen. If we take into account the economic differences, living and social conditions, and the nutritional intake of the children, we will see that the gulf between them is created long before they start school. Thereafter it only widens from year to year, making fair competition impossible. The gap between the generations born in Israel is greater than between the generations which came from abroad. In Israel two peoples have developed who avoid each other, not only on a class level, but also culturally. The authorities claim that elementary education (from 6-14 years of age) is free, but the parents of the pupils have to pay for the following:
1. registration fees
2. school building expenses
3. parent teachers association dues
4. music, drama, dance and other special subjects.
5. government education tax
6. life insurance for the child
7. materials for vocational subjects

8. school trips
9. school dentist fees
10. other health and general services
11. textbooks and exercise books, pens and school uniform.
12. local authority education tax.[2]

At secondary school, that is between 9th and 12th grades, in addition to the above expenses, or most of them, parents had to pay steep fees from the time of the British Mandate until 1978. Though these fees are levied proportionately on the income of the parents, most Sephardim could not afford them. Shlomo ben Ya'kov estimated that the proportion of Sephardi pupils in secondary schools (excluding vocational schools) was never more than 2-3 percent as a result.[3] Dr Smilansky observed that out of 1,300 secondary school students in Tel Aviv there were only 13 Sephardim, and that a third of all students between the ages of 6-13 do not go to school, even though attendance is compulsory, and that 95 percent of pupils leave school at the end of the fourth grade (i.e. at the age of 10). This situation prevails in Beer Sheba, in most of the camps, the slum districts and the development towns inhabited by Sephardim.[4]

In 1978 secondary school fees were abolished in favour of a secondary school tax being levied on all citizens. Most of this tax was paid by employees and not by businessmen and industrialists. The workers paid 0.3 percent of their wages, the employers paid 0.1 percent of their income and the industrialists paid 0.4 percent of theirs. The liberal paper Ha'aretz, which published these figures on 21 May 1982, added that the burden of these taxes was greater for the poor than for the middle- or upper-classes and called for them to be lifted. In addition to this tax, parents also had to foot the above-mentioned expenses.

In the 1986/1987 budget, free secondary education was abolished and a tax equivalent to $60 was imposed on each and every family with one child at school, or $120 for families with more than one child at school. And thus 'free' education officially met its demise.[5]

Since the Mandate period, university students have had to pay fees as well as pay for their accommodation and books etc. In Israel university fees rose in the following manner:

1949	minimum £40 sterling
1979/1980	£225 sterling[6]
1980/1981	£500 sterling
1983	£700 sterling[7]

The newspaper explained that the residents of the development towns and the children of large families only had to pay one half to two-thirds of these fees.

1985/1986	$1,100[8]
1987	$1,250, and so forth.

In 1987 the Ministry of Finance was demanding fees of $1,650 per year, whereas the students are calling for fees of $800. (On 17 May 1987 the government decreed that Jewish students had to pay $1,350, and Palestinian students $1,550 per year. Subsequently the universities decided to impose a fee of $2,000 on all students.[9]) There were, for this reason, violent demonstrations and clashes amongst the students and the security forces.[10]

In spite of receiving government support, the expense of studying at university has managed to exclude the overwhelming majority of able Sephardim and Palestinians. According to Avraham Abbas, the proportion of Sephardi students at the Hebrew University was not even 5 percent in 1957 and at the Technion it was just 3 percent, whereas they were then 55 percent of the population.[11] The leaders of Sephardi Jewry had requested donations from Sephardi Jews abroad to help the poor obtain secondary and higher education, but the Jewish Agency feared that such a step would lessen the donations collected abroad by the Zionist establishment. It therefore took over the initiative and set up a system of study grants, funded by the government and the Jewish Agency. In 1954 1,500 grants were given to students, with a total value of I£145,000.[12] Between 1954–1958 15,000 grants were given and the government and Jewish Agency appointed an executive committee to run the programme, whose members were naturally almost all Ashkenazim. An executive council was set up for the programme, but no Sephardim were allowed to participate in it; they were only allowed to take part in the advisory council which wielded no influence. In 1957 the total amount of the grants reached I£612,000, with preference being given to pupils at industrial or agricultural schools – which served to channel Sephardim away from academic and towards vocational training. The small size of the grants meant that secondary school fees were only reduced by about one third. Those without grants still had to pay the school fees in full, which forced significant numbers to drop out. The programme was intended to help Sephardim, but in reality over a quarter of the students were of Ashkenazi origin, with a total of 1,336 Ashkenazi students in the programme compared with 4,005 Sephardim. Only 5 percent of students involved in the programme received grants for university, so it is apparent that the policy was not to help Sephardim get higher education. Thus in spite of all the drum-beating about grants for secondary education, only a tiny proportion of the Sephardim were included, and Sephardi students represented just 6 percent of the student body at academic secondary schools in 1957, that is a 3 percent increase over the previous five years. If we take into account natural increase and mass immigration – that is, the increase in the Sephardi proportion of the population – we can conclude that the increased proportion of Sephardim at secondary schools was negligible. The amount of the grant would differ according to the economic situation of the student, and the major part of the grant only covered a part of the tuition fees.[13] It was a drop in the ocean.

The following figures show how the percentage of Sephardim in Israeli education – Jewish section – diminishes as the grades go up.

Elementary	52%
9th Grade Secondary (15 yrs)	15.8%
10th Grade	13.5%
11th Grade	9.8%
12th Grade	7.8%
Hebrew University	5%
Haifa Technion	3%

Avraham 'Abbas, who published these figures in 1958, wondered how the Jewish communities could be integrated to form one people at a time when the gulf between the two communities was getting deeper from year to year.[14] Even in the vocational schools, the proportion of Sephardim did not exceed 17 percent, and this figure did not include all the students at kibbutz or *ulpan*[15] schools. We should also point out that the total ratio of secondary school pupils in the large cities, where the Ashkenazim form the largest proportion of the population, was 14.1 percent. In the Sephardi camps the ratio was only 1 percent. Ben Gurion admitted that secondary education, whether academic or vocational, was the privilege of a tiny number. Shoshana Arbeli MP asserted that the Sephardim who reach 12th grade in secondary school (17 years of age) came mostly from the wealthy families who had been resident in Palestine before the establishment of Israel.[16]

The following tables will show the ethnic composition of the Hebrew University in Jerusalem and the Technion in Haifa:

Hebrew University students according to country of origin and ethnic background, 1957[17]

Country of Origin	Group	Number	Percentage
Israel	Mainly Ashkenazim	1,888	56.6
Eastern Europe	Ashkenazim	837	25.1
Western Europe	Ashkenazim	350	10.5
America	Ashkenazim	83	2.5
Syria and Lebanon	Sephardim	12	0.4
Iraq	Sephardim	96	2.8
Turkey	Sephardim	13	0.4
Yemen and Aden	Sephardim	6	0.2
Egypt	Sephardim	24	0.7
North Africa	Sephardim	9	0.3
Other Asian lands	Sephardim	16	0.5

Total percentage of Sephardim at the Hebrew University = 5.3%
Total percentage of Ashkenazim at the Hebrew University = 94.7%

Haifa Technion students according to country of origin, 1957[18]

Country of Origin	Group	Number
Israel	mainly Ashkenazim	277
Eastern Europe	Ashkenazim	110
Western Europe	Ashkenazim	29
America and South Africa	Ashkenazim	6
Syria	Sephardim	0
Turkey	Sephardim	2
Yemen and Aden	Sephardim	0
Egypt	Sephardim	2
North Africa	Sephardim	3
Iraq	Sephardim	6
Other Asian Countries	Sephardim	1

Percentage of Ashkenazim = 97%
Percentage of Sephardim = 3%

Yitzhak Moshe Immanuel pointed out that the government directs Sephardi students toward a technical rather than an academic education, as befits the role set aside for them in the state of Israel. In each successive grade in school, the proportion of Sephardi students goes down, as the following figures, for the Jewish section, prove:

Elementary schools	53.2%
Final 3 grades of primary school	41%
First grade secondary (ages 14–15)	22%
Fourth grade secondary (age 18)	8.8%
Academic secondary schools	7.8%
Hebrew University	5.2%
Haifa Technion	4.5%

These figures show the conditions prevailing in 1959, but it is important to compare the proportion of Sephardim in academic secondary schools with those at vocational secondary schools at the same time:

Academic secondary schools	7.8%
Vocational secondary schools	42%
Agricultural secondary schools	48%

Immanuel says that 'the proportion of boys and girls at secondary school is rising quickly. In 1960 this group constituted 25 percent, by 1964 it will be 64 percent, but if the employment situation does not improve and free education is not made available then we will just see a rise in the numbers who neither study nor find employment.'[19]

In an earlier edition of *Shevet va'am* Immanuel had written that the overwhelming majority of pupils at school in the northern districts of Tel Aviv were Ashkenazim, whereas the overwhelming majority in the southern districts were Sephardim, alluding to the ethnic separation and the disparity between the quality of schools in the two districts. He goes on to speak of racial discrimination in the employment of teachers and the imposition of Ashkenazi teachers on Sephardi pupils. In Tel Aviv-Jaffa, for example, there are 106 headmasters, of whom just 5 are Sephardim. He uses official Israeli statistics for 1955 to show that the proportion of teachers of Sephardi origin was only 9.8 percent.[20]

The school population increased from 140,000 in 1948 to 540,000 in 1958.[21] Clearly, mass immigration provided Ashkenazim many positions in the field of education. By 1972 the number of people working in this area was 8 percent of the working population.[22] The proportion of Sephardi teachers at the secondary school level was 3 or 5 percent, and their proportion among teachers in Colleges of Education was 2 percent.[23] At the university level there were almost none, but Sephardim were allowed to constitute 20 percent of the teaching staff at workers' evening schools.[24] In 1953 there were 2 Scphardim out of 67 secondary school headmasters. At vocational schools and Colleges of Education there were none, but they were 14 percent at primary schools.[25] In the rural schools in the development towns and moshavim etc., which were of a lower level and where conditions were difficult, the percentage of Sephardi teachers was higher.

The Ministry of Education used arbitrary dismissal to keep Sephardim out of the teaching profession. It created constant difficulties, employing Sephardi teachers on a temporary basis and making them sign an agreement every year which stipulated that they sought temporary work, otherwise they were not re-employed. In addition it used various methods to destroy the self-confidence of these teachers and humiliate them.

This fact does not just constitute discrimination against Sephardim, but is also one of the reasons for the drop out rate amongst Sephardi pupils, for in Israel there are many Ashkenazi teachers who treat these pupils despicably. The Ashkenazi teachers know nothing about the culture of their Sephardi pupils, often they are neither interested in the fate of these pupils nor in their distress. A psychological and cultural gulf thus arises between the pupils and their teachers and problems of discipline and alienation arise which end with their dropping out of school.

Immanuel confirms that, in spite of the fact that Dr Handel – a secondary school inspector – admitted that Sephardim constituted the most important section of Jewry up until the sixteenth century, only Ashkenazi history and literature are studied. School syllabuses ignore the history and culture of the Sephardim and concentrate on the history and literature of the Ashkenazim and their life in the ghettos of Eastern Europe. Naturally Sephardi pupils find these topics dull which accounts for the increased drop-out rate in each successive grade. Immanuel draws on the study of Moshe Smilansky for the ethnic composition of education in Israel,[26] which is the same study used by Avraham Abbas.

In its 1973 edition, the Sephardi magazine *Shevet va'am* reiterates that Zionist school syllabuses are not appropriate for Sephardi pupils, and furthermore Sephardi parents cannot help their children with homework in these subjects. These Ashkenazi syllabuses are intended to eradicate any Sephardi identity and to make it easier for the ruling class to impose its authority and influence. Professor Betzalel Rot claims that Sephardi Judaism has disappeared from written history – by which he means the history written for Israel school syllabuses.

Matti Ronen considers that 'the poverty of the Sephardi Jew does not allow him to acquire any education, and this does not allow him to raise his standard of living. The foundation of this gulf between the Sephardi and the Ashkenazi will by necessity go on growing ever wider, making it impossible to break out of the closed circle of poverty. The Sephardi thus deems Ashkenazi society unjust and attempts to resist it by means which are deemed uncultivated and criminal.'[27]

REASONS FOR EDUCATIONAL FAILURE

The drastic failure of Sephardi Jews in the area of education was not a result of their 'uncivilized and primitive Middle Eastern origin', as the Zionist rulers claim, but came about due to the colonialist policy of de-education and cultural oppression directed against them and the Palestinian people. The following sums up the reasons for this failure in various levels of education.

1. School Fees. From kindergarten through university, these represent a heavy burden.

2. Poverty. Conditions of poverty and hunger and overcrowding in dilapidated housing or small flats do not encourage the child at school or enable him to do his homework. Families often need their children to leave school and go out to work to help economically. Yitzhak Yativ claimed[28] that the monthly income for an oriental family averaged I£10-20 (at the time, £1 sterling equalled I£8), whereas Ashkenazi income was ten times greater. One result of this poverty may be to create two peoples vying with each in Israel, with all the incumbent dangers. There would be no point in reproducing official government income tables since they only deal with the 'average', and the average always misleads (see chapter nine on social polarisation). The policy of Sephardi impoverishment and proletarianisation cannot be separated from that of de-education and cultural oppression.

3. The standard of education in Sephardi schools in the Black Belt, the development towns, the moshavim and the camps, is very low compared to that of the Ashkenazi schools, due to the quality of the school buildings, the number of class-rooms, the quality of educational equipment, the number of children per class and the quality of the teachers themselves. The number of primary school teachers who lacked the necessary qualifications was 40 percent in 1958 and these teachers, some of whom were soldiers, taught at Sephardi schools.[29] In Bnei Brak, for example, a class of 100 pupils had to study in an air raid shelter due to a lack of class-rooms.[30] A few years ago the Ministry of Education started bussing Sephardi pupils to Ashkenazi schools from the slum districts, hoping to 'integrate' them. They were crammed into 'special' classes and mistreated, resulting in ethnic violence.

On 7 March 1979, *Ha'aretz* wrote about such battles at the Ramat Hasharon school. The newspaper described School Number 14 in Shikun Dan near Tel Aviv. It pointed out that racial integration was unsuccessful in most cases and that pupils from both communities neither mixed nor visited each other. Since pupils from the slum district had not previously been at an academic school, they faced many difficulties with traditional academic methods. Thus they failed their studies and were prone to despair and anger, particularly toward the arrogance and condescension of Ashkenazi pupils. The teachers would try to jettison the weak pupils and concentrate on the promotion of Ashkenazi pupils. The school counsellor, Naomi Nawi, commented on these matters that 'racial integration is vital if we want to head off a social explosion. But the schools cannot go it alone. Integration must begin in the kindergartens and in society in general . . . the main obstacle is the racism which Ashkenazi pupils learn from their families.'[31]

L. Ram, a student, wrote a detailed report which appeared in *Zu Haderekh* of 5 October 1983, in which she described the tragic state of the Sephardi pupils at the comprehensive school in Qatamon in Jerusalem. She spoke of the humiliation and contempt they were exposed to from Ashkenazi teachers and pupils and wrote that some of her friends had started to affect Ashkenazi accents and to be ashamed of their families and their 'primitive' background. The pupils who stuck to their identity were not popular with the management. She described how the school administration insisted on putting the Sephardim in the non-academic classes and keeping them away from mathematics and science. Only six out of the forty pupils were allowed to take the final secondary school examinations, the *Bagrut*.

4. School syllabuses. We have already mentioned that school syllabuses in Israel ignore Sephardi history and culture and set about to destroy their cultural identity. When this history is touched upon, it is couched in untruths about 'Islamic society's racial oppression' of Jews – with the intention of instilling hatred of the Palestinians and the Arabs. The Ashkenazi teacher tends to dwell on the 'primitive and uncultured' Arabs and Muslims and indirectly destroy the status of Sephardi pupils in the class and alienate them from their parents and background. In spite of the fact that the Sephardi *lingua franca* has been Arabic since the Islamic conquests, there are few Arabic classes. Arabic is just another foreign language after English and French. As a result, Sephardi pupils leave the Israeli school system illiterate in Arabic, though it is the language they speak at home. The Ashkenazi Zionist, Aryeh Eliav MP, one of the leaders of the Labour Party, admits that 'first, we snatched from them the valuable treasure that they brought with them – Arabic. We, the Ashkenazim, have been carried away by a wave

of condescension and arrogance toward the Arab world . . . we have made Arabic and Arab culture into something hateful and despicable.'[32] Notwithstanding this illiteracy, there are good Arabic classes in some secondary school final grades. These classes are made up of a very small number of Ashkenazim who are not studying it for peaceful aims, but to use it in the army and the intelligence agencies and they fall under the aegis of the Prime Minister's Office and not of the Ministry of Education. The studies are carried out under the slogan 'Know Your Enemy'.

The tragedy of the Sephardim is that they no longer know the language of their grandparents, or about the Jewish poets and writers from Iraq, Syria and Egypt. They can neither read nor write the language of their fathers, and are unaware that most of the Jewish heritage, or that most of the works of Maimonides and Saadya Gaon, were written in Arabic. They have been pressurised into believing that they, along with the Arabs, are backward and uncivilized in comparison to the Ashkenazim. The policies of cultural nihilism and imperialism respectively have made great inroads amongst the Sephardim and the Palestinians. Even the prayers in religious schools are taught according to the Ashkenazi ritual. In my final oral examination I was forced to recite a Hebrew poem using Ashkenazi-Yiddish intonation and accent.

'Secondary and university education is not for me, it's for the Ashkenazim' – is what many second-generation Sephardi immigrants say, even though their parents were members of the educated classes in Iraq and Syria and Iran etc. Aryeh Eliav admitted that 'we have torn the oriental Jews, particularly the younger generation, from their past, their roots and their pride and we have inculcated in them, as we did with their fathers, that everything started in Eastern Europe – Jewish thought, Zionism, the pioneer concept and the settlement of Palestine. We have told them that beauty, poetry and culture all came from Europe which means that their fathers had nothing of the sort. Thence we quickly arrive at the myth of "illiteracy" and the backwardness of the "oriental" Jews.'[33] 'In fact, we condemned to death the culture and past of tens of thousands of Jews.'[34] Zionist schools thus destroyed the Sephardim's culture and convinced them that they were not suited for more education.

5. IQ testing. At the end of elementary school (age 14), the pupil who wants to get a grant to go to a secondary school must sit a special IQ examination. Since the questions of this test have to do with the life and culture of the Ashkenazim, many Sephardim fail

it – not because their IQ is low but because the questions are outside their field of reference.[35] Sometimes Sephardim fail because the level of education in their schools is so low, something which rules out any competition with Ashkenazi pupils. Accordingly the Sephardi pupils do not get grants which means that they have to pay school fees in full, and since this is beyond their means it often leads to their leaving school.

6. Ashkenazi teachers' condescension and contempt. Most of the Sephardi pupils who attempt to continue their secondary and university studies have to work day and night in factories and restaurants during their vacation in order to fund their studies, but they still come up against condescension and hostility from some Ashkenazi teachers. Some leave school or university but others persevere and find after gaining their degree that the doors are still shut to them because of their ethnic origin. These disheartening experiences reinforce the downward spiral of educational motivation in the Sephardi community.

7. The breakdown of society. Owing to the upheaval of immigration, the tragic life in the camps and slum districts, unemployment, housing conditions and Ashkenazi cultural oppression, the Sephardi family system has all but collapsed and along with it Sephardi traditions and values. Drug addiction, prostitution and crime have appeared. None of this encourages Sephardi children to strive for an education.

8. Foreign vocabulary. The language of tuition in Jewish schools is Hebrew, which, as it has been developed by the Ashkenazi settlers, contains a huge number of Latin and European loan-words. Whereas an Ashkenazi pupil can ask his parents for help with these foreign words, the Arabic-speaking parent is at a loss. Moreover, most Sephardi children still speak Arabic at home, and, more importantly, they still think in Arabic and hence face a linguistic obstacle at school.

9. Cutbacks in educational and social services. This has come about because Israel, as a part of the Western world, is suffering from the same economic crisis faced by the West. After the Islamic Revolution in Iran, all trade relations with Iran were broken and factories which had exported to Iran also shut down. In addition, there were the expenses of the war in Lebanon and funding for the mercenaries there, and the cost of settlements in the Egyptian, Palestinian and Syrian territories. The victims of Israel's policy of reducing educational and social services were naturally the poor, i.e. the Sephardim and the Palestinians. To prove this point, we

should mention that the student body in Israel had risen from 800,000 in 1969/1970 to 1,200,000 in 1980/1981, but the education budget went down from 10.5 percent of the state budget in 1972 to 5.8 percent in 1980. In 1980/1981 alone 35,000 school hours were cancelled in primary and middle schools; 1,300 teachers were dismissed and school dinner budgets were reduced by 70 percent. In 1981/1982 three agricultural training villages for poor students were closed and the special mothers' training centres in the development towns were closed down. In 1982 the budget was trimmed by a further 7.5 percent which in its turn meant the dismissal of yet more thousands of teachers and workers. The result is that out of every 1,000 pupils who entered the first grade at primary school in 1969/1970 only 26 will finish school, and most of them Ashkenazim. The drop-out rate in the Palestinian sector is even greater.[36]

This policy has gone on year after year. In the 1986/1987 budget, the reduction in the Ministry of Education's budget was $47.5 million , which entailed the cancellation of 170,000 school hours, the dismissal of 7-10,000 teachers and the imposition of the afore-mentioned education tax.[37] In 1969/1970 compulsory education was extended to fifteen years, but it was not applied and some schools encourage 'weak' pupils to leave.

The worsening drop-out rate amongst the younger generations

When the figures for the Sephardi drop-out rate were published in the fifties, Israel accused the Arab and Islamic countries of being the reason for this 'backwardness' and for the appearance of the educational gulf between the two communities.

If we take into account that the proportion of Sephardim in Israeli Jewish society rose from 50 percent in the fifties to 65 percent in the seventies and then 70 percent in the eighties, we can conclude from the following figures that the drop-rate continued to worsen. Then another gulf appeared between those Sephardim who had been educated in Middle Eastern countries on the one hand, and those who were born and studied in Israeli schools on the other – to the advantage of the former. This is completely in accordance with the Israeli policy of de-education and shows Israeli claims to be false.

Proportion of Sephardim in schools and universities[38]

Year	69/70	75/76
First grade primary	63%	59.6%
Eighth grade elementary	57.4%	53.9%
Ninth grade academic secondary	35%	36.2%(average)
12th grade academic secondary	24.7%	
success rate final		
secondary examinations	18.7%	23.8%
B.A. Students	14.2%	16.4%
M.A. and Ph.D. Students	9%	10.1%

All other students = Ashkenazim and Palestinians
Proportion of Sephardim in the Jewish population = 65%

At the end of the sixties, 6 percent of Sephardi pupils received a secondary school certificate as against 35 percent of Ashkenazi pupils.[39] In 1972/1973 the data became 7.4 percent against 31.7 percent, and for higher education they were as follows: 2.8 percent of Sephardi Jews born in Palestine versus 13.8 percent of Ashkenazim. Of those born abroad the figures were 2 percent and 9.3 percent respectively.[40]

The moderate Zionist deputy, Aryeh Eliav, said of the Sephardim at university, 'it seems to me that this dishearteningly low proportion . . . will not reach 10 percent. To reach that figure we have to count students at religious colleges [*yeshivot*] and other non-official establishments.'[41] What Eliav was implying is that the proportion of Sephardim at universities has been boosted artificially to show 'what progress Sephardim have made in Israel.' Then he adds that 'Israel cannot blame the Middle Eastern countries for the underdevelopment of the Sephardim, since this second generation was born and raised in Israel.' He concludes that 'it is our society's greatest deficiency. We have managed to transfer the educational gulf from generation to generation.' The author cautioned Israel against creating two different societies over the course of a few generations.

Eliav enumerates the reasons for this failure, as follows: 'inequality of opportunity, large families living in very cramped housing, loss of confidence and cultural heritage, imbalance in political, social and economic representation and preferential treatment for the armed forces.' Eliav then commented on the 'backwardness' of the Middle Eastern countries by saying that 'the young people who have come to Israel from the Arab world twenty years on [i.e. after the founding of Israel], have much better intellectual and vocational resources than their Israeli-born contemporaries. This phenomenon can be clearly discerned if we examine the standard of higher education of the hundreds of thousands of Jews who have emigrated from Middle Eastern countries to France, Spain, Canada and the United States over the last thirty years.' Finally Eliav warns that discrimination in education threatens the security of the state.[42]

Hierarchy of Education:

We shall now examine the summit of the educational pyramid in Israel thirty years after its founding:

Division of Doctoral (Ph.D.) Students by Origin 1977/1978[43]

Born in Israel to a Sephardi father	2.5%
Born in Dar al-Islam	7.4%
Total proportion of Sephardim	9.9%
Born in Israel to an Israeli-born father (generally Ashkenazim)	4.3%
Born in Israel to a father born in Europe or America (Ashkenazim)	44.5%
Born in Europe and America (Ashkenazim)	41.3%
Total proportion of Ashkenazim	90.1%

The following should be noted with reference to the above figures:
1. The wide gap between the proportions of Sephardim and Ashkenazim: 9.9 percent against 90.1 percent.
2. The gap between Sephardim and foreign-born Ashkenazim: 7.4 percent against 41.3 percent.
3. The deep gap between Israeli-born Sephardim and Ashkenazim: 2.5 percent against 48.8 percent. All these students grew up within the framework of the Israeli Zionist establishment, and the great disparity can only indicate the worsening of the ethnic and class divisions and the polarisation of the two communities as they head toward social conflagration.
4. The gap between the Israeli-born Sephardim and those born in Dar al-Islam: 2.5 percent against 7.4 percent. This indicates that educational and economic conditions for Jews were better in the Arab countries than they are in Israel, which is why the Israeli-raised generation has shown such a deterioration. In fact the gap is wider if we take into account Sephardi doctors and PhDs who emigrated to the West instead of Israel.

5. We have mentioned that those born in Israel to a father born in Palestine were usually Ashkenazim, being the descendants of the early Ashkenazi settlers who immigrated from Czarist Russia and Poland. Their Sephardi contemporaries hardly manage to enter higher educational facilities (except for a tiny number of children from rich families). We have also already mentioned that the overwhelming majority of Sephardim in Palestine at the time of the British Mandate did not even finish their primary education.
6. Based on what Aryeh Eliav, MP, said, it is highly plausible that the Israeli Central Bureau of Statistics made the figures look more favourable for the Sephardim, and that the real proportions are worse than we have mentioned.

We should add that in 1984 a census was taken of graduates from universities or other higher education institutions in Israel who totalled 205,700 (the Palestinians make up 4.3 percent of this number, whereas they are 17 percent of the population).
Now we shall examine Jewish graduates in Israel (1984) by origin:

Graduates in Israel by origin and degree, 1984[44]

Origin	Total	1st degree	2nd degree	3rd degree or higher
Israeli-born to an Israeli-born father (mainly Ashkenazim)	6.4%	8.2%	3.5%	2.8%
Asia and Africa – Sephardim (Total)	14.6%	18.7%	7.8%	7.2%
Israeli-born	5.4%	7.6%	2%	0.5%
Born in Dar al-Islam	9.2%	11.1%	5.8%	6.7%
Europe and America – Ashkenazim (Total)	79%	73.1%	88.7%	90%
Israeli-born	32.2%	38.3%	20.6%	30.1%
Born outside Israel	46.8%	34.8%	68.1%	59.9%

With reference to the above figures the following should be noted:
1. The Ashkenazi totals are : 85.4 percent, 81.3 percent, 92.2 percent, 92.8 percent, whereas the Sephardi totals are 14.6 percent, 18.7 percent, 7.8 percent and 7.2 percent.
2. The Central Bureau of Statistics has mixed chalk with cheese, that is, it has mixed those with university degrees and those with degrees from non-academic institutions such as colleges of nursery and primary school teachers, and Yeshivot etc., in order to narrow the gap between Ashkenazim and Sephardim. If the figures were to pick out those with university degrees, the gap would appear much wider.

3. The Bureau classifies Ashkenazim born in Israel to a father born in Palestine in a special category in order to mislead the foreign reader and to even out the high proportion of Ashkenazim.

4. The wide gulf between Sephardim born in Middle Eastern countries and Israeli-born Sephardim who have grown up and studied in Zionist schools, subject to its colonialist de-education policy.

5. The proportion of Israeli-born Sephardim who receive a PhD is 0.5 percent whereas amongst Ashkenazim of the same generation it is 30.1 percent. The number gaining a MA is 2 percent against 20.6 percent, and for the BA the proportions are 7.6 percent against 38.3 percent, making totals of 5.4 percent against 32.2 percent. These figures yet again prove that the gap does not result from the 'backwardness' of Middle Eastern countries, since both of these strata were born in Israel and have studied in Israeli schools and even so the gap is greater between them and their contemporaries than that between their parents and the Israelis who came from Europe and America, which indicates that polarisation is worsening from generation to generation.

6. Polarization seems even worse if we take into account the increase in the number of Israeli universities and the number of students studying at them. In 1948 the only institutions of higher education were the Hebrew University and the Haifa Technion. The universities of Tel Aviv, Haifa, Beer Sheba and Bar Ilan were then founded and the student body went up from 1,635 in 1948 to 52,780 in 1976, but the proportion of Sephardim remained negligible, as we have already mentioned[45] (add to this variable the increase in the number of Sephardim in the general population).

7. The above proportions are nation-wide, but if we focus on the places which have been specifically set up to supply Ashkenazi settlers with cheap labour, such as the development towns, the policy of de-education will appear in all its repulsiveness. In the development town of Shlomi, for example, the proportion of university graduates is just 1 percent (this figure includes the Ashkenazi managers' children). However, in the Ashkenazi settlement of Savyon it is 25.8 percent and in the Ashkenazi settlement of Omer it is 36 percent.[46] Statistics from the Central Bureau of Statistics for 1961 and 1976 indicate that the gap between the two groups has doubled in the academic section, and the gap in subjects such as mathematics, science and medicine has deepened greatly.[47] At the Arts and Science Institute, which is the highest educational establishment in the country, there is almost no non-

Ashkenazi to be found – and the same applies to academic posts in the universities.

THE ERADICATION OF MIDDLE EASTERN CULTURE OUTSIDE THE SCHOOL

The Israeli authorities practise a policy of cultural oppression toward Sephardim, not just in school syllabuses but in all areas of life, such as the radio and television, literature, the theatre, etc. The media portray Sephardim as 'primitives' who have no culture of any value, and they try to crush their Middle Eastern identity. There is only one hour per week of Sephardi culture on the radio. The second channel devotes 11 percent of its broadcast time to the heritage of the various Israeli communities. [48]

The Jews of the Arab world were renowned for their musical skills, and they formed a large part of the Iraqi musical scene. They were some of the best singers of local styles. In his book, *The Baghdadi Singers and the Iraqi Maqam* (1964), al-Hanafi mentioned 188 singers of whom 21 were Jewish, such as Yusuf Horesh, Sasson Za'rur and Moshe Suleyman amongst others. Iraqi Jews formed bands, and Ezra Haroun became particularly famous, having played the *'ud* for King Faisal. The king said to him on one occasion, 'You have made me happier than I have ever been before, my son.' Then the King's chief of protocol, 'You light up the whole of Iraq with your music.' On another occasion he was given a bowl filled with golden 'Abbasid dinars from the reign of Harun al-Rashid. Each dinar had the name of God stamped on it and a gold chain attached to it – but Ezra Haroun was satisfied with just one golden dinar. Ezra sang the compositions of two Jewish composers, Ibrahim and Ishaq al-Mawsili. He also played a prominent role in the musical conference which was convened in Egypt under aegis of King Fuad in 1932. After he emigrated to Israel his life filled with misery, drudgery and hunger. [49] The Moroccan Jewish poet, Erez Biton, said that the Moroccan Jewish singer, Zahra al-Fasia, sang for King Muhammad V in Rabat. He related how soldiers used to fight with knives to get to hear her whenever she was singing. He said she is currently in a transit camp in Ashkelon, near the welfare office, and in a state poverty and humiliation. [50]

That was the fate of most of the Jewish performers from the Islamic world. Their art died with them in the Zionist camps. This state continued into the seventies when the Sephardi community started looking at its own cultural heritage as a challenge to the Ashkenazi cultural establishment. The search for their roots was instigated by the appearance of the Black Panther movement.

Cultural suppression continues under the guise of 'racial integration'. David Ben Gurion, the first Israeli Prime Minister, said that 'the aim of the government is to inculcate the Yemeni immigrant with Israeli values to the point that he forgets where he came from . . .'[51]

Shmuel Rakanti, one of the first Sephardi MPs, criticised the concept of 'integration' in an article. 'Its real meaning is the eradication of Sephardi culture and traditions and the imposition of Ashkenazi culture . . . I am disgusted by the humility and spiritual and social nihilism. It enrages me. We must reject these corrupting opinions and criticise those who humiliate us while imposing upon us generals and patrons.' Rakanti believes that the only way to solve this problem is 'not through integration but by fostering both cultures. Sephardi culture must have an exalted position amongst the people.'[52] The Yemenite MP, Zekhariah Gluska, demanded more air time on the radio for Yemenite music, and stated that Ashkenazi 'experts' prepared the Yeminite programmes on the radio and added that they were ludicrous.[53]

In July 1979, Zevulun Hammer, the Minister of Education, convened a special meeting of the Public Council for Education and Culture to look into the cultural and social gap in Israel. Hayyim Shiran, of the educational television service, admitted that Sephardim were culturally oppressed, and as a result, over the last thirty years, Sephardim had been losing their self-respect. Dr Gabriel ben Simhon, who is of Moroccan origin, reported that 'the media do not broadcast music for Sephardim. Their music is passed around by cassette tapes. Owing to this, they feel frustrated.' The painter, Ziva Leblich, stated that Israel does not draw upon the latent musical treasures of the Sephardim. Nissim Yehoshua', who is in charge of Sephardi Culture at the Ministry of Education, said that there were many people who believed that the Sephardim had no culture but folklore, (this is the most common view among Ashkenazi 'intellectuals') and he called for Sephardi and Ashkenazi culture to intermix.

Professor David Elazar stressed that Ashkenazim wanted Sephardim to adopt their culture, but there was no justification for this claim.[54] In an article in *Ha'aretz*,[55] Professor Shimon Shamir explained that Israeli (i.e. Ashkenazi) society did not allow Sephardim to be part of the ruling elite. The professor said of Israeli-

Egyptian relations that, 'Ashkenazi society doubts the loyalty of Sephardim when the borders to the Arab world are open.' He added that the Ashkenazim, being prejudiced against the Middle East and its culture, fear Sephardi progress and quotes the views of Ben Gurion and Jabotinsky (see chapter eight). Shamir's views can be paraphrased by stating that were Middle Eastern culture fostered among the Sephardim, they would turn against the Ashkenazim if there was peace and open borders.

In a discussion with Leah 'Inbal, a correspondent of *Ha'aretz*,[56] Ben Simhon stated that in order to be able to finish his studies he had to shed his Sephardi culture and integrate into Ashkenazi life. Ben Simhon was born in Morocco and emigrated to Israel with his family when he was 9 years old. He was one of the few Moroccans who beat all the obstacles and graduated in Jerusalem. He then studied theatre and cinema at the Sorbonne. He is a teacher in the Department of Arts at Tel Aviv University. Ben Simhon affirmed that his family emigrated for religious reasons. His father had believed that angels would be hovering around him as he arrived in the Holy Land. Accordingly he dressed his children in their Sabbath best. He suddenly found that he and his family were suffering from poverty and subsisting amongst the mud and overcrowding of Sha'ar Ha'aliya Camp. Though the family's situation has improved over the last thirty years, Ben Simhon's father says, 'We were rich over there in Morocco, because we felt rich. Here we feel poor because we are insulted.' Ben Simhon admitted that for much of his life he had been forced to ape Ashkenazim and deny his identity. He recounted a joke that was common amongst the Ashkenazim, that upon being asked what he wanted to be when he grew up, a Sephardi child would say 'an Ashkenazi'. Ben Simhon added that in Morocco Jewish women believed that each and every one of their ten children could be the Messiah. In Israel, however, these children have ended up in prison. He added that he and his brother were born in Morocco which is why they were able to complete their university studies. The rest of his siblings, were born in Israel had not managed as much. They became labourers. Ben Simhon recounted that when he and thirty-nine other Moroccan academics met Yigal Allon to discuss the sectarian issue, Allon said, 'the mere presence of forty Moroccan graduates sitting here with me in my office points to some accomplishment – we have made progress in this country.' Ben Simhon replied to this, 'It is surely significant that out of the forty academics, only one went to school in Israel. The rest went to school abroad.' In spite of having received his degree in Israel, Ben Simhon says that he is not typical of the Moroccan community – rather an exception or even a miracle. He grew up struggling and he stressed that 'this country did not give me anything.' When he did his compulsory army service, he joined a parachute brigade made up of kibbutzniks in order to be 'included' but they isolated him. He added that the kibbutzniks are the symbol of racism, in various ways. They are completely shut off from anyone who is different. When he went to the Hebrew University he started to work as a labourer to pay the fees and lived in an abandoned army camp which had been given to the university. Ben Simhon, however, was the only student housed this way. He believes that Sephardim now realise that they must organize to oppose the forces which do not represent them. He stressed the following, 'You must set up an organized opposition, ready to fight – a force which by rights is yours.' Ben Simhon described anti-Sephardi cultural oppression as 'cultural annihilation', and mentioned that he learnt nothing of his own history while he was at school. 'They just wiped out your cultural identity, you had no right to exist – according to their outlook . . . the music and the cultural programmes broadcast by the Israeli media are all foreign to me and most Sephardim.' Ben Simhon's play entitled *A Moroccan King*, about the immigration of the Jews from Morocco, describes a Jewish community in Morocco which was told that the long-awaited Jewish Messiah had appeared and had come to help them get to Jerusalem to found the kingdom of heaven on earth. Since the legend foretold that they would fly to Jerusalem astride clouds, they went up to the rooftops and jumped off in order to mount the clouds – but they fell to their deaths! The author thus intimates that the immigration of the Moroccans to Israel was mass suicide. After much effort, Ben Simhon managed to get the play produced in Israel, although with some changes to make it more palatable. (In July 1989, Ben Simhon took an active part in the Toledo Conference between Sephardi intellectuals and the PLO.)

In a special debate organized by the Jewish Agency in Kfar Hamakabiya, Asher Edan (of Tunisian origin), a lecturer in philosophy at the University of Tel Aviv, stated 'the problem is that the European colonialists came to this country and decreed that its culture would be Ashkenazi. Equality will only be obtained when Sephardim gain control of the financial resources of the state and the Histadrut.' Subsequently he became unemployed. Shlomo Tsadoq said that 'Motti Gur, the former chief of staff, fired the opening shots when he stated "We'll screw the Sephardim like we screwed the Arabs."'

The aforementioned Dr Gabriel Ben Simhon took part in the debate, saying that 'we live in cultural exile. They have changed our culture without telling us.' Hayyim Siran, an expert in theatre, added that there was discrimination in the theatre and that it was difficult to produce plays which dealt with the Sephardi problem. He mentioned that in his position in Israeli television, he has to fight to have Sephardim employed.[57]

In an interview with a correspondent of *Zu Haderekh*,[58] the Moroccan singer, Shlomo Bar, stated 'I want to teach my son Arabic, so that he will be able to speak with our Arab neighbours and be a bridge to peace.' Bar formed a group of Moroccan singers, called 'The Natural Choice Band', to revive Arabic music amongst the Sephardim. He said that since arriving from Morocco, he had lived in poverty and cultural deprivation. He had been constantly despised for being Moroccan and made to feel inferior. He added that his parents were so naive that they were not aware of their debased place in society and that he could not explain this to them. He stated that 95 percent of prison inmates were Moroccan owing to prevailing social conditions, and that Jews in Morocco had not been the victims of any massacres at the hands of the Muslims and that their Muslim neighbours in Morocco had always respected and prayed at the graves of Jewish saints.[59]

In the aftermath of the cut-backs of the education budget, some Sephardim demanded that the subsidy to the Israel Philharmonic Orchestra be cut off. The journalist, Natan Donevitz, objected to this saying that 'we must find a substitute for western music so that Orientals will like it too.' He did not, however, suggest setting up an orchestra for Arabic music.[60]

THE END OF THE SEPHARDI HEBREW SCRIPT

As a step toward the 'national unity', the establishment banned the old Hebrew script which had been used by Sephardim for centuries, and imposed the use of the Ashkenazi Hebrew script. This was yet another cruel act, since most of the Hebrew documents and texts and the works written in Arabic by Sephardi intellectuals were written in this oriental Hebrew script. Sephardim had used this script when they wrote letters, diaries and accounts in Arabic, as well as using the Arabic script.

MISPRONUNCIATION OF HEBREW

Hebrew is a Semitic language which developed in the Middle East and was spoken by the patriarchs, Abraham, Isaac and Jacob, as well as the prophet Moses, Kings David and Solomon and later by Saladin's physician Maimonides. The pronunciation of the letters of the Hebrew alphabet thus corresponds with those of the Arabic alphabet. Sephardim who lived in the Middle East have pronounced them thus since the dawn of history. The Ashkenazim, on the other hand, being Europeans, cannot pronounce 50 percent of Hebrew consonants correctly. In any case, the correct pronunciation was distorted and they pronounced *h* like *kh*, the rolled *r* like a French *r*, the guttural *'ayin* like a glottal stop and so on. They preserved these mispronunciations and vaunted them as part of their European identity, laughing at Sephardim who pronounce the letters correctly.

Many Sephardi children have, accordingly, taken up imitating the accents of their Ashkenazi teachers to avoid being laughed at, while others have affected Ashkenazi accents to hide their origins and to overcome discrimination in the labour market. However, since the appearance of the Black Panthers in the seventies, it has become acceptable to keep the original accent.

THE ERADICATION OF SEPHARDI WRITERS AND POETS

The answer to the question Where are the Sephardi writers and poets who immigrated to Israel is that Israel has eradicated them culturally.

The atmosphere of Zionist nationalist racism against the Arabs and everything Arab has forced these writers and poets to desist from further output. In addition, bearing in mind that it is not easy for their descendants, who have been born and raised in Israel, to learn Arabic, most of the younger generation cannot read Arabic even if they speak it at home. Thus, few people read Arabic, and it has become increasingly difficult to publish in Arabic. Some authors have taken to writing in Hebrew, including Samy Mikhael. The Iraqi Samir Naqqash is the only one who has persisted in writing his works in Arabic. It was he who declared 'I still respect myself as an Iraqi.' Naqqash in his works describes the upheaval of Sephardi emigration as 'a catastrophe' which prevented him from settling down anew in Israel after having been arbitrarily uprooted from Iraq. *Ha'aretz* described Naqash as 'a man with a complex':[61] 'He is a Jew living in the Jewish State, but he writes in Arabic.' According to Ashkenazim, this constitutes a 'complex', since they refuse to admit an historical truth – that the Sephardim are an inseparable part of Arab culture. We should mention that Ashkenazi immigrants from Soviet Russia continue to produce literary works in Russian, but this has not been described by *Ha'aretz* as a 'complex'!

The root of the problem is that Ashkenazi settlers attempted and are still trying to erect an iron curtain, to cut Sephardim off from their cultural homeland. Hundreds of thousands of Ashkenazim revisit their original countries and no one accuses them of treason, whereas one Sephardi from Iraq, Nawi, tried to go back to Iraq. Thereafter he was arrested and imprisoned in Israel for five years for simply trying to visit his birthplace – Baghdad.

DISREGARD OF SEPHARDI WRITERS ABROAD

The Israeli media and school syllabuses do not just ignore Sephardi cultural heritage, but also Sephardi writers, intellectuals and poets who now live outside Israel. Currently Ashkenazi Israel lauds every Ashkenazi writer or intellectual who lives in Europe or America and lays claim to him even if he distances himself from Zionism.

The journalist, Benny Tsiper, writing in *Ha'aretz* about Sephardi intellectuals outside Israel,[62] pointed out that it was France, and not Israel, that arranged commemorative services following the death of Albert Cohen, the Greek Sephardi who is considered one of the greatest writers of this century. His popular French novels have been published all over the world and translated into different languages. Tsiper asserted that this author represented Sephardi culture which has been ignored by Israel. He added that France had absorbed all the literary and artistic works that Sephardi intellectuals had created – those same people who in Israel are contemptuously referred to as 'the oriental communities'. He mentioned some of the writers, such as Patrick Modinanu, Edmond Zabas (of Egyptian origin) an eminent poet in France today, and Darida al-Jazairi who represents modern French philosophy. We must also mention Elias Canetti who was unknown in Israel until he won the Nobel Prize, whereupon *Ha'aretz* published an article on him. Although Canetti is not a Zionist, most of the article on him dealt with the 'struggle of the Zionist movement in Bulgaria'.

Sephardi young people in Israel know almost nothing of their history or culture. The Zionist rulers know too well that he who has a knowledge of his culture can develop his identity, and that he who has an identity can shape his own future. In spite of that, incidents of discrimination, which the Sephardi confronts from the cradle to the grave, help to create his identity. We must also not forget that he is surrounded by 160 million Arabs who are proud of their heritage.

RESULTS OF THE POLICY OF DE-EDUCATION AND CULTURAL OPPRESSION

1. Widespread failure and illiteracy at school. The American anthropologist, Arnold Lewis, wrote an important study on this subject entitled *The Power of Misery and Education* (1979), in which he stated that a third of primary school pupils study in 'remedial' schools, or 'need special care'. According to the Ashkenazi Zionist dictionary, these expressions mean 'Sephardi'. Out of 287 pupils included in the study, there were only 22 Ashkenazi pupils. Lewis said that 25 percent of the teachers were not qualified in the subjects they were teaching. The English teacher could only speak a few words of English, and teachers tried to convince Lewis that 'these pupils' had been brought up in a 'primitive' culture, which was why their intellect and motivation were weak. Lewis confirmed that the Ministry appointed under-qualified teachers in that belief that 'these pupils' did not need high-grade teachers. The government inspector appointed a woman to teach English, for example, after she had failed at other schools. When asked about this by Lewis, the inspector replied, 'the truth is that these pupils do not need to study English because they will all be doing very simple jobs.'[63]

The Ministry of Education published the results of its investigation into this problem, which were reported in an article by Nilly Mendler.[64] The report said that 40 percent of nine-year olds in slum districts failed in reading, writing and arithmetic whereas the national failure average was 14.3 percent. The investigation confirmed that the pupils who fail do not even know a few basic words. However, the failure rate in some districts is 20-25 percent, and this is because classes there have just 20 pupils. The headmaster of the Herzeliya School in Tel Aviv, Dr Carmi

Yogev, stated that 80 percent of the Sephardi pupils, who finish their elementary education in the Hatikvah slum district, cannot read or write. They do not know the whole alphabet and have a minimal grasp of the language. In the development towns, 60-70 percent of the children are classified as remedial.[65]

Zu Haderekh, quoting Yizhak Kadmon, Chairman of the Social Workers Union, reported[66] that 14,000 illiterates had joined the armed forces over the previous three years. It also reported that a prison inmate costs the state I£180,000 per annum whereas the treatment of a juvenile delinquent costs much less than that: approximately I£10,000.

Owing to the low level of education available for Sephardim in the slum districts and the development towns, some families have started sending their children to boarding schools. These are generally religious, agricultural, vocational or military schools. The number of boarders between the ages of 13 and 18 is between 15 and 20 percent of the school population. The Public Committee for the Defence of Sephardi Education carried out a study which showed that the level of education in these boarding schools is not much better than in the schools of the slum districts. This means that the child at boarding schools is physically removed from his family, with the resultant psychological problems, but he does not get a better education for all that.[67] In addition to psychological damage, the boarding schools manage to cut the pupils off from their cultural environment, and inculcate them with either religious or political extremism, or both. In the *yeshivot* of Degel Hatora they have to speak Yiddish.

In the Ashkenazi schools, the educational standard has remained high in spite of cutbacks. These schools have started paying teachers of subjects, such as mathematics and science, three times as much as other teachers. The director of the Ministry of Education, Dr Shoshani, is aware of this, but declared that it was an 'necessary evil'. One of the most corrupt acts is to pay a teacher for two or three hours when he has taught only one. Parents have also started paying extra fees so their children can study subjects not on the curriculum, something over which the Ashkenazi Teachers Unions have been remarkably quiet. Teaching in state schools has thus been divided into two parts, one for the rich and one for the poor. Nurit Dovrat, the journalist who published these facts,[68] stated that this phenomenon, termed 'grey education', can also be found in the health service where it is called 'black health'. Nahman Raz of Kibbutz Geva, Chairman of the Parliamentary Education

Committee, admitted that this phenomenon represents the 'bankruptcy of education'.[69]

The Palestinians commit a grave mistake when they compare the standard of Arab education with the average standard of Jewish education to emphasise the gap arising from the policy of discrimination.[70] If they made a comparison between their schools and the Ashkenazi schools (in the kibbutzim and in the Ashkenazi suburbs for example), they would find that the real gap is much, much greater than they had imagined. They commit the same mistake when they compare their economic conditions with the average for the general Jewish population. This does not encourage a common struggle with the Sephardim.

2. The deterioration of school buildings and equipment. After the government declared a moratorium on the construction of new school buildings or extra rooms, some of the teachers were forced to hold classes in air-raid shelters and cow-sheds. Due to cut-backs in the education budget, the government has kept psychologists and social workers away, and Sephardi and Palestinian schools were the first victims. At the same time, since 1967 the government has been spending enormous amounts to build new schools and to buy the latest school equipment for the Ashkenazi settlements in the occupied Arab territories. In these settlements, school classes have between 5-8 pupils, at the expense of the overcrowded classes in Sephardi and Palestinian schools.[71]

3. Increase in the number of boys and girls who neither go to school nor work. In Musrara these children make up 19 percent of the new generation. Nissim Gaon, Chairman of the World Sephardi Organisation, stated that the number of these children between the ages of 14-17 alone had reached more than 25,000, that 60 percent of Sephardi children skip school and that 70 percent of the delinquents in the state come from this community.[72]

4. Underqualification amongst the Sephardi masses. The policy of de-education has led to a situation where the Sephardi masses end up with no educational or vocational qualifications, and this in turn has led to the spread of unemployment and hence poverty. This situation has made it possible to turn most Sephardim into unskilled labour.

5. The spread of delinquency, crime and drug addiction. This is particularly the case amongst the young people who neither study nor work, but it is also a cause for concern in secondary schools and in the armed forces. Police sources state that 50 percent of secondary school pupils have used hashish and that headmasters

turn a blind eye and will not cooperate with the police to stamp this out.[73] A report of the Ministry of Social Services on juvenile delinquency stated that Sephardi juvenile delinquents formed 92.9 percent of the total number of repeat offenders.[74]

6. Alienation, despair and disaffection with the state of Israel, on the one hand, and loss of Sephardi identity by a great number of the community on the other, was widespread. However, the protests by the Black Panthers have roused many to try and recover their culture and identity (see the final chapter).

This process is well explained by Eliav: 'They tell you, from your youth on, that you have come out from a place of darkness and void, and that your background was completely primitive, and they tell you this so often that you end up believing it. Then there is only one step for you to take, consciously or otherwise, which is to hate your family and the country you came from and to be ashamed of your roots. But in the following stage, you begin to hate those who made you believe that, and who hate you, and you start asking questions about yourself. Is it not all a pack of lies?'[75]

Charlie Biton, MP, leader of the Black Panthers, said that 90 percent of those in military prisons are Sephardi: 'they have refused to do compulsory military service because of racism.'[76]

NOTES

1 *Ha'aretz*, 11 January 1980.
2 *Zu Haderekh*, 14 May 1980 and 25 June 1980.
3 *Shevet va'am*, 1958.
4 *Shevet va'am*, A. 'Abbas, 1958 and Dr Smilansky, *Megamot*, July 1957, and see chapter five.
5 *The Times*, 24 December 1985.
6 *Zu Haderekh*, 13 February 1980.
7 *Ha'aretz*, 27 May 1982.
8 *Zu Haderekh*, 16 October 1985.
9 *Ha'aretz*, 10 July 1987.
10 Ibid, 16 April 1987.
11 *Shevet va'am*, 1958.
12 Avraham Khalfon, *Shevet va'am*, 1954.
13 *Shevet va'am*, 1958.
14 *Shevet va'am*, 1958.
15 Schools for teaching Hebrew to new immigrants.
16 Ibid.
17 *Shevet va'am*, A. 'Abbas, 1958.
18 *Shevet va'am*, A. 'Abbas, 1958.
19 *Shevet va'am*, 1960.
20 *Shevet va'am*, 1959.
21 Central Office of Statistics, 1978.
22 Ministry of Education and Culture, 1976.
23 Central Office of Statistics.

24 Ibid.
25 Ibid.
26 *Megamot*, July 1957.
27 *Shevet va'am*, 1973.
28 *Shevet va'am*, 1959.
29 *Shevet va'am*, 1958.
30 *Ha'aretz*, 4 September 1981.
31 Supplement to *Ha'aretz*, 22 May 1981.
32 *Les temps modernes*, 20.
33 Ibid.
34 Ibid, 21.
35 Since the 1970s IQ tests have been imposed on university entrants and army conscripts.
36 *Zu Haderekh*, April 5 1982, based on official figures.
37 Israeli Press.
38 Central Bureau of Statistics, Israel, official publications 1971, 1974, 1976.
39 Deputy Minister of Education, Government Report on Sephardi Youth, 1972.
40 Smooha, 1978, 160 and 161.
41 *Les temps modernes*, 26.
42 Ibid, 26-29.
43 Israeli Central Bureau of Statistics, Israeli Statistical yearbook, 1980, 605.
44 Statistical Abstract of Israel, 1986, 608.
45 *Les temps modernes*, 130.
46 Ministry of Education data 1981, and Population Census, 1983.
47 Ibid, Special Series 418, table 19.
48 *Shevet va'am*, 1958.
49 *Shevet va'am*, 1960.
50 *Minha marocait*, 29.
51 Knesset Minutes, Volume 8, 1102, 14 February 1951.
52 *Shevet va'am*, 1954.
53 Knesset Minutes, 1949.
54 *Ha'aretz*, July 20 1979.
55 6 April 1980.
56 28 May 1980.
57 *Ha'aretz*, 25 September 1981.
58 3 February 1982.
59 Ibid.
60 *Ha'aretz*, 16 April 1982.
61 16 May 1986.
62 6 November 1981.
63 *Zu Haderekh*, 29 May 1985.
64 *Ha'aretz*, 10 June 1983.
65 Swirski and Shushan, 1985, 27.
66 2 April 1980.
67 *Hadashot Hala*, Number 7, April 1987.
68 *Ma'ariv*, 16 March 1987.
69 Ibid.
70 *Al-Mirsad*, 1 July 1987.
71 *Zu Haderekh*, 20 April 1983.
72 *Ha'aretz*, 4 April 1980.
73 *Ha'aretz*, 14 May 1982.
74 *Ha'aretz*, 31 October 1975.
75 *Les temps modernes*, 21 and 22.
76 *Zu Haderekh*, 7 January 1981.

CHAPTER EIGHT

Rationalisation Of Discrimination

The policy of racial discrimination has led to the Israeli 'people' being divided roughly into two economic, social and educational strata – that is a class made up of the Ashkenazim which includes the elite, and an under class of Sephardim (and Palestinians). This divide also extends into the field of culture, with Ashkenazi/East European culture on the one side, and Sephardi/Middle Eastern on the other.

The Ashkenazim try to rationalise this split by means of racist views well-known in the West, particularly in South Africa. These views form an inseparable part of the racism directed against the Palestinians and the Arabs as a whole, and are not just expounded by the political leaders, but by journalists writers, sociologists and most Ashkenazim. Even if they differ as to tactics, all Zionist parties express these same views, even the non-Zionist Left or the self-proclaimed anti-Zionists.

VIEWS OF THE POLITICAL LEADERS

Herzl, the founder of political Zionism: 'Zionism will be an outpost of European culture against oriental barbarism.'[1] Based on this viewpoint, harsh opinions were formed and cruel steps taken against the Palestinians and the Arabs in general, as well as the Sephardim, who were deemed part of this 'oriental barbarism'.

Jabotinsky, the guru of Right-Wing Zionist Revisionism, the Irgun and the Stern Gang, the Herut Party and the Likud Front: 'The Jews, thank God, have nothing in common with the East. We must put an end to any trace of the oriental spirit in the Jews of Palestine.'[2] In his article, 'Jews of the East,' which was published in 1919, he opposed mixed marriages with Sephardim and the creation of a single Jewish people, and also stated that he was opposed to integration because he did not know what this would beget – 'a brilliant people or a dull race. Ashkenazi Jews had to preserve their majority status in Jewish society in Palestine.'[3]

David Ben Gurion, Labour Party (Mapai), and the Histadrut, head of the Jewish Agency and the first Prime Minister and Minister of Defence of Israel. He described the Sephardim, at a meeting with the army high command in 1950 as 'human dust, with no Jewish or human culture. They need a long course of education and civilisation before they can occupy their proper place in society.'[4] He wrote: 'Godliness disappeared from the oriental sects and their influence on the Jewish people has been minimal or nonexistent. Over the last centuries, European Jews have been at the forefront of the people both qualitatively and quantitatively.' Ben Gurion added that he meant the Jews of Eastern Europe.[5] The historian, Tom Segev, commented on Ben Gurion's words that 'it seemed that the state adopted the viewpoint which says that "the Jewish poor-house" in Plonsk (a poor Polish village where Ben Gurion was born) was "godly", whereas the house of a Jewish doctor, a graduate of the Sorbonne, in Algiers was not.'[6] Ben Gurion believed that the real meaning of the Nazi holocaust was that Hitler had destroyed the fundamental strength of the state of Israel before it was founded. The state came into existence but did not find the people it was awaiting, and thus the Sephardim were brought in. Ben Gurion compared these latter to the 'blacks who were taken over to America as plantation slaves.'[7] On 13 July 1949 he said at the parliamentary Constitutional Committee that the Jews of Morocco were 'human beasts', but he did aver that most thieves and pickpockets were Ashkenazi!'[8] In 1956 Ben Gurion stated that Moroccan Jews 'have no culture but are influenced by the Arabs, and we do not want any Moroccan culture here.' Of the Iranian Jews he said 'I cannot see what contribution Iranian Jews can make to Israel.'[9] In 1959, after the Sephardi uprising at Wadi al-Salib in Haifa, he described the Moroccans as 'a primitive community', and accused them of sympathising with 'outlaws, thieves, pimps and murderers.'[10] Of the Yemenites Ben Gurion wrote in a letter to the army chief of staff, Yigal Yadin, 'that this people can be more easily absorbed on a cultural and economic level than other groups since the Yemenite likes to work and is not keen on urban life, but', Ben Gurion continued, 'on the other hand, he [the Yemenite] represents the greater problem since he is 2,000 years away from us and needs to be taught the most basic concepts of civilisation. The Yemenite treats his wife and children as a primitive man. His health is weak and his physical strength is feeble; he has no knowledge of basic sanitary matters . . . '[11] Ben Gurion demanded that Israel 'civilise' the Yemenite when he said in the Knesset that 'the aim of the government is to inculcate the Yemenite immigrant with Israeli mores to the extent where he forgets where he came from . . . '[12]

It is true that Western technology has not spread quickly in the Yemen, but the situation of the Jews there was better than that of the Ashkenazim who were living in the ghettos of Eastern Europe – see the works of the Ashkenazi writer Mendele Mokher Sefarim, particularly *The Travels of Benjamin III*. The Jews in the Yemen were goldsmiths, blacksmiths, cabinet-makers etc., whereas the Ashkenazim were subsisting in the ghettos as pedlars or small shopkeepers with many occupying jobs relating to religion.

In 1960 Ben Gurion declared that 'Jews in Middle Eastern countries have lived in backward and corrupt societies and lack education, independence and self-respect. The old generation cannot be changed fundamentally but we must imbue the new generations with lofty intellectual and moral values – the characteristics of those pioneers who built Israel. If we fail in this, God forbid, we will face the danger that the coming generation will turn Israel into a Levantine state.'[13] Ben Gurion and other leaders demanded that more Ashkenazi Jews should be brought from Russia, Europe and America in order to 'improve' the ethnic composition of the population. Ben Gurion also said that 'we must resist the spirit of the Levant, for it corrupts individuals and communities.' In 1962, when it was suggested to him that another 'oriental' appointed as a minister, he replied angrily, 'Israel will not be a Levantine state.'[14] 'Levantine' is a term of abuse used by Ashkenazi settlers against Middle Eastern people. It means an oriental person of no culture who adopts the external forms of Western civilisation such as Western costume.

Between 1947-1973 Ben Gurion and the Sephardi leader, Eliahu Eliachar, carried out a correspondence, with Eliachar stressing the importance of eradicating anti-Sephardi discrimination and the broadening of Sephardi representation in state institutions – 'for the sake of unity'. In his letters, Ben Gurion dodged the issue of discrimination, pointing out that Sephardim did not constitute a single community. He claimed that he did not feel he was an

'Ashkenazi' but just a 'Jew'. Finally, Ben Gurion admitted in a letter dated 25 July 1973 the necessity to eliminate the 'gap' for the sake of unity'. These letters were published in the magazine *Shevet va'am* in 1973, and in Eliachar's book *Life with the Jews*. Ben Gurion had been the most important leader in all the Zionist institutions since the British Mandate, and in the 1948 war, in his capacity as Prime Minister and Minister of Defence, he was primarily responsible for the expulsion of the Palestinians, the destruction of hundreds of villages and the expropriation of their property and land. He was also responsible for bringing over the Sephardi Jews from their respective countries and cramming them into the camps.

Arthur Ruppin. A veteran Zionist leader who specialised in agricultural settlement. In 1913 he expressed his fears that Sephardi immigration might lower the cultural level of the country. He set aside a special role for the Sephardim in the economic and social infrastructure, which was 'to compete with the Arab workers', for the Sephardi Jew could 'carry out menial jobs for the same wages as an Arab labourer.'[15]

Golda Meir. Prime Minister and Minister of Labour. A leader of the Labour Party (previously Mapai): 'We in Israel need high-level immigrants, for the future of our economic infrastructure. We have immigrants from Morocco, Libya, Iran, Egypt and other [Middle Eastern] countries whose society is that of the sixteenth century.'[16] Golda Meir made other racist statements (see chapter ten for her dispute with the Black Panthers).

Moshe Sharett (formerly Shertok). Minister of Foreign Affairs and Prime Minister, belonged to the Labour Party. Sharett said to the Soviet Foreign Minister, Vishinsky, that 'there are countries, and here I am talking about the countries of North Africa, whose Jews need not emigrate. It is not a question of the number of people, but their quality. Our concern in this state is to be pioneers, and we need people with a capacity to adapt . . . we cannot depend upon the Jews of Morocco to build the state on their own, for they are not qualified to do that . . . we need people who can withstand any difficulty and who possess the power of endurance. You know that when it comes to constructing the country at the present time, the Jews of Eastern Europe are the salt of the earth . . . '[17]

Abba Eban, from South Africa, a Labour Party leader. He referred to Sephardi immigration as the 'danger' threatening the Ashkenazim in Israel. He defined this danger by stating that Sephardi immigration 'may well force Israel's cultural level down to that of the surrounding countries.' Eban opposed the view that the

Sephardim constituted a bridge to the Arab world, and added that the aim of Zionism was to inculcate a Western spirit amongst the Sephardim instead of allowing them to drag Israel toward an eastern culture.[18]

Motti Gur, former Chief of Staff and a Minister, a leader of the Labour Party: 'The oriental communities will not achieve the level of the Ashkenazim over the next 20-30 years. All the efforts expended on their behalf have only had partial results, and only a few of them have achieved high levels and then only after much difficulty . . . no one blocks the road to progress for them. Unfortunately, it will take many years until the oriental communities, including the university graduates, reach a Western intellectual and technological level. It is a problem.'[19]

Motti Gur is correct if the policy of de-education continues, but the case of the Sephardim who emigrated to France and other Western countries belies Gur's argument. Eliahu Eliachar pointed out that the number of Sephardi professors at the Sorbonne was 80 and that 49 percent of Jewish students at the university were North African. General de Gaulle's surgeon was an Algerian Jew, Professor Abu al-Khair. The Baghdadi professor, Eli Kedourie, teaches at the University of London, as does Sami Zubeida, and in the United States the Baghdadi professor, Daniel Khizum, was well-known, and so on. Let us leave the views of Motti Gur and look at his values and methods. In his party's election campaign Gur declared at a well-attended meeting that 'we will screw the Sephardim like we screwed the Arabs.'[20] This shameless provocation was one of the factors which made Sephardim vote for Likud. Finally we should mention a statement of his that he was ready to withdraw from East Jerusalem in exchange for one million Russian Jews.[21]

Moshe Dayan, a leader of the Labour Party and the military establishment. He declared in 1974 as follows: 'the greatest problem facing Israel is that the number of Sephardim is greater than that of the European immigrants.' Those listening to this speech were white settlers in South Africa and understood his message with no need for further clarification.

THE STANCE OF THE ASHKENAZI PRESS

Since 1948 the Israeli press, which is completely Ashkenazi, has been carrying out a racist campaign against Sephardim, whose aim has been to rationalise the government's discriminatory policies. The press wrote that 'these (Sephardim) understand neither toilets nor toilet paper, and grow vegetables under their beds! They hide their babies in cartons to save them from the doctor and medication.' On 22 March 1951, the liberal newspaper, *Ha'aretz*, wrote about Iraqi transit camp inhabitants that 'many parents teach their children thievery and teachers are helpless in face of this phenomenon . . . a girl said "if I don't do as my parents say, they won't give me enough to eat and they'll beat me twice as hard" . . . the children drink wine on occasion, and their parents teach them to lie.'

In 1952 the same newspaper published a series of articles about the Tunisian,[22] the Afghani[23] and the Iranian[24] Jews. The articles highlighted their poverty, disease and disintegration and stated that many the Iranian Jews were opium and hashish addicts. There were syphilitics even amongst the children, since this was hereditary according to the newspaper. On 11 April 1952 the opening article of the newspaper carried the headline that immigration from 'backward' Arab countries constituted a danger to the existence of Israel as a modern state.

The newspaper, *Yedi'ot Aharonot*,[25] wrote that Sephardim were sub-standard, and that one should fear a lowering of standards amongst employees. On 23 February 1952 the same newspaper wrote that employers were demanding 'civilised' employees, 'not from the oriental communities'. We shall examine in detail the view of some journalists.

Aryeh Gelblum

The attacks reached their zenith in an article by Aryeh Gelblum in *Ha'aretz* on 22 April 1949. The following are some passages from it: ' . . . the immigrants belonged to a race previously unknown in Israel. It seems that there are differences between those who come from Tripoli (Libya), Morocco and Algeria. But I cannot say that I have managed to study the essence of this difference, if there be one. They say, for example, that the Libyans and Tunisians are "better", and that the Algerians and the Moroccans are "worse", but it is the same problem. Generally stated . . . we are faced with people which is extremely primitive and whose education is that of complete ignorance. More dangerous than that is that they are incapable of taking in anything spiritual. On the whole, their level only slighter better than the general level of Arabs, negroes or

Berbers in their native countries. Accordingly, their level is below what we were used to in the past with the Arabs of the land of Israel. In contrast to the Yemenites, they have no roots in Judaism. They are completely at the whim of their instinctive and savage natures. Just how can we teach the Africans to queue properly for food in the dining room? There was a Bulgarian Jew who argued with them about queuing up, but one of the African Jews drew a knife and cut off his nose. More than once they have pounced upon officials of the Jewish Agency and beaten them up. In any case, the camp officials are in constant danger of attack. In the corners of Africans' dwellings in the camps you will find piles of filth, gambling, alcoholism and prostitution. Many of them suffer from eye, skin and sexual diseases, in addition to carrying out acts of assault and robbery. This anti-social group is dangerous and no one restrains them "properly" . . . not only luggage disappears but also equipment belonging to the camp. They robbed one of the camps I used to visit and emptied its general warehouse. In another camp, for example, there was a murder. The dead body was prepared for burial in a room near the hospital, and when the undertakers returned after the funeral they found that all their equipment had been stolen. The "Africans'" in the army used to tell me, "when we finish the war, we'll make war on the Ashkenazim." In one camp they had a plan of rebellion which included overpowering the guards and killing all the employees of the Jewish Agency in the camp. When the police come, there sometimes occur disputes. But more important than all that, there is a basic truth of no less significance which is the lack of any readiness to conform to the life of the country, particularly their chronic indolence and their dislike for work. Almost without exception, they all lack a trade and hence they suffer from crippling poverty. They all tell you that they were "merchants" in Africa, but the truth is that they were itinerant vendors. And they all want to live in "town". What can we do with them? How can we absorb them? Have we thought what would happen to this state if they were its citizens? One day the rest of the Jews from the Arab world will immigrate! How would the state of Israel look and what kind of standard would it have if it had citizens like these? . . . '

This article is one of the most scurrilous attacks on the Sephardim and North Africa as a whole. I myself have met just such Moroccans but the overwhelming majority were kind and pleasant people in the full meaning of the words. I believe that Ashkenazi Jews, like Gelblum, have always hated the Moroccans because they stood up for themselves. The year before, the Ashkenazi high command sent thousands of Moroccan and other Sephardim to their deaths.

The Ashkenazi poet, Natan Alterman, renowned for his humanism and his love of peace, does not include the Sephardim in his affections. He has described them in his works as 'dwellers in dark caves and prison cells from which smoke arises.'[26] Even the socialist kibbutznik, Amos Oz, describes the Sephardi girls he played with as a child in Jerusalem as 'cruel, evil, poisonous oriental girls with a penetrating smell of peanuts, sweat, soap and halva, . . . whose big brothers are involved in the world of crime and football, and mothers and sisters go out with English soldiers.'[27] This is the image of Sephardi Jews in modern Hebrew literature which is created by Ashkenazi settlers.

Along with the Yemenites, the racial discrimination directed against the Moroccans was much worse than that faced by other Sephardim. All the vices which Gelblum rails against in his article arose in the terrible camps in France and Israel, and as for 'standing up for themselves', the General Director of the Ministry of Finance of the time, David Horovitz, told David Ben Gurion that 'the residents of the immigrant camps constitute a second nation, a rebellious people who think that we constitute the rich ruling elite. This is a matter which could easily flare up, and it would be dynamite for the Herut and Communist parties. In many ways the Sephardim have taken over from the Arabs and we have come to view them with the same superiority.'[28] David Horovitz was correct in what he foresaw, and we shall see in chapter ten how the Moroccans formed the beginnings of a resistance to Ashkenazi Zionist rule.

Kalman Katsnelson

Ashkenazi Zionist racism has reached its furthest development in the works of this right-wing Revisionist author. He justifies the great number of Ashkenazim in high positions in terms of their European superiority. Moreover, the Ashkenazim constitute a 'one nation', having overcome sectarian divisions. He then adds that the backwardness of the Sephardim is the main cause of their debased situation and discrimination against them by the Ashkenazim. The Sephardim would need 150 years to catch up.

The author asserts that Ashkenazim are capable of representing the Sephardim in parliament, and he is against the concept of equality. He emphasises that proportional representation in government for Sephardim would undermine the concept of 'a chosen people'. He states that this principle should also apply internally within the Jewish state. According to Katsnelson, Jews do not accept the concept of majority government, but a quality government. No intelligent Jew would submit to a Jewish government that was not elected on the basis of quality. He then reiterates that it is the chosen group of the chosen people who should rule. Finally he states that the 'Ashkenazi nation' is ready to admit the Sephardim, but he threatens that if the Sephardim insist on being separate, then the Ashkenazim would declare themselves a completely separate nation and would go to great lengths to strengthen themselves and their quality as well as treating the Sephardim as a separatist community.[29]

The Sephardi magazine, *Shevet va'am*, published this article which contained these views so that Sephardi leaders could comment on it.

In 1964 Katsnelson brought out his well-known book, *The Ashkenazi Revolution,* in which he wrote that 'Sephardim constitute the majority, and their rate of natural increase is greater than that of the Ashkenazi community. They look like the Arabs, and think like them, and hence Ashkenazim must prevent them from uniting against the European minority . . . The superior Ashkenazi nation, which was ordained to govern, made a mistake in allowing inferior non-Ashkenazim to immigrate. The Ashkenazim must take up the reins of power immediately to prevent the deterioration of their rule and the disintegration of Israel.' The author then enumerates the necessary racist means to exclude the Sephardim from power and authority. Prof. Yehuda Nini claimed that this book is the one document which reflects the real stance of the Ashkenazim toward the Sephardim (see the last chapter).

The novelty here is that this author expressed these views in public and angered many Sephardim. There are other Ashkenazim who object to these views, both in theory and in practice, vis-à-vis the Palestinians, but who ignore the racial discrimination directed against the Sephardim since it serves their interests. And then there are exceptions.

Eliahu Eliachar, a Sephardi leader, calls Katsnelson a 'Jewish Nazi', but he confirms that 'there are many Ashkenazim who hold the same opinions but do not express them in writing.'[30] According to David Sitton, even some leaders of the state of Israel held Katsnelson's ideas.[31]

Dr Mosheh Almozelino commented on Katsnelson's article that

Israeli democracy was a 'myth', for Sephardim were not properly represented in parliament. 'The concept of minority rule by the elite is Nazi, racist and undemocratic.' He compares the claims that 'the Ashkenazim form one nation which is prepared to absorb the Sephardim in its culture,' to attempts by Czarist Russia to eradicate the cultures of the small nations and Russify them. Dr Almozelino believes that this is exactly what the Ashkenazi Zionist media are doing. He stresses that the intellectuals, more than others, are resistant to 'Ashkenazi-Westernisation'. He wonders about Katsnelson's vow that Israel would not agree to be turned into an oriental state, 'What does it mean, they would not "agree"? Is it their state? Do they have the monopoly on Europe and its culture?' He goes on to warn that the Sephardim 'have suffered discrimination patiently, but they are at the end of their tether', and reminds the reader that 'the cause of the destruction of the Second Temple [i.e. the Second Jewish State] was internecine conflict.'[32]

Yoel Markus

He justifies Ashkenazi 'superiority' over Sephardim in his article 'Ethnic Degeneration'[33] in which he wrote that the Ashkenazim had lived in Europe in the shade of European culture for a thousand years, whereas the Sephardim came from countries possessed of no culture. Markus appears to forget that the Ashkenazim lived in ghettos, taking little part in European culture until the nineteenth century and unable to speak the language of their European neighbours.

Amnon Dankner

This Ashkenazi journalist wrote two articles about Sephardim which were published in *Ha'aretz* during February 1983 and in which he described Sephardim as 'backward', 'Khomeinist', 'primitive' and 'living in cultural darkness'. He went on to praise the 'Western, humanistic and liberal' culture of the of the Ashkenazi settlers who, according to him, bear 'the heritage of Heine's poetry, Freud's psychoanalysis, and Einstein's physics.'

Dankner had not read the works of these intellectuals; if he had, he would realise that they would have opposed Zionist principles and the inhumane treatment of the Palestinians. Einstein, we should point out, was approached to immigrate and to be the President of Israel, but he refused.

This racist stance taken by the media and followed in education and literature has led to deepening discord and enmity. Ashkenazi discrimination is not covert, but is open and can be encountered in the workplace, the army, on the bus or in the street. Ashkenazi vocabulary is replete with expressions of contempt and derision for Sephardim (and Palestinians and Arabs as a whole), and Ashkenazim use the word 'Arab' as an insult against Sephardim or to describe anything in a derogatory manner.

If peace between Israel and its Arab neighbours comes about, how will the Arabs manage to live and work on a day to day basis with such arrogance? Even the 'Leftist Progressives' amongst the Ashkenazim take a very paternalistic attitude toward the Palestinians.

VIEWS OF THE SOCIOLOGISTS

1. The School of Modernism

This school is headed by S. N. Eisenstadt and his students at the Hebrew University in Jerusalem. Their theory centres on American 'functionalism' which divides mankind into two parts: the progressive which is the Western world, and the backward traditional which is the Third World. These social scientists say that the cause of the gulf between the Sephardim and the Ashkenazim is not racial discrimination, but the backwardness of the Sephardim. They believe that, in order to overcome this gulf, Sephardim must discard their Middle Eastern heritage and accept Ashkenazi culture.

It is important to note that the technological level and development of economic skills in the ghettos of Eastern Europe was certainly no better than that of the Jews who came from Beirut, Alexandria, Baghdad and other urban Middle Eastern centres. Moreover, the acquisition of higher education does not help Sephardim to achieve equality in Israel.

In contrast to the prophecies of the school of 'Modernism', the second and third generation Sephardim, who were born in modern and progressive Israel and study in its schools, have suffered a decrease in their economic and educational standards in comparison to their fathers who came from the Arab world.

218

2. The School of Ethnic Pluralism

This is also an American school, headed in Israel by Yohanan Peres and Sammy Smooha. Their theory is that most nations consist of more than one group, and that all communities participate together in the various fields of national life such as the economy and politics, but they live apart in the areas of the family, religion and culture. Smooha believes that the differences between Ashkenazim and Sephardim in Israel are crumbling and that some progress is being made toward integration. Smooha supports the School of Modernism in this respect, but he stipulates that there must also be a change in government policy. He adds that a halt in the flow of money from abroad and an end to the state of war would cause a sectarian crisis.

I believe that social polarisation contradicts these two theories (see chapter nine).

3. The View of the 'Humanists'

In 1951 the Israeli magazine, *Megamot*, approached five Ashkenazi staff professors from the Hebrew University to discuss the problem of the Ashkenazi/Sephardi gulf in a series of articles. The professors were Akiva Ernst Simon, Natan Rotstreich, Meshulam Grul, Yosef Ben David (Gross) and Karl Frankenstein.

Karl Frankenstein wrote: 'We must discuss the primitive mentality of many of the immigrants from various countries.' His colleagues agreed with this, and he then suggested that in order to understand the Sephardi mentality it had to be compared with that of children, the mentally retarded or psychotics. Yosef Gross believed that the Sephardim were 'mentally backward' and suffered from a 'defective development of their ego'. They discussed the 'essence of primitivism'.

But Professor Simon, who was one of the leaders of 'Ihud', an organisation that fought for Arab-Jewish cooperation at the time of the British Mandate, warned against imposing a foreign culture on the Sephardim, since that would lead to a state of both social and moral alienation. He emphasised the positive sides of the 'primitive mentality', such as 'religion and prayers, emotional reaction to goodness and beauty, and genuine cordiality in personal relations – these are all positive attributes which the Sephardim possess in contrast to the Ashkenazim.'

These articles crystalised Ashkenazi unanimity: some of them were paternalistic and others harboured feelings of superiority or contempt for Sephardim. They also brought out the fear that there was a danger stalking Ashkenazi culture. The participants in this debate expressed the view that the 'absorption' of the Sephardim was a 'cultural necessity', which aimed to inculcate Sephardim with western values in the hope of integrating them into Ashkenazi society.

Finally, Professor Simon warned that 'the absorption of hundreds of thousands with "primitive" mentalities would split society into two camps, with the one distinguished by its feelings of superiority and the other by its inferiority.'[34]

4. The 'Mahbarot lemehkar ulevikoret' Group

This is a progressive Ashkenazi group which grew up around Dr Shlomo Swirski, a professor at the University of Haifa, and included Deborah Bernstein and Sarah Katsir. It started publishing 'files' about the conditions of the Palestinians and Sephardim in 1948, and hence its name – 'Research and Criticism Files'. Even though they did not use expressions such as 'discrimination' and 'racism', they collected important facts and figures on these matters. They ignored the historical perspective and missed an important point, which is that relations between the settler community and the Sephardim did not start in 1948 but had been developing since the beginning of Zionist colonisation. They create the impression that the conflict is between the 'host country' (i.e. the foreign settlers) and the 'immigrants' (i.e. the native Jews of Palestine and the neighbouring countries). They also overlooked the cultural and political suppression carried out by the establishment.

Swirski and Bernstein wrote that 'even good intentions cannot alter the gulf which has occurred.'[35] Anyone who has lived in Palestine since the British Mandate knows that the intentions of the Ashkenazi settlers were never good toward the natives, whether they were Palestinians or Sephardim. In the third part of his book,[36] Swirski believes that the extension of public services will not create equality or change the 'division of labour' in society. Public services actually deepen and cement the gulf for most of those who benefit from them are Ashkenazim.

As for setting up a Sephardi political party, he says that even if they manage to form an 'oriental' government, it would face strong opposition from the Ashkenazi establishment, such as the wealthy, the Histadrut leadership and the state apparatus. He adds that the Ashkenazi parties have strong financial backing from Histadrut concerns, the banks, and industry etc, and this is the source of their power, which is much more important than the parliamentary political organizations which represent them. Therefore, Sephardi political organization will remain without any financial footing and, according to Swirski, will thus not be able to effect any change in the social infrastructure of the country.

It does not occur to Swirski that an 'oriental' government might make peace with the Palestinian people, redistribute land for the benefit of its inhabitants and reorganise the economy to benefit the underprivileged – as happened in Algeria and Zimbabwe.

Swirski points out that even Sephardi uprisings, such as that at Wadi al-Salib in Haifa and in Jerusalem with the Black Panthers, will end up with promises, the improvement of services, the setting up of committees of enquiry, the expansion of the welfare budget and the absorption of some leaders. But the division of labour and the social structure will not change.

Swirski then recommends setting up an economic and organisational infrastructure under Sephardi governance, centred on the trade unions and places of residence, on the assumption that this will have an effect on the parliamentary and political level, enabling the Sephardim to participate in all strategic departments of the state.

The author also suggests that cooperatives be set up to run a slum improvement programme and the participation of Sephardim in ownership and control of the firms in development downs. He states that these cooperatives could wield enough economic influence to pressurise the government and to help ameliorate conditions in the Sephardi development towns. All the agricultural moshavim inhabited by Sephardim could form a federation either inside or outside the general moshav movement – then all these establishments and moshavim could unite in a national federation. On the subject of the Histadrut, the author suggests that the Sephardi majority change the institutions of the Histadrut, or secede from it and set up their own unions to work with the Arabs and the Ashkenazim. Swirski believes that in the slum districts teachers and social workers from the Sephardi community should be appointed, the school syllabus should be changed to revive Sephardi culture, and that some form of community service must be set up to deal with the problems of the Sephardim. Swirski claims that an 'oriental' economic and organizational foundation would represent a step forward not only toward ameliorating the conditions of Sephardim, but also toward renewing the original aspirations of the Zionist movement, that is, to create a society founded on 'justice and equality'. The author presents no proof to support his last claim.

Unlike the Communists and Trotskyists, the author says of the remark that the Sephardi struggle should be a general 'class struggle', that the class struggle in Israel cannot be compared to the class struggle in Britain, for example, where the bourgeoisie and the workers are from the same ethnic background. Economic development in Israel has not created a general class division but a division of labour along ethnic community lines. For this reason the 'class' struggle is not that of simple workers but of Sephardim since the bourgeoisie is Ashkenazi and the proletariat is Sephardi. This also applies to the Arab workers who are not like workers in Europe since they have been proletarianised by the policy of land confiscation and the non-development of the Arab areas, and accordingly theirs must be a national struggle. The Ashkenazi workers will not effect this struggle since they receive preferential wages. The left-wing parties do not defend the rights of the down-trodden Sephardim since they are taken up with nationalist matters. He does not mention that the parties, being Ashkenazi, benefit from ethnic discrimination – he only says that this merits a separate study.

Swirski warns that the Ashkenazi establishment might try to foil any plan to establish a Sephardi economic and organizational infrastructure by buying out Sephardi activists. This is exactly what has been happening since the beginning of Ashkenazi settlement. In addition to oppression, a policy of dismissals and impoverishment. Professor Swirski lives within the University of Haifa, does not experience this problem, and is unaware that conditions are much worse than he imagines. Even though he deconstructs many myths in his work, he is still influenced by the Zionist myth that the gulf between the Sephardim and the Ashkenazim is incompatible with the aspirations of the Zionist movement which aimed to establish 'a new Jewish society to be an example to the nations' – according to his own words.[37] I do not wish to refute this opinion by quoting the pronouncements of the Zionist bourgeoisie, right-wingers or capitalists, but I shall quote Ber Borochov (1881-1917) the ideological father of the Zionist Marxist Mapam Party: 'The foundation upon which our future society will be built, will be as follows: healthy Sephardi or Yemenite labourers who can be made into a proletariat, and a large number of diggers, camel-drivers and porters.'[38] Swirski's greatest contribution has been his analysis of the ethnic division of labour in Israel.

THE POLITICAL PARTIES' POSITIONS

The Ashkenazi Zionist parties – from the far left to the far right – form the ruling establishment in the state, private capital, the nationalised industries, the Histadrut and the World Zionist Organisation.

Fundamentally there are only tactical differences between the parties on the Palestinian issue or with regard to the Arab world and Sephardim.

The Zionist parties try to ignore the Sephardi problem since they believe that any discussion of the issue could shatter the 'unity of the people'. The official line is that there exist neither a problem nor discrimination, and that if there be a gulf, it is a transient phenomenon. In the lead-up to elections, the parties co-opt some workers from the ranks of the Sephardim, in the hope of winning Sephardi votes with promises. After the elections, everything reverts to normal.

We must point out, in this regard, that the right-wing nationalist Herut Party has exploited the hardships of the Sephardim by condemning discrimination. Some members have also treated Sephardim humanely, for reasons of national unity. This party, more than any other, has opened the doors to party advancement to the Sephardim, except for ministerial and parliamentary positions, which have remained mostly the preserve of Ashkenazim. The bitter struggle in 1986, between Polish Yitzhak Shamir and Moroccan David Levi, was not a personal struggle but one between two ethnic factions within the party. This does not mean that the Sephardi faction represents the interests of the Sephardim. In any case, the main reason why almost half of the Sephardi electorate voted for Menahem Begin in 1977 was the policy of discrimination followed by the Labour Party since 1948.

The Israeli Communist party wins 40 percent of the Palestinian vote inside the Israel of 1948's borders for, until the later emergence of Progressive List, it was the only party to represent the interests of the Palestinian people inside Israel. Arabs constituted more than 50 percent of the party cadres and members, and the rest were, and still are Ashkenazim. The Communist Party won a very small portion (perhaps 2 percent) of the Jewish vote, both Ashkenazi and Sephardi. Ashkenazim do not vote for the party for a number of reasons including its proclaimed anti-Zionism, and pro-Palestinian and pro-Soviet stance.

One can well wonder, why do the down-trodden amongst the Sephardim not vote for the Communist Party which has always defended them? We should consider the following reasons.

Whereas the Communist Party defends the Palestinians as a people and a working class simultaneously, it defends the Sephardim only as workers. The communist press which supports the slum areas, the development towns, the unemployed, etc., does not make any reference to them as an ethnic community suffering from racial discrimination. In the party newspaper, *Zu Haderekh*, of 19 March 1986, in which are described the conditions of the agricultural moshavim, the communists wrote that the rich moshavim might confiscate the property of the poor moshavim, but they did not mention that the rich moshavim were in fact Ashkenazi moshavim controlling most of the fertile land, whereas the poor moshavim were the ones with no economic foundation, into which the Sephardim had been crammed.

The communists ignore the ordeal of the educated and middle-class Sephardim, because they cannot fit them into the artificial mould of 'the working class'.

However, the Sephardim are not a 'working class', and they do not desire to be. The Sephardim who immigrated from the Middle East were merchants, professionals and artisans. The Sephardim who have become a working class in Israel were forced into it. They are not exploited by abstract capital, but by alien capitalists. According to Swirski, the situation in Britain, where the workers and the employers constitute the same ethnic group, does not apply to South Africa or Israel. If it were a class issue in Israel, the conditions of Ashkenazi workers would be comparable to those of the Sephardim.

The people who governed the Sephardim (and the Palestinians) and who destroyed them economically, socially and culturally from 1948 until 1977, were not capitalist but members of the Socialist Labour Party. During this period the conditions of the Ashkenazi workers improved at the expense of the Sephardim and the Palestinian people. Ashkenazi kibbutzim, more than businessmen, exploit Sephardim, and discrimination in state and Histadrut industrial projects is worse than that in the private sector. Unfortunately this situation is what pushed many Sephardim into joining the Likud.

The Sephardim are not just fighting for food, drink, clothing and housing, but against the extirpation of their culture. A crude theory of 'class struggle' excludes this.

On 14 January 1981 a Communist Party leader published an article, signed 'a Brother', in the newspaper *Zu Haderekh*. The 'Brother' ascribed Sephardi under-representation in the political apparatus to a lack of Sephardi capital, for, according to him, 'Israel is a bourgeois dictatorship.' If this explanation were correct, the Ashkenazi Labour Party would not have ruled Israel from 1948-1977. The 'Brother' tries, indirectly, to whitewash Israeli discrimination, by pointing out that discrimination in Israel is not enshrined in the law, as it is in South Africa (as if illegal discrimination is preferable . . .) The only concession which this party makes to the Sephardi community is the inclusion of four words in its lengthy resolutions: 'opposed to ethnic discrimination.'

From time to time, the communist press mentions that there are 'oriental communities' in addition to 'the working class', and compares them to 'Israeli society' (i.e. the Ashkenazim). This also means that the Communist Party, just like the other parties of the Zionist establishment, does not recognise the cultural unity of the Sephardim, just as Zionism does not recognise the unity of the Arab nation but supports Arab centrifugalism.

When Emil Habibi, a communist leader, was asked, at a meeting he convened in London a few years ago, about the Sephardim in Israel, he refused to answer, claiming that he was not knowledgeable on the subject! Which other communist leader is not knowledgeable about 80 percent of the 'working class' in his country?

When the president of the state of Israel attended the Communist Party Conference which was held in 1986, he praised the party for its defence of the 'foundations of the state of Israel'.

50 percent of the members of the Central Committee of the Israeli Communist Party are Palestinians, and 50 percent are Ashkenazi settlers. The same composition exists throughout the party apparatus, and means that the party institutions do not represent Sephardim.

THE STANCE OF THE ASHKENAZI FAR LEFT

In the seventies, the Ashkenazi far left supported the struggle of the Sephardim and helped the Black Panthers, but when they failed to dominate them they desisted. Subsequently some leftist extremists started to propagate a spirit of discord between Palestinian Arabs and the Sephardim, accusing the Sephardim of fascism, racism and hostility to the Arabs. This stance effectively prevents any solidarity between the two down-trodden communities and helps the Zionist establishment and the secret police.

THE KNESSET AND RACISM

On 26 May 1982 the Knesset rejected a resolution which would outlaw discrimination, incitement, the publication of hatred and the committing of acts of violence for racial or religious reasons. Voting against this resolution were the parties of the government coalition and the opposition Labour Party. The Marxist Zionist Mapam Party did not attend this session.[39]

In 1985, a parliamentary majority voted against a similar resolution on the basis that there was no need for such a law, since 'Israel is not racist.'

Finally, in May 1985 the Knesset did pass a law against racial incitement alone, but reserved the right of prosecution solely to the state and not to the persons involved. Racial discrimination carried out by the government or Zionist groups or individuals remained, as previously, not against the law. It is true that the Israeli declaration of independence in 1948 promised the citizens of the country equality, regardless of origin, religion or sex, etc., but this declaration has never been considered as the law and the Knesset has never accepted it as one of the state's precepts.

THE UN RESOLUTION 1976

It was due to the racist nature of the Zionist state of Israel that the General Assembly of the United Nations declared on November 10 1976 that 'Zionism is a form of racism and racial discrimination.'

The Moroccan Jew, Mikha'il al-Baz has said that 'this internal colonialism over Sephardim, which is based on Jewish ideology, has become legal owing to ongoing ethno-centricity. In this context, the emergence of a Sephardi ethnicity indicates the rejection of an inadequate Israeli identity and could become the catalyst for the formation of a society in which Arab and Jewish citizens are equal.'[40]

NOTES

1 *The Jewish State*, 30.
2 His article entitled, 'The East', 1926.
3 *Ha'aretz, 22 July 1983.*
4 *Ben Gurion, Netsah Yisrael*, 34, 'Ayyanot Publications, 1964.
5 Ibid, 17.
6 Arabic translation, 167.
7 *Netsah Yisrael*, 9, 14, 23, 34 and 37. Also, Zionist Executive Committee 1949, p 118.
8 Ben Gurion Archives, Diaries, 20 July 1949.
9 *Al Hamishmar*, 28 September 1981.
10 Ben Gurion to Judge Etzioni, 3 August 1959, Ben Gurion Archives.
11 Ben Gurion Archives, 27 November 1950.
12 Knesset Minutes, Volume 8, 1102, 14 February 1951.
13 *New York Times*, 25 October 1960, quoted by Elie Kedourie, 1970, 448.
14 Israeli press.
15 Quoting Dr Shitrit, *Al Hamishmar*, 28 September 1981.
16 Mikhail Albaz, *Les temps modernes*, 120.
17 Report by Sharett, 12 December 1948, State Archives, Ministry of Foreign Affairs – 130/11/2502/8. Quoted in Segev, p 183, Arabic translation.
18 *Society*, Part IX, May 1972, 42.
19 *Ha'aretz*, 21 May 1978.
20 *Ha'aretz Supplement*, 4 September 1981.
21 *Ha'aretz*, June 1987.
22 5 May 1952.
23 21 May 1952.
24 2 June 1952.
25 31 March 1951.
26 *Yom Hamillion*, Alterman, Volume I, 120.
27 *The Hill of Evil Counsel*, Am Oved, 1976 (Hebrew), 16 and *A Perfect Peace* (English), The Hogarth Press, 18.
28 12 April 1949, State Archives, Ministry of Foreign Affairs, 130.02/2447/3.
29 *Shevet va'am*, 1959.
30 *Life with the Jews*, 413.
31 *Shevet va'am*, 1959.
32 *Shevet va'am*, 1960.
33 *Ha'aretz*, 23 April 1982.
34 *Megamot* B/3, April 1951, and also issues B/4 and C/1, and weekly supplement to *Ha'aretz*, 19 March 1982.
35 *Mahbarot lemehkar ulevikoret*, No. 4, 7.
36 1981.
37 Swirski, 1981, 361.
38 *The Question of Zion and the Country, Selected Works* (Hebrew), vol. 1, Am Oved Publications, Da'at Library, 1944.
39 *Zu Haderekh*, 2 June 1982.
40 *Les temps modernes*, 125.

CHAPTER NINE

Economic Development, Exploitation And Polarisation

We have seen in chapter five how the Zionist establishment made a 'working class' of 750,000 Sephardim from countries in the Middle East and North Africa in its camps of various kinds. In this chapter, I shall explain how both 'Socialist' and capitalist Ashkenazi Israel exploited them for the sake of its economic development and political domination and go on to the social polarisation which has resulted from this policy.

1. INDUSTRIAL DEVELOPMENT

During the British Mandate, Zionist industry was under-developed. It had a small workforce and market and lacked investment and modern equipment. Its small factories concentrated in the main on assembling imported components. After the founding of the state of Israel, the Arab-Islamic countries furnished Israel with hundreds of thousands of workers, and it is these people, in addition to those who came from the socialist countries, who expanded the consumer market. This mass immigration helped Israel to import funds in the form of Jewish donations, American grants and German reparations, etc. Thus Israel was provided with all the necessary conditions for rapid economic development: a work force, funds and a consumer market.

The percentage of the development budget of the government's budget invested by the government in industry was as follows:
1948-1953   11 percent
1954-1955   16 percent

1956-1959   19 percent

Between 1955-1958 17.5 percent of imported machinery came from Germany as reparations,[1] and in 1958 the Bank for Economic Development was founded.

As a result of this economic policy, between 1959-1965 the number of workers in industry averaged 25 percent of the total work force. Unemployment went down from 9 percent in the fifties to 4 percent starting from 1961. The basic catalyst for this speedy development was access to cheap labour, which helped business owners to reap massive profits. Between 1958-1963, which was a period of speedy industrialisation, the distance between top and bottom incomes widened considerably.[2]

Those who benefitted from the state policy of industrialisation were private and Histadrut projects which were controlled by Ashkenazi settlers and which received enormous sums of state money in the form of low-interest loans, paid low taxes and enjoyed various financial inducements, not to mention access to armies of cheap labour.

By dint of this industrial development a new Ashkenazi class came into being – a service stratum of engineers, managers and university teachers who trained and taught the specialists, the marketing people and bankers, etc. By 1975 this class formed 32.4 percent of the total Ashkenazi work force (compared with only 11.8 percent Sephardim who were second-grade compared to Ashkenazi officials and managers). This gulf between the ethnic groups widened in the generation of those born in Palestine, with 42 percent Ashkenazim and only 12.5 percent Sephardim.[3] Clearly, this accelerated industrialisation enabled relatively lowly Ashkenazim to ascend the socio-economic ladder on the backs of the Sephardim.

The gulf in the working class can be seen in the following figures: 25.5 percent of Ashkenazim work as labourers (generally skilled), and 42.1 percent of Sephardim (generally unskilled). The gap is greater among the generation born in Palestine: 17.4 percent Ashkenazim and 42.4 percent Sephardim.[4] Even the Sephardim who have managed to scale the Ashkenazi fortress and gain government positions only form a servile sector in the ruling Ashkenazi aristocracy.

By 1965 there were 43,750 workers in the textile industry, that is, double the number of 1955, and this caused production to rise by 250 percent.[5] The value of exports went up from $5.7 million to $46.6 million over the same period.[6]

The establishment favoured the textile industry because of the low investment needed for its development, the large profits it produced and the existence of a proletariat in the development towns such as Dimona, Kiryat Shemoneh, Ofakim and Kiryat Gad, etc.

The number of workers in the clothing industry went up from 13,490 in 1961 to 30,590 in 1972. The number of Sephardi workers in this industry went up four times whereas the number of Ashkenazim only went up by 170 percent.[7] Wages were less than the national average and Sephardim had leadership positions in only 46 out of 334 factories. All the large factories were controlled by Ashkenazi settlers.[8]

There were 168 metal factories with more than 80 employees, whereas there had only been 28 prior to the founding of Israel.[9] Most of the metal factories were controlled by Ashkenazi companies such as Kur, Klal, the Investment Company of Bank Discount, etc. Only 17 of the 170 metal factories employing more than 80 people were controlled by Sephardim and these were effectively subsidiaries of the large firms.[10]

Ashkenazi would-be entrepreneurs were actively assisted by the state. At the end of the sixties, the government gave the owners of the diamond industry easy low interest loans for up to 80 percent of the cost of their raw materials and 90 percent of exports costs and helped them to find and train their work force. Subsequently profits went up 360 times (1949-1970) and production went up from I£2 million to I£700 million over the same period, that is 350 times and the number of workers rose from 800 to 9,500.[11] Ashkenazi capitalism has been massively state-aided.

2. THE DEVELOPMENT OF THE CONSTRUCTION INDUSTRY

Mass immigration led to the development of the construction industry to the extent where 18-19 percent of the gross national product was invested in it, compared to 9-13 percent in Western Europe in the period 1956-1965. 10 percent of the work force was involved in construction and new housing units increased from 843,000m^2 to 3,373,000m^2 over the period 1949-1962.[12]

This branch of the economy can be divided into two parts: the public sector, that is housing built by the state, local authorities and Zionist agencies; and the private sector, that is housing built by private capital. Naturally, private capital built better and much more spacious housing, which was specifically for privileged new immigrants. The public sector built shoddy, small dwellings for Sephardim, even though they had much larger families than the Ashkenazim. The flats allotted to Sephardim had a ground area of between 45 and 61m^2 over the period 1955-1965, whereas an Ashkenazi family was allotted between 75-92m^2.[13]

Additionally, the Histadrut undertook the construction of 70,000 luxury dwellings for Ashkenazim[14] in the central districts of the country. Sephardi housing was constructed in remote areas and they had to pay a 65 percent cash deposit with the remainder to be paid over instalments carrying a high interest rate. Moreover, in these remote districts the Sephardim had to pay an additional sum of 22 percent for roads, the development of neighbouring lands, the construction of a sewer system and an electricity network. The work force used in this construction activity was made up overwhelmingly of Sephardim and Palestinians, particularly in the unskilled jobs (that is, 'black work'). Exploitation in this field was particularly ugly, since the labourers worked intermittently and were considered 'non-permanent'. Even Solel Boneh, the Histadrut company, employed 70-80 percent of its construction labour on a non-permanent basis and paid them less than Ashkenazim who worked in Histadrut cooperative industry. Accordingly, the Histadrut gained greater profits from construction than from all other branches of production, particularly cooperative industry (36 percent against 11.5 percent from cooperative industry).

Avraham Cohen stated that state sector and Histadrut construction in 1960 produced returns of 30-35 percent profit compared to 60 percent in the private sector.[15] One of the phenomena of economic development in this area was the emergence of the Histadrut company, Solel Boneh, as a powerful force – not only in Israel but also in third world countries – extending Israeli influence and building military bases for the Americans in Turkey and elsewhere. In 1948 the turnover of this company was I£5 million and by 1953 it was I£60 million. In 1958 the Kur company, which supplies South Africa with arms, broke away from Solel Boneh.

Construction activity was paralleled by the emergence of new banks to form a link between the government housing companies and the residents of the new housing developments. One of these banks is the Mishkanta'ot Leshikun Bank (Mortgage Bank) which the Histadrut set up in 1951. Banking activity expanded along with their funds and profits – all under Ashkenazi control. We must also add that industrial development, particularly in the metals industries, helped the development of the military armaments industry to the extent that Israel is now a major arms-exporting country, particularly to countries where Israeli weaponry has killed many innocents.

3. AGRICULTURAL DEVELOPMENT

Mass immigration necessitated increased food production. Citrus production used 250,000 *dunums* in 1945, which figure rose to 430,000 *dunums* by 1978, whereas other agricultural lands rose from 1,650 million *dunums* in 1948 to 4,110 million *dunums* in 1958. These figures include expropriated Arab lands, that is the lands of the refugees and also the Palestinians who remained in Israel. During this period, vegetable production went up 330 percent, egg production by 240 percent, milk by 330 percent and wheat by 340 percent, and the number of tractors rose by 510 percent. This development took place at a time when the population doubled in size. (Israeli sources ignore the fact that this population increase was equal to the number of Palestinians expelled from their homes.) Moreover, the government undertook irrigation and afforestation works, soil improvement, the revival of the citrus industry and the exploitation of Arab lands.

The value of agricultural production went up from I£274.2 million in 1949 to I£586.5 million over the following five years, and then doubled again by 1959. Exports went up from $18 million in 1949 to $35 million in 1964. Investment in agriculture went up 300 percent between 1948-1965, and Israel thus managed to supply its inhabitants with the necessary vegetables, and to develop the citrus and industrial agricultural produce as well as its livestock and poultry industries. Between 1958-1960, the new moshavim produced approximately 60 percent of total vegetable production, 42 percent of fodder, 46 percent of sugar cane and pistachio, 35 percent of milk production, and 25 percent of poultry products. All other production took place on the rich 'veteran' settlements which used low-paid Sephardim and Palestinians to expand their production and profits, particularly for the seasonal work involved in fruit-picking and the agricultural products used for industry, such as cotton. The citrus workers were often paid 'emergency wages'. These workers earned I£28 per month, compared to I£40 for a construction worker, and I£41 for a factory worker. Profits from citrus-growing multiplied, as a result of state support and the modern equipment which Israel had received American loans to buy. Between 1956-1959 the turnover per *dunum* was I£450 of which I£210 was profit. The children of the Palestinians and Sephardim who worked on these plantation often went hungry. I would go so far as to say that seasonal work in agriculture was the greatest dividing factor between the Ashkenazi oppressor and the Palestinian and Sephardi underclass.

In addition to the citrus industry, exploitation was also widespread in the cultivation of commodities, such as cotton, sugar and olives – in spite of state support paid to the owners of these businesses.

Agriculture helped the state budget. Cotton, for example, was first cultivated in 1954. After only 10 years the area of land dedicated to cotton was 129,500 *dunums*, production reached almost 20,000 tons, and the profit was I£92 per *dunum*. Sugar cane and pistachio cultivation developed along the same lines, using modern machinery, and cheap labour, particularly on the Ashkenazi kibbutzim.

In addition, the Ministry of Labour used Sephardim for irrigation and afforestation works and to drain Lake Hula, which gave the kibbutzim 40,000 extra *dunums*, and for which works the government paid 'emergency wages'.

Agricultural development was paralleled by the expansion of various services such as marketing (the Tnuva and Ha-mashbir companies), export projects, industries linked with agriculture, banks and financial institutions. All the former, along with the employers, earned huge profits.[16]

4. THE DEVELOPMENT OF THE GOVERNMENT APPARATUS

Mass immigration together with its high birth rate, necessitated the expansion of the government apparatus. This enabled the Ashkenazi settlers to better themselves and occupy the highest positions of the state, including the government, the army, the Histadrut and the Jewish Agency. In addition, the poverty of the Sephardim necessitated the establishment of welfare institutions and prisons to deal with their social and economic problems. Most of the officials of these institutions were members of the settler community, and the situation was the same in education where the number of students rose from 140,000 pupils in 1948 to 540,000 in 1958.[17] This created thousands of well-paid jobs for the Ashkenazi settlers (see chapters six and seven). Dispersal, the destruction of families and traditions and the degrading life in the camps, unemployment and poverty all led to disaffection among the young, prostitution, drug addiction, divorce, crime and other social problems. 90 percent of those in need of welfare services are Sephardim, and 90 percent of the welfare officers are Ashkenazim!

Israel set up four special educational institutes in the universities to train social workers. Instructors were appointed, which meant more jobs for Ashkenazi intellectuals and social workers who were inculcated with reactionary and discriminatory social theories.

Consequently, four distinct social groups came into existence in Israel. They are:

1. The state apparatus, which includes the government, the Histadrut, the army and the Jewish Agency.
2. Business owners and bankers.
3. Engineers, professionals and skilled workers.
4. Semi-skilled and unskilled workers, the prison population, the unemployed, the marginal sub-cultures, etc.

The first three groups are in essence the Ashkenazi community, whereas the lowest group is in the main the Middle Easterners – that is, the Sephardim and their Palestinian brethren. In every Israeli establishment the whites are on top, with very few exceptions. Mass immigration from the Middle East (and Eastern Europe) helped the Ashkenazim to secure their economic, political and military position.

In a lecture he gave to soldiers on how to suppress the identity of the Arabs in the occupied territories, the American (Ashkenazi) officer who specialised in psychological warfare said, 'The Arabs have to be trained the way a man trains a dog.' When an Ashkenazi soldier asked him if this was also applicable to the Sephardim who had come from Arab countries, the officer replied, 'Yes! Most of them are like the Arabs, but if we do our utmost, many real Jews will come from the United States.'[18]

ELIACHAR'S WARNING

Zionist history in Palestine is characterised by provocation, polarisation and explosion. This does not apply solely to relations between the Ashkenazim and Sephardim but also to those with the Palestinians. The struggle of the Palestinians started with the Ashkenazim only, but it was escalated to become a general Jewish/ Arab schism, and thence an international quarrel with the threat of nuclear war.

The harsh conditions for Sephardim in the Zionist camps and the aforementioned speedy economic developments, led to a quickening of ethnic polarisation. This was not a post-1948 phenomenon, but had been in existence since the very beginning of the Ashkenazi Zionist presence in Palestine, as we have described in previous chapters.

On 30 November 1941, the greatest intellectual of the Zionist labour movement, Berl Katsnelson, wrote in *Hapo'el Hatza'ir*[19] that 'the Ashkenazi workers organized within the Histadrut [the General Trade Union Federation] form a quasi-aristocracy in comparison to the Sephardi worker who lives on the fringes of the Histadrut. This deprived class will one day rise up against the Histadrut if its conditions are not improved.' Eliahu Eliachar, the leader of the Jerusalem Sephardim, quoted this statement (of Katsnelson), but commented that since its publication the conditions of Sephardim had become ten times worse.[20]

In his article,[21] Eliachar wrote that 'anyone can absorb Western technology if he is given the opportunity, as Sephardi intellectuals have proved.' Eliachar dramatically accused the Zionist establishment and its agents within the Sephardi community of being responsible for the spread of misery and suffering, starting each sentence with the words 'I accuse.'[22]

Eliachar blames the Ashkenazi leaders who have wasted millions of the state's funds instead of using them to solve economic problems such as poverty and housing. He apportions blame for the spread of prostitution to Sephardi girls, pointing out that there are more than 200 of them. He emphasises that prostitution was non-existent amongst Sephardim before they came to Israel. He mentions that he asked the Ministry of Finance for a credit of I£30 million to improve housing conditions, but the Ministry turned down the request. He adds that the leaders have built palaces for themselves instead of granting free secondary and university education.

Eliachar goes on to say that whereas the state encourages Sephardi families to have many children, it neither helps them nor invests more than a paltry percentage of its I£10 billion annual budget in this. At the same time, the state uses the children from these families for compulsory military service. Representatives of Israel abroad make much of the miserable conditions of the Sephardi families to raise funds for the state. Eliachar criticises Sephardim who have accepted token or honorary positions in government, but who do not help their own community, and have objected to the establishment of a non-political organization to defend Sephardi rights.

Eliachar enumerates the organisations which Sephardim have set up in Palestine since the British Mandate, and ascribes to the Zionist establishment the failure of them all and its strengthening of narrow sectarian, class and party hegemony which has led to the non-representation of Sephardim in the higher institutions of the state, with the exception of the Minister of Police, Bekhor Shitrit, who represented the Mapai Party.

Eliachar warns that the continued state of poverty and grievances amongst the Sephardim represent a danger to the security of the state, for most of the army is made up of Sephardim. He demands the establishment of an organization to work on bridging the gap between the communities. He warns that 'in the future, there could well arise a group of demagogues bent on inciting the down-trodden Sephardi masses.' Nilly Arkin warns that poverty, cultural backwardness and degrading living conditions would affect the military capability of the young generation and that those children might constitute a danger for Israel in the future.

We should draw the reader's attention to the fact that Israeli militarism has reached a point where one cannot speak of right and wrong, but only in terms of 'security'. Those who have tried to bring up the subject of discrimination have been labelled traitors, and only the euphemism 'gap' is used to hint at the great divide.

BEGIN AND THE SLUM
REHABILITATION PROJECT

When the state of Israel came into existence in 1948, Begin was the leader of a small right-wing party called Herut (Freedom). Begin knew that he would only be able to defeat the 'Labour' establishment which had governed the settler community for many years by exploiting the anger of the Sephardim. He promised to set up a new system built upon total ethnic equality, not only in the state but within his party also (this party together with business interests and liberals formed a right-wing bloc called Likud). Begin spread the fiction that he was 'Moroccan' whereas he was in fact Polish, having fled at the beginning of the Second World War from the Polish nationalist army to Palestine where he led the Irgun. In 1977, Begin finally managed to win a large portion of the Sephardi vote because of his calls for equality – and not because of his anti-Arab policy. He formed the first right-wing government (the Labour government had been no less hostile to the Arabs than Begin, being the government which had expelled the Palestinian people, destroyed hundreds of Arab villages and towns, expropriated the lands and property of the Arabs in 1948 and annexed a large part of the Palestinian territories (according to United Nations declarations), invaded Sinai in 1956 and occupied the West Bank, Sinai and the Golan in 1967 etc.).

In 1978 Begin started a new programme to 'improve the people's conditions', as he had promised. This programme was called the 'Slum Rehabilitation Project'. It took in 169 slum areas, including the Black Belt areas of the large cities, the development towns and the bankrupt 'cooperative' villages. *Ha'aretz* wrote on 5 January 1979 that the number of inhabitants in these areas was 300,000 and that $1.2 million dollars had been set aside for the first stage of the project. Begin's government agreed to match the contributions of American Jews to this project.

It soon emerged that the project was a complete failure. It had only tidied up a few sites in the slum districts, and most of those who had benefitted from the project were Ashkenazim.

This came about because the government refused to allow the Sephardim involved to elect their own committees to run the project and to spend the funds on the necessary housing, jobs and education, etc. The government instead set up an enormous bureaucracy of Ashkenazi officials co-opted from various authorities, such as the central government, local authorities, the Jewish Agency, etc. Amongst these committees were a Ministerial Committee, a Civil Service Committee, with a Project Comptroller in the Prime Minister's Office, a Project Director in the Jewish Agency and a Project Director in the Ministry of Labour and Social Services. On the local level there was participation by the following committees and individuals: Director of the Steering Committee, Director of Construction and Housing, municipal employees, and civil servants from various districts who dealt with matters of housing, education, labour and health. The central government supplied experts in geography, sociology and engineering, and the Amidar and Amigur

Housing Companies played an active role.

When these bureaucracies became aware of the vast sums of money and the political influence which the money brought with it, a mighty struggle broke out amongst the various agencies vying to control the project.

Out of I£400 million budgeted for 1978, I£200 million were set aside for public buildings, and another sum to pay the salaries of Ashkenazi experts. Only a small sum was set aside for services to the slum districts.[23]

The Israeli press reported that 60 percent of the project's funds were paid out as salaries to the army of Ashkenazi officials, and that most of the remaining funds were spent on sprucing up the slum districts with public buildings, and parks to impress foreign visitors, instead of being spent on building residential units, ameliorating living conditions and fighting unemployment, delinquency, crime and disaffection.

The local authorities, which are controlled by the Ashkenazim, started to spend more and more on Ashkenazi neighbourhoods, at the expense of municipal services to the poor districts. The municipalities thus managed indirectly to exploit the project to improve Ashkenazi areas. The residents of Shekhunat Hatikvah in Tel Aviv for example say that the Art College which was set up in the district used up a large amount of project funds, even though students at the college are Ashkenazim who commute from the rich suburbs. The residents of the district demanded that the college be moved away, and recently the municipality agreed to this.[24]

In addition to this, the central government started to make cuts in the social services budget. Local authorities then had to turn to the Slum Rehabilitation Project to ask for financial help. This practice enabled the central government to spend more of the funds on Ashkenazi settlements in the occupied territories.

On 4 April 1980, *Ha'aretz* wrote that the residents of the Amidar district had left the project's steering committee, because they were only represented by 4 out of the 24 members, and they wished to take the initiative. The newspaper on 23 May 1980 quoted residents of the poor districts in Kiryat Ata who claimed that the project only served to give employment to Ashkenazim and who demanded that local committees be set up to administer the project. After describing the harsh conditions in the slum districts, the newspaper wrote that the Sephardim were threatening to carry out a 'revolution' together with the Sephardim in the slum district of Tel Hanan and Tirat Hacarmel, and the Ohalim organization in

Jerusalem. The newspaper added that in one building there were 200 children who had to play in the street because there was no garden for them to play in, and that the neighbourhood was full of crime, drug addiction and prostitution.

On 1 August 1980, the historian Tom Segev published an article in *Ha'aretz*, under the heading 'It's all a big cheat!', in which he described these developments and affirmed that 'it all exists on paper only'. He enumerated all the departments involved in the project and described their ongoing quarrels. He stressed cuts were being made in the social services budget by the government, that some committee chairmen had enriched themselves through this project and that much money was being spent on 'window-dressing for propaganda purposes'.

On 8 October 1980, *Zu Haderekh* wrote that 'out of the $6 million collected in America for this project, the government only spent $700,000 by February 1980 – the rest having been swallowed up by the (Ashkenazi) bureaucracy.'

The most important article written on this subject, appeared in *Ha'aretz* on 29 January 1982. It was by Ze'ev Yefet and appeared under the headline 'The Flight of the Budget'. Yefet wrote that the project administrators had built incomplete pavements in the slum districts of Kfar Saba. In Ashdod they set up a large park at a great distance from the slum area. In Amidar at Ramat Gan, they planted flowers instead of treating the problems of housing, crime and violence. He wrote that the mayors control the project, and it is they who have ignored these districts for many years. They have now taken over the project's funds and spend them as they wish. Some municipalities spend the project's funds to provide the regular services which should fall under the municipalities' own budgets. In D Street in Jaffa, for example, there is a music conservatory which used to be funded by Tel Aviv, but the mayor, Mr Lahat, declared that from now on the municipality could not afford to fund it, and that the 'Project' had to support it. Leaders of the Social Services' Workers Union say that the municipalities dismiss their employees in order to re-employ them again on the payroll of the Slum Rehabilitation Project. In Bet Shemesh, the local council received 300,000 shekels from the project, and spent it on garbage collection. In Kadima the Ministry of the Interior reduced its financial help by 800,000 shekels claiming that the municipality could receive this sum from the project. Out of the 6 million shekels set aside for the project, 3 million shekels are spent on regular government services which do not do anything for 'Slum

Rehabilitation'. At Hatzor in the Galilee, the government stopped paying the extra cost of afternoon school hours and the project was forced to step in. In Safad the Ministries of the Interior and of Housing cut back the regular budget and demanded that the Mayor use project money instead. The project has also had to fund the intermediate classes in secondary schools, instead of the Ministry of Education, and this Ministry has cancelled other educational programmes which were intended to help Sephardim.

After these shocking facts were published, the government declared that funds invested in the project had reached $600 million, that 50,000 apartments had been renovated and 20,000 apartments enlarged. The government did not disclose the meagre part of the total $600 million that it used for this. Its communiqué only mentioned that the government spent project funds to set up clinics, nurseries, sports centres and public buildings[25] – which should all have been built with funds from its own budget and not with project funds.

Thus the Slum Rehabilitation Project met its demise, and the remaining funds were swallowed up by central government, the municipalities and the Ashkenazi apparatus. Menahem Begin, the Prime Minister who had come to rescue Sephardim from injustice and oppression, saw all of this but took no positive action (while he was Prime Minister). He simply sent the slum children off into the army, perhaps to die in the Lebanese war, and it may have been this last fact which led to his physical and psychological breakdown.

In her report for 1984/85, Rina Gottman, the Jewish Agency Comptroller, did not publish the serious shortfalls in the project administration. However, she admitted that posts were not advertised. The project administration did not look too carefully at the qualifications of its officials, and there was no system of prioritising the project's various schemes in progress. The Jewish Agency has spent $175 million to date.[26]

POLARISATION

In addition to the failure of the Slum Rehabilitation Project, the policy of economic 'opening-up' which has been taken by the Likud governments has led to the increased polarisation between the two Jewish communities (except for a small group of Sephardim which has managed to better itself and has joined the small bourgeois class of restauranteurs, garage and boutique owners and which has accordingly linked its fate to the Likud bloc for economic reasons).

As for the recent economic crisis in Israel, as part of the Western world, the Sephardim and Palestinians were the main victims.

Moreover, the severance of all trade relations between Israel and the Islamic Republic of Iran including the imports of oil, has resulted in closure of all the Israeli factories which exported to Iran before the revolution.

To make matters worse, there was the invasion of Lebanon whose cost Israel offset by cutting back social and educational services, etc.

The setting up of Ashkenazi settlements in the Arab territories occupied after 1967, and 'defence' expenses in addition to debt repayments took up two thirds of the state budget.[27] In the 1986 budget, this amount was 69.2 percent whereas social and municipal services were allocated only 17.8 percent of the state budget.[28]

Consequently, unemployment, cut-backs in food subsidies, inflation and the concomitant erosion of wages worsened. *The Times*[29] pointed out inflation was running at almost 1,000 percent, and that the new economic programme included reducing inflation by 30 percent, cutting the budget by $500 million and reducing the work force in the public sector by 10 percent, that is 14,000 workers. The newspaper reported that there was a danger of violence spreading and damage to the regime owing to its austerity policy and that the police were drawing up plans to deal with this. In September 1981, the monthly expenses of a family with 3.4 members living in a city were 8,898 shekels. By September 1984 this amount had reached 257,000 shekels.[30] A vendor in one of the large markets told a correspondent of *The Times* that 'people are ready to kill over a frozen chicken.' *The Times* correspondent did not mention the expenses of the large families.

There is no doubt that the percentage of Sephardim who live below the poverty line had doubled since Begin's accession to power in 1977. Charlie Biton, MP, stated that between 1977-1979 this section of the community had increased by 78 percent, and that the reduction of taxes on consumer luxuries such as cars and televisions had not helped the down-trodden. At the same time, the government was paying reparations of $100,000 to Ashkenazi settler families who left Sinai – in total a sum which could have been used to build 17,000 residential units for the poor.[31]

The annual statement of the state Social Security Institute in 1980 added that during the Likud administration (1977-1980) the gap deepened and that the number of babies born in poverty doubled. There was an increase of 300 percent in the number of families with

4-5 children below the poverty line. These families came to form 11.7 percent of the national total. Families with more than 5 children below the poverty line increased by 400 percent, forming together 25 percent of the national total. The report stated that one of the reasons for this phenomenon was the abolition of some taxes which had been previously imposed on the rich (property, commercial and inheritance taxes, etc.) The Liberal MP, Amnon Rubeinstein, described this poverty as 'a time bomb placed in our midst by Begin.'[32]

In 1977 3.8 percent of children, that is 28,200, were living below the poverty line. By 1981 this figure was 8.4 percent, or 67,000.[33] The Milk Marketing Board stated that since the government withdrew its subsidy, milk sales had gone down by 13-29 percent. The Ichilov Hospital in Tel Aviv said that it had started treating children for malnutrition.[34]

We must mention that the poverty line in Israel is lower than that in Western countries, and that the families who live below it in Israel are those who earn less than £36 sterling per month. There were 547,000 such people in 1983,[35] that is 13 percent of the population. On 22 May 1985 the Central Office of Statistics published a special report on workers' income, in which it stated that the standard of living of most labourers had gone down in 1983/84. The income of rich and middle-class (Ashkenazi) families had dropped by 1.5 percent whereas that of the (Sephardi) bottom tenth of the population had fallen by 11.5 percent.[36]

When Israeli (that is, Ashkenazi) sources speak of the poor and the inhabitants of the development towns and slum districts, they do not mention that they are Sephardim for reasons of 'national unity'. Instead, they make out that the problem is purely a gap between the rich and the poor.

The Moroccan intellectual, Mikhail al-Baz, said that 'the dependency of Sephardim on the welfare institutions of the state is becoming more acute from one generation to the next. In 1964, 34.5 percent of families in the development towns were in need of welfare payments, compared to 17.4 percent nationally. By 1973 the number of destitute went up. 40.3 percent of the destitute were concentrated in the development towns even though these towns only held 17 percent of the Israeli population.' Al-Baz adds that 83 percent of elementary school pupils have comprehension difficulties, compared to 45 percent nationwide.[37] Al-Baz concluded that ethnic inequality is institutionalised.[38]

Even Ashkenazi intellectuals admitted these facts ten years before al–Baz wrote his comments. Yonah Rosenfeld and Avraham Zlatschwi stated in 1965 that the ethnic inequality tended to increase in the Israeli-born generations.

Zionist propagandists say that the condition of the Sephardim has improved in Israel in comparison to their previous condition in their countries of origin but DrYa'akov Nahon disproved this statement. In his analysis, which was published by the Jerusalem Institute for Israeli Research, Dr Nahon demonstrated that the number of Ashkenazi white collar workers had increased by 90 percent compared to the number of Sephardim while the number of the blue collar Sephardim had gone up by 90 percent! There were five times more Ashkenazim in academic positions than Sephardim. When it came to the menial jobs, there were 200–350 percent more Sephardim than Ashkenazim.[39] If there is any hint of equality, it is only to be found amongst the petits bourgeois who represent 18 percent of both ethnic groups.

Poverty and polarisation have worsened to the extent that Hesqel San'ani, of Yemenite origin, declared that he was prepared to sell his eye and kidney in order to buy a flat instead of having to sleep in buses, as he had done for the past eight years. Sara Barneya declared that she would sell her unborn baby to be able to buy a small one-and-a-half room flat.[40]

Yohanan Peres, a social scientist, observed that the ethnic and social gulf in Israel was greater than in any other country in the world, including the United States.[41] In 1984 the rate of pay for one hour's labour in the United States was $13 and in Canada it was $11.5, whereas in Israel it was only $4.5.[42] These figures are for the average and this is always misleading since the Sephardi and Palestinian masses earn wages much lower than the average.

Dr Yohanan Peres suggests, 'If we do not eradicate the sectarian gap, the preponderant feelings of injustice may well lead to a destructive explosion'.[43] He added that 'the second generation [of Sephardim], born in Israel, is more aware of injustice than the first foreign-born generation . . . [44] He wrote that an average Ashkenazi family had an income 400 percent greater than that of an average Sephardi family,[45] and that 'the sectarian gap between the whites and the blacks in the United States in the area of labour, the professions, administrative and technical jobs is less acute than it is in Israel.'[46]

The number of Israelis who married outside their community was 18.5 percent in 1971,[47] but this does not mean that the two communities are moving towards integration. It signifies just the opposite – that 81.5 percent of Israelis do not marry spouses from the other community. Moreover, those who do intermarry, marry partners from the same social class.

Travelling from Haifa to Marseilles on a Turkish ship, most of whose passengers were Israelis, both Ashkenazim and Sephardim. . . I noted that when we first set off, relations between the two groups were restrained but correct and the Sephardim spoke amongst themselves of their lives and work in Israel, and then about their problems in Israel. Gradually the conversation turned to their hardships and finally they all said that if they found suitable work in France they would stay there. Contact with the Ashkenazim cooled as we approached Marseilles, and when we disembarked the Ashkenazim and Sephardim formed separate groups, hired separate taxis and parted without a word. In London there are many Israelis, from both communities, and I have seen little evidence of friendly relations between them.

The deepening of the gap between the two communities in the Israeli-born second generation in the 'upper classes' is to be noted. 12.9 percent of Sephardi immigrants (1977) belong to this group, compared to 30.9 percent of Ashkenazim. In the Israeli-born generation the relative figures are 14.6 percent compared to 45.6 percent. These figures also prove that the downward trend amongst the Sephardim is an Israeli-created phenomenon.

Break-down of Occupations amongst the Jewish population according to ethnic origin[48]

Occupation	Born in Africa & Asia		Born in Europe & America		Born in Israel of Sephardi Origin		Born in Israel Ashkenazi Origin	
	%		%		%		%	
	1974	1977	1974	1977	1974	1977	1974	1977
Liberal, technical, and managerial professions	11.4	12.9	27.8	30.9	11	14.6	41.4	45.6
Services and commerce	39	41.5	28	28.2	40.6	43.1	33.8	31.1
Agricultural, and skilled and unskilled labourers	39.5	45.7	34.2	30.8	48.4	42.1	24.8	22.2
Total (000s)	306.7	302.6	393.3	390.2	91.9	122.5	150.8	75.2
Total (%)	100	100	100	100	100	100	100	100

The reality is much worse, since in every occupational class the Sephardim are normally at the bottom.

The disparity in income can be seen in the following table. It can be shown clearly that the disparity in income appears among the higher grades. At the lower end of the wage scale in 1966, wages were only 30 percent of the national average, that is ten times less than the highest wages.

Segments of the population[49]	9–12 years of education		Over 13 years of education	
	Sephardim	Ashkenazim	Sephardim	Ashkenazim
Lowest fifth	10.8	12.0	15.5	7.6
Second fifth	21.6	16.4	8.5	9.7
Third fifth	26.0	17.3	9.9	13.0
Fourth fifth	24.6	24.8	36.6	23.2
Top fifth	17.0	29.5	27.3	46.5
TOTAL	100	100	100	100

The picture is worse if we take into account the income of Sephardim who did not have a chance to finish 9 years of education. In 1979 19 percent of the Israeli population (that is 445,000 people) were classified as poor, and 75 percent of whom were Sephardi. According to G. Habib's statistics, 78 percent of poor children, (92 percent according to Katz) come from large Sephardi families. Their misery was not relieved by the welfare payments they received, for these were only 43 percent of the national average.[50]

The report on income prepared by the Social Policy Research Centre stated that the distribution of income in Israel was just less that in the Western countries.[51] Those in the top tenth of the income scale (excluding businessmen) – generally Ashkenazim – earn 40 percent of the total income for all workers. The richest 1 percent of the population in 1984 controlled more than 11.5 percent of total national income.[52] Data point to the fact that the rich (Ashkenazim) are earning more, and in 1980 their average individual income reached $86,900. By 1984 it had reached $100,700.

The polarisation of the Ashkenazi settler community on the one hand, and the Sephardim and Palestinians on the other, becomes apparent in the sample data on family income: on the first and second lowest rungs of the social ladder the average family income was $150–200 per month in 1984 (mostly Sephardim and Palestinians). On the sixth rung, family income was $500 per month, on the eight rung $900 (generally Ashkenazim) and in the ninth rung it was $1,200 per month (generally Ashkenazim).[53]

The latest official data confirm that poverty is spreading amongst

Sephardim and Palestinians. The newspaper *Yedi'ot Aharonot* quoted official sources that 'the number of people who live below the poverty line has reached 267,000, of whom 120,000 are children. Their number increased by 25 percent during 1983 and 1984.'[54] Since the beginning of 1985, the new economic policy has led to wages being eroded by 35–40 percent. The minimum wage has gone down from 40 percent to 23 percent of the average wage. Unemployment has gone up to a national average of 10 percent, but in Sephardi and Palestinian districts it is 30–40 percent. Steps are continually being taken to cut back the amount of welfare payments, child support and other educational and social services. (In Beer Sheba, for example, the Soroka Hospital admits 300 children a month, including 20–30 who, because of the extent of their malnutrition, look like concentration camp children. These are the children of Sephardim, Palestinians and American Black Hebrews.)[55]

CRIME AND TORTURE

The reader may wonder: How is it that the Sephardim have accepted the Ashkenazi Zionist régime? Did they accept it as a *fait accompli*, or did they struggle?

Defeatists surrendered and accepted what the Ashkenazi chose to give them. A large portion of this group belonged to the rich and middle classes and is relatively very small.

The group of Eliahu Eliachar, which belonged to the native Jewish 'aristocracy', struggled and compromised at one and the same time, and failed abysmally. Another group of the native Jewish 'aristocracy', which included Bekhor Shitrit (former Minister of Police) and Yitzhak Navon (formerly President), cooperated with the Zionist establishment, particularly with the Labour Party.

There is also a large group of people who have been silently and patiently waiting. In contrast to them there is the vociferous group which has refused to acquiesce and which includes the Black Panthers, the Shahak, Oded, the East for Peace and Ohalim Organisations, as well as other small and ad hoc organizations which mainly arose in the slum districts. We shall cover these organisations and their struggles and solidarity with the Palestinians in the next chapter.

Finally, there is the group of offenders. These are people who live in the slum districts of the large towns, the development towns and the moshavim. Social scientists claim that crime and misconduct are sometimes the means of struggle used by the down-trodden against the ruling establishment and the dominant society. The crime rate in Jewish society in the Muslim-Arab world was 0.1 percent, but in Israel 90 percent of the prison population is Sephardi. The same percentage applies in the brothels. The Chief of Police of Tel Aviv, Moshe Timokan, pointing to the worsening situation, stated that 'in one district alone there are 2,000 boys (between 10 and 16) with criminal records.' Israeli social scientists warn that 'social segregation is a graver danger than the enemy outside.' In these districts there are border police armed with guns and truncheons, and exchanges of fire between them and the youths of the slum districts have become a daily occurrence.[56] Some of these youths belong to resistance groups, or to be more precise, they have been pushed into throwing in their lot with resistance groups.

In 1970, Sephardi Jews represented 78 percent of those committing criminal acts, and Sephardi youth represented 93 percent.[57]

The Israeli establishment confronts all these challenges with a policy of pitiless oppression, that is, the imposition of harsh punitive measures, severe beatings, torture and corruption. 88 percent of the Israeli police force comes from the Sephardi and Druze communities (which also provide 90 percent of the prison officers). It also appointed the Sephardi Bekhor Shitrit and Shlomo Hillel as Ministers of Police. Israel thus was employing the same means as Rhodesia/Zimbabwe and South Africa where they use blacks to police blacks. Israeli sources state that most of the mercenaries in South Lebanon are Shi'ites.

The press throughout the world has published much material about torture in Zionist prisons and the various punitive measures employed against the Palestinians, but nothing about torture inflicted on Sephardim, except for the British *Tribune* newspaper, which publicised this in a letter from Ya'kov Yeruba'al.[58] Zionist influence has been able to suppress these facts out of fear that they might cause an outcry of indignation from world Jewry, and particularly from the hundreds of thousands of Sephardim in the West.

The following are some of the facts of this issue.

Yahya Hazzan: Torture has meant the possibility that he could lose his sight in his right eye. His lawyer, Oded Dovrath, states that Yahya was taken to the police station in Rehovot where he was beaten, punched and kicked by police officers hoping to force him to make a statement, until he collapsed on the floor. When he raised his head, they kicked his eye until he fainted. He was then forced to sign a 'confession', but had no idea of its contents. When he started to vomit blood he was transferred to a hospital for an operation on his eye.[59] *Ha'aretz* took up his case again on 2 March 1979 with a picture of the victim, and added that police officers had almost strangled him. After the operation on his eye, he was sent to Rehovot prison. Shortly thereafter he was examined by a specialist who found that damage to his eye was causing him to have double vision and that this could be a permanent condition.

Uri Naqqash: He was arrested when he was on a bus because a policeman did not like his manner or the way he spoke. His ill-treatment led to a perforated ear-drum.[60]

S. Nunikashvili: A soldier from Georgia (Georgian Jews belong culturally to the Sephardi community). He is 19 years old and was tortured in a police station in Petah Tikvah. He was embarrassed to describe what they did to him there: they started by beating him on the face, then a policeman urinated on him. They stripped his clothing from him and sodomised him twice with a broom-handle. They stuffed a urine-soaked rag into his mouth to stifle his screams. When he asked to see a doctor he was taken to the police headquarters where he was beaten again. A policeman said to him, 'If you ask to see a doctor I'll string you up and say that you hanged yourself.'[61]

Anonymous: the lawyer Ladisky stated that one of his clients was forced to remove his clothing, upon which point he was beaten, punched and kicked by a policeman using a stick. Cold water was then thrown on him. They sprayed tear gas into his eyes, stuck a broom handle in his mouth and then did the same with the barrel of a rifle. When they interrogated him they held a knife over his genitals and threatened to cut them off. Then they threw him onto the ground which was covered with water.[62]

Pinhas Bahbut: Tortured until he signed a statement.[63]

Binyamin Shitrit: He was tied up with chains and tortured until he needed hospitalisation. The previous year he had been so badly tortured that he tried to commit suicide by throwing himself out of an upper-storey window of the police station. He did not die and the police proceeded to harass him.[64]

Elie Avraham: He has a long history of being tortured by the military police because he refused to do his military service. He stated that he refused to be conscripted because of racial discrimination in Israel.[65]

Shim'on Abu Tubul: Committed suicide in prison. An adolescent who, after his death, became a hero in the folk songs of the Sephardim.[66]

Another sadistic method used in Ramla Prison was the use of enemas.[67]

General Moshe Nativ, head of all armed forces personnel, stated that 16 soldiers had committed suicide over a period of only six months.[68] Charlie Biton, MP, sent a letter to the Minister of Justice decrying the treatment meted out to Sephardim in the army and mentioning the names of some of the soldiers in question: Elie Avraham, Moshe Bahbut, Albert Danino, Atyas Ricardo and Me'ir Badusa. He wrote that these soldiers had complained of being tortured with tear gas. Biton added that the military authorities had refused to look into these complaints.[69] In December 1980 Israel Radio announced that the parents of soldiers were complaining of the mental breakdown of their boys in the army as a result of the dreadful treatment they received in the army and that some of them had to be sent to psychiatric hospitals.

Natan Dunevitz, a correspondent of *Ha'aretz*, admitted that only Sephardim were the victims of torture, which is why the Ashkenazi public showed no interest in the matter.[70] A high-ranking officer in the Israeli police admitted to torturing prisoners with electrodes attached to their genitals. He boasted that 'these methods are "effective", and when we employ them the accused is prepared to sign anything.'[71] A high court judge, Hayyim Cohen, condemned torture, and *The Jerusalem Post* which reported this said that such a denunciation in a Western country would lead to the resignation of the chiefs of police.[72]

In *Zu Haderekh* on 13 February 1985, Yosef Algazi published an article based on a report of the Israeli Human Rights Organisation. Algazi wrote 'a day does not pass that we do not submit a complaint about the torture and violence practised by the police. Often no complaint is made out of fear of police reprisals. In spite of that, the number of complaints has risen over recent years. In 1982 there were 2,098 complaints and this rose to 2,230 in 1983. Three times as many policemen were tried in disciplinary hearings in 1984 as in 1983. Since the judge and the accused were policemen, the severest punishment meted out to those accused of torture was a fine which was the equivalent of £5 sterling.' The report names the following Sephardim who have been tortured:

Yosef Baraka: He had a hemorrhage and his spinal column was broken.

Shlomo (Salim) Zurihan: Tortured with electrodes eighteen times consecutively, causing grave damage to his nerves and sight.

Menashe Ezra: Beaten harshly for a number of hours, then pins were stuck in his wounds, was kicked in the groin. Then they spat on it and verbally humiliated him.

Marcelle and Yaffa Ohna: Both beaten and gassed with tear gas.

Yohai Cohen: Died on 20 January 1985 after being strung up and tortured. Eleven days before his death, he was seen by a witness, suspended and being tortured. The police claim that he hanged himself. When *Ma'ariv* and *Hadashot* published the circumstances of his death at the hands of the police, the journalists involved were called in to the police station and threatened.

Rahamim Salim: Harshly and continuously beaten by a group of policemen.

Yehuda Idri: Beaten and kicked in the genitals, stomach and neck.

From polarisation and alienation the road to resistance was wide open.

NOTES

1 Prime Minister's Office, 1968, 413–418.
2 Bank of Israel, 1968.
3 *Mahbarot lemehkar ulevikoret*, No. 1, 41.
4 Ibid.
5 Ministry of Trade and Industry, 28, 29 and 40.
6 Ibid. See also Kleiner, 1966, 153.
7 *Mahbarot lemehkar ulevikoret*, No. 4, 46.
8 Ibid.
9 *Dunsguide*, Tel Aviv, 1979.
10 Ibid.
11 *Mahbarot lemehkar ulevikoret*, No. 4, 42.
12 Central Bureau of Statistics, 1973.
13 Heffer, 1975, 93.
14 *Riva'on lekalkala*, 1963.
15 'Profits in Israel', *Basha'ar* 6, 1963.
16 Swirski and Bernstein, 1980, 18–26.
17 Central Bureau of Statistics, 1978.
18 *Zu Haderekh*, 1980.
19 No 13/14.
20 *Shevet va'am*, 1960.
21 *Shevet va'am*, Second Series, No. 1. 1970.
22 A reference to Zola's famous words 'J'accuse' regarding the Dreyfus case – which was event that inspired Theodor Herzl to write his *Judenstaat*.
23 *New Society News*, 1979, quoted by Swirski, 1981, 344–355.
24 *Ha'aretz*, 4 April 1986.
25 *Ha'aretz*, 28 March 1986.
26 *Ha'aretz*, 12 July 1985.
27 *The Times*, 22 February 1982.
28 *Zu Haderekh*, 29 January 1986.
29 25 October, 1984.

30 Israeli Office of Statistics.
31 *Zu Haderekh*, 9 April 1981.
32 *Ha'aretz*, 6 November 1981.
33 *Zu Haderekh*, 9 March 1983, quoting the Annual Statement of the Institute for Social Security.
34 *Zu Haderekh*, 28 December 1980.
35 *Ha'aretz*, 22 February 1985, quoting the Annual Statement of the Institute of Social Security.
36 *Zu Haderekh*, 29 May 1985.
37 *Les temps modernes, The Second Israel*, 112.
38 Ibid.
39 *Zu Haderekh*, 15 August 1984.
40 *Zu Haderekh*, 28 January 1981.
41 *Ha'aretz*, 26 June 1981.
42 *Zu Haderekh*, 31 December 1985 quoting a statement from the Institute of Productivity.
43 Peres, 1977, 82.
44 Ibid.
45 Ibid. 132.
46 Ibid, 143.
47 Ibid, p 147.
48 Mikhail al-Baz, *Les temps modernes, The Second Israel*, 1981, 116.
49 Ibid, 119.
50 Ibid.
51 *Al Hamishmar*, 6 September 1985.
52 *Ha'aretz*, 6 September 1985.
53 Q.v. Article by Ahmad Sa'ad in *Falestine al-Thawra*, 9 November 1985, and also the article by Salim Jubran in *Falestine al-Thawra*, 13 July 1985..
54 11 September 1985.
55 See the statement of Professor Stanley Yudetsky of the Soroka Hospital in *Zu Haderekh*, 22 July 1987.
56 Shalom Cohen, *Les temps modernes*, 95.
57 Central Office of Statistics, 1970: Special Series 417, Table B, and Special Series 408, Table E.
58 25 March 1980.
59 *Yedi'ot Aharonot*, 17 January 1979.
60 *Yedi'ot Aharonot*, 22 February 1979.
61 *Ha'olam Hazeh*, 7 February 1979.
62 Israeli press, 15 January, 1979.
63 *Yedi'ot Aharonot*, 1 July 1979.
64 *Zu Haderekh*, 5 March 1980.
65 *Zu Haderekh*, 9 July 1980.
66 *Zu Haderekh*, 3 February 1982.
67 *Ha'aretz*, 26 February 1982.
68 *Ma'ariv*, 25 December 1980.
69 *Zu Haderekh*, 28 January 1981.
70 11 April 1980.
71 *Yedi'ot Aharonot*, 30 March 1979.
72 29 June 1979.

CHAPTER TEN

Sephardi Resistance And Solidarity With The Palestinians

RESISTANCE

The Beginning Of Popular Protest Demonstrations

After the founding of the state of Israel in 1948, the Zionist establishment, with the help of the Western powers and their sympathisers in the Arab countries, displaced most of the Sephardim and brought them to Palestine where they joined with native Palestinian Jews to form the overwhelming majority of the new state. The tragic conditions in the refugee camps, and the urban and rural slums, which we have described in earlier chapters, brought about the emergence of a new type of resistance – involving popular uprisings, strikes, demonstrations and bloody clashes with the police force and the border guard.

This kind of *Intifada* has often spread among the soldiers too, in the form of hunger strikes, indiscipline and verbal and physical violence against Ashkenazi officers, but reports have been suppressed by censorship.[1] In the city of Ashkelon, a local leader, Na'im Khlaschi, led many thousands of Sephardim against the policy of racial discrimination. In the seventies, Na'im helped to set up the Black Panther organization.

Toward the end of April 1949, 300 Sephardi residents from the town of Ramleh staged a noisy demonstration in Allenby Street in Tel Aviv. They demanded 'bread and work' and tried to storm the old Knesset building, until the Israeli police managed to turn them back, whereupon they went off to the government offices at Hakirya and were met by some officials who promised them that the government would employ them in 'emergency work'.[2] Two weeks later Sephardim stormed the Jewish Agency building in Haifa and went on the rampage inside the Department of Absorption. They demanded 'work and housing' but this time the police only managed to overpower them by bringing in reinforcements. Some of the demonstrators were injured during the clashes, and a number were arrested.[3]

In July of the same year, demonstrators from Jaffa attacked the former parliament building in Tel Aviv, using sticks and destroying its doors. At the last moment, the police managed to stop them getting into the hall itself. Yosef Shprinsak refused to meet the demonstrators and declared 'We cannot talk with those who break down doors.'(Knesset Minutes 26 July 1949.)

At the same time as the Zionist establishment was bringing in hundreds of thousands of immigrants and sending them to inhuman camps, the Jewish Agency was listening to detailed reports of their misery and hunger.[4] Hungry children attacked other children on the way to school and stole their food.[5]

The Events Of Wadi Al-Salib

These were the culmination of the popular uprisings undertaken by the Sephardim, and the Moroccans in particular. They took place in July 1959. The immediate cause was the granting of comfortable housing to new Ashkenazi immigrants from Poland whereas hundreds of thousands of Sephardim were still living in filthy tents and dilapidated housing since 1948. Moreover, the government bought additional flats from private companies for these Polish immigrants, and flats which were built for Sephardim were given at the last minute to the Ashkenazi newcomers. We should also mention that most of Israel's leadership was of Polish origin, including Ben Gurion, Peres, Shamir and Chaim Wisemann.

The spark was provided by the police when they shot down a Moroccan in the street. The Sephardim considered this to be a racist provocation, and the Moroccans who were living in the slum district of Wadi al-Salib in Haifa, staged demonstrations under the leadership of David Ben-Harush, secretary of the North African Association. The demonstrators, who included many women and children, destroyed the local Histadrut headquarters and then thronged out of Wadi al-Salib making their way toward the Ashkenazi area of Hadar, breaking shop windows in the main street.

The police and the border guard hurried to the area, and behaved as if they were putting down an incipient revolution, causing serious casualties amongst women and old men. Eventually they managed to corner the leaders of the uprising, including David Ben-Harush, who opened fire on them as they moved in. However, the police managed – albeit with great difficulty – to arrest him and his colleagues. Some of the ringleaders were beaten up and sentenced, whilst others were bought off. There was a simultaneous outbreak of violence in most of the Sephardi camps, with the masses staging spontaneous demonstrations, acts of sabotage and arson against government buildings, causing millions of dollars worth of damage. The protest movement called upon Sephardim to leave the Ashkenazi political parties and to join the North-African Association.

In order to calm down the protesters, the Prime Minister, David Ben Gurion, formed a committee to look into the problem under M. Etzioni, a member of the High Court. The committee produced a detailed report about the social gap between Ashkenazim and Sephardim, together with lengthy recommendations on how to eliminate it. The government, naturally ignored the report.[6] The committee of investigation denied the existence of any racial discrimination in Israel. Subsequently Ben-Harush was given a new flat and a job.

In 1963 the secret 'Front for National Equality' emerged, and was eliminated by the secret police and for 'security reasons' there was a complete media blackout.[7]

The Intifada *of The Black Panthers*

In 1971, Sephardim from the Musrara district of Jerusalem formed the largest protest organisation – the Black Panthers. They adopted the name of one of the black organisations in America because they believed that there was no fundamental difference between anti-black discrimination in the United States and anti-Sephardi discrimination in Israel in the fields of occupation, education, housing, etc. They set out to challenge the 'Labour' establishment's concepts of 'equality', 'socialism', 'democracy', 'Jewish liberation' and 'the ingathering of the exiles'.

One of the crudest provocations which gave rise to this ethnic organisation was the way the Ashkenazi immigrants from Russia were being received: In March 1971 they were given a royal reception by the government and the Jewish Agency, granted luxurious furnished housing and jobs which matched their qualifications. The [Russian] Prime Minister, Golda Meir, rushed to Lod airport on Mondays and Thursdays with tear-filled eyes and a voice cracked with emotion to welcome them: 'You are the real Jews. We have been waiting for you for 25 years. You speak Yiddish!' She added 'Every loyal Jew must speak Yiddish, for he who does not know Yiddish is not a Jew.[8] You are a superior breed – you will provide us with heroes.'[9]

This welcome aroused a cry of indignation among the Sephardim who took it as a slight that Golda had divided the Jews into two: the real Jews who spoke Yiddish, and the lower classes, that is the pseudo-Jews who spoke Arabic instead of Yiddish, the dark Jews from the Middle East. The receptions laid on by the leaders of the state for newly-arrived Ashkenazi immigrants angered the Sephardim who had been welcomed at the airport, upon their arrival in the country, by being sprayed with DDT.

The new Russian immigrants were also provided with the following:

1. A long-term low-interest mortgage. This enabled every family to pay less than one quarter of the price (of a flat). The mortgage repayments then shrank to almost nothing because of the chronic inflation.

2. Luxury flats. Every family of three received a flat with two large bedrooms, usually in the large towns. The area of a flat was 80m^2, whereas Sephardim with large families had been allocated flats averaging 30–40m^2. In Tel Aviv, the Ashkenazi immigrants were housed in a plush suburb, Neveh Sharet, which lies next to the Sephardi slum district of Shekhunat Ha'argazim.

3. The postponement of compulsory military service, whereas the state sent the Sephardim straight to the front, where they died in their thousands in 1948.

4. No income tax for a certain period.

5. No customs duties or import tax, which meant that every Russian could buy a car or a fridge at less than half price on an instalment basis.

6. Employment commensurate with the immigrant's qualifications.

Even though these privileges cost the people, the majority of whom were Sephardim and Palestinians, more than $25,000 per family,[10] the new immigrants treated their Sephardi (and Palestinian) neighbours contemptuously. They sent petitions to the

Tel Aviv Town Hall to express their indignation at having to live next to 'Black' Jews whom they claimed were 'Levantine' and uncivilised, and they threatened to leave the country.[11] The Ashkenazi authorities gave in to some of their demands and removed Sephardi children from Ashkenazi schools and youth clubs, and in some places kept them out of the local swimming pools. These outrageous measures led some of the slum residents to stone the new Russian immigrants, many of whom left Israel for America in search of a higher standard of living.[12]

One of the immigrants, a certain Oltchik, became quite notorious. This Oltchik received a spacious and luxurious flat in the neat 'American' suburb of Kiryat Yovel. He found a position in the Solel Boneh company – and, he could not stand Sephardim. Upon being told that there were eighty thousand children who did not have a bed to sleep in, he snapped, 'You make all these children and then ask me to pay for their education and food? Is it my concern if you must have ten children?' During the summer break, Solel Boneh employs a number of school-children for a daily wage of I£12, but Oltchik's son was paid I£47. Charlie Biton, a Black Panther leader stated, 'if this immigration [of Russian Jews] continues, there will be a civil war.'[13]

Though these Russian immigrants were born and raised in the socialist Soviet Union they, along with American extremists such as Rabbi Kahane, form the racist extreme right-wing and are the backbone of Zionist settlement on the occupied West Bank.

In addition to this provocative wave of immigration, there was another cause for the groundswell of support for the Black Panther uprisings which was the plot to gentrify Musrara for the Ashkenazim. After the occupation of the old city of Jerusalem in 1967, Musrara suddenly gained economic importance, located as it was between the old and new cities, which is why the ruling establishment wanted to raze the old Arab houses and make Musrara a 'redevelopment area' with luxury housing for the Ashkenazim. That implied the expulsion of the poor Sephardim. Sephardi families would have to be ripped apart and crowded into the ugly tower blocks which had been built around Arab Jerusalem. We should add that most Sephardim instinctively refused to settle in the occupied Arab territories, perhaps because they realised that the settlements were being built on sand, and that sand in the East is fickle!

There was another provocative factor: much of the youth of Musrara and other Sephardi slums was made up of those who had not studied, had no jobs and had not served in the army. The police would goad, arrest and expose them to humiliation, torture and 'dry beating', and in prison they were exposed to buggery. At the age of fourteen, Charlie Biton MP experienced this treatment for a crime which he had not committed. The courts would impose the heaviest sentences on them for delinquency whereas they were lenient with big Ashkenazi criminals, sending them off to mental institutions instead of prison. Accordingly, Sephardi youth from Musrara and the slum districts started to consider the state as their archenemy and inimical to Sephardi society as a whole. These youths also heard long stories from their parents about the treatment they had received from the Jewish Agency and the Israeli government after they immigrated to Israel since 1948.

Finally, these youths were influenced by the popular uprisings which were staged by the blacks in America, South Africa and the third world against racism and colonialism. The Ashkenazi settlers 'helped' these youths to become politicised by calling them 'blacks', 'shvartses', 'Arabs' and so on.

Conditions in Musrara were no better than those of the black areas in the United States. S. Malka described the district and the conditions obtaining there as follows: 'Musrara is a district which falls within the boundaries of Jewish Jerusalem and at the edge of the old city. It was hastily founded on the second day of 1948 to house immigrants from Morocco and Iraq. The authorities then paid no attention to it and it stayed in a state of neglect. Its dark coloured stones . . . washed clothes speak of poverty and despair? . . . fluttering from windows and in the streets. The dilapidated houses lean against each other and inside the inhabitants live six or seven to a room . . . suffering from poverty and hardship. The families here are large . . . with members being spread over three or four floors of a building. A nerve-wracking din rises from the incessant chattering of the people outside. Inactivity wears the people down, and finally there is crime. That is the natural result of filthy hovels and the human material: the majority are working class, migrant workers, unemployed, a whole class without qualifications . . . a whole society suffering from economic, social and educational deprivation . . . Musrara is the kingdom of the poor – of the Sephardim.'[14]

At the same time as the Sephardim (and Palestinians) had to make do with such miserable conditions, Ashkenazi Jews were enjoying an unprecedented economic boom due to the occupation of the remaining Palestinian territories in the West Bank, the Gaza Strip plus Sinai and the Syrian Golan Heights. They eagerly improved their material situation, snatching up cars, televisions and hi-fi sets. A nouveau riche class arose which rushed madly towards land speculation and alarming financial activities. Inflation rose fast and there were price rises which delineated more sharply the contours of social inequalities and Ashkenazi/Sephardi polarisation (which phenomena were even more drastically manifested amongst the Palestinians).

This was the soil in which the Black Panthers arose and flourished. They were not struggling for the Sephardim alone, but for the rights of the Palestinian Arabs also. Their leaders started to be proud of their Middle Eastern origin and their Arab ethnicity, which sent a shiver through the Ashkenazi ruling establishment which had been relying on 'divide and rule'. This was particularly the case of the extreme Ashkenazi left-wingers who purported to like the Palestinians. The following are some of the claims of the Ashkenazi leftists as to the reasons for the emergence of the Black Panthers:

1. The residents of the slum districts started to confront the danger represented by the cheap Arab labour from the occupied territories. (The fact is that most of the jobs carried out by Arab labourers from the territories had been turned down by the Sephardim, who realised that the expropriation of Palestinian lands and the establishment of settlements would push the Palestinians into the labour market in Israel.) In order to create a schism between the Sephardim and the Palestinians, these 'friends' add that the occupation serves the interests of the Sephardi whereas the truth is exactly the opposite, since the state spends millions on Ashkenazi settlements in the occupied territories at the expense of social services, and at the cost of neglecting the slum districts and the development towns where the Sephardim live.

2. Israel's victory in 1967 encouraged the Sephardim to demand their share of the booty, having fought against the Arabs. The truth is that most youths in the Black Panther movement and their supporters did not take part in that war. They had refused to do military service and the military establishment could not force these 'marginals' into military service.

Black Panther Demonstrations

On 1 March 1971 the Black Panthers asked the police to allow them to stage a peaceful demonstration against discrimination in front of the Jerusalem Town Hall. The decision came from the Prime Minister, Golda Meir, who rejected the request decisively for no stated reasons. On the evening of the same day, the police made a series of provocative arrests of Black Panther members and supporters in Jerusalem. The French newspaper published by Moroccan students of the Hebrew University in Jerusalem commented on the arbitrary arrests as follows: 'Yesterday evening freedom passed away in Israel. It died without a whimper, with no funeral or cries of grief. . . when the police arrest 15 young members of the Black Panthers who had resolved to demonstrate in front of the town hall . . .'

On 3 March 1971, a demonstration took place and registered a dazzling success. The five hundred demonstrators in front of the town hall consisted of Panthers, students, leftists and passers-by. There resounded the call of 'set them free' and 'enough of discrimination'. Then the Mayor, Teddy Kollek, appeared on the balcony in his night-clothes and addressed the demonstrators sneeringly, 'Demonstrate if you wish, but keep off my grass.' This policy of contempt was consciously used by the Zionists against the Sephardim and the Arabs in the hope of undermining their self-confidence. But this time, it did not work, and the government instituted a paternalistic campaign to deal with these 'unpleasant children' – as the Prime Minister, Golda Meir, termed them during her meeting with them.[15] Golda Meir started to pamper them as if they were her children, always reminding them 'we are all Jews'. However, she did not succeed and one of the members of the movement said, as he came out of a meeting with her, 'her vision is superficial and emotional. . .nice children and wicked children . . .' In that meeting the Panthers presented thirty-three demands, e.g. participation in social projects. The Prime Minister answered that 'there will be no such thing' and refused to discuss them. She tried to 'buy' the leaders, but failed.

Subsequently, the Black Panthers worked on developing a social movement against racial discrimination. They called for decent housing and for fully qualified teachers. They demanded that the school syllabus include Maimonides instead of Bialik and Chernihovsky. The whisper became a shout, as the cries for help issuing from Musrara and Qatamon turned into public displays, bloody clashes between the Black Panthers and the police force and Molotov cocktails . . . 'bombs thrown by Jews against Jews in the Jewish state' as Golda Meir stated. Often the clashes were provoked by the police under the leadership of the Iraqi Minister of Police,

Shlomo Hillel, who was nicknamed 'the Black Collaborator'.

The fire which was kindled in Musrara spread to all the slum areas inhabited by the Sephardi poor and jobless. When the demonstrators saw that the Israeli police were using the same repressive measures they used on the Palestinians, that is beatings, arrest and torture, the walls separating Sephardim from Palestinians crumbled. There came about a solidarity between them, as Kochavi Shemesh, a Black Panther (Iraqi) leader, declared, 'It is unfeasible for one people to exist at the expense of another people. We must quickly find a common language with the Palestinians.'

On 18 May 1971 the Panthers staged one of their largest demonstrations with 5,000 participants which lasted seven and a half hours and during which the police arrest 260 people. The police promised to release them if they joined a moderate association – 'The Alliance of Moroccan Immigrants'. The police used batons to beat up the demonstrators and the public saw police brutality for themselves.

Demonstrations by the Panthers continued throughout the summer of 1971 although the media only reported them if there was violence. In the meantime 5,000 Sephardim joined the Panthers' organisation and others offered help. Some rich Sephardim provided money and advice, but secretly.

On 23 August 1971 the largest demonstration took place. It was joined by six or seven thousand people who set fire to a picture of Golda Meir. There were prolonged clashes between the demonstrators and the security forces which led to many people being wounded and held in custody for long periods, among them the majority of the Black Panther members. This demonstration was considered the zenith of Panther resistance. The next demonstration they staged was in January 1972 outside the building in Jerusalem where the Annual World Zionist Conference was being held. The police had to employ one thousand officers. University students and poor young couples joined the demonstration. The protesters declared that the Zionist conference did not represent them. In the end they succeeded in presenting their demands to the conference. On 1 May 1972 the Panthers' demonstration was broken by the police. On the following day the Jerusalem students demonstrated in support of the Panthers. A few days later Ovadia Harari was shot by the police, which sparked off further demonstrations.

A mature political consciousness amongst the Panthers was slow to emerge for they had little education; most of them had not had the opportunity to finish elementary school. During those days (May 1972), the Panthers stole the milk delivered to the houses of the rich in Rehavia and distributed it to poor Sephardi children. They also constructed a bier and carried it through the streets in a long funeral procession, repeating 'we shall bury hatred and the social gap', and then they returned their army reserve cards to the authorities indicating that they refused service as a form of protest.

When residents of the slum district of Hatikva in Tel Aviv staged a demonstration against the racial discrimination directed against one of their football teams, the government used the notoriously cruel border guard to crush them. The border guard laid siege against the district on 7 and 8 June 1971, using all forms of oppression. When Ashkenazi business owners were asked about the suppression of the district, they replied, 'the authorities ought to beat that riff-raff up even more . . .'[16] Thereafter the state used the Mafia, under the leadership of Mintsch – a known criminal – to attack the Panthers.[17] On 14 June 1971 the Panthers' demonstration in the Hatikva slum district was crushed by the right-wing Herut party, and on 5 July of the same year 7,000 people demonstrated in Jerusalem without any violent incidents.

Views Of The Black Panthers

Kochavi Shemesh became one of the most courageous leaders of the Panthers by declaring his revolutionary views in public. In a discussion with a correspondent of the magazine *Israleft* on 20 November 1972 he stated that 'the problem of sectarian inequality between the Ashkenazim and the Sephardim can only be solved after the solution of the Palestinian problem. I accuse the government and the media of inciting the Sephardim to hostility against the Arabs.' He emphasised the necessity for solidarity between Arab and Jewish workers in order to reduce the tension that existed between them and to move them toward a common struggle against the rulers of Israel. He added that the government could not change the conditions of the Sephardim without changing the social make-up of the country, but it did not want to do that, and so the Panthers had to undertake that operation, to redistribute the national income and resources and to reform social services such as education, housing, welfare etc. He stated that criminality amongst the Sephardim was a result of social injustice and spoke of the path of struggle to be followed by other sections of youth. He stated that the Panthers had established party branches throughout the country and had no difficulty in finding support everywhere, but that it was more useful to stage demonstrations in Jerusalem than in the remote villages.

When Shemesh was questioned about the concept of Zionism as a solution to the problem of Jews throughout the world, he replied, 'the Zionists have solved the problem of the Ashkenazi Jews in Israel, but the Sephardim are worse off in Israel than they were in the Arab countries, and they also face greater dangers to their security in Israel than they did in the Arab countries.'

Shemesh also mentioned that anti-Semitism did not exist except when Iraq allied itself to Germany in 1941. He emphasised that there is anti-Semitism in Israel, against the Sephardim and that what happened to the Ashkenazi Jews in Europe is happening now to Sephardim in Israel. The derogatory terms used to describe Sephardim in Israel, such as 'primitive' and 'Frank' epitomise racist thinking. Shemesh added that 'I witnessed an Ashkenazi child on a television programme saying that his mother told him not to play with Sephardim.'

Shemesh goes on to speak of the Ashkenazi left, which he claims is helping the Sephardim in their struggle, but it cannot lead them to victory since it is bogged down unnecessarily with internal feuding. In any case the Panthers must lead the struggle of the down-trodden until the end.

He was then asked: 'Has the ruling establishment tried to buy you out?' and he replied, 'They tried many ways, but with no success. When they failed, they tried to destroy our organisation through arrests and police harassment, and two or three of our members have decided to desist from any further political activity.'

Shemesh said that 'the Sephardi question, in my opinion, starts with Zionism, for adherence to Zionist ideology means abandoning your original culture. Anyone who understand Zionist ideology knows that it is based on the culture of the European Jews and stands in direct contradiction to the native culture of the area. One of the establishment's greatest mistakes, for example, was to state that Sephardi culture is no more than a Jewish folk culture, for they were afraid that we would accept the concept that our culture is Arab. This is where the huge gap appears between Ashkenazi and Sephardi culture. We do not have any theatres or newspapers and so on, our customs, traditions and culture were Arab, whether we came from the Yemen, Iran, Iraq, the Middle East or Morocco. We are culturally part of the Arab world. That is what the Zionists fear most. Accordingly, they have done everything possible to deprive us of our past. In other words, they have presented a distorted image of Arab culture as "backward" . . . they ridiculed our accent . . . they despised us . . . if I were to support Zionism that would mean that I would be working against my own identity. We Sephardim must thus sever our connections with the Zionist movement and say to them: "Yes. We are Sephardim. Yes. We are 'Orientals.'" This term is positive and not negative. We are not against Arab-Oriental culture, on the contrary we are part of it. I believe that we must make it easy for the Sephardim to reclaim their identity.' Shemesh mentioned that he did not want to study the literature which described the life of the Ashkenazi Jews in Eastern Europe, or the history of Ashkenazi Jews whilst he knew nothing of his forebears' history. He declared, 'I will say it aloud: we are in the East and if Zionism wants to survive it can only do so through constant warfare. Thus, the only way for Israel to survive is for it to become a Middle Eastern country and to integrate with the area.'[18]

Sa'adya Marciano, the leader of the Black Panthers at that time, stated that 'Sephardi culture and the Sephardi way of life have been suffocated over the last thirty years. I am speaking of art, music and creativity. The establishment has been intent on suffocating all of that to stop it flourishing. It has wilfully neglected it, out of fear that Sephardi culture would destroy the way of life they have been trying to create here. In fact, the Ashkenazi establishment almost succeeded but for the renaissance of Sephardi culture amongst my generation. We are a generation which likes Arab music because it is beautiful and fascinating and which is not only moving away from being ashamed of its culture and traditions but is proud of them, and upon whose shoulders has fallen the burden of preserving that culture. The new state of peace with Egypt will bring about the most significant development for this generation. The bond will become natural when the borders are opened, and at that time our Ashkenazi brothers will see the majesty of Middle Eastern values. . . . They will accept it without fear, and it will be possible to take the best from both cultures . . .'[19] Although Marciano supported the Palestinian cause, he stressed the Sephardi cause in order to widen his base among his community. On the other hand, Biton stressed, 'Zionist society is unjust. We started our activities with the struggle against poverty, but slowly we realised that the struggle is for the oppressed Palestinians as well . . . we should fight against a government which lets a minority govern a majority and we should support the poor against the rich.'

The longing of the Sephardim for their Middle Eastern homelands planted in their heart the hope that peace with Egypt would expand to include the Palestinians and the other Arab countries and that the borders would be open for them to revisit their homelands. The events which followed the 'peace' have proved that their belief was only political naïveté.

After the Black Panthers elected a chairman, a treasurer and a legal adviser, and had set up an administrative apparatus for their activities, they drew up a political and economic manifesto as follows:

1. The rehabilitation of the slum districts
2. The availability of free education from the kindergarten to the university levels for all families of limited income.
3. Free housing to be built for all the poor.
4. The replacement of remand homes by agricultural children's villages.
5. A general increase in the wage levels for the heads of large families.
6. Comprehensive representation for Sephardim in the power structure.

The ruling Zionist establishment believed that the Black Panther Movement constituted a grave danger for the following reasons:

1. It was a revolutionary political movement which was born in the poor Sephardi areas, and was trying to unite the Sephardim and increase their representation in the organs of state and it expresses the feelings and the aspirations of most Sephardim.
2. It was opposed to the Ashkenazi settlers who controlled the state and the economy, although it was willing to work within the establishment and it did cooperate with Ashkenazi progressives.
3. It sympathised with the struggle of the Palestinian people.
4. Its pride in Sephardi–Islamic culture was destroying all the efforts of the ruling establishment to eradicate the Sephardi identity. These last two points could lead to forging an alliance between the Sephardim and the Arabs based on common culture, history and cause.
5. In order to meet its demands, Israel had to change its infrastructure.
6. It used mass demonstrations which threatened the existing order.

In 1973, Marciano and his followers joined the new and radical Israeli Democratic Party which had been formed by the journalist Shalom Cohen (of Iraqi origin, educated in Egypt and then the editor of the magazine, *Ha'olam Hazeh*). The party suffered failure in the parliamentary elections of 1973 but gained three seats on the Executive Committee of the Histadrut and 28 seats on 7 workers councils (of the Histadrut).

When prices rose sharply in 1974, the Panthers organised several demonstrations and strikes. Biton was sent to prison for a crime he did not commit, but thanks to public support he was pardoned. On 23 September 1975, the Black Panthers' Convention called for the elimination of discrimination and the establishment of a Palestinian state. From now on the Ashkenazi left diverted the Panthers to 'class struggle' rather than ethnic equality. The most active Ashkenazi groups in the work were Ya'ad, Moked and the Communist Party.

In 1977 the Panthers started aspiring again to enter the legislature, but they split up into small groups with each one sheltering behind a different Ashkenazi left-wing party. Charlie Biton joined the Democratic Front (Hadash) which included the Communist Party, the local Palestinian Councils and some Jewish revolutionary factions. He was placed third on the electoral list and was appointed a Member of Parliament, although his organisation was still called the Black Panthers. In 1990 he left Hadash. Sa'adya Marciano joined the Sheli Party which represented the Zionist far left and whose leadership was made up of Aryeh Eliav, Uri Avneri and Matti Peled. Shalom Cohen, Yehoshua Peretz (a Moroccan trade unionist) and the famous Israeli author, Ephraim Kishon, formed a new group. Another group of Panthers joined the Dash Party which was headed by Yigal Yadin. The Black Panthers then ceased to exist politically and all its leaders disappeared , except for Charlie Biton and Kokhavi Shemesh.

Charlie Biton's membership of the Democratic Front under the leadership of the Communist Party had advantages and disadvantages. The advantages were as follows:
1. He was elected to Parliament to represent the interests of the Palestinians and the Sephardim.
2. The Panthers received financial support from the Front.
3. Sephardim worked together with Palestinians since the overwhelming majority of the Front's and the Communist Party's members were Palestinian Arabs. Generally the Front won 40 percent of the Palestinian vote.

The disadvantages were that the Panthers, before they joined the Democratic Front, used to stress that they were struggling against Ashkenazi Zionist racism, but they now have to talk in terms of 'class struggle' – which is the exact stance of the Ashkenazi left. This transformation has led to the alienation of most Sephardim from the Panthers (see chapter eight, pp 223–25).

Why The Black Panthers Failed To Become A Mass Movement

1. Fear of state terrorism, violence, arrests and torture used by the government against the Black Panthers paralysed many of their supporters.

2. The government incorporated some of the Panthers by providing them with jobs or housing.

3. The policy of 'divide and rule' which the left-wing parties employed. We must mention that all the factions of the Panthers which joined the left-wing Zionist parties, such as Sheli and Dash, disappeared. This belies the belief of some who claimed that 'we must work from within the establishment in order to change it to our advantage.'

4. Membership of the Panthers in the Democratic Front limited the Panthers' independence and alienated those who refused to apply the theory of 'class struggle' to ethnic division. We must emphasise that the worst form of McCarthyism in the West took place in Israel. It destroyed the lives of thousands of Jews and Palestinians – most of whom were not communists. In addition, the Democratic Front paid no attention to the struggle of the Sephardi intelligentsia and professionals against racial discrimination.

5. The lack of any economic base. All parties in Israel have an economic base to fund them. The party in turn represents and defends the interests of this economic base in the institutions of state. The economic base of the Mapai (Labour) Party, for example, is the Histadrut and its economic institutions such as the Histadrut factories, banks, the construction and development companies, the communications and marketing companies, etc., as well as the settlement movements which subscribe to the party, such as kibbutzim and moshavim. These utilities together form the largest employer and control most of the workers and jobs, that is they control the standard of living of the majority of the population. When a disagreement arose between Ben Gurion, the head of the party, and most of the other party leaders, he seceded and formed a new party – 'Rafi' – in the belief that he would be able to attract the party membership over to his side. He failed however, and the new party remained small and weak. The party apparatus and the

economic empire behind the party is stronger than any single leader. The left-wing Zionist Mapam Party has its base in its own kibbutzim which are members of the Kibbutz Ha'artzi Federation. The power base of the Likud bloc is private sector capital. The Black Panthers, on the other hand, do not have an economic base, and their membership was, and still is, made up of the poorest sector of the population. As a result, the organisation cannot fund its activities or help its supporters. In addition, the state funds the parties and their electoral campaigns in proportion to the number of members they have in parliament and the local councils, making it almost impossible for the new or small parties to compete with the well-established 'veteran' parties. Hence, the participation of the Panthers in the general elections meant certain failure, and it would have been better for them to remain an extra-parliamentary movement representing the Sephardim of all political beliefs. They could thus have worked at uniting to fight against racial discrimination and for a just peace.

6. A large part of the Sephardi population lives outside the Panther's field of influence (which is mainly in the Black Belt districts where they live). These are the people who live in the development towns and the remote cooperative settlements under the economic, political and organisational control of Zionist settlers, and they receive their daily bread from Zionist overseers (see chapter five).

7. All the Panthers' leaders come from the 'margins' of society, having very little education and being alienated from the trade unions, the professions and the Sephardi bourgeoisie.

8. Whereas the trade unions and the left-wing parties in other countries support down-trodden and oppressed communities, these organisations in Israel form the backbone of the Ashkenazi Zionist establishment. Even the Communist Party only supports the Sephardim as workers, and not as an ethnic community with its own cultural identity.

9. The Ashkenazi media depicted the Panthers as riff-raff and criminals, which alienated the 'respectable' Sephardim from them. Charlie Biton says that 'we published our abhorrence of racial discrimination wherever we could, hoping that we could attract Sephardi university students, the elite of the youth, but to no avail. They sympathised with the reasons which pushed us to rebel and even helped us, but only from afar – unfortunately, since the great majority of them feared for their status and achievements.'[20] The truth is that for the Sephardi intelligentsia the threat of 'job loss' was a very effective weapon which neutralised them.

10. The 1973 war enabled the government to engross the masses in the 'external' danger. Since the time of the British Mandate, the Zionists have exploited the 'Arab danger' to dilute the struggle against racism. They used the slogan 'the unity of the Jewish people against the Arab enemy'. The same 'danger' helped them to spend most of the resources on military expansionism and to maintain the economic gap between the two Jewish communities. Obviously the Israeli rulers are afraid of peace. In the fifties, they said that they needed thirty years of tension and siege by the Arabs so that the 'desert generation' would die out – that is, the Sephardi Jews who were born and raised in Arab countries – and for Israeli society to be fully integrated.

11. Lack of experience and knowledge in political work.

In addition to state-sponsored harassment and terror, the Jewish Defence League, headed by the American Rabbi Martin Kahane, 'declared war' on the Black Panthers in 1973. In the eighties, after this fascist gang formed the Kach Party, its members starting demonstrating outside the home of Charlie Biton in Jerusalem, shouting 'Where is Charlie Biton, the Arab? We are not the foreign settlers!'

The bulk of Kach's membership is made up of Jews who immigrated from America and who held anti-black views there. They, together with Russian immigrants, have now turned their racism against the Sephardim as well as the Palestinians.

Claims of the Ashkenazi Far Left

The far-leftists who took up the Palestinian cause published their reasons for the failure of the Black Panthers. It will be noticed that their claims are based on dubious Zionist sources.

1. Sephardim (or 'Orientals' according to their paternalistic terminology) do not constitute a single society with a culture of its own, there are Iraqis, Moroccans, Yemenites, etc. Each group has its own culture. This view is in complete accord with Zionist claims that there is no single Arab community and culture. Most of these leftists are ignorant of the true state of affairs in the Arab world, and can only communicate with their Palestinian 'brethren' in English.

2. Lack of cooperation with the Palestinian people. Firstly, the Sephardim believe that the Palestinians would be a danger to their

livelihood, and secondly, the Sephardim are hostile to the Arabs because of the 'oppression' they suffered in the Arab world which is why they started supporting the 'hawks' in Israel.

The truth is that the Black Panthers have always supported the principle of solidarity with the Palestinian people. The Sephardim did not begrudge the Palestinians from the occupied territories their jobs road-sweeping, cleaning Ashkenazi toilets, dish-washing and so on, since these were very low-paid jobs and the Sephardim had refused to do them. The Sephardim believe that the real conflict is not between them and the Palestinians but with the Ashkenazi overseers who try to keep them down so that they can preserve their privileges. Funds spent on rehabilitating the slum districts would mean cut-backs in the amount available for Ashkenazi settlement in the occupied territories. It would not mean a cut-back in the budgets of Arab villages, since they function almost without government funding anyway.

The myth that the Arabs oppressed the Jews in Arab countries has been propagated by the Zionists. There were, in fact, some regrettable incidents, but how can the new generation of Sephardim remember this 'oppression' when they have not lived in Arab countries, but were born in Israel? Their parents, who were born in Iraq, Iran, Egypt etc., and suffered from the so-called 'Arab oppression' did not vote for the 'hawks' but for the Labour party – until 1977. Thereafter half of them voted for the right-wing Likud, but not for ideological reasons, rather it was an economic protest vote. Far left-wing Ashkenazim always blame the Sephardim for having voted for the hawks and forget that all these 'hawks' are Ashkenazim. When they speak of the settlements on the West Bank they forget that they are all Ashkenazi, and when they speak of the fascist media in the slum districts they forget that the fascist machinery is totally Ashkenazi.

Who are Kahane, Begin, Sharon, Eitan, Shamir, Levinger and the other right-wing party activists who form the core of the Likud? They are all Ashkenazim. Who are the left-wing hawks such as Ben Gurion, Rabin, Dayan, Yadin, Peres and others? They are all Ashkenazim. The same goes for the leaders of the army, the intelligence services, the police and the whole Zionist establishment. When Ashkenazi left-wingers speak about these people, they forget that they are Ashkenazim and do not refer to their ethnic origin. When they speak about 'their following' they emphasise their ethnic origin – Sephardi. This is not to say that the Sephardim have no negative characteristics or that there are no traitors amongst their ranks, but to stress these negative phenomena does not help the common struggle for a just peace. It seems to me also that there is a division of labour amongst the Ashkenazim themselves. The Ashkenazi right incites the Sephardim against the Arabs, and the Ashkenazi left incites the Arabs against the Sephardim. The far left presents another 'reason' for the failure of the Panthers: they refused to cooperate with the Ashkenazi working class. The truth is that the Panthers were fragmented, as we have seen, because of this cooperation.

The Ashkenazi far left accuses the Sephardim of anti-Ashkenazi racism because Sephardim on the whole believe that the Ashkenazi community is responsible for the racial discrimination directed against them and against the Palestinians. This is exactly the position of the progressive world toward the whites in South Africa, and toward the French settlers in Algeria before independence. The international community has accepted this principle with regard to the responsibility of the German people for the policies of the Nazi era. This stance cannot be termed racist. The high standards of living of the Ashkenazim are founded on the exploitation of the Palestinians and the Sephardim.[21]

Establishment Reaction

Following the Panthers' demonstrations, the government formed the Horovitz Committee to enquire into the problem. The brief of the Committee was to look into the government's official stance that 'the lower educational level of the Sephardim has caused them to be discriminated against.' The Committee, however, came to the opposite conclusion, which was that 'as the educational level of the Sephardim is raised, they meet more discrimination' – that is to say that Sephardi intellectuals are exposed to greater discrimination than their under-educated brethren.[22] This indeed is the secret of the worsening of the economic and educational gap between the communities.

The committee of enquiry added that the standard of living of the Sephardim went down between 1959-1969.[23]

At the beginning of 1972, Dr Katz, the Director of Israeli National Social Security, published an article entitled 'Who and what is preventing the narrowing of the social gap?' DrKatz concluded that national insurance was not capable of narrowing the economic gap between the two communities, and that many children from large (i.e. Sephardi) families cannot benefit from university education because of their economic condition. Only 6 percent of the children who began their elementary schooling in 1951/1952 finished their secondary schooling successfully. In the Ashkenazi community, the percentage is 35 percent.[24] Dr Katz does not reveal how many Sephardi students were accepted by the Hebrew University or the Technion in Haifa.

On 28 June 1973, *Ma'ariv* published the report of the Prime Minister's Committee on Youth which dealt with the harshness of their material and psychological conditions. The report mentioned that 80 percent of youth belonged to the working class, and that 92 percent were Sephardim. The criteria used in the study were as follows:

1. A monthly income of $20 per person
2. Poor housing conditions with 3 or more persons to a room.
3. The parents' lack of education.

The Prime Minister, Golda Meir, when receiving the Black Panthers, had declared, 'In the past they were good children, and I hope that some of them will continue to be good. But I am afraid that others are not!'[25] This is the paternalistic attitude which runs through the state at all levels. None of the social services provided for the Sephardim acquit themselves honourably, rather they provide 'acts of charity to help the Sephardim to be better off than they were in the Arab countries they came from.' One of the means of psychological control used against the Sephardim is 'the cult of the state' whereby they serve the state and not vice versa.

Let us return to Dr Katz, who chaired the government committee made up of 113 members to look into the problems of poverty, and which did not include a single non-establishment Sephardi. The committee set up 14 sub-committees, and finally presented a lengthy report with their recommendations. Neither the government of Golda Meir, nor those which followed, did anything to diminish discrimination. Nor did Dr Katz himself, who subsequently became Minister of Employment and Social Services in the Likud government in 1980.[26]

The author, Matti Ronen, commented on this report,[27] that 'the government feared the spread of the Black Panther organization throughout the country which is why it set up the Katz Committee to appease the moderates in the Panther movement, and to persuade them that the government was undertaking some action to solve the problems of the Sephardim.'

The Katz Committee was authorised:

1. To define issues concerning underprivileged youth.
2. To look into the services which deal with the youth and children.
3. To make suggestions on how to improve their conditions.

The report issued by this committee comprised 11 topics which covered all the branches of the social services and included 289 recommendations. However the government only implemented a small portion of them. The following are some of the recommendations:

1. An effort should be made to reduce the gap between the two communities in the areas of housing, health and education, etc. The report stressed that 25 percent of the country's children were living in misery owing to their parents' lack of education as well as overcrowding in the home. This high percentage represents a danger to social equilibrium and could well push the underprivileged sector of the population to take revolutionary steps against the establishment, since 94 percent of the poor are Sephardim who believed that racial discrimination is the reason for their poverty. Matti Ronen commented on this recommendation that the government decided to upgrade social services without giving any priority to the needs of the poor. Therefore some Ashkenazim were able to benefit from this action and the social gap between the communities worsened.

2. A special government bureau should be set up to deal with the welfare of the poor (i.e. the Sephardim). However, the government rejected this recommendation and instead set up advisory committees without any executive authority. There was a prevailing belief that the government was only taking cosmetic measures.

3. Sephardim should participate in welfare plans by decentralising government, granting extensive powers to the local authorities. Furthermore they should be allowed to form local leaderships. Ronen comments that the ruling establishment has always tried to strengthen the central authority and has steadfastly treated the Sephardim paternalistically, justifying this with claims that Sephardi culture is debased and that their Arab culture cannot cope with the demands of a modern state. However, the Government rejected this recommendation.

4. Public consciousness should be dealt with for the sake of 'social cohesion' – that is, the racist opinions of Ashkenazi society should be countered. (However, what in fact happened was that racist views

about Sephardim and Palestinians became more firmly entrenched after the beginning of the seventies.)

In conclusion, we can state that Ronen was correct. The Ashkenazi government did not try to solve the problem of the two communities mutual incompatibility, and only tried to quell the Black Panther movement's popular uprisings.

At the same time, foreign journalists were sending out detailed reports about the bloody clashes between the Black Panthers and the security force. International circles received these reports with incredulity – 'Jews fighting Jews? Racism within the Jewish people, itself the victim of racism?' World Zionism, which had managed to cover up these problems since the end of the last century, very quickly started up its propaganda machine, which is one of the slickest in the world, to persuade public opinion in the West that racism does not exist in Israel and that the economic gap between the communities was a result of the Sephardim being educationally so far behind the Ashkenazim who were qualified, experienced and trained to deal with the latest technology. It also churned out the old story that Israel too was beset by the same hardships as the Western countries with their third world immigrants.

Sephardim and Likud

After the disintegration of the Black Panthers' unity in 1977, the Sephardim had only one way of getting rid of the Zionist establishment's rule as represented by the Labour Party, and its parliamentary bloc, Ma'arakh, that was to vote for the opposition – the right-wing Likud under the leadership of Menahem Begin, leader of the Herut Party. Many Sephardim took the view that 'my enemy's enemy is my friend'. From then on, the Sephardim started to gain more influence in the Herut Party, until the party conference of 1986 when there were clashes between the interests of the Sephardim and the Ashkenazim over the leaders of the party.

In a letter to *Falestine al-Thawra*,[28] Na'im Kedourie Ruben discussed the reasons which had made Sephardim vote for Begin and the growing position of his community in the Likud Bloc which had managed to oust the Labour Party from power in 1977.

He writes:

. . . Begin started off as the leader of a small party. After 29 years

273

as the leader of the Opposition to the Labour (Mapai) Government he won the elections in 1977 for the following reasons:

1. He exploited the plight of the Sephardim who had been condemned by the Labour government to become the 'proletariat', after having been members of the middle classes in Arab countries and in Palestine before Zionist settlement. Begin promised them complete equality, not just in the state but in his party too.

2. Begin encouraged Sephardi party activists who had a local following. He helped to establish local leadership such as that of David Levi who led the poor of Bet Shean.

3. By believing in economic liberalisation and encouraging private sector capital, Begin helped the Sephardim, who suffered from racial discrimination in state and Histadrut workplaces, to improve their situation and to become part of the petit bourgeoisie. Many became restauranteurs, or garage- and boutique-owners. He thus tied them economically to his right-wing party, and at the same time many [Sephardi] workers went to work for the private sector since advancement was much easier there that in the state or Histadrut factories.

Since work conditions in state and Histadrut factories were much better than in the private sector, competition between Ashkenazim and Sephardim was more aggressive, with the Ashkenazi managements giving preference to their own. On the other hand, promotion for Sephardim in the private sector was much easier. Moreover, the Sephardim were, and still are, subjected to much worse exploitation by the Ashkenazi kibbutzim than by the private sector.

Consequently, half of the Sephardi workforce moved into the private sector, and was tied economically to the Herut party. This analysis disproves the propaganda which states that the Sephardim support Herut because of their hostility to the Arabs.

The foregoing shows how the Sephardim gained influence in the Herut movement by flocking to the conference in large numbers. This development could well lead to their complete control of the party and its leadership with the help of their Druze and Bedouin comrades in the party.

The 'Sephardi danger' instilled fear in the hearts of the Ashkenazi settlers and businessmen and Shamir has only managed to stay in power by manipulating the figures . . .

This was the reason for the break-down of the party conference.

Many Sephardim believe that the Herut Party is going to be the Sephardi party, (although the balance of power favours the rich Ashkenazi minority over the poor majority). Accordingly, the Ashkenazi minority in the party has managed to attract to its ranks some Sephardim, such as Moshe Katsav and Meir Shitrit.

At any rate, 40 percent of Sephardim are currently voting for Labour and far left wing groups.'[29]

Since the Likud did not fulfil its promises to the Sephardim, and the poorest section became worse off as described in chapter nine, it lost many votes in the 1984 election. Neither of the two large parties was able to form a government, causing a real parliamentary crisis until the Americans forced the two blocs to form a coalition government. Henceforth, this government has been paralysed, spending most of its time in quarrels and mutual backbiting, leading to the present crisis (1990).

The Impact of the Black Panthers on the Sephardim

The Black Panther Movement encouraged the Sephardim to discuss ethnic discrimination publicly, to condemn it and fight against it. It also provided an active incentive for the renaissance of Sephardi culture and provided a groundswell of support for the struggle of the Palestinians.

Previously the Sephardi masses had been afraid to discuss the problem openly for the ruling establishment accused anyone who complained of racial discrimination of 'incitement', 'sectarianism' or 'exploiting the sectarian plight for his own personal interests'. It often accused him of what it termed 'dividing a united people', or it sneered that he was suffering from an inferiority complex. In fact the ruling establishment had, and still has, a terror of people like Eliahu Eliachar, David Ben Harush and others, who fought back. The Israeli intelligence services have always placed Sephardim who criticise racial discrimination under surveillance.

Not all of those who started speaking about this subject publicly were 'marginals' or anti-Zionists – there were also people who had served the Zionist establishment. Amongst these was Professor Yehuda Nini, of Yemenite origin, who was a commander in the 1948 war. He was later appointed secretary to the Minister of Education, Zalman Aran, and professor of literature at the Hebrew at the Hebrew University, participating in various committees of the Zionist media. We mentioned in chapter two his writings about the abhorrent treatment meted out to the Yemenites in Palestine by Ashkenazi settlers. In the spring of 1971 Professor Yehuda Nini wrote an important essay entitled 'Thoughts on the Destruction of the Third Temple'. The author foresees that the destruction of the state of Israel will come about through anti-Sephardi racial discrimination. Nini states it was necessary to go to the Yemenite Jews and 'tell them that they died (in 1948) for the Abramovitches and their like; sons of small shop-keepers, textile merchants and profiteers became the princes who rule us. The government and administration are Ashkenazi Jews. Statistics show that among them are a few from Eastern countries, but note well to what posts they are relegated. You will find them at the bottom of the ladder, among the waiters in the cafés, the clerks and small administrators.'

Professor Nini accused Israeli judges of being racists and swindlers: 'Let an Oriental commit the smallest crime, even if acquitted he gets thrown into prison. Let an Ashkenazi contravene the law, eyes are shut to it and he is even acclaimed publicly and if he must be penalised he can "aspire" to an open prison.'

Nini presents the Abromovitches (i.e. Ashkenazim) as 'bloodsuckers' on the body of the Sephardi community: 'those from Islamic countries have been expelled with trifling opposition from any corner of good earth which could be the object of a development programme so that the "others" may prosper.'

Nini demolishes the myth of complete equality in the army, saying that 'there is not a single Sephardi general, and there are very few Sephardi colonels or lieutenant-colonels. In rank below that of major, there are 10 percent Sephardim. The other military professions, such as pilots and specialists are staffed by the kibbutzniks and Western immigrants. The soldiers who have to do the cooking, the cleaning and other services are all Sephardim, and these latter hate their military duties and sometimes beat up their Ashkenazi officers. In some units you will find that a third, or a half, of the soldiers have served time in prison for insubordination or violence.'

It should be pointed out that Nini's study was not published in the anti-government press, but in *Shdemot,* a magazine of the Kibbutz Organisation.[30] The essay caused an outcry. It was not easy to make vicious attacks on Nini, for he was not a 'marginal' or 'an agent of Moscow'. The magazine which published his article was an establishment publication and *Ha'aretz* therefore concluded that Nini was worse than Matzpen (i.e. the extreme left).[31]

Cultural Renaissance

The awakening of the Black Panthers coincided with social developments which led to a radical change in the stance of the Sephardim toward the Ashkenazi rulers and their culture. Until that point, the Sephardi position had been characterised by fear, vacillation and shame over their culture and history. The fear was a result of the government's iron fist which employed the weapon of job dismissal in a harsh manner against any Sephardi who raised his voice in protest. Control by the ruling party (Mapai, or Labour) over the Sephardim was total as the party controlled the government, the government apparatus, the trade unions, the Jewish Agency and the factories and economic projects of the Histadrut. Hesitancy was a result of the crumbs dropped by the authorities to those who kept quiet, and the Sephardim exhibited shame toward their culture as the Ashkenazi-controlled media and educational system, literature, theatre, etc., managed to condition the new generation into believing that Sephardi culture is 'primitive, backward and barbarian'. Now their courage started to appear anew, not only because of the emergence of the Black Panthers, but there were other developments too which reinforced their identity.

The rise in the proportion of Sephardim – for example, from 30 percent in 1948 to 65 percent in 1971 – was a catalyst in this process. Wherever they were, in the fields, the factories or the coffee shop, they started to see that they were surrounded by members of their own community, they heard Arabic spoken, and they started to discover their common traditions again, notwithstanding that they had different countries of origin. They became increasingly aware that the Ashkenazi/American culture imposed on the country was what had pushed some of them into crime, prostitution, cultural bankruptcy, corruption and the breakdown of their families. They concluded that their Sephardi culture was better than the culture of the Zionist state and they started to take pride in it and tried to revive it. Their lowly position in Ashkenazi society only made them more aware of the honoured position they had held in Arab society, in Baghdad, Cairo, Beirut and Damascus, etc. They realised that Zionism had misled them.

In the fifties, most Sephardim were immigrants from the Arab world who did not understand Hebrew or the ins and outs of government. Some of them clung to the false premise that Israel was the long-awaited Messianic state which had come about to save Jews and mankind from injustice . . . By the seventies most of them were Israeli born and educated. They could speak the language of the régime, and understood the ruses and cruelty of their rulers and started to disdain their parents' naïveté and weakness. They started to rebel.

There was another reason: in the fifties, unemployment was widespread amongst the Sephardim and forced them into submission – the welfare state did not exist. Those without work were in danger of dying from hunger. However, in the seventies the economy was in a better state, unemployment had gone down and the private sector had expanded and was not controlled by the ruling party. Many Sephardim left the public sector and the Histadrut sector and joined the private sector, particularly the *petits bourgeois* – divesting themselves of the formerly omnipresent fear of unemployment or dismissal.

On the other hand, the Ashkenazi government has used the Sephardim as front-line soldiers resulting in considerable loss of life and fostering systematic evasion of army service. In the slum districts most young men refuse to join the army. There are 'no go' areas for the military authorities, which call this phenomenon 'social shortcoming' (in addition to claiming that they are 'drug addicts' and 'criminals' or 'lunatics'). They issue a document which indicates that the bearer has been 'exempted' from military service under Article 24. Those holding it boast that they belong to 'Commando Unit 24'. The minority who join the army are considered stupid and are the butt of jokes and objects of scorn in the slum districts.

The journalist Shalom Cohen (of *Ha'olam Hazeh*) asked one of these youths if he would like to join the armed forces. He replied, 'Me, serve in their army! No chance. When they summoned me for the medical examination, I stuffed myself full of drugs, and they sent me to a psychiatrist and got my papers stamped with Article 24. I'd have to be a real sucker to throw away three years of my life doing nothing.' The journalist added that this youth lived in Pardes Katz where those exempted from the army constitute over 50 percent.[32]

In the realm of culture, the Sephardim started to show an interest in Arabic poetry and music in public. Having previously listened to the Arabic radio stations half-secretly, they now started to tune into the Arabic radio and television of the Arab states openly, throwing down the gauntlet to the Ashkenazim's distaste for what they termed 'primitive' Arabic music. They started to form Arabic music and dance groups and set up a cassette and video industry to make up for the almost complete absence of Arabic music and films in the Israeli media, which only broadcast one half hour a week of 'ethnic programming', as if the Sephardim were a small minority.

In addition, they started to criticise the school syllabuses for only covering Ashkenazi culture and history and for depicting the Sephardim as having been primitives who were straight out of the desert – until the settlers 'civilised' them. The curriculum included no mention of Sephardi history, because it was part of Arab history, and Palestinian history was studied in a way that accorded with Zionist views. That is to say that it was studied up until the fall of the Jewish state in 70 A.D. and then taken up again with the start of Zionist settlement at the end of the last century – as if Palestine had been empty for 2,000 years until the Ashkenazi immigrants discovered it and set about planting trees, draining the swamps and 'making the desert bloom'.

Sephardi intellectuals in France applied themselves to studying their history and publishing it. Hayyim Za'afrani stated 'we are witnessing now the awakening of the Sephardi mind . . . a mind which is giving impetus to the development of an ethnic group, a culture which is different from the other cultural, ethnic and intellectual groups which make up the Jewish world . . . we have set about rediscovering the culture and history inherited from the golden age of Jewish-Arab cooperation which occurred in the Middle East.'[33] Professor Za'afrani continued, 'Our studies in Jewish thought in North Africa have been completed. Our findings show, and will continue to show, the Jews' constant devotion in those countries to producing excellent works in the fields of philosophy, law, poetry, literature, commentaries, sermons, and collections of oral folklore which were written down in the Hebrew dialects which were a mixture of Hebrew, Arabic and Berber.'[34]

Sephardi intellectuals were proud of the tolerance of their Judaism (which was undoubtedly influenced by Islamic tolerance), compared to the Ashkenazi rite which is much stricter and more dogmatic.

Naim Khlaschi, of Iraqi origin, pointed out that 'Sephardim are part of Arab culture. They have common traditions, they honour the teacher and the father, they respect the family framework, strive for their children's education, eat the same food and listen to the same music. Rich and poor alike, they prefer the music of Farid al-Atrash to that of Wagner. Charlie Biton and his colleagues are promising to resurrect Sephardi culture, which is being suppressed and destroyed. Israel does not deserve to carry on as a foreign Western state here in the East.' Khlaschi added that when he attempted to defend Sephardim in the transit camps, the establishment threatened to make him a simple worker. However, he refused to do other than preserve his human dignity, and his culture as an Iraqi, at any cost. 'Once the Minister of Police was invited to Ramat Gan, a small town near Tel Aviv whose population is 25 percent Iraqi, to discuss foreign and security affairs. Invitations were sent to all the Iraqis, including the deputy mayor. 600 people attended the meeting, but there were only 6 Iraqis. The rest were Ashkenazi pensioners. When the minister asked why the Iraqis had stayed away, he was told that a concert of Umm Kulthoum was being televised.'

Khlaschi ascribed the spread of prostitution amongst Sephardi girls in Israel to the destruction of Sephardi culture and the imposition of Western culture. He spoke of his optimism that Middle Eastern culture would eventually prevail in spite of the difficulties. He said that instead of a perfunctory glance at the history of the Jews of Iraq and North Africa which is how schools teach now, pupils would be taught in depth about the ancient Jewish universities in Iraq, such as Sura and Pumbedita. He added that Ashkenazi teachers claim that these were only religious seminaries whereas in fact they taught a wide range of subjects.[35]

In the field of singing, Shlomo Bar, of Moroccan origin, set up a group called 'The Natural Choice Band' which was received enthusiastically by the nostalgic Sephardi public. Bar stated that Moroccan Jews never suffered from oppression in Morocco. Jews and Muslims coexisted so closely there that Muslims prayed at the graves of Jewish saints. Bar added that he wanted to teach his son Arabic so that he could get along with his Palestinian neighbours.[36]

Amongst the tapes which have been distributed on cassettes were the songs of Muhammad 'Abd al-Wahhab, Umm Kulthum, Farid al-Atrash, Asmahan and Nazem al-Ghazali.[37] An eager Iraqi public lapped up tapes of Milo Hamama, and of the Iraqi singer, Murad Salman Basun, who re-recorded and reissued his songs.

A number of intellectuals have started to write their memoirs of life in Arab countries. Because of the climate of cultural repression, most of these works are published in Hebrew. The best-known of these books is *A House in Baghdad* by Yitzhak Bar Moshe, in which he describes the warm relations which prevailed between Jews, Christians and Muslims in Iraq. Y. Qujman published his valuable book, *Contemporary Classical Music in Iraq*, which was published in London by ACT in Arabic in 1978. Ezzat Sasson-Mu'allim published the memoirs of his family in a book entitled *By The Rivers Of Babylon* in 1980 (in Arabic). Nissim Rejwan wrote *The Jews of Iraq* in English and was published by Weidenfeld and Nicholson.

One of the best-known intellectuals who did not give up his mother tongue, that is Arabic, is Samir Naqqash. On 28 June 1986 *Falestine al-Thawra* published an article by him in which he condemns the way he was arbitrarily uprooted from Iraq and he explains why he persevered in using Arabic as follows:[38]

'Language is the most important means of communicating with people. Communication is the basic objective of the writer. Language is the raw material and the writer's expressive power and energy is in proportion to his grasp of the raw material.

'Arabic is my first language. The first words I spoke were in Arabic. It is my natural language and I have always loved it. I have a great passion for it. Moreover, Arabic is well known for its beauty and richness. Hebrew, which was a dead language for thousands of years until it was resurrected very recently, can just not be compared with it in terms of richness or utter beauty.

'In modern Iraq, some of the most outstanding poets and writers were Jews. Studies in the development of contemporary Iraqi poetry and literature concluded that the first short story was written in the twenties by a Jewish youth – Murad Mikha'il (who recently passed away in Israel). These Iraqi/Jewish writers and poets continued writing in Arabic in Israel. However, there are those who continue to express their surprise at the fact that I write in Arabic although I left Iraq when I was 12 years old . . . Some people repudiate the fact that I have personal and artistic reasons for writing in Arabic and simply consider it a "complex" I have.

'All the problems, which I and my family went through after the catastrophe of being uprooted from Iraq and transplanted here, have made me more nostalgic. My love for Arabic was redoubled and I made an effort to absorb every word of classical and colloquial Arabic that I come across. I have never become assimilated in this country. On the contrary, I have opposed everything 'Israeli', and I, like many people of Iraqi origin, still consider myself an Iraqi. That is the truth, notwithstanding that some people try to deny it.'

However, Sephardim were unable to revive their Arabic-Islamic art and craft and their skills died with them. Only a fraction of their works found their way to Israeli museums.

The Emergence of Other Protest Movements

Since the British Mandate, all the Zionist parties have set up special branches for the Sephardim, that is, a bureau for Sephardi affairs within the party. In fact the purpose of the bureau was to solicit Sephardi votes in parliamentary and local elections. The officials of the bureau were salaried and their duties included bribing, intimidation and patronage. These methods are still employed. When Na'im Khlaschi was brought to Tel Aviv in 1951 to work on *Al-Mirsad* (the Arabic newspaper of the left-wing Mapam party) he was sent to party headquarters where he was told to go to room number 8. It was labelled 'Bureau of Sephardim and Yemenites', next to the lavatory and the 'Arabic Section'). He was thunderstruck. When he was asked to come in, he replied 'No. I'm going home. I am having an attack of diarrhoea. Perhaps tomorrow. . .' Khlaschi described a Sephardi meeting which took place in Mapam under the banner 'For Socialism and Zionism and the Brotherhood of Peoples'. Ashkenazi leaders gave speeches of mind-boggling lengthiness. He asked to be allowed to say a word and they shut him up. Finally he was permitted to speak for five minutes. He addressed his words to the head of the party, Me'ir Ya'ari: 'We do not want a special department for Sephardim and Yemenites. We don't want a "Negro's Department"' Me'ir Ya'ari refused to countenance absorbing the Sephardim and Yemenites into the main body of the party, so Na'im threw away his party card and left the meeting. The department was only abolished ten years later. 'My quarrel with those leaders is not new,' Na'im added. 'I have known how they behave for a long time. In the Mapai (Labour) Party too there is a special Sephardi Department – next to the toilets too, but the room number is different!'[39]

Ezra Sofer wrote about Zionist party agents in Sephardi society in *Ha'aretz* on 22 May 1981. 'In the past people used to boast about their thoroughbred horses but now the party leaders compete over the Sephardim. Menahem Begin won over David Levi, Moshe Dayan has Ben Porat and Shimon Peres uses Shoshana Arbili. Soon they will start comparing the relative values of their tame "natives".'

Against this background, Gabriel Ben Simhon (of Moroccan origin) said to a correspondent of *Ha'aretz* on 28 May 1980 that 'Sephardim realise that this government does not represent them . . .

They must create an organized opposition, a force which is ready to fight – a force which by rights is theirs.' (See chapter seven for a précis of the article.)

The formation of the Black Panthers was followed by Sephardi youth organisations which aimed to improve conditions through positive action, and not through popular uprisings. The most important of these organisations are Oded, Ohalim, Ela, ShHQ and the Eastern Front.

Oded

This movement was born in the Israeli universities. It believes in positive action to improve the conditions of the Sephardi community, such as helping weak pupils with their studies. It also aims to raise the level of social consciousness and independence of action of the Sephardim so that they can solve their own problems instead of waiting for the progressive Ashkenazim to come along.

It cannot be denied that the Ashkenazim have imbued the Sephardim with an inferiority complex. The membership of Oded says that in order to throw off this complex they must help their community and prove that they have freed themselves from this psychological domination and that they can succeed independently in a new society.

Since the community was always autonomous under Islamic and Ottoman rule, it was the individual's duty to serve his community. This autonomy has been destroyed in the state of Israel, and those who want to work for their community were told 'Leave it to the government or the Jewish Agency,' or 'you are a sectarian and are shredding the unity of the Jewish people'. Thus the Sephardi community, particularly the poor, were left to the mercy of those in power – the Ashkenazim. When things got worse, they criticised the government and the Jewish Agency, but they did nothing because the state of Israel had made them forget how to work on behalf of the community and had conditioned them through the media to believe that they, and the Arabs as a whole, were incapable of carrying out social action, or cooperating with each other, because they suffered from the individualism and corruption which had been prevalent in the Ottoman era. Of course that is the racist view point from which Oded tried to free people.

Oded also encouraged 'help exchange' groups to work with pupils who were weak at school, to organise summer holidays for Sephardi children and to run preparatory courses for new pupils. It encouraged political activity at the university level, and its activity spread throughout the country.

Initially the authorities had reservations about the organisation, but then became hostile and cut off all financial help for two reasons: firstly, because the movement helped the community to work independently of the establishment, and secondly, because the organisation was accused of 'political activity'.

The organisation does admit that its activities can be somewhat condescending in the way help is meted out by the intellectuals to the masses, but the Sephardi masses have reached such a state of degradation that the organisation has to customise the help it offers to them. The organisation hopes, however, that by helping the down-trodden to set themselves aright and achieve positions within the ruling establishment, these same people will perhaps be able to change government policy towards their community by means of ethical pressure and by stirring up opposition – not against the Ashkenazi community, but against existing conditions in the country.

The weak points of Oded are very apparent and can be summarised as follows:

1. Dependence on government funding means that the government can destroy the organisation whenever it wants. It is the ruling establishment which created the social structure, and thus it is pure political naïveté to demand the government's help to destroy it.

2. Its paternalistic attitude toward the masses: if the Oded Movement believed in independent action it would have joined the Black Panther Movement, and/or worked at the grass roots level. The way to confront the problems should be for the intellectuals and the workers to unite in their struggle.

3. If the Sephardim are the victims of the Zionist state, why does the movement insist on the principle of supporting Zionism and the state of Israel? This is reminiscent of the stance of the Communist Party which states 'We are against Zionism, but we support the state of Israel', even though the state of Israel with its institutions and policies is the true embodiment of Zionism.

The Oded people proved their political naïveté when they joined with Mapam for two years. This marriage ended in failure because Mapam is a Zionist colonialist party whose kibbutzim exploit Sephardim. Mapam wanted to use Oded as a bridge-head to control the Sephardi community, particularly to win votes in the elections, but it refused to grant any significant positions in the party leadership apparatus to Oded people. When they insisted that such positions would help the whole community to improve its lot in the social ladder, the party fobbed them off. Subsequently it started to fight them by bringing in unknowns to vote against them at party meetings, which eventually led to their departure. The Oded people said later that the Mapam kibbutzim were not in the least bit interested in the Sephardim of the development towns.

There is also a 'psychological' reason for the failure of this 'marriage' between the North Africans and Mapam: the Ashkenazi members of Mapam, particularly from the 'Hashomer Hatza'ir' kibbutz federation, are the most arrogant in the country. They form a political, social and ethnic closed group, which believes that it is the ideological, socialist, Zionist, Marxist and pioneer élite. They believe that their socialism is the most perfect brand known to mankind, and that the Sephardim are still living in the jungle. The strange thing in the Zionist political scene is that the more left-wing the Ashkenazim are, the more they tend to denigrate the native culture of the Middle East (with a few rare exceptions, such as Felicia Langer), and here we are not talking about politics, but about personal relations and prejudices. This was one of the strengths of the Herut right-wingers and what made them so attractive to the Sephardim.

Shelly Yehimovitz claimed that the Oded Movement failed because it was a bourgeois movement, made up of highly educated or rich North Africans. The author agrees with this, but the nationalist bourgeoisies of the Third World have scored decisive victories against colonisation. If the members of the North African bourgeoisie in the Oded Movement were to ally themselves with the other opposition movements, such as the Black Panthers – instead of the with the ruling establishment, they too would score some impressive victories. We only have to cast a glance at the Palestinian bourgeoisie, or the struggle of the Palestinian intellectuals.

Charlie Biton points out that 'Oded has operated as a part of the ruling establishment, but the Panthers work for radical social change. We are sure that our way is correct – whereas they get a salary from the régime'. F. Ezran, a former leader of Oded, admitted that 'the Panthers' participation in social change was outstanding.'

In the final analysis, the Oded movement has had a positive result – which is the lesson its members learned from having requested help from the régime. This lesson is a necessary stage in the development of Sephardi consciousness about the nature of Zionism.[40]

Dr Asher Edan (of Tunisian origin) of the University of Tel Aviv and some comrades followed the path of Oded and started arranging crash courses to train Sephardi youth for leadership work. The Zionist Organisation funded their activities, but when they became too popular, they were dismissed from their jobs and their activities ground to a halt.

Ohalim [Tents]

Alongside Oded which functioned in the universities, Sephardim in the slum districts set up other organisations, the most important of which was the Ohalim, or Tents, Organisation. The name recalled the tragic camps Sephardim lived in when they were brought to Palestine after 1948. On 16 June 1979 Ohalim announced 'the end of the Ashkenazi colonialist mandate over Palestine and the founding of the Ohalim Slum Districts Council in order to carry out the Declaration of Independence' which contained the movement's manifesto with regard to complete equality amongst the citizens. At the beginning of this declaration the organisation mentioned that 'the Declaration of Independence of the state of Israel, dated 14 May 1948, promised that the State would develop for the benefit of all of its inhabitants regardless of religion, race, etc.,' and that it would be 'founded on principles of justice, freedom and peace' and would 'implement social equality'.

Ohalim accuses the rulers of Israel of having ignored the 'Declaration of Independence'. Instead of setting up a democratic country founded on equality, they have divided the people into two 'and condemned us to be hewers of wood and drawers of water'. The signatories to the declaration continued 'and you have imprisoned us in slum ghettos and in your tower block cages and you have debased our humanity through overcrowding in your desire that we should be in your shadow with no self-expression or cultural identity. You have done everything to keep us out of political decision-making and the central subjects to do with the conditions of our life. You have created the conditions for crime to burgeon and to transform our children into prisoners.' The signatories then address the Likud government:

'Since you tricked us after having promised the slum districts that you would repair the damage wrought against society by past

Israeli governments since the founding of the state, and over the last two years have added other failures to the list, we, the youth of the Ohalim slum in Jerusalem and the second generation in the slum ghettos, have decided to put an end to this state of affairs and to embark upon a struggle to create a new society. Today [16 June 1979] we announce the end of the disgraceful and unjust mandate which has practised discrimination against 60 percent of its citizens. To this end, we have set up the Ohalim Slum Council and have written the Declaration of Independence of the Ohalim Slum Camp. We, the residents of the slum districts, will not rest until this Declaration is made an intrinsic part of the basic law of the state . . . ' The Declaration contains the following: 'We the Ohalim Slum Youth, call for the building of a Society which will have as its aim the following:

1. A revolution in education and culture in order to liberate our children and families from servitude.
2. A change in the realm of housing in order to allow every family to live in human conditions with decent educational and health facilities.
3. The extension of free health services.
4. Acknowledgement of our equal rights in order to determine the content and aim of welfare policy.
5. The departure from the slum ghettos must be paralleled by the development of our authentic cultural identity.
6. Rehabilitation to be extended to those who have fallen victim to injustice.
7. The provision of decent living conditions for bread-winners, children, the aged, pensioners and the sick.

Ohalim categorically rejects the idea of collecting donations for the slum districts. It calls for an end to the amassing of funds at the slum districts' expense. We aim to set up a society founded on equality with no social gap, and we demand to be a centre for social reform to start immediately under the leadership of the Ohalim Slum Council.

Jerusalem, 16 June 1979.

Signed: Members of the Council.

We should mention that the seventh article of the Declaration includes the Palestinian people. The organisation does not deal with their political problems but with social, economic and cultural matters with particular emphasis on the slum districts.

In 1984, Ohalim under the leadership of Yamin Suwisa joined

the Labour Party. Although the residents of the slum disricts represent 22 percent of the country's population, the organisation was only granted three seats in the Party Bureau, whereas the kibbutzim which represented 3 percent of the population had 12 seats. Suwisa stated that peace with the Palestinians, the liberation of the occupied Arab territories and the expenditure of funds on helping the underdogs, as opposed to war-mongering and the establishment of new settlements, were the principal reasons that made him join the Labour Party. He stated that Peres, the leader of the Labour Party, believed in a true peace. Suwisa stressed 'the Occupation does not only corrupt, but is the single most important cause for the current conditions in the slum districts.'[41] He personally would like to be a member of parliament one day.[42]

Defiance

Alongside 'positive' struggle as practised by members of the middle class, poor Sephardim under the leadership of the Black Panthers, Ohalim, Shahaq and Elah challenged the authorities with other means of struggle, such as establishing camps on public lands in pre-1967 Israel to house homeless young families. These camps were not set up to be permanent but to act as a protest against Israeli settlement policy in the West Bank and the Gaza Strip at the expense of social services inside Israel. These activities led to bloody clashes between the youths in the camps and the police which ended in the demolition of the camps and mass arrests.

Ohel Moreh was one of these camps. It was established in June 1980 and named after one of the West Bank settlements.[43] In the same month 'Ohalim City' was set up in Nahalat Yehuda in the centre of the country. This new site was hurriedly besieged by the police and the border guard, and after a bloody battle the camp was demolished and a large number of its dwellers were wounded. As usual there was a campaign of arbitrary arrests.[44]

In July 1980, two hundred Sephardim occupied empty flats in Hadar Yosef in Tel Aviv, condemning the settlement policy in the West Bank. Four women were wounded by the border guard during the ensuing clash.[45]

On 1 August 1980 *Ha'aretz* reported that two hundred Sephardi families were building a camp near the town hall in Mevasseret Tsion. The mayor, Elias Moyal, warned that the social gap between Ashkenazim and Sephardim could well lead to a social explosion.

He censured the Ministry of Housing for not having built any new residential units over the past five years.

On 4 July 1980 *Ha'aretz* reported that 30 families had put up 20 tents in the town of Yahud, near Petah Tikvah. The newspaper added that 85 percent of these families had been living with their in-laws. The security forces and the border guard quickly arrived and demolished the camp. We should note that the border guard, which is notorious for its cruelty, is only ever used against the Palestinians and the Sephardim.

The second method of struggle was to build unlicensed extensions. The Palestinians and the Sephardim both did this to ease their housing needs. If a son or daughter got married and had nowhere to live, the family would add a room to their old houses – but the government refused to grant licenses for this. The Ashkenazi controlled municipalities tried their utmost to have these old houses demolished and to sell the land off to companies greedy to build luxury housing for Ashkenazim. Often these plots were in the middle of the large cities and worth millions. There was another reason that made the government demolish these districts, which belonged to Palestinians who had been expelled from them. Moshe Smilansky, a writer and humane, veteran settler, commented on this common phenomenon that 'the ruling establishment is trying to destroy anything built by the Palestinians in this country to prove to the world that Palestine was an arid desert and that everything was built there through the efforts of the Zionist settlement.'

Sometimes the authorities simply bulldoze these extra rooms. This action is followed by violent clashes between the police force, the border guard and the inhabitants and ends with many arrests being made.

The racial discrimination inherent in these acts of demolition makes the Sephardim particularly angry, since the authorities take no action against the illegally built rooms on Ashkenazi homes in the north of Tel Aviv.

Ha'aretz wrote on 9 June 1980 that 'the authorities have demolished the house of the Mondani family in Holon even though the family had bought and paid for the house. The government claimed that the land was state property. The family with twelve children became homeless.'

In Segev in Galilee, the authorities demolished six houses which belonged to Me'ir Azulai, Shimon Buonaparte and other Sephardim. These victims screamed at the rulers 'You are treating us like the Nazis.' *Ha'aretz* added on 12 December 1980 that the government is removing the town's Sephardi residents as part of its plan to establish an Ashkenazi settlement to be called Moshav Atsmon. Two hours after this event the police and the border guard attacked the Palestinian village of 'Arraba. They demolished a workshop which belonged to Tawfiq Shalash and Othman Asali because it had been built without a permit. On the same day the South African Minister of Finance arrived in Israel and gave a televised speech in which he affirmed the similarity between Israel and South Africa.[46]

On 23 December 1982 the police carried out a shocking provocation at Kfar Shalem in Tel Aviv by demolishing the extra room that Shimon Yehoshua, of Yemenite origin, had built with the help of a Palestinian friend on to his house for his marriage. When this young man tried to resist the police, they shot him dead. On the day of the incident, his father had won a stay of demolition from the courts, which the police disregarded. They claimed that the deceased was armed although eye witnesses said that the gun could have been taken from him without having to shoot him at point blank range. Yehoshua had to build the unlicensed extra room since his family, with nineteen members, was living in only three rooms. The incident aroused the anger of the Sephardim in the slum districts. The newspapers which reported this claimed that orders had been issued to demolish Ashkenazi property also in the Dizengoff Centre, and the Plaza Hotel, but that they were not carried out. Sephardim, who staged noisy demonstrations, pointed out that the police did not open fire on the armed Ashkenazi settlers who commit acts of violence and pick quarrels with the Palestinians in the occupied territories. They did not open fire on the Ashkenazi settlers who forcefully resisted the orders to evacuate Yamit in occupied Egyptian territory. After the murder of this Yemenite, youths from the district blocked streets, burnt tires and wrote anti-Ashkenazi slogans on the walls, such as 'Ashke-NAZIS'. The irony is that 'Ashkenazi' means also 'German' in Hebrew.

A few days later, on 1 January 1983 demonstrations broke out in various towns over the demolitions and the Member of Parliament, Tewfiq Tubi, stated in his report to parliament that a similar incident had taken place on 8 November 1977 when the police killed a Palestinian called al-Masri in the village of Majd al-Kurum. He mentioned another incident in Nazareth in which forty-four Palestinians had been injured.

The Knesset decided to delay the Yemenite youth's burial until nightfall to prevent any other disturbances.[47] One of the reasons for the murder of this youth could well have been his friendship with a Palestinian. The authorities try to make sure that the only 'friendly' relations with the Palestinians take place via the secret service. The Ashkenazi progressives keep the secret services and the Ministry of Foreign Affairs up to date on any 'secret' peace talks they hold with Palestinians abroad.

Two years after the murder of the Shimon Yehushua, there were more bloody clashes between the residents of Kfar Shalem and the security forces following the demolition of some buildings. The demonstrators closed off the main streets and set fire to a warehouse which belonged to the municipality and the police arrested five people including Moni Yakim, a Black Panther leader. The demonstrators shouted 'Ashke-NAZIS'! at the police. *Ha'aretz*, which reported this incident on 28 December 1984, stated that the municipality of Tel Aviv had demolished 100 houses and more were slated for demolition. It mentioned that a Member of Parliament, Michael Eytan, and a police officer were injured in the demonstrations and that the police had managed to stop the demonstrators storming the residence of the mayor, Shlomo Lahat. As the value of land in this slum district (formerly Kafr Salama) rocketed, the authorities sold it off to private companies and asked the residents to leave. When they refused, the municipality cut off all services, and filth and rubbish started to pile up in the district (the desperate conditions in Kfar Shalem are similar to those of the Palestinian refugees in the occupied Gaza Strip and the West Bank). The Sephardi residents of the district threatened to kill the mayor. One of them, Elias Mizrahi, stated to a correspondent of *Ha'aretz* that 'people here suffer from racial discrimination. The state has crushed them and the situation is very explosive.' The demonstrators then demanded that the United Nations intervene to protect them against the state of Israel. The MP, Charlie Biton, stayed with the demonstrators throughout the day.[48]

Hada Bosem wrote in *Ha'aretz* on 15 February 1985 that the mayor of Tel Aviv was waging a war for the sake of law and order. However, he was only waging it on the weak and not demolishing buildings erected by the Ashkenazim in the Dizengoff Centre or elsewhere. On Friday, the municipality carried out the demolition orders in Kfar Shalem as the residents carried out demonstrations and threw fire bombs into the main street (*Ha'aretz*, February 14 1984).

Eliezer Dammari, of Yemenite origin, admits to having built an unlicensed room, but he claims that Avraham Shapira, a Member of Parliament, also broke the law and the authorities did not demolish his home. A municipal engineer corroborated this claim. The correspondent of *Ha'aretz* pointed out that for every six demolitions carried out in the slum districts of south Tel Aviv, the authorities carry out only one in the Ashkenazi northern suburbs. The newspaper condemned this discrimination. In the Palestinian sector this policy is much more severe, particularly if we take into consideration that the number of Palestinians doubles every ten years. The government generally refuses to grant licenses for new Palestinian houses or to extend existing houses.

Since the emergence of the Black Panther Movement, there has been a great increase in Sephardi disturbances, demonstrations and riots aimed at improving their living conditions and their children's school, as well as against the cut-backs in social and health services and the policy of unemployment.

In December 1980, about 30 youths from the Hatikva district in Tel Aviv locked the mayor, Shlomo Lahat, in his office with 7 of his senior aides and nailed the door shut because he had refused to fund a youth organisation in the district. 400 policemen and border guards rushed to the scene and attacked the youths. The incident ended with some of the protesters being injured and their leaders arrested. The youths declared that the municipality was trying to paralyse the activities of the local leadership in Hatikva.[49]

Five days after this incident, the police arrested twelve youths from the district without warrants, and confined them to house arrest from six p.m. until seven a.m. One of the leaders of the district emphasised that the police did not treat the Ashkenazi extremists, such as Gush Emunim, the same way when they committed acts of violence against the Arabs.[50] The police beat Motti Levi and Smadar Batish so badly that they lost consciousness and had to be taken to hospital.[51]

Ha'aretz stated on 3 April 1981 that the youth of Hatikvah carried out a protest demonstration against the closure of the Ohel club. They blocked the crossroads of Lod and Nitzahon Streets and stopped all traffic. They threw stones at the police who had to use force to reopen the roads. In Natanya, the mayor fled from his office to avoid having to meet Sephardim from Ramat Herzl who were carrying out a noisy demonstration over the closure of the youth club in their district.[52] The authorities had closed down these clubs because they were afraid of the anti-establishment political activities which the Sephardi were planning in them.

During the election campaign of 1981, the Sephardim used the dispute between the two major parties, the Labour and the Likud Bloc, to carry out violent attacks against the Labour party in revenge for the policy of discrimination. There was also another reason: during this election campaign the Labour leaders provoked the Sephardim, one of whom said 'the Labour Party is supported by the generals and the intellectuals, whereas Likud is only supported by the *chakh chakh*.'[53] Accordingly, many Sephardim started to put stickers on their cars which read 'This *chakh chakh* votes Likud'. The media joined in the anti-Sephardi campaign as did the Ashkenazi actor Dudu Topaz. One of the reasons for this was the emergence of a new North African electoral list headed by Abu Hatzerah. This list – Tami – won four seats. On the other hand, Motti Gur a former chief of staff and a Labour Party leader, uttered the statement that 'we'll screw the Sephardim like we screwed the Arabs.' These racist comments led to an increase in acts of violence. *Ha'aretz* wrote that the Sephardim set fire to a police station in the (Yemenite) township of Rosh Ha'ayin and caused extensive material damage. Sephardi youths threw stones at the police and harassed and insulted them in various other places. Shimon Peres, the leader of the Labour Party, was pelted with tomatoes and driven out of Bet Shemesh.

Likud naturally exploited these incidents to garner the Sephardi vote and won by forty-eight seats to form its second government in 1981.

The Sephardi president, Yitzhak Navon, condemned ethnic tension and the hostile language used by the Ashkenazim. When asked about Israel being on top of a sectarian time-bomb, he replied, 'the fuse has become very short and must be put out.' A correspondent of *Ha'aretz*,[54] who described the televised discussion in which Navon made these remarks, pointed out that 'the president knows as well as we do that we are sitting on a volcano.' The president attributed the bitterness of the Sephardim to their exclusion from active participation in the state's affairs. The newspaper commented on the programmes for Balkan Jews (who are Sephardim) by stating that even in the death camps in Europe the Ashkenazim discriminated against the Balkan Jews.

Shlomo Tsadok, a member of Tami, wrote an article in *Yedi'ot Aharonot* in which he suggested that the way to solve the problem of anti-Sephardi racial discrimination was through armed struggle against the Ashkenazim.[55]

Two days later, Natan Dunevitz commented that 'even the Sephardim who have done well for themselves get angry when they think back . . . they will not forget the time their parents were humiliated, how they were sprayed with DDT and pushed into the transit camps for years. They want revenge upon the Ashkenazi establishment which is led by the Labour Party. This party will not get back into power by granting symbolic representation to the Sephardim, for this has now been unmasked and lost the people's trust.'[56]

The string of insults directed against the Sephardim is not new. We have become accustomed to hearing them since the British Mandate. All these terms of abuse – Arab, Oriental, Black, primitive, Iraqi, Persian, Egyptian, etc. – express the racism and arrogance of the Ashkenazim toward the Muslim, Christian and Sephardi inhabitants of the Middle East. What is new is that the insults now appear in the media, at political meetings and on the street where previously they were only used in the private domain. This change has come about because the Ashkenazi rulers in the Labour Party lost their nerve and their reason when they realised that these 'slaves' were starting to raise their heads and had managed to oust them from power in spite of their political weakness. It is true that owing to the political economic and parliamentary system the Sephardim cannot form a political party able to compete with the Ashkenazi parties, even though the Sephardim form two thirds of the Jewish population, but they can sway the balance in a general election to keep an Ashkenazi party in or out of power. This numerical power has strengthened the importance of the Sephardim and they have started using their 'numbers' to uphold their dignity on both a political and a grass roots level.

Let us examine some other examples of the protests carried out by the Sephardim against the settlers. In the township of Or Yehuda (made up of the former camps of Saqiya and Khairiya and Kafr 'Ana), all the schools and kindergartens went on strike in protest at the poor level of teaching. The children and their parents, who were mostly Iraqi, demanded that the school and its equipment be improved and that qualified teachers be appointed. Strikes spread to the township of Bnei Brak where overcrowding in the school building forced a class of one hundred pupils to study in an air-raid shelter.[57]

In February 1986 all civil servants in the development towns went on strike and demonstrated in front of the Knesset demanding a meeting with the Prime Minister, Shimon Peres. However, he refused their request and sent out a huge number of mounted policemen and border guards armed with the latest riot-control equipment. The demonstrators shouted 'We want bread and work',

'Bread for the townships, not for the settlements', etc. They summarised their problems as follows:

1. Unemployment.
2. Low wages (£100–160 per month).
3. Delays in getting paid.
4. The municipalities' debts which had reached $31 million.
5. Lack of economic development.
6. A shortage of skilled work for the educated.
7. The exodus of inhabitants from the townships.
8. The atrocious state of housing and the towns in general.[58]

In the township of Yeruham, where a third of the workforce are unemployed, the residents struck for five days. They then sent representatives to meet the Histadrut leadership in Shfayim. They demonstrated in Dizengoff Street and Kings of Israel Square in Tel Aviv, asking the people to sign a petition of support with their struggle. Then they travelled to Jerusalem and set up tents in front of the houses of the Prime Minister and the Deputy Prime Minister. Residents of all the development towns went on strike at this time in sympathy with Yeruham.

In its leader article on 4 April 1986, *Ha'aretz* wrote that some of the development towns had been condemned to death. The MP, Charlie Biton, confirmed that the ruling establishment was setting up hi-tech industries in Ashkenazi areas, but that the development towns had only the textile and food industries which need unskilled workers because the towns were planned as a source of cheap labour. His colleague, Asi Arma stated that 'the government's heart is in the West Bank and we must struggle to regain it and help the development towns and Yeruham.'[59]

Discrimination is leading to alienation, and alienation is leading to solidarity with the old neighbours – the Arabs and the Palestinians in particular.

SEPHARDI SOLIDARITY WITH THE PALESTINIANS

Anti-Sephardi racial discrimination was undoubtedly one of the main catalysts for the Sephardi cultural renaissance and their growing sense of pride. Even though the Israeli-born generation had never lived in the Arab world, their solidarity with the Palestinians was born of their common culture, language, history and fate as oppressed natives.

At this historic moment, parents and grandparents who were still alive, started to tell their children about the amicable relations which they had had with their Muslim compatriots in their countries of origin. They also recalled the good relations that the Palestinian Jews had had with the Muslims and Christians of Palestine before Ashkenazi-Zionist settlement. The old-timers mentioned the heroic efforts they had made to find a peaceful solution to the Zionist-Palestinian conflict.

Dr Eliahu Eliachar, the most prominent Sephardi leader, stated in his book *Life with the Palestinians* (1975) that from 1921 native Jewish notables offered to mediate but the offer was categorically rejected by the Zionist establishment, as was any idea of a peaceful solution. Some of the Zionist leaders, including Dr Ruppin and Brener, believed that there could be no understanding or peaceful coexistence with the Arabs and that the problem would sooner or later be decided by resorting to arms.[60] (Menashe Eliachar recalled that 'during the reception ceremony for the British General Allenby who conquered Jerusalem, the Mufti, Kamal al-Husseini [his uncle] and Musa Kazim Pasha sat at the door of the hall. The VIPs sat on the dais. I said to one of the "organisers" that the Mufti, the Mayor and Kamal al-Husseini are protesting and wish to leave. He replied, "So let them go."'[61])

Eliahu Eliachar stated that he and his native Jewish friends supported the principle that the Jewish community in Palestine should be integrated in the Middle East, but the Ashkenazi Zionist leadership feared becoming 'Levantised' and objected vehemently.[62] Equally it opposed the principle of a joint education system for Jews and Arabs, and instead it set up Jewish schools which taught Arabic only as a third foreign language[63] and operated the principle of 'Jewish labour'.[64] Eliachar goes on to condemn the cultural oppression of the native Jews and Arabs.[65]

Eliachar describes as suicidal the policy of force which does not relinquish a square inch of land.[66]

At the World Conference of Arab-Jewry in 1925, which was convened in Vienna, the Chairman, Moshe de Figiatto a Syrian from Aleppo, criticised Zionism for its lack of concern for Palestinian interests.[67] Rabbi Hayyim Nahum (a former Ottoman Chief Rabbi) supported this peaceful stance. Dr Yitzhak Levi and Rabbi Toledano demanded that an Arabic newspaper be established for the Palestinian Jewish community.[68]

After the foundation of the state of Israel, Jewish communities in the Middle East wanted to help the warring parties to find a peaceful solution, but the Jewish Agency opposed this on the grounds that 'such mediation could be harmful for Israel's future.'[69]

Dr Eliachar stated that with regard to the future there is no possibility of a settlement with the Arab countries without a solution to the Palestinian problem.[70] He demanded that meetings be convened between Jews and Palestinians to increase mutual understanding.[71] He opposed the Zionist views which do not recognise the rights of the Palestinians on the grounds that 'they do not constitute a separate people.'[72] He also opposed the establishment of boundaries between the Sephardim and the Arab world, or between the Arab nation and the non-Arab Muslims in the area. Dr Eliachar mentioned that the Israeli government has not allowed a Sephardi to speak about the Zionist-Arab dispute at the United Nations, or in any other international fora. He called upon Ashkenazim to relinquish their policy of force, and to withdraw from the Arab territories occupied in 1967, as well as from the villages of Bir'im and Iqrit (on the Lebanese border). Eliachar supported the recognition of the Palestinian people's right to independence and to setting up a Palestinian entity based on justice and self-determination.[73]

Despite the lip service the author pays to Zionism, as is the case with all Sephardi notables, this book bears witness to the sympathy that Sephardim have for the Palestinians, as well as highlighting the evil intent of future Zionist expansionism. We should point out that Dr Eliachar was born in the old city of Jerusalem. He studied medicine at Beirut University and then law at Cairo University. In the First World War he was a medical officer in the Ottoman Army. He was appointed director of the Bureau of Trade and Industry in the British Mandate Government and the editor of the *English Trade Bulletin*. In 1937 he was elected head of the Jewish community in Jerusalem, and in 1946 head of the Sephardi community, whereupon he became active in organising world Sephardi conferences. When the state of Israel was founded, he was elected to the first and second parliaments as well as deputy mayor of Jerusalem.

In 1975 Dr Eliachar publicly demanded the establishment of a Palestinian state, and this in turn inspired some of his colleagues to hold discussions with representatives of the Palestine Liberation Organisation in London and Paris. The Zionists plotted against him, however, and ousted him as leader of the community. In his place was appointed David Sitton, the Deputy-President of the

World Sephardi Federation headed by Nissim Gaon. However, David Sitton supported the plan to establish a federal state which would include Israel, a Palestinian state and the Kingdom of Jordan, explaining that 'even if this plan is not realised now, the Palestinians cannot be denied the right to establish their own national entity.'[74]

Even Shlomo Cohen-Sidon, a well-known Likud 'hawk', declared after the peace treaty with Egypt that 'the establishment of settlements in the occupied Arab territories has become meaningless. If Arafat were to come to Jerusalem I would agree to withdraw from the West Bank and to the establishment of a Palestinian state. I know the Arabs, and I am convinced that we can live with them.'[75]

After the 1948 war, some Sephardi leaders who came from Arab countries offered to mediate for Israel with the Arab states. They had very warm relations with the leaders of the Arab countries. The best known of these Sephardim were Eliahu 'Eni, Mahlab Ibrahim and Siyon Efraim from Iraq; Sa'ad Maliki, who was a good friend of Nasser; Yehuda Maslim who was a friend of King Hassan of Morocco; Albert Maimun who was a friend of President Burguiba; Shalom Cohen who was a friend of the Algerian leader Belqasim and Hashem Jawwad, the Iraqi politician. The Israeli Ministry of Foreign Affairs however rejected their offer even though these high-ranking Sephardim had covert encouragement from the respective Arab leaders.[76]

The Zionists' rejection was based on the following:

1. Their expansionist ambitions (note Israeli territorial expansionism since 1948).

2. A fear of peace, since this would renew the friendly relations between the Sephardim and the Arab world at the expense of the privileged settlers. Therefore, the ruling establishment has tried to preserve the wall of hostilities between Israel and its Arab neighbours for more than 40 years – waiting for the death of the generation which was born and brought up in the Arab and Islamic world.

3. Zionist leaders believe that the state of war, tension and siege will forge all the communities into one people, otherwise the conflict between the Ashkenazi settlers and the Sephardim will tear the state apart.

4. The state of war helps Israel to collect donations from world Jewry, as well as backing from the Western world and the United States in particular.

5. The participation of Sephardim in peace negotiations would

strengthen their hand and influence in the power structure.

Notwithstanding the brave efforts made by the Sephardim for the sake of peace and in support of Palestinian rights, the Ashkenazim claim that Sephardim are anti-Arab. The Ashkenazi settlers have apparently split into two groups: the first is made up of left-wingers who incite the Palestinians against the Sephardim, and the second is made up of the right-wingers who incite the Sephardim against the Palestinians! The Israeli security services stand on the sidelines pulling the strings and erecting a steel barrier between Sephardim and Palestinians lest they unite and revolt.

The MP, Charlie Biton, claims that anti-Arab discrimination does not stem from the Sephardim but arises in the imported Euro-centric political philosophy of various movements and groups and that most of those who vote for the extreme right-wing parties such as Tehiyya and Gush Emunim are not Middle Easterners. The Sephardim who vote for the Likud Bloc do not do so out of right-wing nationalist beliefs, which is why Menahem Begin and the Ashkenazi leaders of the party united against the North Africans and their leaders, such as David Levi, during the Herut Conference in 1986. Biton adds that the settlers in the West Bank are not Sephardim but Ashkenazim and that Rabbi Meir Kahane and his supporters are American Jews. Their views are those of the American 'Jewish Defence League' as are those of Finkelstein in Upper Nazareth, the racist of Tiberias and others. Biton goes on to claim that 'Sephardim are far from being racist, since they have not lived in the West. They are not opposed to intermarriage with Arabs, whereas the Ashkenazim are against intermarriage with Sephardim, never mind with Arab Muslims or Christians . . . Those who believe in the concept of "Eretz Yisrael Hashlema"[77] and support the expulsion of the Palestinians from their homeland are not Sephardim, but Ashkenazim in Kahane's movement and the Tehiyya Party, such as Levinger, Sharon, Ne'eman, Eytan, Druckman and Shapira, etc. The Sephardim who continue to vote for the Likud bloc and some of the religious parties only do so as a protest against the Labour Party which embittered their lives for decades.' Finally Biton emphasises that the Sephardi supporters of Likud are not interested in its nationalist policies. If the Likud bloc were to decide to withdraw from the occupied Arab territories it would win the approval of the Sephardim, as happened when it resolved to withdraw from Sinai.[78]

During their national conference which was held in Beer Sheba

in 1975, the Black Panthers decided upon the following principles:
1. The necessity of peaceful coexistence with the Arab states and the Palestinian people.
2. The condemnation of the continued occupation of the Arab territories since 1967.
3. Temporary agreements, such as the one already concluded, cannot guarantee peace. It is with the Palestinians above all that the future of the occupied territories must be discussed.
4. There can be no peace without a solution to the Palestinian problem.
5. Both peoples in Palestine must have the right of self-determination.
6. The Sephardim have the capacity to be a bridge for peace by dint of their common culture with the Arab world and through their participation in the struggle for equality in Israeli society.[79]

From its very inception the Black Panther Movement declared common cause with the Palestinian people as follows:
1. A people which oppresses another people cannot be free.
2. The Palestinians have an inalienable right to self-determination and nationhood.
3. Peace is a vital concern for the people, security and economy of Israel. No peace can be achieved in the Middle East without the support of the Palestinians.
4. The Palestinians have a right to their own state in the land of Palestine.
5. The struggle against racism and discrimination is a basic tenet and anti-Sephardi and anti-Palestinian discrimination cannot be distinguished from one another.[80]

In September 1982 80,000 Sephardim protested over the Sabra and Shatila massacres.

We should mention that on 11 November 1979 the Panthers occupied the settlement of Elazar on the West Bank. In spite of the fact that they did not use any weapons, they managed to disarm the Ashkenazi settlers, members of Gush Emunim. The settlement remained under the Panthers' control until army reinforcements arrived.

The Panthers linked solidarity with the Palestinian people to their struggle against the economic policy which had abolished most state subsidies on foodstuffs and caused the continued inflation. During the bloody clashes which took place on 20 and 21 November

1979, the security forces arrested seventeen demonstrators. *Ha'aretz* added[81] that Sephardi children in Qatamon in Jerusalem taunted Jewish American tourists with cries of 'We are all Arafat . . . all Arafat.'

This thinking had been developing since the emergence of the Black Panthers. On 11 April 1972, *Ma'ariv* published a report on the discussions held between the leaders of the Panthers and members of the left-wing Zionist party, Mapam, in the Hashomer Hatza'ir Cultural Centre in the Bet She'an Valley. The following is a summary of the Panthers' points:

'Our aim is a social revolution which will be left-wing, but will not resemble the Russian or Chinese revolutions. We shall build a society founded on complete equality, and we shall struggle with the oppressed Arabs against Zionism. We are the only segment of society which can be a bridge to the Arabs. We oppose colonialism which is intent upon monopolising citizens' funds, and therefore we do not differentiate between military or settler colonialism. That is the difference between us and the Mapam Party (whose kibbutzim had taken part in the plunder of Palestinian lands after 1948). We want to found a large socialist party . . . There is no difference between the leaders of the Zionist right or left. They all belong to the two hundred families who control Israel's destiny. The offer to make the Yemenite member of Parliament, Yesha'yahu, the Speaker of Parliament makes us laugh. It is sheer hypocrisy, since Yesha'yahu and his ilk belong to the two hundred ruling families. We shall not participate in the next election campaign since changes cannot be effected in this country through the parliamentary system. We are not concerned that the parliament is totally Ashkenazi, since parliament is insignificant. Senior civil servants, appointed by the government, decide the affairs of the country. There are three hundred civil servants between the grades of 1 and 3, which number includes only 9 Sephardim and even they are members of the oligarchy. The Sephardi revolution will explode within 30 years.'

Kochavi Shemesh stated that Sephardi hatred for Arabs is no more than a myth. It is the establishment which has dwelt on hatred. Jews had lived in Iraq in peace and quiet until Zionist agents arrived there and bombed Jewish institutions in their attempt to cause a Jewish/Muslim schism.

With regard to cooperation with the Palestinians, the Panthers declared 'we have organised meetings with the Jewish poor and the Palestinians in Arab Jerusalem, Nablus and elsewhere . . . the Palestinians sympathise with our activities. We must strive toward a common struggle with the Arabs against the ruling establishment.'

Charlie Biton said of the acts of violence, 'the use of violence is permissible as a response to government violence. The laws of the state defend the system and not the citizen, and therefore we have been forced into answering violence with violence.' Shemesh said that the Black Panthers chose their name because it shocks. It was used for the first time by Ms Meyuhas, a member of the Jerusalem Town Council, when she delivered her report on these youths.

Solidarity with the Palestinians is only a part of the psychological revolution and cultural revival which has exploded amongst the Sephardim in Israel. An intellectual told the journalist Shalom Cohen (of Iraqi/Egyptian origin), 'they told us for many years that we were just like the Arabs. That was the greatest insult they could find for us. Gradually we were beset by an inferiority complex with respect to the Ashkenazim . . . When someone called me an Arab, I beat him up. Some time after this incident I said to myself "In fact . . . it's true . . . I am an Arab Jew," and the word "Arab" stopped being an insult, not just for me but for everyone in my position.'

Many Sephardim in Israel took to saying, 'We know the Arabs very well. We can live with them better than the people we are living with now.'

When the first wave of Israeli journalists returned from Egypt in February 1978, an Israeli broadcaster described how twelve Israeli journalists were making a boat trip on the Nile. Amongst them were two Sephardim, one of whom, Shlomo 'Anbary, responded to the impact the scenery had on him by stating 'I am an Arab Jew. My real name is Salim and I feel happy here.' This vexed his Ashkenazi colleagues, and no sooner had 'Anbary returned to Jerusalem than he was requested to clarify exactly what he had meant. He replied, 'I was born in Iraq, part of my education took place in Egypt and I was imbued with Arab thought. I am fluent in their language and I love their music. Obviously I am an Israeli by nationality, a Jew in religion, but I cannot help being Arab in culture and thought.' All the journalists on this first trip observed that the Sephardi journalists got on much better than the Ashkenazim. The Sephardim could mix freely and openly with the public, whereas the Ashkenazim preferred to be accompanied by Egyptian security police. At a soirée, the editor of *Yedi'ot Aharanot* posed the question 'What would happen to Israeli society if we made peace with the Arabs, and the majority of the people feel that they are closer to the Arab than to us [the Ashkenazim].' He followed this question by stating 'it is obvious that peace has not come yet.'[82]

The Black Panthers were amongst the first Israelis to challenge the Ashkenazi Zionist establishment by declaring that Sephardim constituted part of the Arab world. Kochavi Shemesh stated, 'There is no difference between me and an Arab with the exception of religion. Would those who claim that religion is what defines nationality also claim that Arab Catholics and French Catholics, for example, belong to the same nation?' When Shemesh met Ashkenazi immigrants from Russia, he realised that they did not have common national ties with him. He added, 'the Sephardim and those Ashkenazim come from two different cultures . . . we even differ in our physiognomies. The only thing that we have in common is our religion.' Shemesh believes that the state of Israel is trying to combine religious groups of different nations into one nation. 'That is Zionist theory, whereas in fact Zionist practice is to treat the Sephardim like the Palestinians.'[83]

An Israeli soldier claimed that during one of the battles of the 1973 war, he witnessed a group of soldiers leave their positions and start playing cards with each other. When he advised them to return to their positions they refused, since they did not consider themselves part of the Zionist entity.[84]

The MP, Charlie Biton, said in Parliament on 7 January 1981 that anti-Sephardi discrimination was the reason why they avoided conscription and that 90 percent of those held in military prisons were Sephardim. Obviously, of the Sephardim who do join the armed forces a large number disobey the orders of Ashkenazi officers and are jailed. Natan Dunevitz ascribes this phenomenon[85] to the fact that the army is a symbol of the ruling establishment and it is more usual for Sephardi youths to avoid conscription. (The number of draft evaders was 10,000 in the years 1985/86. Emil Elimelekh, commander of the military police, stated that 72 percent of the Sephardi prisoners are serving sentences for desertion.)[86]

An extract of a letter, which was sent by one of the Black Panthers to his brother in the army, may explain the state of alienation between the repressed section of the population and the establishment.

He says that his wife has given birth to his fifth son, who will have to sleep in the same bed as his brother Ezra and sister Geula. Ya'akov, his oldest son, has been arrested for stealing a bar of chocolate and he will be sentenced to three years in prison where he will learn how to take drugs and rob. His daughter, Ruti, who

is seven years old, has rheumatism, and coughs up blood all night. When he requested help from the Ministry of Housing, the official screamed at him that the government only deals with housing for new immigrants. The father is bemused by the fact that they seem to have money for immigrants, settlements and security, they have funds to invest in (pre-revolutionary) Iran and Uganda, to build a new Hilton, to cover financial losses for the banks . . . so why can they not save the life of his daughter! Even death is expensive in Israel! His monthly salary is less than $50! He writes to his brother, the soldier: 'You are not defending me. I don't own anything that needs defending, not even my life. You are defending my oppressors, and you are defending them, my brother, so that they can oppress me.'
Signed: the poor citizen.[87]

Draft resistance on such a large scale led to a lowering of morale amongst the privates in the army, most of whom are Sephardim. Since the Lebanese war, the Army High Command has not been able to depend upon these soldiers and has had to rely upon the Ashkenazi-controlled air- and sea-borne weapons to destroy Syrian and Palestinian positions. This change has led to increased destruction and more carnage of innocent civilians.

FIRST STIRRINGS OF ARMED STRUGGLE

Animosity to the ruling establishment and belief in violence as an inevitable means of struggle developed to the point where they were embodied in a number of small organisations, such as the Red Front, which was a secret movement in the early seventies and was involved in armed struggle against Israel in support of Syria, and the Palestinian Resistance, and whose membership included Sephardim, Ashkenazim and Palestinians. One of those arrested on suspicion of membership in the Front was Hesqel Cohen, a former member of the Black Panthers. He was sentenced to seven years in prison.

On the other hand, there was the Ma'atz Organisation which was comprised of Sephardim only. This organisation undertook extensive sabotage and arson operations against large factories. As it was a secret organisation and trials of its members were carried out in camera, no details are available about it other than those published in the Israeli press. On 13 October 1978 *Ha'aretz* reported that the police had sent six members of the organisation to trial charged with having carried out thirteen acts of arson between 1975–1978 in the Tel Aviv area. In addition they were accused of having caused I£2.5 million worth of damage to the Bulgat plant in Kiryat Gat and I£3 million worth of damage to the Bulgat plant in Lod, where the fire raged for three days. (Bulgat produces the boxes used in the export of citrus fruit.) The police tortured the suspects during interrogation. They were then tried in camera and sentenced to long stretches in prison, at which time they disappeared from the Israeli media. The group also carried out other acts of sabotage against furniture shops and the building which housed *Ha'aretz*. The group was accused of plotting to blow up the police headquarters in Tel Aviv and kill senior officers.

The well-known journalist, Shalom Cohen (who worked for many years as an editor of *Ha'olam Hazeh*), stated that Ma'atz had a 'Prime Minister' and stolen army weapons. After an investigation which took a few months, Ma'atz members admitted that their organisation was 'the Israeli Red Brigade'. They all stem from the Black Belts and in fact the organisation started its activities in the Hatikvah district of Tel Aviv. One of their aims was to kidnap the Minister of Justice, Shmuel Tamir, who opposed a general amnesty. They set fire to a number of industrial plants, including a textile factory where they caused damage in the value of I£40 million. A representative of the public prosecutor claimed that these arson attacks were aimed at the national economy and that Ma'atz members were enemies of Israel.[88]

There were also numerous acts of sabotage undertaken by individuals. In these cases the police were unable to arrest any suspects, and the attacks were described as 'accidents'. Many in Israel believe that the Israeli secret service (the Shin Bet) secretly assassinated individuals who they believed were 'cooperating with the Arabs' and whose guilt they could never prove in a court of law. The killings take place during army reserve duty. The Shin Bet would then inform the family of the victim that he had been murdered by Arab infiltrators or during a military operation.

After the Ma'atz operations, the Panthers continued their struggle against the government and the Ashkenazi settlers in the West Bank. On 23 March 1980 *Ha'aretz* reported that the Panthers had stormed the offices of the Minister of Labour and Social Security, Israel Katz, leaving behind eight rabbits as a symbol of the helplessness of the poor. Sephardim in the Ezra, Hatikva and Argazim slums of Tel Aviv then staged violent demonstrations on 14 April 1981 following the municipality's demolition of four houses. The demonstrators set fire to shops and municipal property after which the police instituted a campaign of arrests. In November 1980 the police opened fire on students in Ramallah on the West Bank wounding ten. On the same day the police, for no reason, fired on a Sephardi youth in Jerusalem, seriously wounding him. Charlie Biton condemned these incidents in Parliament: 'This government is the enemy of Sephardim. What you will be seeing is the establishment of a united front among Sephardim from Musrara and youths from the University of Bir Zeit against an oppressive government.'[89]

During this period of mass struggle, on 30 August 1980, all the slum organisations united in the framework of a single independent national organisation. At the founding meeting, which took place in Tel Aviv, the speakers condemned the following:

1. Racial discrimination
2. Condescension towards Sephardim and Sephardi culture.
3. The paternalistic treatment of Sephardim by Ashkenazim.
4. Neglect of the Slum Revival Programme.
5. Neglect of economic development in the development towns.

The participants demanded complete social, economic and cultural equality with Ashkenazim. They affirmed that the organisation was independent and apolitical but stressed in the Israeli press that 'money must be spent by the state on the slum districts instead of the Ashkenazi settlements in the occupied territories.'

Acts of violence continued to take place in the slum districts. After one such incident when a bus, a car, a municipal warehouse and other public buildings were set on fire, *Ha'aretz* reported that nine people were arrested in the Hatikvah district, including Shlomo Khoja, Eliahu Siso, Dalia Batai and others.

Dan Margalit wrote in the same newspaper[90] that the Black Panthers had succeeded in their political work, for they expressed the people's true feelings toward racial discrimination and the social predicament and that the establishment was in a state of alarm. He attributed the Panther's election failure of that year to a new form of protest by the Sephardim, that of an election boycott.

Sa'adya Marciano, a Panther leader, predicted in 1978 that acts of violence against the authorities would increase. He stated 'the Ashkenazim are not prepared to give up even a small part of their hegemony . . . In this context I therefore expect that the explosion which took place in 1971 will repeat itself. When that happens the generation of the new movement will have greater resolve, better planning and be more active and violent. As a result, the explosion will have more force.' Marciano expected that 'the generation of tomorrow will move towards partition.'[91]

Kochavi Shemesh considered that it was vital for the Panthers to join the Democratic Front (which included Arab Local Councils and the Communist Party). 'By electing to do that, we will have forged for the first time a real bond between the Sephardim and the Palestinians who are both the butt of discrimination. This bond is very important to us, the Sephardim, for we must see the Arabs as our natural allies.[92] I am a Sephardi, or to be more precise, I am an Arab Jew and my culture is Middle Eastern.' However, he denied the existence of any cultural link between him and the Jews who came from the Balkans (apparently he was not aware that they are Sephardim whose ancestors were expelled from Spain along with their Muslim brethren after the fall of the Muslim state).[93]

Three years later, Moni Yakim, another Black Panther, expected that armed struggle would begin. He stated, 'it is impossible to challenge anti-Sephardi racial discrimination in Israel through democratic means. Regrettably the Ashkenazi ruling class could well be pushing us into armed struggle against them in order to achieve our just aims.'[94] He continued, 'the Black Panther movement constitutes a political movement which defends the Sephardim who have been proletarianised in Palestine. These oppressed believe that democratic means have been discredited since the world only recognised the Palestine Liberation Organisation after it carried out commando operations.' Yakim addressed the following words to the Ashkenazim, 'The new generation of Sephardim will not speak with you, they will act.' He expressed his opposition to the immigration of Soviet Jews, since 'these immigrants are reactionary and the government is bringing them over to settle them in the occupied territories.' Charlie Biton added during the same newspaper interview that 'the Ashkenazi immigrants from the Soviet Union are not wanted here, as they come to take over our houses.' (We should point out that the government allotted to these new immigrants the houses which had been built for the Sephardi poor who had been waiting for them since 1948.) Yakim stated that the Ashkenazi kibbutzim 'represent the ugly face of Israel and their profits should be distributed amongst the workers – who are the Sephardim.' He expressed the Sephardim's distaste for these settlements, because they are exploited by them, stated that in the future the Sephardim would take over the settlements and demanded that half of the kibbutzim's lands be granted to the poor. He claimed that the Black Panthers' victory should not be measured by the number of votes they get in the elections, but by the spread of their revolutionary ideas amongst the various parties. Yakim emphasised that America was hindering a rapprochement between the Sephardim and the Palestine Liberation Organisation.

These radical declarations raised an outcry of indignation in Ashkenazi society. Aharon Stern accused Yakim of aiming to complete what Hitler started. Stern threatened that 'the Ashkenazi settlers will not just stand by and watch.'[95] Yakim then asked *Ha'aretz* to allow him to respond to these accusations, and on 30 October 1981 they published an article by him in which he stated 'regarding armed struggle, I believe that the Ashkenazi ruling class had always used force to monopolise economic and political power. In the light of historical developments, we must defend ourselves, we must meet acts of violence by the state with acts of violence by the masses and respond to the use of arms with the same. We have been pushed into this sorry state of affairs by the folly and arrogance of the ruling Ashkenazi class which has shut in our faces any democratic means of alleviating Ashkenazi-Zionist oppression.' Finally Yakim demanded 'a fundamental change which could stop Zionism being worshipped, and the implementation of an anti-racist policy based on cooperation with the Middle East.'

SEPHARDIM AND PEACE NOW

In December 1982, an alliance of the Peace Now movement and the Sephardim from the slum districts emerged to oppose Zionist settlement in the occupied territories. Marciano and R. Ben-Harush pointed out that the means of repression employed on the West Bank would soon be turned against the Sephardim. On the same day (23 December 1982), the police demolished a part of a Yemenite's house – Shim'on Yehoshu'a – in Kfar Shalom in Tel Aviv. The police fired at him and shot him dead, as mentioned above. Reuven Ben Harush, a representative from Musrara in Jerusalem, stated 'Before 1967 they taught us that the enemy was over there [he pointed to Arab Jerusalem], but afterwards we realised that the real enemy is here' [he pointed to the Ashkenazi suburbs of West Jerusalem].[96]

S. Abu Tubul, a Sephardi youth who was drafted into the

Lebanese war, published the following poem in *Ha'aretz*,[97] in which he expresses the tragedy of his fellow Sephardim in the Lebanese arena. He also speaks of the wall which has been constructed to keep Sephardim from the Arab world.

A Naïve Poem for the Neighbour Behind the Border
She stood before me, gazing at me,
I saw her eyes.
How like my mother's are her eyes,
in which I saw her pains!
How like my mother's are her pains.
I wish I knew what to say to this mother's glances.
The mother, behind the valley,
The mother who is gazing at me,
her eyes telling me everything,
everything they don't tell me here.
I wish I knew, how to meet this scream in her eyes.
They did not teach me how to witness screams in eyes –
eyes behind the valley,
They did not teach me how to witness eyes behind the valley.
They did not teach me how to witness
life behind the valley.
Consider! What did they teach me?
O, Neighbour! O, Neighbour behind the valley,
to you I say They didn't teach me,
they blocked my path
to you – to your emotions,
they forbade any contact,
I want to say to you,
Now I know
that one gets to know by seeing.

A month later the Sephardi Slum District and Development Town Committee organised a commemoration for the victims of the Lebanese war. The slogan of the organisers was that the war must be stopped and the principle of equality must be instituted. David Hamu, the Haifa representative of the organisation stated that 'during this ceremony we will light two candles: one for the souls of the Palestinian and Lebanese martyrs, and the second for the Israeli dead. In so doing, we are calling for the cessation of this war. We, children of the Middle East, believe that Israel must join together with the peoples of the region by means of peaceful dialogue and that Israel must respect the indigenous peoples of the area and their customs and traditions.' David Hamu criticised the lack of recognition of the Palestinian people, saying that this is against democratic principles. He added that the lack of equality in the use of the state's resources represented the corollary of the policy of force used by Israel against the Arabs. Domestic policy had created two tiers of Jewish citizens, he claimed. 'Inequality would worsen due to the war, since the economic burden was being placed upon the weaker classes. At the same time, the warmongers would get richer, and the gap between the Ashkenazim and the Sephardim would deepen.' Candles were lit, and those assembled expressed their solidarity with the Arab nation across the border. In the second part of the ceremony the group 'Natural Choice' under Sholmo Bar sang solidarity songs. One of the slogans of the meetings was 'The Ashkenazim have failed to manage both society and peace.' Another slogan called for Sephardi unity in Palestine.[98]

On 10 February 1973 Peace Now demonstrated in Jerusalem against Sharon and the policy of warmongering. Fascist gangs attacked the demonstrators, beating and cursing them. A bomb was thrown at them killing Emil Grunzweig and wounding a number of demonstrators. The Ashkenazi press wrote hundreds of articles about the death of the Ashkenazi peacenik, but ignored the case of Eddie Levi, a Sephardi, who was demonstrating with Grunzweig and was seriously injured. The media also ignored the rest of the Sephardim who exposed themselves to fascist hostilities. The well-known writer, Shulamit Har-Even, who was an eye-witness to these events, wrote about the case in the March/April 1983 issues of New Outlook. Amnon Dankner published a number of articles in which he portrayed the Ashkenazim as peaceniks and the Sephardim as a fascist mob, ignoring the fact that Sharon and the rest of the fascist leadership are Ashkenazim (see above p.217).

In Musrara, Kiryat Menahem and Hatikva slums the Sephardim staged a demonstration and marched to the settlement of Efrat on the West Bank under the slogan 'Spend money on the slum districts and not on the settlements.'[99]

However, the coalition of Sephardim and Palestinians on the one hand and the Peace Now movement, which is supported by the rich kibbutzim, on the other, cannot be a lasting one, for these kibbutzim have increased their property and profits a number of times since 1948, by exploiting the development towns and grabbing the most fertile Palestinian lands through various legal means, such as the land appropriation law. Moreover, the kibbutzim provide the state of Israel with its military élite, who form a class similar to the Mamelukes of Egypt or the Janissaries in the Ottoman state. We saw during the Lebanese war that most members of this élite opposed the invasion or wanted its speedy end, but they carried out all orders except for one officer – Officer Geva.

Ha'aretz reported on 8 February 1985 on the class conflict between the kibbutzim and their hired workers. There was a 'rumour' going round that the leadership of the Kibbutz Federation had convened a secret meeting at the kibbutz of Kiryat 'Anavim (near Jerusalem) to discuss the possibility of an attack on the kibbutzim by unemployed Sephardim, particularly those who had been laid off by the kibbutzim. When a correspondent of the newspaper contacted leaders of the Kibbutz Federation, such as Yehuda Harel and Shlomo Leshem, he felt that they were not happy with his question. The correspondent was told that after the meeting had listened to a talk by Hayyim Barkai, a professor of economics, it went into closed session, not to discuss armed clashes, according to them, but the demonstrations. They did not discuss how to confront the possible events, but how to prevent them by allowing Sephardim to participate in their factories or by setting up integrated schools.

We do not wish to detract from the significance of Peace Now's struggle, but we must state that the alliance is only a stepping stone until the nature of the kibbutzim changes.

THE BLACK BELT MOVEMENT

In the neighbourhoods of West Jerusalem the Sephardim set up a resistance organisation called ShHQ[100] in 1982. Its activities were concentrated in the districts of Eyn Ganim and Kiryat Menahem which contain 18,000 inhabitants, 80 percent of whom are North Africans. The most important leaders of the movement are Yehuda Ashraf and his brother Daniel Odani. The organisation is a broad front supported by individuals from various parties. It demands funds to be invested in the slum districts instead of in the settlements in the occupied territories. The inhabitants of these districts declared that it was they who bore the cost of the Lebanese war and the new settlements. The Sephardi inhabitants staged noisy demonstrations in protest at having to pay 30 percent of their income to cover 'free education'. After the government announced the start of the Slum

Revival Project in these districts, the municipality stopped providing services and stated that the new project would provide them. The correspondent, Lili Galili, wrote that the inhabitants would use peaceful means, but would also use less peaceful means such as closing off streets, in their struggle.[101] This organisation later formed a united front with the Ohalim organisation under the leadership of Yamin Suwisa, and with a branch of the Black Panthers led by Sa'adya Marciano. The chief factor in this step was the new economic policy and the cutbacks in social services.[102]

In June 1983 the ShHQ Organisation pitched an illegal camp near Jerusalem to protest against the housing shortage. The movements leader, Dada Ben Shitrit, declared that Sephardim refuse to be moved into the new houses built in the occupied territories, because they oppose the expropriation of their Arab neighbours' lands. He continued, 'in the Arab countries we lived in peace and friendship with the Arabs and we are prepared to support any party which will help the Palestinian people, but not the right-wing who build settlements in the occupied Arab territories.' Another leader of the movement stated that 'for twenty years we have been exploited, but we refuse to be fodder for their cannons any longer.' A few days later, police and border guard reinforcements demolished the camp and forcibly dispersed the inhabitants.[103]

In 1985 all the Sephardi organisations from the slum districts united under the leadership of the Black Panthers and started the '1985 Struggle', which was an extensive series of uprisings against the policy of poverty and de-education and the policy of suppression and settlement in the occupied Arab territories. In Tel Aviv, for example, the five district committees organised noisy demonstrations against budget cutbacks in education, adult-education and youth clubs.[104]

On 25 February 1985 Charlie Biton and Sa'adya Marciano presented a petition to the High Court to allow the Sephardi movement to stage a protest march on the West Bank against the Prime Minister and his settlement policy. The Prime Minister had already decided to visit the settlements on the West Bank at the same time, and the leaders of 'the 1985 Struggle' planned to demonstrate along the Prime Minister's route. However, the establishment took fright and the Minister of Defence, Yitzhak Rabin, banned the march.

On 11 March 1985 *Ha'aretz* reported that 'the 1985 Struggle Organisation', under Charlie Biton and Sa'adya Marciano, was preparing for demonstrations against the Lebanese invasion and to demand the withdrawal of Israeli forces from Lebanon. Biton and Marciano stated to the correspondent of *Ha'aretz*, 'the time has come to use the firm hand of the slum districts to apply pressure to the government's throat.' The correspondent, Lili Galili, met a leader of the slum districts, Afi Ben David, and asked him why he was supporting these demonstrations when he had been a supporter of the policies of Likud and Sharon for fifteen years. He replied that 'the people can be duped sometimes, but not all the time.' He added, 'they told us that they had finished off the terrorists and then the Shi'ah emerged . . . when Israeli soldiers started being picked off in Lebanon like sitting ducks the residents of the slum districts wised up and for the first time they went out into the streets to demonstrate – not for economic reasons but for political reasons.' Ben David criticised the accusations of the Ashkenazi left and the Ashkenazi press which claimed that the Sephardim are anti-Arab, oppose peace and like war, etc. He confirmed that Sephardim realise that the policy of war is one of the reasons for their economic hardships.[105]

In District C in Beer Sheba on 15 December 1985, five hundred Sephardi men rushed to try and prevent Kahane, who was accompanied by a gang of his bullies, from coming to their district.[106] Charlie Biton, MP, pointed out that anti-Kahane demonstrations in Giv'atayim (near Tel Aviv) had forced the racist Rabbi to pay $500 dollars to every poor person from Afula to join him in an anti-Arab demonstration. Biton went on to wonder where Kahane gets his funds.

Lili Galili wrote in *Ha'aretz* on 23 August 1985 that 55 young activists from the slum districts such as Musrara and Qatamon in Jerusalem had met to discuss the problem of racism. At the end of the meeting they declared 'Racism is an expression of extremism, and extremism has never been a part of Sephardi culture. Those who harm the Palestinians, harm the Sephardim and will push the nation into civil war.' The correspondent added that the movement would publish a paper on life in the slum districts and would institute a political and social awareness campaign in the 'Black Belts' and the development towns.

THE INTELLECTUALS' MOVEMENT

The Movement for Solidarity with the Palestinians did not just spread in the slum areas, but its activities encompassed Sephardi intellectuals also. On 1 June 1983 *Ha'aretz* wrote that Sephardi intellectuals had founded a new movement called East for Peace, which aimed to encourage the cause of peace with the Palestinians and the Arabs and to struggle against racial discrimination in Israel.

Professor Menahem Amir, a social scientist, declared that Israel was on the verge of civil war owing to ideological and political polarisation and ethnic disintegration. The President, Yitzhak Navon, commented that 'there are dangers, and I am worried. They are more serious than the threat posed by the Palestine Liberation Organisation or an external war.'[107]

In July 1983, Palestinian and Sephardi university students in Haifa set up The Black Force, an organisation which believed in strengthening the alliance between the Palestinian people and the Sephardim. This movement operated under the leadership of Menasheh Aharoni, the Chairman of the Students' Federation at Haifa University and a member of the Tami Party (the North African Jews' party headed by Abu Hatserah). Also active in the movement's leadership was Yisrael Ben Bast of Beitshan, who was a member of the Ma'arakh bloc (Labour). Ben Bast declared 'I believe that the Palestinians and Sephardim must unite and struggle for their common interests, as it is incumbent upon all those who are downtrodden to join ranks.' Nissim Dahhan, the former chairman of the Students Union expressed his radical opinions regarding the anti-discrimination struggle. *Ha'aretz Supplement* commented on 22 July 1983 that a Palestinian student, Nizar Hassan, had instigated the founding of this movement.

The organisation believes that the state's resources should be channelled toward the amelioration of living conditions in the Black Belts areas, instead of for the establishment of Zionist settlements on plundered Palestinian land. The organisation supports the principle of peace with the Palestinian people and the Arab world. Members of the organisation set up a workcamp in the Haifa suburb of Halisa to help the Palestinian and Sephardi residents. The Black Force gets complete support from the Palestinian and Sephardi communities as well as from Tami and the Labour and Communist parties.

In 1972 a common front was set up along the lines of this organisation and managed to win 32 out of the 40 seats in the Haifa University Students' Union Committee. A year later, members of the Labour Party and the Likud Front united and destroyed it.

Authors and politicians, who had previously cooperated with the Zionist establishment, joined this protest movement. We have already mentioned Dr Eliahu Eliachar, but we must also mention the historian Nahum Menahem who originates from Qamishly in Syria. He wrote a valuable book, entitled *Tension and Ethnic Discrimination in Israel*, which was published in 1983 by Ahdut Press in Tel Aviv. In this the author condemned discrimination and the arrogance with which the Ashkenazim have viewed the Palestinians and the Arab world since the start of Zionist settlement. In an interview with the journalist Amnon Dankner,[108] he expressed his horror at the massacres of Sabra and Shatila, and pointed out that the Ashkenazi Zionists have always requested imperialist governments, such as Britain and the Ottomans, to help them against the Arabs, whereas the Arabs always wanted to negotiate directly. He stressed that the Palestinians always stretched out their hands in peace to the Jews, but were rejected. In 1920, Menahem added, the Arabs were ready to accept a compromise with the Zionists and those who said that the Arab-Israeli dispute was insoluble were not telling the truth. He added that the West considered the Arab countries primitive and backward, an opinion which heavily influenced the Zionist movement which, for the same reason, founded the kibbutzim as societies closed to the Arabs. Later the Ashkenazi settlers displaced the Palestinians and founded settlements on their lands. The first military organisation to be set up by the Zionists was the 'Hashomer' organisation, which aimed to separate Jewish society from Arab society in Palestine. The author also reveals that landowners in Syria and Lebanon offered to sell huge tracts of land to the Zionists for very low prices in exchange for help against French imperialism. Herzl, however, was not interested in the rights of the Arabs.

Menahem provides details of the conversation which took place on 24 June 1919 between the Zionist leader, Ussishkin and the Mayor of Jerusalem, Musa Kazem.[109] When Ussishkin arrived in Palestine, he was met and welcomed by the mayor. Ussishkin started to criticise the Arab municipality and its services and then went on to the Arab-Zionist dispute and threatened the Palestinian nationalists with force. Menahem continued his interview with the correspondent of *Ha'aretz* by referring to what Moshe Dayan said after the 1967 war – 'If Nasser and Hussein want peace, they should telephone me.' Menahem condemned the destruction of the town of Yamit in Sinai before it was handed back to Egypt. He stated that the Ashkenazi leaders do not know how to deal with the Arabs or how to avoid offending them.

The historian went on to describe Ashkenazi-Sephardi relations since the start of Zionist colonisation. He stressed that a civil war would break out if politicians could not find a solution for the problem of anti-Sephardi racial discrimination. The cover illustration to his book shows a broken and bleeding star of David.

Nahum Menahem was not the first to warn of the danger of civil war in Israel. The author Natan Dunevitz had already written[110] that 'the animosity between the Sephardim and the Ashkenazim is a time bomb which will explode one day if it is not defused.' He went on to say that a hundred years ago the Palestinians and Sephardim were the aristocracy in Palestine whereas the Ashkenazim were poor and not overly clean. The situation is now much more dangerous since the Sephardim are hostile to anything which represents the ruling establishment. Their state of alienation is so acute that they explode over any incident such as an industrial dispute, a quarrel with neighbours and so on. Sephardi youths express their bitterness by overturning police cars and arson – according to Dunevitz.

THE DIALOGUE COMMITTEE 1986

In addition to the previously mentioned university circles which support the Palestinian cause, there emerged in 1986 another intellectual movement – the Committee for Israeli-Palestinian Dialogue. It was founded by Sephardim to support the Palestinian right to self-determination and the struggle for peace and democracy. The Committee convened a press conference attended by its leadership:
Dr Shlomo al-Baz (of Moroccan origin) – Professor at the Hebrew University of Jerusalem.
Professor Sasson Somekh (of Iraqi origin) – Professor of Arabic literature at Tel Aviv University.
Dr David Tsemah.
Latif Dori (of Iraqi origin) – Director of the Arab Bureau in the Mapam Party and leader of this committee.
Etti Danino – a social scientist.

Shlomo al-Baz declared that the signatories to the Committee's manifesto would work to counter the common slur that Sephardim hate Arabs. He added that Sephardim do not belong to the leadership of the chauvinist nationalist camp, and added that Sephardim have the power and the will to build a bridge between the Arab world and Israeli society in order to revive their common history and to integrate in the region.

Dr Tsemah made it clear there had indeed been contacts with Palestinians in the occupied territories over the possibility of setting up a common organisation. These contacts had been with two mayors who had been removed from their positions, with Rashad al-Shawa of Gaza, and Mustafa al-Natsha of Hebron.

One hundred Sephardim signed the Committee's manifesto, including the lawyers Ezra Gabbai and Nissim Eli'ad, Dr'Ada Aharoni, Dr Sa'adya Rahmi, Menashe Khalifa a member of the Central Committee of the Communist Party, Efraim Katsav, head of the Workers' Committee in the Teva Factory in Petah Tikvah, the authors, Sami Mikhael and Dr Shimon Balas, and the singer, Shlomo Bar.

The Likud bloc expressed their anxiety over the course of events in the Sephardi community. A Likud official described them as 'a deleterious ideological virus which has been carried over into Likud from the Labour party grass-roots.'[111]

The founding of the Committee for Israeli-Palestinian Dialogue was announced at a press conference at Bet Agron in Jerusalem on 26 January 1986. The answers given by those participating in the press conference showed the new direction developing amongst the Middle Eastern communities towards a greater understanding of the dispute.[112] Latif Dori stated that the Palestine Liberation Organisation was the representative of the Palestinian people whose responsibility was to speak on behalf of the Palestinians in any negotiations. The participants handed out a declaration in Arabic, Hebrew and English as follows:

Support The Israeli-Palestinian Dialogue
We the undersigned, a group of Sephardi Israelis, are worried by the situation of the people in this Jewish/Palestinian country. We recognise the inalienable right of each people to live in peace under its own leadership. Through our duty to play our role in the struggle taking place for peace and democracy, we propose to:
1 Persevere in the fight against all forms of national and ethnic discrimination in Israel and to strive for peaceful cohabitation.
We reject the abject generalisation which claims that the Sephardim 'hate the Arabs'.
The Sephardim have the ability and the desire to build a bridge between the Arab world and Israeli society and to renew our common culture whose roots go back hundreds of years so that

we can be integrated into the Middle East.

2 To persevere in the struggle to attain a peace which will put an end to destruction, suffering and bloodshed. We propose that the two parties start political negotiations on the basis of reciprocal recognition of the two people's respective right to self-determination. When such an agreement is reached it will guarantee a secure and prosperous future for our people and the peoples of the region.

3 To continue to encourage an Israeli-Palestinian dialogue amongst those concerned with fostering a peace consciousness. In order to highlight the afore-mentioned aims we announce the formation of the Committee for Israeli-Palestinian Dialogue which will be open to all those desire peace.

Committee for Israeli-Palestinian Dialogue

On 1 June 1986 the newspaper *Al Hamishmar* reported that the Sephardi members of the Committee for Dialogue had convened their first meeting with Palestinian leaders inside the country. Amongst those present were Ibrahim Qarain, the editor of the magazine, *Al-'Awda*, Dr Najwa Muhawwil, a professor at the Hebrew University in Jerusalem, Latif Dori, the secretary of the Committee for Dialogue, Hana Seniora, the editor of the newspaper, *Al-Fajr*, and Kokhavi Shemesh from the Black Panthers.

In May 1986, Latif Dori met the editor of the Palestinian weekly, *Sawt al-Bilad*, and had stressed the Sephardim's struggle against racism and the efforts to solve the Palestinian problem.[113]

On 14 April 1986 Latif Dori sent a telegram to Yitzhak Navon, the Minister of Education, demanding the withdrawal of all textbooks which describe Arabs pejoratively and stated that such action would constitute an additional measure against racism. Dori expressed his gratitude for the withdrawal of textbooks which portrayed Sephardim in a negative light.

On 20 February 1986 *Al Hamishmar* claimed that most of the leading lights of Kahane's racist party were Sephardim. Dori asked the leaders of this party for the names of its leaders and he was given a list of names of which two were Sephardim and the remaining 11 were Ashkenazi. Dori condemned the newspaper's attempt to denigrate the reputation of Sephardim.[114]

This does not however mean that all the Sephardim have rushed to join in the struggle. The ruling establishment continues to control the minds of the majority by manipulation of the media, schools, the draft and the economic and political scene. What it cannot do is to solve the structural contradiction between the Ashkenazi and the Sephardi communities inside the Zionist régime.

The bloody clashes between the Sephardim and the Zionist establishment aroused much interest in international, Arab and Palestinian circles and the Palestinian resistance movement started to consider it an important phenomenon.

THE COUNTER-TERRORISM ACT

In response to the meetings between Sephardim and the Palestinian leadership, the Knesset passed into law on 6 August 1986 a new motion forbidding such contacts. This law was called the Counter-terrorism Act and its aim was to prevent meetings between Israelis and PLO representatives.

The Committee for Dialogue called a press conference in Jerusalem in which they condemned the new law. Latif Dori stated 'this law is despotic and has no equal in any state in the world, it is out of accord with the laws of logic and democratic values.' Dori affirmed that he and his colleagues would continue their contacts with PLO representatives at any time and anywhere. Hana Seniora stated to the press conference that 'this law destroys any opportunity for dialogue and peace, for peace cannot come to pass without talks and meetings between Israelis and Palestinians.' He added that the only impediment to peace was the Israeli refusal to negotiate with the Palestine Liberation Organisation, the single legitimate representative of the Palestinian people.[115] Dori commented on the meeting between Shimon Peres and King Hassan of Morocco that 'every Israeli leader who meets an Arab leader without announcing his recognition of the right of the Palestinian people to self-determination will return empty handed. We suggest that the leadership of the state follow in our tracks and instigate a real Israeli-Palestinian dialogue which would lead to a fruitful dialogue with the PLO and the Arab peoples.'

THE FIRST SEPHARDI-PALESTINIAN CONFERENCE IN ROMANIA 1986

The first meeting between Latif Dori and his colleagues and the PLO took place in Romania on 6 November 1986. The magazine *Falestine al-Thawra* published a number of articles about this meeting in its edition of 15 November 1986, including the following, filed by Ziyad Abu al-Hayja' from Bucharest:

In its successive sessions, the Palestine National Council decided to move toward a meeting and dialogue with individual Jewish and Israeli democratic forces which support the right of the Palestinian people to self-determination and to establish an independent state and which consider the PLO the sole legitimate representative of the Palestinian people.

To counter this declaration, which was issued by the highest legal authority of the Palestinian people (the Palestine National Council being the Palestinian people's Parliament), the Knesset on 6 August 1986 outlawed all meetings with representatives of the PLO under pain of a three-year prison sentence.

Abu al-Hayja' went on to say that both the PLO and the Israeli peacemakers decided to defeat this law and to hold this conference in Romania.

The meeting opened at five-thirty on 6 November, in the presence of over one hundred journalists from all over the world who had come to cover this event.

At the start, Latif Dori confirmed his support for the right of the Palestinian people to self-determination and to establish an independent state. He stated that the meeting showed that there can be no peace in the Middle East without the PLO as the sole legitimate representative of the Palestinian people.

Latif Dori went on to comment about the law passed by the Knesset. 'In fact it is not an anti-terrorist law. It is a terrorist law.'

Dori concluded by quoting some verses by the Tunisian poet Abu al-Qasim al-Shabi.[116]'My Palestinian brothers, the night of occupation will be dispelled, the shackles of occupation will be broken and destiny will respond to your aspirations by establishing your independent Palestinian state.'

Colonel 'Abd al-Razzaq al-Yahya, a member of the PLO's Executive Committee and the head of the Palestinian delegation, then spoke. He welcomed the courage of the Israeli individuals in standing up to the Knesset law and attending the meeting with the PLO. He reasserted that the PLO was interested in fostering peace-loving forces in Israel and that it was always ready to meet them in accordance with resolutions passed by the Palestine National Congress . . .

He added, 'Israel is waging war against representatives of the Palestinian people from its representatives on the village council level up to its representative in the leadership of the PLO.'

Father Ibrahim 'Ayyad, adviser on church affairs to the chairman of the Executive Committee of the PLO, called upon peaceloving forces in Israel to transform their struggle into real action. 'Imad Shaqur, adviser on Israeli affairs to the chairman of the Executive Committee, addressed the Israeli delegation. 'Tell your children, tell your people that you found the hands of the PLO extended to you in peace.' The Palestinian journalist Raymonda Tawil, who lives in occupied East Jerusalem, praised the courage of the Israeli delegation.

At seven o'clock that evening the meeting ended and the Palestinian delegation distributed to the journalists the following communiqué:

In accordance with resolutions of the Palestine National Council in its various sessions with regard to a positive dialogue with Jewish democratic forces which recognise the PLO as the sole legitimate representative of the Palestinian people and its inalienable rights and which believes in and struggles for a just and lasting peace based upon the right of the Palestinian people to self-determination and the establishment of an independent Palestinian state, there has taken place a meeting between a number of Israelis and Palestinians.

The Palestine Liberation Organisation reaffirms its deep commitment to struggle by all means to achieve a just and lasting peace within the framework of an international conference with the participation of the Soviet Union, the United States, the permanent members of the Security Council and the parties concerned, including the Palestine Liberation Organisation.

After the meeting, the Israeli authorities decided to try some of the Israeli delegates on a charge of being in contact with an enemy 'terrorist organisation'. Latif Dori, the secretary of the Committee for Israeli–Palestinian Dialogue and head of the delegation to Romania, together with a number of other leaders of the delegation lodged a complaint with the police after they received anonymous death threats.

Dori stated that the Prime Minister, Yitzhak Shamir, and the security authorities, would bear responsibility for any attack upon himself or his colleagues and mentioned that Shamir had already accused them of treason.

The Kach Movement of Rabbi Kahane distributed leaflets in Jerusalem containing the names, addresses and telephone numbers of four members of the delegation under investigation by the police. The movement announced that it intended to have them tried for breaking the new law by meeting members of Palestinian organisations.[117]

THE SECOND PLO-SEPHARDI CONFERENCE: BUDAPEST 1987

On 9 June 1987 in Budapest two PLO leaders, Mahmud 'Abbas (Abu Mazin) and 'Abd al-Razzaq al-Yahya, received a Sephardi delegation headed by Charlie Biton, MP. The delegation included fifteen Sephardim from the slum districts and the development towns, members of the Black Panthers. Before he left Israel, Biton stated that the authorities had employed terrorism and intimidation to stop his mission and that they had pressurised the East for Peace organisation into withdrawing from the delegation. He added that the Sephardim in Israel would prove that there was another Israel, an Israel in which the Sephardim denounced the attacks made by Gush Emunim and Kahane's gang on Deheisha Camp. In Budapest he made a statement in which he said that 'this delegation recognises the Palestine Liberation Organisation, the sole legitimate representative of the Palestinian people and calls upon Israel to recognise the national rights of the Palestinian people including the right to establish an independent state alongside Israel. This delegation calls upon Israel to participate in the proposed international conference with the Palestinian Liberation Organisation and the superpowers.' Biton stated that he condemned the anti-democratic Israeli law which forbids meetings with the PLO, and called for it to be retracted.[118]

On 15 June 1987 *The Guardian* reported that Biton and members of the delegation might be tried for having contact with an 'enemy' organisation, a crime which carries a maximum sentence of three years. Mahmud 'Abbas Abu Mazin, declared that the PLO strongly supported the delegation's proposals. *Ha'aretz* added that the Israeli delegation comprised twenty-two members[119] including members from the Mapam and the Communist parties.

The Palestinian Delegation included:
Mahmud 'Abbas (Abu Mazin), member of the PLO Executive Committee and head of the National and International Relations Department.
'Abd al-Razzaq al-Yahya, member of the PLO. Executive Committee, and its representative in Jordan, former commander of the Palestine Liberation Army.

Nabil 'Amru, Director of Broadcasting for the Palestinian Revolution.

Ramzi Khuri, Director of the Office of the Chairman of the Executive Committee.

Sa'id Abu 'Ammara, PLO representative in Moscow.

'Imad Shaqur, Adviser on Israeli Affairs to the Chairman of the Executive Committee.

Khalid Salam, Editor of the newspaper, *Sawt al-Bilad*, published in Nicosia.

During the meeting, Dr Vilner had stated 'I do not want to say that most Israelis of Sephardi origin do not support the Likud – but their reasons have nothing to do with the Arab-Israel dispute. They do not support it for its policy of expansionism and settlement. It was their economic and class situation which pushed them into supporting Likud. Ma'arakh [Labour-Alliance] and the Ashkenazim, as an *haut bourgeois* class, oppressed the Sephardim. Now, the Sephardim have started to learn how their exploitation has been started by the Right.'[120] Abu Mazin then spoke. 'Friends, let us speak as frankly as we can about a subject which deserves some clarification, both by us and by you – that is the picture painted over the years about Sephardim in Israel, most of whom had lived with us in peace and harmony for many years. The ruling establishment in Israel together with influential Western propaganda machinery have gone to pains to depict the Sephardim as Arab-and Palestinian-haters. However, your presence here with us as representatives of significant sectors of public opinion in Israel proves the invalidity of this claim. Your peace proposals are heading inexorably towards a lasting peace founded on justice, and as we agree, that means the realisation of the inalienable national rights of the Palestinian people. Hence our welcome to you is founded on your deep awareness of the benefits of a just peace in whose shade we all need to live. Our National Council, particularly in its last session, has made all these positive ideas the subject of consideration and respect. The Council has passed unambiguous resolutions according our meetings and dialogue all the necessary support and legality. We met yesterday for the sake of peace and we are meeting again today for the sake of peace. It is our common desire to forge peace and through our shared awareness we are putting an end to those who want this region to remain a permanent theatre of war and destruction. With peace it will be possible for all our children to live in security, stability and freedom just like children the world over.'[121]

It is significant to note that Ashkenazi settlers from the Zionist, non-Zionist and anti-Zionist Left have held many meetings with the PLO over recent years, particularly with 'Isam Sartawi, but they have not been prosecuted – perhaps they were secretly encouraged by the government which received briefings about their talks. The new law was not passed until the Sephardim founded the Dialogue Committee and resolved to start a dialogue with the PLO. The law is in complete accord with Zionist policies, which are to erect a barrier between the Sephardim and the Palestinians. A secret serviceman, named Reuven, admitted in court that the government had requested Ashkenazi Israelis to establish contacts with the PLO. and that prior meetings had all taken place with government permission.[122]

Ha'aretz reported on 19 June 1987 that Latif Dori met the delegation upon its return from Budapest. He declared 'no power in the world that can halt the dialogue which will continue anywhere and at any time. We are ready to pay the price for our struggle for a just peace and peace co-existence amongst our two peoples.' Charlie Biton took the opportunity to mention the threats directed against members of the Palestinian and Israeli delegations. Ze'ev Even, the chief of criminal investigations in the central region, summoned Biton, who then claimed parliamentary immunity. The delegation's lawyer, Amos Giv'on, stated that the members would retain their right not to answer questions from the secret service. In 1988, Dori and three other Israelis were sentenced to six months in jail or community service for meeting PLO officials in Romania, and Dori received the Kreisky Peace Award in Vienna.[123] Abbi Nathan, the owner of the pirate 'Voice of Peace' radio station and originally from Iran, was sent to prison for meeting PLO officials in 1986. Unrepentant, he claimed that as soon as he got out of prison he would go and meet Arafat.[124]

THE THIRD PLO-SEPHARDI CONFERENCE: TOLEDO 1989

'While the Ashkenazi Establishment of Israel is refusing to negotiate with the PLO,' stated Abu Mazin, 'it is important to deal directly with the Sephardi Jews who represent the masses of the Israeli people. Since the Sephardi Jews are the majority in Israel, matters of peace and war will be dependent on them. They are an organic part of our culture, our Arab Islamic society, part of our history and memory. We ought to renew our memory to use our common cultural dimension in order to overcome the present and plan for the future.'

The Toledo Conference was held between 3-6 July 1989 and organised by the Spanish Institute for Peace and International Studies and two Jewish Moroccan groups based in Paris: 'Perspectives Judeo-Arabe' and 'Identity and Dialogue'. The choice of Toledo is highly significant since it symbolises the cultural and political co-operation between Sephardi Jews and Muslims in Spain over many generations.

The Jewish communiqué published at the end of the deliberations describes 'the common culture of Jews and Arabs is an important basis for the future of the Israeli and Palestinian peoples'. The statement praises PLO moderation and calls upon the government of Israel 'to respond to the challenge of peace offered by the PLO and to begin negotiations in order to attain a just and peaceful solution based on self-determination and the establishment of a Palestinian state next to Israel.'

The Palestinian group was led by Mahmud 'Abbas Abu Mazin, and the poet Mahmud Darwish, both members of the PLO Executive Committee.

Darwish pointed out that peace must be based on mutual interest and cultural heritage, and Sephardi Jews are more able than others to live with this idea since it does not lead them into the unknown.

Thirty-eight Sephardim from Israel attended. They included Latif Dori, Secretary of the Committee for Israeli-Palestinian Dialogue, Rabbi Mordechai Malka, Rabbi Moshe Suwisa, Professor David Tzemah, Dr Shimon Balas of Tel Aviv University, Professor Shlomo al-Baz of the Hebrew University, the actor Yosef Shiloah, the poet Erez Biton and Naim Giladi-Khlaschi, Secretary of the World Organisation of Jews from Islamic countries.

Interestingly, many of them preferred to address the conference in Arabic, their mother tongue, rather than Hebrew or English. Sephardi Jews living outside Israel were also present, among them Seraj Berdugo, head of the Jewish Community in Morocco, Seraj Eyda, Deputy President of the Tunisian Human Rights Organisation, Amiel Alcalay, a researcher and interpreter from the US, Elie Baida, a Syrian economist and Naim Katan, an Iraqi writer and Chairman of the Royal Academy of Science in Canada.

Progressive intellectuals from Arab countries were present in strength. Hamadi al-Sayyid, head of the Arab League in Paris, writers Lutf Allah Suleiman, Mahmud Hussein and Burhan Ghalyun among many others.

Seraj Berdugo observed that although many Moroccan Jews in Israel vote for the right, for social reasons, 'deep in their hearts they are not anti-Arab.' He revealed that 30 percent of Moroccan Jews did not emigrate to Israel but to the West where they are better off. As for the Jews in Morocco, he stressed, 'we are living evidence of the form of life which will exist in the Middle East after the achievement of peace.'[125]

MORDECHAI VANUNU – 1986:
A MOROCCAN IN CHAINS

The story of Mordechai Vanunu, the Israeli of Moroccan origin who divulged information about Israel's secret nuclear plant to *The Sunday Times*, can only be explained within the framework of anti-Sephardi racial discrimination and Sephardi solidarity with the Palestinian people's struggle. Israeli newspapers have published a number of scurrilous articles about this brave man with the aim of covering up this truth.

Mordechai is the son of Salman Wa'anunu who immigrated with his family from Marrakesh in 1963 and lived in one of the Sephardi slum districts in Beer Sheba. Vanunu went to elementary school and was then transferred to a religious secondary school, subsequently entering the department of geography and philosophy at Beer Sheba University. His father still sells religious artifacts in Beer Sheba market.

During his university education he made friends with Palestinian students and started to defend their rights. In November 1985, for example, Vanunu took part in a meeting on Middle Eastern culture attended by Arab students, at which the Palestinian flag was raised and enthusiastic speeches were given. Vanunu gave a speech in which he said 'every Arab student must continue to struggle against Zionist racism which also oppresses the Sephardim.' He called for the establishment of a Palestinian state. M. Artzi'eli, who published the declaration[126] noted that Vanunu neither added 'alongside Israel' nor 'in its place'.

During his studies, Vanunu stated that the Ashkenazi establishment treated the natives the way the whites treat the blacks in South Africa and that the Ashkenazim had blocked all means of advancement for the Sephardim. He demanded that the number of rooms allotted to Arab students on the campus be doubled and he was in constant contact with the Progressive List and the Democratic Front.

After working in the Israeli nuclear programme, Vanunu determined that the publication of Israel's nuclear secrets would save the Middle East from destruction. It is possible too that the security services knew about Vanunu's movements and did nothing, hoping that the publication of the nuclear secrets would intimidate the Arab states. Now (1990) solitary confinement in prison and the abject treatment meted out to him both aim at destroying him psychologically.

In July 1987 Mordechai Vanunu sent a letter to the MP, Charlie Biton, asking him to speak out about the dangers of nuclear arms in Israel. He stressed that he was neither a spy nor an agent of any organisation and had not acted for financial reasons, but because he wanted the average citizen to know the truth. Vanunu referred to the fact that he was kidnapped by the Mossad and Shin Bet in contravention of international and Israeli law, and that he was undergoing humiliation in prison and had been fair game for the press (e.g. the seizure and publication of his diary). However, according to Vanunu, he was still strong and believed he was right as much as he did before he was kidnapped. He asked for help to obtain the rights legally allowed for prisoners as he was in solitary confinement and not allowed to receive visits from anyone except his brothers and his girlfriend. He was not allowed to make a telephone call, even to his lawyer. He added that he was not a prisoner but a captive of the Shin Bet. Vanunu accused the Israeli authorities of disgraceful behaviour in the Lebanese war and other scandals. He asked Biton to visit the prison to 'see for himself how he is deprived of all his human rights in the name of security'. *Zu Haderekh* published this letter[127] with parts cut out by the censor.

At the beginning of August 1987 the Bertrand Russell Peace Foundation convened a press conference in London at which Me'ir Vanunu described how Mossad kidnapped his brother. *The Sunday Times* published the details[128] and it appeared that a Mossad agent named Cindy (a Jewish American immigrant married to an Israeli army officer) enticed Vanunu into travelling from London to her 'sister's' apartment in Rome where two men pinned him down as Cindy gave him an injection. He woke up shackled in irons and on a ship to Israel. The abduction took place just a few days before *The Sunday Times* published Vanunu's information about the Israeli nuclear bomb.[129] In prison Vanunu was forced to 'confess' his crime and went on hunger strike for thirty-five days. He was informed that he would be tried for treason and could face the death penalty. Vanunu is now demanding that the court acquit him immediately as he was transferred to Israel in contravention of international and Italian law. His brother revealed details of the case but the threat of 15 years imprisonment has decided him not to return to Israel.

At his court appearances, Vanunu was forced to wear a helmet to hide his face from distant cameras. His trial was held in camera and he was not permitted to tell the court certain facts in his defence. Two security officers flanked him, ready to gag him should he attempt to disobey. Finally convicted, he was sentenced to 18 years in prison.

In the short history of the state of Israel, there have been others convicted of treason and espionage but they were not treated so brutally or given such long sentences because they were of European origin while Vanunu is 'only a Moroccan Jew' belonging, according to the Zionist mentality, to the 'inferior Arab–Islamic society'.

Actually, Vanunu did not spy for another country, as convicted Ashkenazim had done, but published, in a 'friendly' country, information which had been common knowledge throughout the world.

Although Vanunu's main motive was to aid the cause of peace, there is no doubt that he was deeply marked and embittered by the racism which he and his family have been subject to for many years.

As a nuclear technician, there is no doubt that he was aware of the strategic alliance between Israel and South Africa, aiming at the possibility of using nuclear weapons against the 'inferior races'. This is the social and ideological environment in which Vanunu formulated his bold action for peace.

The most crucial question is: how did the 'most efficient intelligence service in the world' allow a man with his political ideas to work for nine years on a nuclear project, to collect secret information, to photograph Israel's nuclear installations and to leave the country (which has very tight exit controls) with all this documentation?

It is reasonable to suppose that the Israeli security services knew about his movements and turned a blind eye, assuming that he would go abroad, publish his material and alarm the Arab world. Israel knows that sooner or later the balance of power will shift in favour of the Islamic world, so the nuclear option could be held up as a deterrent.

There is no point in building up a deterrent force without

informing the other side of its existence. Vanunu appears to have been allowed to do this job and pay a heavy price for it.

The last question must be: can Israeli nuclear bombs deter a combined Arab-Islamic attack? The answer must be no. A nuclear assault on any of her near neighbours would have disastrous consequences for Israel: even with no retaliation, Israel could not survive the fall-out from her own weapons used close at hand.

In any case, Israel's paymaster, America, would not permit the use of nuclear weapons, not out of love for Islam, but because they would destroy vital oil supplies and thereby the Western economy. However, the Arab states reacted with the development of chemical and long range missiles.

THE EASTERN FRONT

Kochavi Shemesh and Sa'adya Marciano – both veteran Black Panthers, founded this new organisation in solidarity with the Palestinian people. On 11 October 1986 *Falestine al-Thawra* published an interview with these two leaders.

Shemesh's view was that 'life taught us, as did events and their repercussions, that we could only expect poverty as long as "war" remained a weapon in the hands of the Ashkenazi bourgeoisie and that in order to distribute more bread and milk to our children we needed "peace". Thus a common front with the Palestinian people was inevitable in order to put an end to the problem of discrimination.

'The concept of the Eastern Front arose as an organisation which would work for peace with the Palestinians as a prelude to the struggle for equality amongst all the communities in Israel and to purge it of the plague of racism.'

As for the dangers of war, Shemesh pointed out that the 1967 war showed that Israel, not the Arabs, was the aggressor.

Despite the activities of Rabbi Kahane's group, Shemesh asserts that most educated Sephardim support the peace movement in Israel.

How do you differ from Peace Now?

Shemesh: 'Firstly, we stem from a Sephardi cultural background and we represent the poor Sephardim. The Peace Now people are members of the intelligentsia and have their roots in the state of Israel which masquerades as a Western state and looks for its cultural stimulus to the countries of origin of the Ashkenazim. Hence we are struggling inside Israel for equality and social justice.

'Our cultural background is Middle Eastern. The issue of equality and that of being Middle Easterners is a vital issue for us whereas it does not concern the Peace Now movement at all.

'We differ from Peace Now in that we have a programme. Where is their programme?

'We understand peace with the Palestinians to mean the establishment of an independent Palestinian state. Peace Now does not demand this, and we have not heard that they see it as a basis for peace in spite of the fact that many members of Peace Now support the establishment of an independent Palestinian state. We believe that the borders of the Palestinian and Israeli states can only be drawn by mutual recognition and negotiations. We accept the pre-1967 borders, but Peace Now has not taken a stance on this matter.'

Support for the Palestinian Intifada

Sephardi Jews, along with other progressives, took part in noisy mass demonstrations in support of the Palestinian people's uprising. One of those who refused to serve in the army in the occupied territories during the Intifada, which started in December 1987, was M. 'Amur, an officer of Moroccan origin and a member of the Eastern Front. He was sent to Megiddo prison. The Eastern Front, along with the Yesh Gvul ('There is a Limit'), Day Lakibbush ('Stop the Occupation') and Year 21 organisations staged a demonstration in front of the prison. Yosef Shiloah, an Eastern Front representative stated that 'Me'ir 'Amur is a hero, since he is challenging the occupation authorities by rejecting the means of oppression wielded against the Palestinian people, and we support him for that.' Shiloah pointed out that 'Amur had refused to do military service for another reason, which was the racial discrimination suffered by Sephardim in Israel.'

The demonstrators chanted, 'Rabin, Rabin, how many bones have you broken today? No to shooting, no to crying, no to military service on the West Bank and the Gaza Strip.' Amur's colleagues in the Department of Social Science at Tel Aviv University published a petition in *Ha'aretz*[130] in support of his refusal.

At the same time, Erez Biton, the poet of Moroccan origin, stated at a meeting of progressive writers, 'the Palestinian intifada is a boon in that it brings Israel back to its senses. The Jordanian option is dead . . . We cannot live as crusaders or colonialists. We have to learn that the Palestinians are part of our life.'[131]

After he came out of prison, 'Amur spoke with Rahel Sa'ar, a correspondent of *Ha'aretz*.[132] He blamed the Ashkenazi 'doves' for ignoring anti-Sephardi discrimination.

Lili Galili reported in *Ha'aretz* the words of a youth in the streets of Dimonah. 'Poor Israel. Who is there to defend her in the next generation? All her young people are alcoholics and drug addicts. They prefer non-combat positions in the army. Yasser Arafat doesn't need his intifada. He just has to sit tight for another ten years and Israel will blow itself apart.'[133]

During the course of the Sephardi struggle against occupation, two soldiers won a great moral victory. Angelo 'Idan (of Libyan origin) and Rami Hasson (of Sephardi Palestinian origin) served several prison sentences in 1989 for refusing to serve in the occupied Arab land. Eventually the military command released them.

Hasson (33) said after 140 days of imprisonment that he also refused to accept any command in the army and that most Sephardi soldiers did not want to keep these territories. He stated that they had good memories from Iraq and Morocco – their original countries. However after five terms of imprisonment he was called up again in October 1989 but refused to go . . .

Charlie Biton, MP, went to Shabura refugee camp, near Rafah, where five Palestinians were shot dead and a curfew had been imposed for 18 days. He demanded that the soldiers involved should be tried.[134]

Sephardi inhabitants of the slum districts began to hold meetings with their Palestinian neighbours in order to help them. In Jerusalem, Professor Shlomo al-Baz hurried with his friends to the nearly Arab village when he heard shots (fired by the Border Police). His very presence stopped another disaster.[135]

Even Sephardim who have joined the Zionist Establishment tend to be more moderate than their Ashkenazi colleagues. When Navon, for example, became the head of the Foreign Affairs and Defence Committee in the Knesset in 1983, he demanded that talks be held with the Palestinians instead of with Jordan and he believed in a peace based on Israel's withdrawal from the occupied territories.[136] When Menahem Begin refused to form a committee of enquiry to look into the massacres at Sabra and Shatila, Yitzhak Navon went on television and demanded that such a committee be formed. He intended to resign as president if the government rejected his request. Navon also opposed the principle of the Judaisation of the Galilee, saying 'We should develop the Galilee for all its inhabitants.'[137]

Mordechai Ben Porat and Aharon Ozan, of Iraqi and Tunisian origin respectively, demanded the withdrawal of Israeli forces from Lebanon without preconditions.[138] Whilst recent Ashkenazi religious fundamentalism is serving as a vehicle for extreme nationalism inspired by the Book of Joshua, Sephardi reaction to Ashkenazi permissiveness is driving towards non-Zionist traditionalism. The vehicle for this trend is the fast growing support for the new Sephardi religious movement, known as SHAS. Rabbi Yitzhak Perets, its leader who is considered 'reactionary right-wing', demanded the participation of the Palestine Liberation Organization in the proposed international conference, making reference to the harmony and good relations that had prevailed between Jews and Muslims over their common history, in contrast with the sufferings of Ashkenazi Jews in Europe.[139]

Rabbi Ovadia Yosef, regarded as the primary spiritual leader of Israel's Sephardim and SHAS and whose dovish views have long been known, was invited to Cairo in July 1989 by the Egyptian president. In their talk, Rabbi Yosef advocated withdrawal from parts of the occupied territories if Israel could be guaranteed a secure and lasting peace.

The Cairo visit provoked outrage in Israel's right wing, but reports that Rabbi Yosef would issue a formal religious ruling along the same lines caused near panic.

The right wing fears that a declaration by Rabbi Yosef that Jewish religious law obliges Israel to give up territories if it would spare bloodshed could have a serious impact on opinion.

Rabbi Yosef was to deliver a religious ruling on the subject at a religious meeting in Jerusalem in August 1989. However, the Prime Minister, Yitzhak Shamir, and other leading right wing politicians reportedly pressed him not to speak out formally on the subject for fear it would invite political pressure and even bloodshed.[140]

In fact the Rabbi had already stated in 1980 that 'blood is more important than land', and thereafter he was removed from office as Sephardi Chief Rabbi. In April 1990 this party decided to support Labour to form a Peace Government, but its economic weakness enabled the Ashkenazi boss, Rabbi Schach, to veto the move, demanding support for Likud (*Hadashot*, 27 April).

THE SEPHARDI MOVEMENT ABROAD

Ever since the emergence of the Black Panthers in the streets of Jerusalem, progressive Sephardim have been active in the West, trying to raise the consciousness of world and Jewish public opinion, particularly among the hundreds of thousands of Jews who emigrated from the Arab world and Israel to the West.

Members of this movement take an active part in pro-Palestinian meetings and demonstrations as well as writing letters and articles for Western and Palestinian newspapers on anti-Palestinian and anti-Sephardi discrimination.

Amongst these organisations are the World Sephardi Organisation which is headquartered in New York, the Sephardi Organisation for Israeli-Palestinian Peace with its headquarters in Paris, and the 'International Committee Against Oppression of Sephardi Jews in Israel' whose headquarters are in London.

Sephardi organisations in the West have come up against a great many difficulties for the following reasons:

1 Western, and particularly American, support for Israel as a fundamental policy notwithstanding moral considerations. This is because Israel constitutes a Western military outpost against the socialist bloc and the Middle Eastern peoples.

2 The ability of the World Zionist Organisation, Israeli embassies and Mossad agents to penetrate Western news media, such as radio, television and the press, and political parties as well as philanthropic organisations and trade and student unions, in order to defend Israel by suppressing the truth.

3 The Israeli government's ability to exert complete control over the religious, political and social life of the Jews who live in the West, including the Sephardim who emigrated from the Middle East. This takes place through the synagogues, the Zionist press and the World Zionist Organisation.

The World Zionist Organisation has exploited synagogues to collect funds for Israel and to spread Zionist propaganda. All the donations are handed over to the Zionist Organisation, which pays no tax on them to the British government, since it is ostensibly a 'charitable' organisation whereas every Israeli knows that these funds are used to establish settlements in the occupied territories and to purchase war material, directly or indirectly.

I asked an experienced journalist why the press did not publish material on the oppression of the Sephardim in Israel. He replied, 'I am afraid to. The Zionists would accuse me of anti-Semitism.'

If a newspaper publishes an item which Israel wants retracted, scores of letters are immediately sent to the editor.

When the BBC broadcasts a news item which is not favourable to Israel, it receives scores of letters of complaint. There are more Muslims than Jews in Britain, but they are not as well organised and unable to orchestrate phone calls and letters.

4 The massive financial resources at the disposal of the pro-Israel lobby abroad could buy up an army of journalists, politicians, unionists and parties.

5 The United Nations does not deal with organisations which do not represent member states.

6 Some of the Arab states show no concern about anti-Sephardi racism in Israel and are not aware of the significance of this internal conflict.

7 Israeli pressure (via America and the Arab governments) on the PLO to stop any cooperation with Sephardi organisations.

8 The anti-Sephardi lies spread by the extreme Ashkenazi left amongst the Palestinians in order to prevent them uniting in struggle. The most vicious of these lies is that the Sephardim are anti-Arab. We believe that the Israeli secret service is the source of this libel.

The most important of these factors is Western, and particularly American, support for Israel. The Western powers will change this policy when they realise that it does not serve their national interests. This analysis does not mean that we should sit by and wait.

Notwithstanding the importance of political work in the West, the crucial struggle will take place, not in London, New York or Paris, but in the Middle East – in Nablus, Nazareth, Jerusalem and the Black Belts, in the development towns and the Sephardi moshavim.

That will happen when the Arabs recognise the root of the dispute in the Middle East. It is not a religious war, between Jews, Christians and Muslims, but an anti-colonialist struggle between foreign settlers and the natives, who are the Christians, Muslims and Sephardi Jews.

The callous attitude of the East European Zionist leaders to genuine grievances and human life seems to be imported from their countries of origin; and the collapse we are witnessing in that part of the world will probably repeat itself in Israel with much more catastrophic consequences.

NOTES

1 *Zu Haderekh*, 13 September 1989.
2 *Ha'aretz*, 26 April 1949.
3 *Ha'aretz*, 9 May 1949.
4 Jewish Agency Minutes, 7 March 1949 and 29 April 1949.
5 Knesset Minutes, Volume 3, 618, 24 January 1950.
6 See *The Educational and the Social Gap*, Hedim, October 1978.
7 *Bama'arakha*, No. 25, July 1963.
8 Hodar, *Israca*, 1973, 18.
9 Woolfson, *Prophets in Babylon*, 267.
10 Hodar, Israca, 1973. Even now, in 1990, poor Sephardim and Palestinians are being forced to pay heavier taxation in order to finance the new influx of Soviet Jews!
11 *Ha'aretz*, 22 March 1971.
12 Hodar, *Israca*, 17 and 18, and Woolfson, *Prophets in Babylon*.
13 The Black Panthers, 9 November 1972.
14 *Les temps modernes, The Second Israel*, 169, and see Appendix V.
15 13 April 1971.
16 *Ma'ariv*, 8 June 1971.
17 *Ha'aretz*, June 1971 and *Israca*, January 1973.
18 *Les temps modernes, The Second Israel*, 188.
19 Ibid.
20 Mordekhai Soman, *Les temps modernes, The Second Israel*, 181.
21 See *Israel and the Palestinians*, Ithaca, 1975, and also *Israca*, January 1973.
22 Rafael Shpira, *Khamsin*, No. 5, 24.
23 *Israleft*, 20 November 1972.
24 *Israleft*, 20 November 1972.
25 *Yedi'ot Aharonot*, 28 May 1971.
26 'The Report and the Social Gap', Uzi Benziman, *Ha'aretz*, 18 May 1973.
27 *Shevet va'am*, 1978.
28 26 March 1986.
29 *Koteret Rashit*, 27 July 1988.
30 Number 41, 1971.
31 *Israca*, January 1973.
32 *Les temps modernes, The Second Israel*, 95.
33 *Les temps modernes, The Second Israel*, 33.
34 Ibid, 35.
35 Swirski, 1981.
36 *Zu Haderekh*, 3 February 1982.
37 Stars of the Arabic film and music industry in the fifties and sixties.
38 Originally published in *Liqa'*, the magazine of the Jewish Arabic Institute of the Histadrut on 3 July 1987.
39 Swirski, 1981.
40 *Al Hamishmar*, (Hotam), 4 July 1986 and 11 July 1986, and *Zu Haderekh*, 30 July 1986.
41 *Ha'aretz*, 5 June 1987.
42 Ibid.
43 *The Times*, 17 June 1980.
44 *Ha'aretz*, 27 June 1980.
45 *Zu Haderekh*, 16 July 1980.
46 Ibid.
47 *Herald Tribune*, 31 December 1982 and *Zu Haderekh*, 29 December 1982.
48 *Ha'aretz* 4 January 1984.
49 *Ha'aretz*, 5 December 1980.
50 *Zu Haderekh*, 10 December 1980.
51 *Zu Haderekh*, 17 December 1980.
52 *Ha'aretz*, 9 January 1981.
53 A derogatory term mocking the sound of Arabic.
54 28 September 1981.
55 *Zu Haderekh*, 24 February 1982.

56 *Ha'aretz Supplement*, 26 February 1982.
57 *Ha'aretz*, 4 September 1981.
58 *Zu Haderekh*, 19 February 1986.
59 *Zu Haderekh*, 16 April 1986.
60 P. 26.
61 *Ha'aretz*, 9 January 1987.
62 P. 20.
63 P. 26.
64 Pp. 20, 21.
65 Pp. 227 and 228
66 P. 9.
67 P. 17.
68 P. 18.
69 P. 27.
70 P. 233.
71 P. 242.
72 P. 248.
73 P. 296.
74 *Les temps modernes, The Second Israel*, 89.
75 Ibid.
76 Na'im Giladi-Khlaschi, *The Black Panthers Bulletin*.
77 The greatest territorial extent of the biblical kingdom of Israel.
78 *Ha'aretz*, 20 May 1986.
79 *Les temps modernes*, 88.
80 See also Charlie Biton's interview, *Falestine al-Thawra*, 17 January 1987.
81 30 November 1979.
82 *Les temps modernes, The Second Israel*, trans. Fu'ad Jadid.
83 Matzpen, January 1973.
84 Swirski, 1981, 296.
85 *Ha'aretz*, 6 February 1981.
86 The Israeli press, 22 September 1986.
87 *Black Panther Bulletin*, 9 November 1972.
88 *Les temps modernes, The Second Israel*, 96.
89 *Zu Haderekh*, 26 November 1980.
90 17 April 1981.
91 *Les temps modernes, The Second Israel*, 182.
92 Ibid.
93 Ibid, 186.
94 *Ha'aretz*, 11 September 1981.
95 *Ha'aretz*, 18 September 1981.
96 *Ha'aretz*, 24 December 1982.
97 25 June 1982.
98 *Zu Haderekh*, 28 July 1982.
99 *New Outlook*, March 1983.
100 An acronym for 'For Improving the Life of the Community'.
101 *Ha'aretz*, 26 September 1982.
102 *Ha'aretz*, 23 September 1983.
103 *Ha'aretz*, 17 June 1983.
104 *Zu Haderekh*, 16 January 1985.
105 *Ha'aretz*, 15 March 1985.
106 *Zu Haderekh*, 18 December 1985.
107 *New Outlook*, May 1983.
108 *Ha'aretz Supplement*, 29 July 1983.
109 Pp. 349-354.
110 *Ha'aretz Supplement*, 9 January 1981.
111 *Zu Haderekh*, 29 January 1986.
112 *Al-'Awdah*, 30 January 1986.
113 *Direct Line*, May 1986.
114 *'Al Hamishmar*, 27 February 1986.
115 *Al- Mirsad*, 27 August 1986.

116 The opening verses of the poem 'The Will to Live' from the collection *Songs of Life*.
117 *Al-Mirsad*, 7 January 1987.
118 *Zu Haderekh*, 10 June 1987.
119 *Ha'aretz*, 12 June 1987.
120 *Falestine al-Thawra*, 20 June 1987.
121 Ibid.
122 *Ha'aretz*, 19 June 1987.
123 *The Jerusalem Post*, 5 July 1988.
124 *Middle East International*, 20 October 1989.
125 *Falestine al-Thawra*, 16 July 1989, *Kul al-'Arab*, 12 July 1989, *Zu Haderekh*, 12 July 1989, *Ha'olam Hazze*, 12 July 1989.
126 *Ha'aretz*, 7 November 1986.
127 22 July 1987.
128 9 August 1987.
129 5 October 1986.
130 17 February 1988.
131 *Zu Haderekh*, 24 February 1988.
132 1 April 1988.
133 *Ha'aretz*, 1 April 1988.
134 *Zu Haderekh*,12 April 1989 and 31 May 1989.
135 *Falestine al-Thawra*, 21 May 1989.
136 Yoel Markus, *Ha'aretz*, 4 February 1983.
137 *The Guardian*, 3 May 1983, 19.
138 *The Times*, 22 April 1983.
139 *Hadashot*, 8 May 1987.
140 *The Guardian*, 15 August 1989.

APPENDIX I
TRANSIT CAMPS: MA'BAROT

To throw more light on the suffering of the Sephardim in these 'Ma'barot', we will quote here the stories of two people.

NA'IM 'ABDUSH

They settled my uncle Menahem and his family, and my grandmother Kehela, in Har Tuv camp in the Jerusalem district. My grandmother had lost two sons in the First World War and was blind. She was unable to deal with the biting cold in the tent and fell ill and died. Subsequently, Uncle Menahem took his family to one of the slum areas in Tel Aviv where he tried to start up the same type of business he had carried on in Baghdad, but he came up against numerous difficulties as a result of which he had a heart attack and died when he was forty-eight (his father had lived to be eighty in Baghdad), leaving behind a widow and ten children.

My father lived in Petah Tikvah Camp for ten years, until he died in his hut. Samra, my paternal grandmother, was placed in Pardes Hanna Camp on her own and she remained there until she died a few years later at over one hundred years of age. My sister Lulu was settled in Saqiya Camp until her husband took to drink and gambling and the family fell apart. The rest of the family was ripped apart as follows: my sister, Marcelle, and her family were sent to Tel Mond Camp. Ten years later her husband died of a heart attack which was a result of the hard agricultural labour he had to do. My uncle, Salim, was sent to Khairiya Camp. He had been a senior civil servant in Baghdad, but stayed unemployed for the rest of his life. His grandson committed suicide in 1989, as a result of racist harassment in the army. Uncle Ya'qov refused to emigrate and stayed in Iraq until he died, but his family was settled in one of the camps – I don't know which one! I don't remember which camp the wife of my uncle Tsiyon was sent to. My aunt Rosa and her family went to Lod Camp and I never saw her again! I don't know which camp aunt Baliha and her family went to. My aunt Najiya and her family were sent to Ra'anana Camp where her middle-aged husband died. Uncle Avraham and his family went to a camp near Haifa, I'm not sure which one exactly! Uncle Kabi and his family went to a camp in the coastal plain. The children of my father's uncle were split up amongst different camps. Had the whole family been settled in the same camp we could have made up a commando squadron to defend our interests!

JIHAD KHEDOURIE

'When I was nine years old, in 1941, fascist gangs in Baghdad attacked and looted our house. Our family was almost killed. Those incidents affected me, and I was happy to immigrate to Israel in 1950. As soon as I got to the Sha'ar Ha'aliya Camp I was conscripted, but I did not object. During my military service Ashkenazi officers would treat me and other Sephardim like slaves. I was well-known for my temper in Baghdad . . . I would not accept that! We used to curse the officers whenever they humiliated us. Eventually I came to the conclusion that this is a colonialist state which oppresses Sephardim and Palestinians and which in turn would be finished off by the Arab nation. I cursed the state whenever they wronged me or my mates. At one point they took my unit to the Egyptian border and demanded that we attack an Egyptian position. We said that the Egyptians had not carried out any hostile actions against us, and that we did not wish to start a new war. The Ashkenazi officers seethed and threatened us with guns, but got nowhere and we returned to the military camp. One morning an officer came to wake me up, and started treating me rudely, so I spat in his face. Following this, a number of officers beat me up quite badly. When I finished my military service I refused to do reserve duty, I would tear up the military call-up order and tell them that I had not received it. An officer from the Reserves came and asked me "Don't you want to serve the flag?" to which I replied "It's your flag, not mine!" I lived for a while in one of the transit camps near some Arab villages and started going to one of the villages and would sit in the coffee shop and talk to the Palestinians – in Arabic naturally. I became friends with them, and they liked me. I was happy there. But then a secret policeman paid me a visit and demanded that I desist from those visits, for security reasons . . . I refused. I bought a room in Tel Aviv and I would let the villagers come and sleep on the floor when they came to work in Tel Aviv, but the police warned me that it was against Israel's security interests. I told them to go to hell. In the end they trumped up a charge against me and I was sent to jail. At that time I decided that I would not live in Israel any more. So I went off to Europe, and after a few days an Israeli Jew I knew approached me and asked if he could put his suitcase in my room for a few hours. After he left the room, the police came and looked through everything . . . They opened the suitcase and found drugs. They did not believe what I told them, and I was put in prison for a second time. After that I returned to Israel against my will, but I decided not to recognise Israel or to pay any taxes. I had bought a little piece of land near that camp, and the municipality sent a tax demand. I refused to pay it and they put me in prison. I refused again and they imprisoned me again . . . '

I lost contact with Jihad, but his sister Su'ad continued his tale: 'After he had been put in prison a number of times, he had a nervous breakdown, became apathetic and depressed. He did not work and would speak only occasionally. He did not visit his family and spurned marriage, preferring to be left completely alone. He became an ascetic like Abu al-'Ala' al-Ma'arri.[1] Finally in 1982, aged 48, he had a heart attack, and his neighbours took him to the Ichiliv hospital in Tel Aviv. When the doctors saw that he did not belong to the Sick Fund or any other health plan, they sent him home where a few hours later he was found dead.'

We shall finish this discussion of the camps by quoting the words of camp residents, in the novel *Hama'bara* by Shimon Balas, which we have referred to previously. The theme of this true story is the struggle of the Iraqi transit camp residents to elect a committee to represent their interests to the authorities. Balas describes the bloody clashes between Sephardim on the one hand, and the police, hired ruffians and the Ashkenazi camp director on the other.[2] The violent confrontation ends with the defeat of the police. Women from Baghdad participated in this battle by throwing mud at the police. There follows some of fragments of conversations which take place among the camp residents:

Woman: God doesn't listen to us . . .
David: The god of Israel is Ashkenazi too . . . [3]
A Mother: Abroad (i.e. in Iraq) you could bring up children. Here everything is up the spout. What camp children stay at home? Is this shack what you call a house? That's why they're never here . . . [4]
Abu Nu'man: If you have no work, with all due respect, you don't even get looked up to by a dog. Anyway, listen to me. I have lived longer than you and I can tell you that life in those days was more decent. (Abu Nu'man had been a merchant

who travelled around the Iraqi countryside.) Whenever I came to a Muslim village, the men and women would rush to tell the Sheikh that Ezra the Jew had arrived. The Sheikh would receive me in his guest room and would put me up in his house as long as I had business in the area.[5]

When a government doctor came and ordered a villager to hospital for an operation, the villagers would say, 'Let's ask Ezra first.'[6]

A resident: All the heart disease and the sudden deaths at an early age are due to our way of life . . . [7]

'Eini: It seems to me that since the days of the Babylonian exile, Mesopotamian Jews have suffered no catastrophe as awful as the one which has been visited upon us. That old and enlightened Judaism has been trampled into the earth and scattered over the arid and muddy lands which they call 'transit camps'. I said to the camp administrator, 'How long do you intend to treat us like your slaves?'[8]

This is our fate . . . they have trampled on our dignity. Everything is topsy-turvy, our values and dignity crushed . . . [9]

My family was well-known in Iraq. We used to mix with ministers, senators and sheikhs. When I entered the Sheikh's reception room, everyone would stand up. Who knows me here? I'm just a peasant here.[10]

A woman: Moshe ate some cheese from the dustbin, and his stomach is hurting him now . . . [11]

Wife: Na'im the baker's wife gave birth to a still-born child, it was too muddy for the doctor to come to the camp.[12]

Hayyim: Who will make peace with the Arab countries? The Ashkenazim? No – we will. Who know who the Arabs are. We can speak to them. They'll listen to us and trust us. That's what we'll do, Abu-Suhayl – not just sit in transit camps.[13]

Yosef: The judge is the tool of the authorities, just like the police. Except that the police are a violent tool, but the court covers up crime and violence in the name of law and justice.[14]

Meir: You and your friends still think things are going to get better. I stopped believing that a long time ago. The communists write and speak about 'Work Opportunities' and 'Housing Opportunities' . . . Just who's going to give that to us? The Jewish Agency? The Histadrut, the Knesset, who? Yes. They're all against you.[15]

Abu Nu'man (to the Zionists): You made our lives hell in Iraq. We had been independent there, living by the sweat of our brows. We were our own masters until you brought us this catastrophic Palestine thing of yours. You said we had to get up, leave everything and come here . . . And what did you do? We got up and came – to graveyards.[16]

Nu'man: Bear up, father. Bear up.[17]

Abu Nu'man: Why should I? Is this a life? (*He sits upright and grimaces*)

Nu'man: Don't you feel well?

Abu Nu'man: My back is hurting me. We worked in the rain yesterday.[18]

Hayyim: Madness reigned over the camp. There were quarrels, fights, disturbances, police! The labour office was shut . . . The Ashkenazim are laughing at us. They say that we Iraqis are primitive. The Ashkenazim who are not worth two-pence in their own countries – they come here and lord it over us.[19]

Avraham told me that the director of his camp used to stir up sectarian quarrels amongst the Iraqis and the Moroccans, between the Jews from Mosul and the Kurds. There were disturbances every day. Then Avraham gathered together the leaders of the communities and formed a committee. The committee members marched up to the camp director and informed him: 'We are the camp administration'. He jumped into his car and sped off and he came back with the police . . . [20]

Moshe: (singing) They led us here like cattle

They brought us to the black camp
They taught us how to build
And we were as blind as beetles.[21]

Hayyim: The parties share us out . . . there is an abundance of parties in this country. But let me ask you, who are the heads of these parties? The same Ashkenazim who despise us.[22]

Camp Director: You are primitive people. You don't know how to run your own affairs. You have no concept of what a democratic way of life is. You just know how to stab people in the back.

Yosef: That is an insult and a blatant fabrication. Who stabs whom in the back? Us or him? Who sent Ya'kov and Shafiq and hired bullies from other camps to come and attack us on the Sabbath?[23]

NOTES

1 She is referring to Abu al-'Ala' al-Ma'arri (973–1057), outspoken poet and author. He was born just outside Aleppo, visited Baghdad and returned to his village where he retired to his house. He became blind and lived in a permanent state of fasting. His most famous work was the *Epistle of Forgiveness*.
2 Pp. 67 and 102.
3 P. 16.
4 P. 29.
5 P. 34.
6 P. 35.
7 P. 50.
8 P. 51.
9 P. 54.
10 P. 52.
11 P. 58.
12 P. 96–97.
13 P. 102.
14 P. 109.
15 P. 109.
16 'Graveyards' in Arabic (*maqabir*) is a pun on 'Transit Camps' (*ma'abir*).
17 P. 119.
18 P. 120.
19 P. 128.
20 P. 130.
21 P. 146.
22 P. 149.
23 P. 184.

APPENDIX II
KIRYAT SHEMONAH: A DEVELOPMENT TOWN ON THE LEBANESE BORDER

In his book (1981), Dr Shlomo Swirski quotes conversations with residents of Kiryat Shemonah, from which the following are extracted.

M: My brother-in-law came to Israel in 1948, but he left because of the discrimination . . . my daughter has told me to change our Moroccan surname because it is stopping her getting on. She wants us to have a nice Russian name. We do not differentiate between Ashkenazim and Sephardim. There is an Ashkenazi man in our town and we voted for him.

D: Why does the government not institute the plan for the industrial development of the Upper Galilee in Kiryat Shemonah instead of in the kibbutzim which already have vast landholdings and factories?

B: I worked for kibbutzim for 18 years and then was fired because I objected to the way they snatched up the lands of the Hula. All the money invested in the town goes straight into the pockets of the kibbutzim and not to residents of the town.

G: A shirt costs 500 Israeli pounds here, and 150 Israeli pounds in Tel Aviv. Trousers cost 1200 Israeli pounds here, and 300 Israeli pounds in Haifa. I have to go to Tel Aviv tomorrow to buy the basics for my family. I'll lose a whole day's work and the travel expenses. We had an Ashkenazi committee chairman. They arranged a party for him and gave him presents – a calculator, a lump sum, and the post of project director in one of the branches of the company. They gave him a car and doubled his current salary. Why? Because they discovered that he had been embezzling, and they wanted to cover it up. And we had followed him like sheep, trusted him, and now they have appointed a new Ashkenazi who knows nothing about the project. Why don't they appoint one of us . . . someone who has worked here for 18 years? That's discrimination. Once, they promoted one of us who then started to help us. The director said to him, 'Are you with us or with them?'

S: Since the kibbutzim preached socialism and were non-exploitative, they resolved not to employ labour in any settlement. But they established an industrial concern comprising all the settlements in the area, and that employed hired labourers. That's hypocrisy. Had they built the factories in the development towns it would have been a different matter. Once, we requested a car for one of our workers. The director said to us, 'The budget won't allow it.' Then they appointed an Ashkenazi kibbutz member and gave him a Renault 12. The Russian and Polish Jews who rule this state are out for themselves . . . Is this a democracy? Democracy is a fine word, but if you have power and authority you can do what you like.

B: They told the people who came from the Yemen, Iraq and North Africa that the culture they brought from those countries was worthless. They destroyed the system whereby the father was the head of the family. Then they gave Sephardim all sorts of bad names, such as 'Morocco Sakkin'[1] implying that we are all criminals and murderers.

S: The kibbutz kids have lots of educational opportunities . . . our kids have only one – to do labouring jobs.

B: The Black Panthers proved that the government has a policy of divide and rule.

G: Why doesn't the government bring higher education and technological jobs to our town? Why does the government only give benefits to people who leave the large towns to come and live in Kiryat Shemonah,[2] but we the residents get nothing.

342

That type of discrimination will lead to civil war. How is that suicide, crime and prostitution only take place among Sephardim?

D: Why do you think?

G: Because the government, whether it's Labour or Likud, created this social gulf through discrimination. These days people don't just think of leaving Kiryat Shemonah but Israel too. Three workers from our plant got redundancy money and left the country. Then there is the man who is taking his seven children to France . . .

M: Why do they ask us in the army where your father is from?

G: In the army all the cooks, chauffeurs and sanitary workers are Moroccans. Why is that? I don't have the strength any more to carry on the political fight for equality. I go to work every day at three in the morning and don't finish until six at night. My average day is between 14 and 15 hours, including overtime. In spite of that my wages only last for 15 days out of the month. The rest of the month I have to borrow. They've fixed my life so that I don't have any free time for political activity. What's more, we are not united.

M: When they see us try and unite, the policy of divide and rule starts. I was travelling with the union secretary who said to me, 'Give up that nonsense. I'll speak to so and so and get you a job . . . Come to your senses!' So they tried to get me over to their side. Naturally some people are weak . . . Once they reduced my employment hours and I asked the committee chairman for help. He went to the manager who told him, 'If you leave the committee I'll give you a nice job.' So he left the committee. See how they divide us! We had committees going in Galilee, Haifa, and Bet She'an, but they were all broken by graft.

G: We have to use violence and stage demonstrations like they did in Wadi al-Salib in Haifa.[3] If you don't turn the wheel by hand, the cart will not move. We must use force to put an end to the discrimination against us. It's got to change. We need someone to unite us.

M: We have got to get rid of the director who bribed the committee chairman, in order to foil his divide and rule policy.

G: You need money, time and strength. You don't have that strength. Neither the government or its economic policy will allow you to be strong. So you can't fight them. If you do, they'll arrest you for something. Look what they did to poor Peretz. He was only acting for the workers.[4] When David Ben Harush organized the demonstrations in Wadi al-Salib in Haifa they tried to buy him off. When we started to strike, they sent the police against us. But the police from Kiryat Shemonah and Safad refused to use force. Then they sent the police from Shfar'am against us. They brought in the minorities [i.e. the Druze police].

M: Look at Charlie Biton, the head of Black Panthers. He went around looking for a party which would help him and joined the communists.

MN: Why don't we get together and fight for our town. And you, G! You've got influence in the committee – you head the struggle.

G: I don't have any strength. The Histadrut is over me, and if the Histadrut doesn't help me and the workers abandon me, what can I do on my own?

B: I understand, a member of the workers' committee is just a person with problems and children to bring up. If he's got five or six children and no salary, and limited opportunities, even if he has noble views . . . how can he help the workers and live as well if the struggle were to last two years? Naturally, everything would fall apart piece by piece.

A: In spite of G's influence on the committee, he cannot depend on his comrades, because they'd abandon him if they were given money and their conditions were improved.

G: They tell us 'Well go then, go back to Morocco. We have Arab workers and don't need you!' They have no regard for union agreements. When we go to the Histadrut they tell us that they have to form a committee to look into the matter. I suggested to them that we take over the administration of the plant ourselves. They said that would just lead to the failure of the plant.

D: That's just a sign of weakness. The solution is to persist until we eventually succeed.

A: We need internal organization in order to change the conditions.

B: In 1977 the development towns voted Likud, thinking they would help us. But Likud is worse than the previous party. The rich have just got richer.

A: Comrades, we have to accept the situation as it is. There is no solution.

B: No, don't say that.

M: Here in Israel everyone is out for himself.

A: If we don't unite, it'll just go on like this.

G: Our organization cannot just be local.

A: It will need money.

M: They'll stop you getting it.

A: We'll never have time and money, because we are workers.

B: We need a leader like the leader of the blacks in America who was killed.

D: You mean you want them to assassinate us (laughter) . . .

G: Suppose we establish an organization, and we organize demonstrations and meetings, and then they throw me in prison on some pretext. Who'll defend me? That's what they did to the Sephardi leader Peretz. They put him in prison and we don't hear anything about him. He's sitting silent now because he has ascertained that silence is better.

D: Are you going to organize demonstrations for him?

G: I supported him, but a demonstration . . .

D: No. The problem is that we only supported him in our thoughts.

G: That doesn't cost anything. If we had had a half-day strike for him here and in Bet She'an and Ma'alot, that would have constituted strength.

M: If they thought that you could organize a strike, they wouldn't try and harm you . . . on the contrary, they'd be afraid of you, they'd know that you are strong.

G: They'd invent some legal clause showing that you were against the state.

D: People will gain strength when they believe in themselves. The only way forward is to be self-confident and to organize for the struggle. If the organization comes from outside it will be no use.

G: It's no use anyway. They will destroy us economically. They use bribes and inducements to break us. We have to have one aim – power.[5]

NOTES

1 Literally, 'knife-wielding Moroccan.'
2 I.e. migrating Ashkenazim, e.g., teachers, managers, etc..
3 See chapter ten.
4 Peretz was a Moroccan who challenged the Histadrut and organized a general strike in the port of Ashdod – which was broken.
5 P 104–118.

APPENDIX III
DEVELOPMENT TOWNS

SHLOMI

This town in the Galilee was established in 1949 to house Tunisian, Moroccan, Yemenite and Bulgarian immigrants. David Oren says in his report that if we were to compare economic development in the neighbouring Ashkenazi settlements to the situation in this town, we would have to conclude that development here is zero. This is why 40 percent of the town's residents have left since 1961. The establishment had hoped to settle 15,000 people here, but they only managed to settle 3,000. Homes are in a state of neglect and most people work outside the town, earning low wages compared to the big towns, that is £90 a month. The reductions in services have only made things much worse. People suffer from unemployment and there are no opportunities for the young generation or those just out of the army. There is no cinema in the town, no ambulance and no decent air-raid shelter; the few shelters that exist are full of rubbish. The residents complain of government discrimination in the way money is invested in the local economy, and threaten to end the Labour Party's control of the local council. The authorities brought over these Sephardim to provide cheap labour for the neighbouring Ashkenazi settlements, which have got rich on it. This led to 47 percent of the town's residents voting for the Likud bloc in the 1981 elections as a provocation to the bosses on the settlements who belonged to the Labour Party, which only won 27 percent of the vote. In the 1977 elections the majority voted for the Labour Party, and the Likud government therefore refused to include the town in the relief project for poor neighbourhoods. The article stresses that the government has spent money on Ashkenazi settlement on the West Bank and the Gaza Strip instead of helping Shlomi. A group of women reacted by starting a self-help project. Then the Sephardi Oded organization (see chapter ten) started to help the town, but the government foiled both plans because it wants the town to remain subservient.[1]

KIRYAT YAM

By 1986 the debts of this town of 3,600 had reached 600,000 New Shekels, 90 percent of which, according to the mayor, were interest repayments to the banks. The mayor also stated that the problem had not been solved by a reduction in services. In the past the town paid wages on the fourth of every month, then on the ninth, then employees were forced to pay the interest on the overdrafts. Now the banks refuse credit to municipal employees because the town cannot make the interest repayments. On 13 January 1986 the employees went on strike, staged a stormy demonstration and blocked off the main road. They sent a delegation to Jerusalem where they demonstrated in front of government buildings, met the Minister of the Interior and heard the usual promises.[2]

YERUHAM

This town to the south of Beer Sheba was founded in 1951. According to research figures published by the Ben Gurion University in Beer Sheba in 1980, Yeruham is one of the poorest development towns. 30 percent of its residents leave every year, including 80 percent of those just out of the army. The town is full of garbage and its houses are dreadful. Private industry uses its inhabitants as a pool of cheap labour, and thus the standard of living is low. Due to the poor school facilities, many teachers refuse to teach at its school, so the Ministry of Education uses unqualified teachers including soldiers.[3] On 28 November 1980 *Ha'aretz* reported that 1,000 people leave the town every year.

Reports published in the Israeli newspapers at the end of 1984 stated that the town's population was between 6,500 and 7,000, including 700 unemployed. This caused an increase in demonstrations and acts of violence against the authorities. The town hall was set on fire. The Sephardi Jews of the town threatened to return their army reserve- and identity-cards to the authorities. The reasons for the uprising were as follows:

1. Lack of food in the shops.
2. Shortage of teachers in the schools.
3. No local doctor.
4. The dismissal of the local headmaster.
5. Dismissals and unemployment.
6. The abject poverty: 50 percent of the residents require welfare payments, including 25 percent who receive welfare permanently.

There is no bakery in the town, no shop and no garage. Doctors and teachers refuse to live there. Moroccans form 50 percent of the inhabitants, the remainder being Iranians, Indians and some Rumanians together with their Israeli-born children. The economic base of the town is weak. It is far from the main highway and the industrial and agricultural centres. The residents elected an emergency committee to fight for their rights, which was joined by Charlie Biton, leader of the Black Panthers and a member of the Knesset.[4]

The government wanted to house 60 Ethiopian families in this town, but Barukh al-Muqayyis, the head of the local council, refused to accept them because of the rampant unemployment affecting two-thirds of the employees. Al-Muqayyis stated that it was up to the government to house the Ethiopians on Ashkenazi kibbutzim where there was no unemployment.[5]

Members of the local council joined the popular uprisings against the authorities, protesting against the lack of work and their overdue wages. A correspondent of *Zu Haderekh*, Miriam Galili, spoke to some of the residents about this, and there follows an abridgement of her article which appeared on 26 December 1984.

Rahel 'Ammar: She is divorced and has to feed four children. Her father is paralysed and has a heart condition. She is out of work even though she has qualifications and experience. She lost her job two years ago and received no unemployment benefits for six months. She said bitterly, 'I feel like a dead person. It seems that we are just good for military service and nothing else . . . '

Meir Shim'oni: Worked as a policeman for 25 years, and has been out of work for a year and a half. His wife is also out of a job. He was appointed as an inspector in the town and then was dismissed. Shim'oni wonders, 'why do they send people to this town when there is no work for them here?'

A youth: Said that the ruling establishment set up development towns in the Negev for strategic reasons to do with Egypt. After the peace treaty, the government started channelling funds into the colonies on the occupied West Bank. There are ten students from the town at university, but they have no future in the town.

S. Peretz: Father of four children, his wife is disabled. He says that in spite of the existence of skilled workers in the town, 70 percent of the labour on projects in the area is from elsewhere.

Esther Amslan: 22 years old. Completed three courses at the College of Technology.

Currently unemployed.

Tamar Omar: 20 years old. Unemployed even though she has finished secondary school. Her three unemployed brothers have left the town. She is thinking about leaving too.

Shim'on: Completed his army service, and has been unemployed for two year. He says 'What do I do? I bum around the streets and eat melon seeds!'

Tsippora Za'afrani: mother of seven. She works only four days a week. Her husband is out of work. Her daughter has finished her army service and is now unemployed.

The mayor, Barukh al-Muqayyis says that the number of unemployed has reached 700, and that between 180 and 200 of those who finish the army each year cannot find work and are forced to leave the town. He blames the government bureaucracy which gives preference to the colonisation of the West Bank. He adds that industry in the area is deteriorating, the plastics factory has shut down, the Venezia Factory is in an unsettled state, the Ackerstein tobacco factory is in danger of having to close, and sales are slow at the Negev Ceramics and Tamruqé Leggis factories. Al-Muqayyis had received members of the unemployment committee and discussed the possibility of staging demonstrations in front of the Knesset. Asi Armah, leader of the popular protest in the town, said that the unemployment crisis started two years ago. I would add to that 28 years of economic stagnation.

On 30 March 1986 the *Ha'aretz* wrote that Minister of Absorption, Ya'akov Tsur, had developed a programme to absorb Ashkenazim from South Africa whereby each family was to receive a $40,000 mortgage. Avraham Asis abjured this policy in his letter to the newspaper, and asked 'What about the unemployed in Yeruham?' In his letter published in *Zu Haderekh* on 26 March 1986, Sammy Harush states that he is married with two children. His family came from Morocco and he is a driver of heavy machinery, but that he has been dismissed four times. Then he wonders where the Histadrut is and why it does not stand up for him. He concludes that the whole of the government apparatus, from top to bottom, is built on lies.

In April 1986, the protest movement of the Sephardim in Yeruham reached its zenith, particularly in Tel Aviv and Jerusalem. Charlie Biton travelled to Yeruham and took part in the Sephardim's demonstrations there and gave a speech in which he said 'We must stir up the government, and work against it with means stronger than the Black Panthers.' He condemned the channelling of the state budget towards the Ashkenazi settlements which are colonizing the occupied West Bank. He appealed to the inhabitants of development towns to shut down their towns, to block off the roads and to march on Jerusalem so that the government would not be able to ignore their existence.[6] The residents of Yeruham sent 36 local leaders to demonstrate in Tel Aviv and Jerusalem and they staged a general strike in the town. Then the strikes spread until they included development towns in the north and south, who struck for two hours in solidarity with the residents of Yeruham. Mordechai Artzieli, a correspondent of *Ha'aretz*, wrote in his report on the protest movement that there had been 35,000 residents in this town, but that there were now only 6,200 left. 1,000 people were leaving every year. University students from Yeruham are ashamed to admit where they come from, and army officers serving in the area refuse to settle there. He concluded that 'Yeruham has no future, and there is no hope that it may have a future.'[7]

David Mesiqi, Secretary of the Trade Unions in the town said, 'The government has decreased the apparatus of local government throughout the country by 3 percent. But in Yeruham 25 percent of local government employees have been dismissed.'[8] The aim of these dismissals was to avoid having to lay off Ashkenazim in the large towns. In the protest movement of 1985, many residents of this town called for separation from Israel.[9]

In his conversation with T. Dekel,[10] Mayor B. al-Muqayyis demanded the return of the occupied territories to their owners. He opposed the occupation of the Syrian Golan Heights, and the attempts at occupying Beirut. He supported an international conference to find a permanent solution to the strife. Al-Muqayyis is from Morocco. He studied economics at Bar Ilan University, and is currently a member of the central committee of the Labour Party. He was troubled when he saw the arrogance of the occupiers in Gaza after the Six Day War of 1967, and how they intimidated Arab business owners into selling at low prices. 'I felt like dreadful,' he said. Al-Muqayyis said that in spite of Israel's victories, it will always lose. 'We must understand that the correct way forward is through negotiations, and we must not keep looking backwards. The crux is that we must love life and people.' Al-Muqayyis objected to the common opinion that Arab women are not affected by the death of one of their sons, because they have many others. Al-Muqayyis supported the principle of compromise and coexistence with the Palestinian Arab people. He suggested that the Jewish masses need to be appraised of the fact that the Palestinian people must be respected. Al-Muqayyis said that 85 percent of the residents of his town voted for Likud, but when he discussed the matter with them, they were convinced of the correctness of a policy of peace. Then it turned out that they do not support Labour, not because of its left-wing views, but because it is an anti-Sephardi party of Ashkenazim. Al-Muqayyis said that even though his family was right-wing, his father always spoke about the good relations they had with Arabs (in Morocco). He added that from a young age he learnt to confront the sectarian problem, his colour, his Arab name and his second class citizenship. The Sephardim were cannon-fodder, proletarianised and subjected to attacks for being religious. Since becoming active in the 'Oded' campaign (see chapter ten), he believes in positive action and severely criticises Ashkenazi religious fanaticism imported from Eastern Europe. He calls for a return to the 1948 borders, the opening of Israel's borders with the Arab world, the dismantling of barriers, peaceful coexistence and religious tolerance.

DIMONAH

Founded in 1955 to absorb Moroccans. Mordechai Artzieli's article in *Ha'aretz* on 19 September 1980 states that these Moroccans were taken off the ship and put into two trucks. They were told that they were being taken on a half-hour journey from Haifa to a new town. The trucks did not stop for eight hours. When they arrived at the spot in the Negev desert they were greeted by a fierce sand storm. They could see no houses there, and refused to get down from the trucks. After a sharp dispute they got out and were housed in simple huts with iron beds, cheap blankets and straw mattresses. The huts had no water or electricity, and there were primitive outdoor toilets. They lived in those huts until they managed to build their own flats with a floor area of 48m². Teenagers were conscripted immediately. The 30,000 inhabitants of Dimonah suffered from abject poverty. Their dreadful houses were like uniform cement boxes. The quality of life was the very lowest with filth piling up everywhere. The town suffered from chronic and violent juvenile delinquency involving recently the use of hand grenades. The youth of the town has no social or vocational opportunities, since work in the textile mills is just about the only work in the town. Most of the youth are unemployed.

In its edition of 24 February 1980, *The Jerusalem Post* wrote that the monthly wage at the Kitan Textile Factory was between £41 and £80 sterling, the lowest wages in Israel. The standard of education is also very poor due to a lack of continuity among the teaching staff. *Ha'aretz* wrote that conditions in Dimonah a considered to be better that those prevailing in other development towns such as Yeruham and Mitzpeh Ramon. Dimonah is termed as a 'jewel among the development towns', and the article concludes that Dimonah represents the failure of the state in this sphere.

On 1 January 1982, David Oren published an article in *Ha'aretz* about the family of Pinhas Albaz who live in Dimonah. The following is a summary:

Pinhas left school nearly-illiterate at the age of eleven. His family had come from Casablanca, where his father worked in a lottery office. They were quite well-off. In Dimonah they have undergone many hardships. His father dislikes the prevailing social relations in the town, such as permissiveness and rudeness, the neglect of traditional values and the lack of respect for parents and elders. He also dislikes the overcrowded living conditions, and the isolation and the alienation of a remote development town. He complains about his livelihood – the fact that in order to earn a living he has to work as a labourer by day and a guard by night. His son Pinhas says that he left school because the teachers did not care about him. He would play truant, but the authorities paid no attention. Finally he left school to help his poor family. His brother was sent to a religious school to reduce the number of mouths in the house. His older sister was sent out to work, whereas his second sister stayed at home to help out with the housework. His third sister went to school. After a while his older sister turned to prostitution. The father was overcome with despair and took to drink until he was killed in a car accident. At that time Pinhas started to believe that the ruling establishment was Ashkenazi and that Moroccans were considered an inferior race. He thought that Ashkenazi Jews passed their time in the cafes on the beach in Tel Aviv and that they were destroying the Moroccans who lived in the slums of Dimonah deprived of everything except dirt and sand. In his eyes and the eyes of his friends, Dimonah was nothing more than a graveyard in the middle of nowhere, with no future. Pinhas said that the waves of Sephardi resistance had not yet started. Then he stated unambiguously 'I hate the state of Israel, I hate the army. I hate them all. When I get out of the army I am going to leave the country. I hate the Ashkenazim and don't wish to talk to them. I have read what Shlomo Tsadok wrote about Sephardi armed struggle against the Ashkenazim, and I am with him. There are thousands of kids like me.'[11] When he was fifteen, Shlomo was sent to a religious school in Britain, but he left it and stayed in London in the hope of avoiding army service. He continued, 'We used to poke fun at the Sephardim who were conscripted. We'd ask them "Why? What has the state of Israel done for you?" Moreover, I felt no compulsion to sacrifice myself for this state, because I didn't feel part of it.' Pinhas stayed in London for four years and no one ever asked him whether he was Ashkenazi or Moroccan. When his visa expired, he had to go back and join the army. Since the army could not make use of him because he was illiterate, the military authorities started teaching him to read and write. His little brother has already become a delinquent.

David Oren, the author of the article, asked David Burkan, the local social work inspector, about the fate of young people like Pinhas. The inspector replied that the state has failed to make 'those people' citizens, due to bad education, the lack of relations between them and the social workers, the arrogance of civil servants and their feelings of racial superiority toward Sephardim.

I do not know what happened to Pinhas after that article appeared. However I do know that kids like him get killed during their military service, or end up doing long sentences in military jails, then they return to civilian life with no jobs.

By 1984 the local council's debts in Dimonah had reached 290 million shekels. As for the youngsters who managed to attain higher education, the mayor remarked 'How can I ask university graduates to come and work in textile factories when members of the Ashkenazi settlement, Ma'aleh Adumim, in the occupied lands, work with computers?' Most of the inhabitants vote for Likud as a protest against what happened to them under Labour Party rule.[12]

Yosef Alghazi wrote in an article in *Zu Haderekh*[13] that unemployment and despair have made the inhabitants turn to drink and other intoxicants. There were seven alcohol-related deaths in 1985 alone.

SHDEROT

The most important projects employing the inhabitants of this town are the Sha'ar Hanegev Projects which are owned by the neighbouring kibbutzim. Due to burgeoning unemployment, the employees of the 'Of Kur' factory have had to relinquish some of their rights and to work a four-day week[14]. Overtime pay has been reduced from 131-157 percent to 125-150 percent, and wages have gone down 25 percent. Moreover, wages have gone down in real terms too because of inflation. As a result of all this, the workers resorted to a strike and won a five-day week. There are approximately 170 workers in this factory, most of whom live in Shderot or the Gaza Strip. Woman are 60 percent of the work force, and most of the workers have between three and five children. The afore-mentioned newspaper article stated that their wages do not suffice for their bare necessities and are spent before the end of the month. Unemployment and resentment are destroying the residents' morale.

The secretary of the Workers' Committee described Shderot as 'a black town in the United States' at the turn of the century. He said that there was now between 16 percent and 20 percent unemployment amongst heads of large families. There are 2700 heads of family, out of whom 1070 are out of work, and the young people who leave the town to study elsewhere do not return.

OFAKIM AND NETIVOT

These two towns are in the Negev. They depend on the low-paying textile industry. The industrial project there is called 'Keshet' and the residents live under threat of dismissal and unemployment.[15]

On 9 January 1981 *Ha'aretz* reported that the OP-AR factory in Ofakim would shortly shut down. That meant that 460 workers would be laid off. The workers thus flocked to Jerusalem to demonstrate in front of the Knesset. Ofakim was founded in the fifties and settled by Moroccan immigrants. Residents of both towns were used by the neighbouring Ashkenazi settlements as a pool of unskilled labour. By 1981 50 percent of the inhabitants were working in the textile industry, but this then went down to 20 percent because Palestinians from the Gaza Strip were employed. In spite of the abject poverty prevailing in the Ofakim, housing is more expensive than in the old-rich settlement of Rehovot, where a flat costs 270,000 shekels. The same costs 320,000 shekels in Ofakim. For the same reasons as in other development towns, 2500 of the residents voted for Likud, while the Labour Party only got 1200 votes.[16]

Netivot has chronic unemployment, and protest has become fiercer.[17] Demonstrations took place throughout 1985 as the number of unemployed reached 300. Yosef Eno, head of the local council, and Yosef Shawqi, one of the trade union stewards, warned that unemployment was endemic. Hesqel Yegna, the town's trade union chief, demanded that more money be invested in the town, and not in the occupied territories. The mayor of Beer Sheba, Eliahu Nawi, demanded the transfer of factories to the Negev.[18] A. Dahhan from Ofakim stated to a reporter from

Ha'aretz[19] that 'this place is shit. Stay until dark and you will see that everything is dead.' A. Vaqnin said that 'Ofakim is a graveyard for the living.' Then Dahhan added 'The whole place is falling apart.'

During the sixties, the OP-AR Textile factory employed more than 600 people. This was then cut back to 460, and at the beginning of the eighties it was further pared down to 380. Currently it only employs 160 workers. At the end of May 1986 workers were not paid. They went on strike and demonstrated. Then they went and demonstrated in front of the Knesset in Jerusalem. Had they not received loans from the Histadrut they would have just been left to starve. The factory owner is an Ashkenazi called Yakobovitz. Abu Qasis, Union Secretary in Ofakim, stated that during 1985 three factories shut down, raising the number of unemployed to 220. During the coming month 60 young people just out of the army would swell their ranks. There are also 330 people who have only seasonal work.

At present Ofakim has 14,000 inhabitants. It was founded along with Shderot and Netivot in the northern Negev, on the Beer Sheba-Ashkelon axis. Unemployment causes most of the young people to leave the town.[20]

When the government announced that it was authorizing millions of dollars to establish six new settlements in the occupied territories, the head of the local council expressed his abhorrence for this policy and said that those who demand the establishment of settlements on the West Bank are the people who are causing unemployment in the development towns. He added that during the last six years 625 people have been laid off, and new jobs have only been found for 214 of them.[21]

MITZPEH RAMON

This town too lies in the Negev, 85 kilometres from Beer Sheba. The planners wanted to settle 5,000 people here over the first five years, 25,000 within twenty years and then 50,000 within 30 years. The residents who settled there in 1955 were told that the economy of the town would be based on the natural resources found in the area of Ramon, and that it would become a centre for all the settlements of the area. The inhabitants suffered from a lack of water, which had to be trucked in. There was not a single doctor, nurse, teacher or shop. They were provided with no municipal services for a number of months. Thus, before the end of the first year, most of the residents fled from the town.[22] The ruling establishment then shipped in more immigrants and settled them in the empty residential units, but after a while these newcomers fled too. By the end of the ninth year the number of flats was just 800, half of which were empty. The lack of any means of earning a living pushed the residents into staging fierce demonstrations during which they raised black banners and closed down the main highway to Eilat.

At the beginning of 1986 the town had 3,800 inhabitants, but nine months later there were only 2,000. There are 1,600 residential units in the town, out of which 1,100 are standing empty, including 400 new units. The number of school pupils has gone down from 1,200 to 650 over the last three years. At the beginning of the 85/86 school year the secondary school lost 20 percent of its students. The dentist left town, leaving behind a general practitioner and a pediatrician. Most of the shops have been boarded up since their owners went away. After nightfall Mitzpeh Ramon is like a ghost town where fear descends on the streets. Most of the towns industrial concerns have shut down, and a large proportion of the owners and workers in the remaining small businesses live outside the town. Tension and anger are the prevailing emotions of the residents who have formed the 'leadership of the struggle' and have come up with the following points for action:
1. Close off the town and the roads leading to it.

3. Demonstrate in Jerusalem.
4. Hunger and work strike.
5. Occupy the empty houses in the town which belong to the Ministry of Housing.
6. Demolish the empty houses in the town.
7. Demand reparations comparable to those paid to the Ashkenazi residents of Yamit.[23] (Yamit was an Ashkenazi settlement in the Egyptian occupied territory.)

UPPER YOKNA'AM

Founded in 1950. By 1980 it had 5,500 inhabitants, 70 percent of whom were working in the Saltam factory. The town, which lies in the Haifa area, does not have an ambulance, a fire-engine, a street-cleaning machine or a constabulary to protect the residents from the gangs which have arisen in the slum districts. There is no cinema or coffee shop, and just one pharmacy which opened in 1980. The residents depend on the neighbouring Ashkenazi settlement of Tiv'on for all these services.

In the vicinity of the town there is a small Ashkenazi settlement, with 450 people, which controls Upper Yokna'am. It is called 'Upper' to 'throw the enemy off', as they say in the Israeli army. The Ashkenazi settlers treat the Sephardim from Yokna'am with arrogance and naturally there is animosity between the communities. After the Iranian Revolution, the Saltam factory lost one of its export markets and had to lay off workers. The number of unemployed rose to 400 in 1980.[24] Since then unemployment has risen further, and resentment has grown. The annual turnover of the Saltam factory, the only one in the town, has dropped from $150 million to $50 million . The secretary of the trade union who issued these figures, Rafael Toledano, added that 500 workers had been laid off over the previous four months, and that according to management plans 300 others were about to be laid off.[25]

BETH SHEMESH

This town lies in the district of Bab al-Wad, on the Jerusalem road. It was founded in 1948 as a transit camp for Moroccans. By 1981 it had 13,000 inhabitants. People there still recall in anger how the Israeli establishment degraded those who had been members of the middle class in their country of origin, and how privileges helped Ashkenazi Jews raise their own station. The residents of Beth Shemesh also point out that the neighbouring Ashkenazi kibbutzim refuse to build schools where their children can all study together. They say that 'the Ashkenazim come to our town once every four years to try and get our vote in the elections.' Economic conditions do not differ from those in other development towns – unemployment, housing problems, bad housing stock etc.

These are the reasons why the ruling Labour Party, the party of the neighbouring Ashkenazi settlements, lost its majority in 1977. In 1981 Likud won 56 percent of the votes, whereas the Labour vote went down from 35 percent to 22 percent.

On 28 May 1981, members of Likud managed to break up a Labour Party meeting and throw Shimon Peres, the party leader, out of town. Peres fled under a barrage of tomatoes and stones. The immediate reason for the flare up of emotions against the Labour Party was the fact that some Labour Party leaders had made racist statements, such as Motti Gur who said 'We'll screw the Sephardim like we screw the Arabs.'[26] The Sephardim of Beth Shemesh shouted at Peres and his comrades, 'We don't want you here, you fucking Ashkenazim, go back to Tel Aviv!' Then they shouted, 'Arafat – Arafat – Arafat!' and others shouted, 'Begin – Begin – Begin!'

Since the Labour Party represents the nucleus of Ashkenazi Zionist establishment, many Sephardim believe that Begin and his party offer the only means of breaking this establishment. Residents of the town state that it was the Labour Party which ruled all aspects of life before 1978 and which gave preference to Ashkenazim in everything and considered them 'Israelis' while terming Sephardim 'the Oriental sects' and 'primitives' and had forced them to give up their cultural identity. The leader of the Labour Party had deemed them 'human refuse' whose culture needed to be forgotten Ben Gurion claimed that 'they do not have their own language, but speak jargon.'[27]

Amos Elon who had a dialogue with them, added that some of the Sephardim could join the Zionist establishment by copying their Ashkenazi masters and by conforming to establishment structure.[28] When this Ashkenazi reporter was asked by Patrick Seale about this problem, he denied the existence of anti-Sephardi discrimination and described those who write on this subject as 'fringe' (British TV, 1989; see his report on Kiryat Shemonah).

The motor works, which is the biggest factory in town, faced serious financial problems, causing 600 workers to be laid off. If the factory were to shut, the whole town would shut down too. The secretary of the workers council, Hayyim Harush, said that those laid off had already gone through their redundancy pay and were now just hanging around the streets. All the workers committees had thus got together and formed one committee. The secretary of this new committee, S. Cohen, said that 'The erosion of wages is causing much resentment, and strikes will spread like wildfire.' It is worth mentioning that, at the start, the town's residents believed that the motor factory would teach their children advanced technology and that they would stay in the town. However, it turned out that the overwhelming majority of the engineers were Ashkenazim from out of town.[29]

BET SHE'AN

By 1985 this town had almost 13,000 inhabitants. Due to economic clashes between the town's residents and their employers from Ashkenazi kibbutzim, most of the residents voted Likud. Their local leader, David Levy, rode this wave of discontent to reach the leadership of the Herut Party and the Likud Bloc. Voting for the right, however, does not benefit the residents, and most of the factories have shut down causing wide unemployment here also.[30] A third of Likud supporters have therefore decided not to vote for it again.

Most of the town's inhabitants work in the textile or food-processing industries, which are notorious for paying low wages. They suffer from abysmal social and health services. Labour Party leaders came here and gave enthusiastic speeches, except that the locals refused to listen. 'Suddenly a woman grabbed the microphone and shouted, "We don't want political parties, we want decent wages."'[31] The correspondent for *Ha'aretz* indicated that the residents were fed up both with the politicians ruling from Jerusalem and the state. Benny, a driver at the Eyn Harod Cooperative Co., told the journalist, 'This country is worse than a ghetto!' Another man told him, 'This ghetto ought to be shut down!' A third said, 'It's time to close down this whole shitty state', to the agreement of all present. The journalist, R. Prester, concludes 'At this calm general meeting there was something ominous and discomforting. In spite of that, the peoples' comments were more convincing than the pronouncements of the Party leaders at the microphone.'[32]

In another article, by N. Barnir,[33] we see that 800 people, or 20 percent of the working population, is out of work. One of the workers says that he does not participate in the demonstrations lest he lose his job, and that he cannot express his opinions because he is deprived of his rights. 'We work like robots, and they despise us and treat us as if we were worthless.' There was an American industrialist in the town called Julius Ber. He invested government funds in his factory, exploited cheap local labour and then disappeared. While he was still around, he treated the Sephardi and Palestinian workers harshly, firing them if there was a disagreement, subjecting them to humiliation and intimidation.

Now the local council is threatening to close the town and to stop providing general services.[34]

Dr Swirski of the University of Haifa carried out a dialogue with some of the residents of Bet She'an, and I shall give here an abridgement of it, leaving out those portions which repeat the views of the resident of Kiryat Shemonah.

H: (Vis-à-vis the middle-aged men who had just been laid off) If the Trade Union council were made up of Likud people, it would be able to fight for them with the kibbutzim which belong to the Labour Party and own the industries in the area. If the town were to expand and need more land, it would definitely have to confront the kibbutzim then, since they monopolise all the lands around the town.

S: If they develop 'Upper Bet She'an' for the Ashkenazim, then the Sephardi part of town will be 'Lower Bet She'an' (this is a reference to Nazareth where Israel has constructed 'Upper Nazareth' for the Ashkenazim).

H: The kibbutzim don't invest a single pound in industrial projects to employ Sephardim. But they do invest their profits from government hand-outs on the stock exchange and in other projects. Everything for the future is planned along party lines. Why don't they combine our schools with the kibbutz schools?

Z: Because the kibbutz kids hate our children.

D: Why is it preferable to combine the schools?

H: Because educational opportunities are better in their schools.

Z: Educating our children in the kibbutz schools would mean taking our children out of their own environment and placing them in an environment which is supposedly more developed. When our children come back home after they finish their studies, they'll face the same problems, but their sense of alienation will be more acute.

H: 99 percent of the Sephardi children who do study on the kibbutzim don't come back to us.

S: Educating Sephardi children in kibbutz schools just creates schizophrenic children, who are not accepted by the Ashkenazim but have assimilated so much of their culture that they cannot go back to Sephardi society.

M: I lived in Kiryat Shemonah. I and some other families managed to send our children to the school at Kibbutz Dafna, but the children remain segregated. One time they had a field trip, but the school refused to provide lunch for our children. This was only made clear to the kids during the trip. The kibbutz provided food for its own children, but ours went hungry during the trip. After that the kids from Kiryat Shemonah did not go on any other field trips. My son won't take part in any of the student clubs or societies, since he has come up against numerous problems which have scarred him emotionally.

R: They have turned these towns into Sephardi ghettoes. In Bet She'an for example, 85 percent of the town consists of Moroccans. That's a mistake. The government gives preferential treatment to Ashkenazi teachers to come from out of town, but after a short while they leave again.

V: It's a transit camp here.

Z: What happens to a teacher who has been brought up here?

S: The poor wretch!

MY: They help the teachers who come from outside, but they don't help local teachers. It's our fault because we don't fight it. When we do fight, we come up against government repression.

M: Why don't you revolt?

H: Because council members are working for the ruling party, it's in their own interest.

M: Why don't you oppose them?

H: We had a popular uprising in 1957/58. We smashed everything up and cried 'Bread and Work'. But the uprising was forcibly put down. The police arrested some of the demonstrators and threw them into prison. Then they were run out of town. The leaders of the town took bribes.

MY: We'll succeed, if everyone takes part in a revolt, like Wadi al-Salib.

Z: We won't be able to organize that!

H: We have to set up political groups in the development towns, the Black Belt and the large towns . . . the inhabitants of the development towns voted for Begin, to improve their situation. But that hasn't happened, and the new leader ought to be one of us, not Begin or Katz . . .

H: The government has treated us with contempt. It erected a textile factory to employ 700 people and placate the seething resentment. But the young leave the town, leaving behind just the old folk. Over the last seven to nine years the population has gone down from 12-14,000 to 12,700. What has happened to natural increase? Every year between 250 and 300 people get out of the army, and there is no work for them. The settlements managed to grab all the economic programmes, thanks to their members who are in the central government, the agricultural administration or Hamashbir (the Histadrut stores), and so forth. That's how they are effective. We don't have that power. Even though the programmes were aimed at helping places like Bet She'an, they built a factory on Kibbutz Mesillot, and at Bet She'an's expense they got allowances, loans and grants as well as vocational training programmes.

A: Because in the Kibbutz Federation they are united.

N: Take the settlement of Neveh Etan for example. It has built the Plasgon factory. When it was doing well in the first two years, they sent some members to Britain and America for training, at the expense of other settlements.

D: The government has various ways of covering up the losses of the kibbutzim.

H: The kibbutz monopolies are destroying our enterprises. 10-12 years ago, people from our town who worked with heavy machinery set up a cooperative, but it was soon swallowed up by the kibbutzim. Then we set up a truck cooperative, but it was snuffed out by the kibbutz-owned Bet She'an-Harod Company. Why don't we set up our own political and spiritual leadership?

D: People who own the smaller companies, employing up to 25 workers, come from all the communities. But the owners of the large companies which use the latest technology are almost all Ahkenazim. How is it that the Ashkenazim have managed to get ample funding, but we Sephardim have failed? Why do we have more drunkards, prostitutes and alienated youth? And we don't have any ministers, or generals or pilots.

B: And if our children graduate from university, they cannot get a job.

S: We ought to tell the managers who come from out of town that we don't want them. Then we should employ managers from here.

H: Businesses won't accept that.

N: Because we don't encourage our own – the Moroccans.

S: Because they've brainwashed us.

A: The Moroccans don't help each other.

S: Because the state tells you that Moroccans are incapable of running a company?

H: The state and business should adopt the principle of equality of opportunity.

B: We have to define our aims.

N: We ought to set up our own local leadership. Why should we not be able to create a political force through organization?[35]

Finally, we must mention that the development town of Arad does not suffer from any of the afore-mentioned problems, since its inhabitants are Ashkenazim. The government classes it as an 'Ashkenazi settlement' and therefore its economic structure is completely different from that of the Sephardi development towns.[36]

NOTES

1 *Ha'aretz*, 4 September 1981.
2 *Zu Haderekh*, 15 January 1986 and January 22 1986.
3 *Zu Haderekh*, 15 October 1980.
4 *Ha'aretz*, 28 December 1984.
5 *Ha'aretz*, 28 December 1984.
6 *Zu Haderekh*, 2 April 1986.
7 *Ha'aretz*, 4 April 1986.
8 *Zu Haderekh*, 23 July 1986.
9 *Zu Haderekh*, 26 June 1985.
10 *Zu Haderekh*, 4 June 1987.
11 The writings of Shlomo Zadoq appeared in *Yedi'ot Aharonot*.
12 Roman Prester, *Ha'aretz*, 24 August 1984.
13 *Zu Haderekh*, 9 July 1986.
14 *Zu Haderekh*, 15 January 1986.
15 *Ma'ariv*, 25 December 1980.
16 *Ha'aretz*, 27 July 1981.
17 *Ha'aretz*, 28 December 1984.
18 *Zu Haderekh*, 9 January 1985.
19 30 May 1986.
20 Ibid.
21 Al-Ghazi, *Zu Haderekh*, 9 July 1986.
22 M. Artzieli, *Ha'aretz*, 19 September 1986.
23 Ibid.
24 *Ha'aretz*, 7 November 1980.
25 *Zu Haderekh*, 1 July 1987.
26 *Ha'aretz Supplement*, 4 September 1981.
27 Meaning, the different dialects of colloquial Arabic (see chapter eight).
28 *Ha'aretz*, 28 September 1981.
29 *Zu Haderekh*, 2 April 1986.
30 *Ha'aretz*, 21 June 1985.
31 Quoted from an article by Roman Prester in *Ha'aretz*, 21 June 1985.
32 Ibid.
33 *Zu Haderekh*, 24 July 1985.
34 Ibid.
35 Swirski, 1981, 119–138.
36 *Ha'aretz*, 27 June 1980.

APPENDIX IV
MOSHAVIM (COOPERATIVE VILLAGES)

Moshav Porat: By 1980 it had one thousand inhabitants. The fathers, or grandfathers, came from Libya. As the average number of families members was 10, there was an acute housing problem with parents, children and grandchildren living in the same unit. The average total individual annual income was £17 sterling. The moshav has debts of £193,333 sterling. The youth cannot leave the village because they have no vocation and are not able to find accommodation. On 26 September 1980 Ha'aretz reported that the moshav's problems were highly explosive, had caused widespread crime and led to acts of violence to the extent that the Eged bus company was afraid to send its buses to the moshav. Due to a lack of water for irrigation, most of the moshav's orchards have become dry – that is, 1,300 dunums of citrus fruit and 303 dunums of flowers. The primary emotion of the inhabitants is resentment in face of the policy of racial discrimination. At the present time, they have overcome their jealousy of their rich Ashkenazi neighbouring settlements and just want to leave the moshav, but where to? Even though the correspondent of Ha'aretz writes of the despair and misery in the moshav, he is condescending towards them. Asher Kishner claims that 'they are a few centuries behind' because they have preserved some aspects of their Sephardi culture. The title of the article is 'Cave-dwellers dilemma' implying that Sephardim and Arabs still live in caves. A year later a Libyan Jew, Shelmon Kardi, stated to a correspondent of Ha'aretz, Y. Hamizrahi[1] that Libyan Jews had held high positions in the Libyan police, army and government, and that even the Germans and Italians had treated them deferentially.

Moshav Eliakim: This moshav was founded in 1949 for Yemenites. Two years later, when the residents realised that no one had studied the soil and that it was uncultivable, they left the moshav. A few years later Yemenites from Tsemah Camp were taken there. When they found that the land was uncultivable, they went to work as labourers on Ashkenazi settlements. Sara Avraham said that her husband's monthly wage was £120 sterling, and that her children left the moshav because the authorities would not let them stay. She added, 'We would like to be able to farm, but we cannot because of the discrimination against us.' Sa'adya Sirri, a member of the local town council, said that 'the land could be farmed if the farmers were able to get some financial support from the government.' He continued, 'They have money for the settlements in the occupied Arab territories, how come they have none to help us?' Half of the inhabitants of the moshav live on welfare and a third are out of work.[2]

Moshav Avivim: Founded in 1963 to settle Moroccans. By 1982 its debts had reached 15 million shekels. The housing conditions are lamentable. Children are only educated between the ages of 8 and 12. The school has no library or science laboratory and its educational standard is extremely low. Parents cannot afford to pay income tax and the government therefore impounded their telephones, television and furniture. Mounds of foul-smelling garbage surround the houses. The unemployed young people of the moshav hang out in the streets. The village has one nurse and a doctor comes twice a week. As a result of their seething resentment, the inhabitants declared a general strike and were joined by the inhabitants of neighbouring moshavim, such as Shefer, Netoa' and others.[3]

Moshav Zar'it: This village lies on the Lebanese border and is inhabited by 48 families. The greatest cause of resentment is the debt situation and the fact that egg production is limited to just 320 per annum per farmer, whereas the residents wish to produce 550 eggs per annum to pay off their debts which have now reached $2.2 million. On 26 June 1986 *Zu Haderekh* reported that the inhabitants had declared a general strike and locked the gates of the village after the failure of their negotiations with the authorities. They also decided to return their arms to the army and to desist from carrying out reserve duty.

Roman Prester, a correspondent of *Ha'aretz*, accused the Zionist establishment of neglect, particularly with regard to education, in Kiryat Malakhi.[4] He called this moshav 'an angel-less village' making a pun on the name of the village and the Hebrew word for angel (*mal'akh*).

On 6 March 1970 *Ha'aretz* reported that a representative of the BBC in Israel had met Sephardim from the northern moshavim who were suffering from poverty and discrimination. He commented that these Sephardim would probably leave their moshavim and development towns in the north, not because of attacks by members of Fateh, (the largest Palestinian military organisation) but because of the cold-heartedness of the bureaucrats in Tel Aviv.

In his article in *Ha'aretz* on 2 April 1982, David Oren wrote that 'the government does not intend to rescue the moshavim from bankruptcy, but hopes rather to eliminate them and transform them into residential areas.' That means that the lands will be taken from the residents and handed over to private companies which will then employ the residents in various agricultural and industrial projects, thereby removing any differences between the development towns and the moshavim. Five years after this article was published, the parliamentary finance committee recommended eliminating 30–40 moshavim, as David Oren had forecast. The amount owed by the moshavim rose from $550 million in 1985 to $2,000 million in 1987 due to an increase in the interest rate of between 100 percent and 150 percent in the second half of 1985 followed by another 40 percent increase in 1986. Thus, the additional interest due on the loans during 1985/1986 was 600 million shekels ($350 million).[5]

NOTES
1 2 October 1981
2 *Ha'aretz*, 27 November 1981
3 *Zu Haderekh*, 31 March 1982, 24 March 1982
4 6 March 1970
5 A. Shushan, *Zu Haderekh*, 29 July 1987

APPENDIX V
SLUMS

Musrara: One of the slum neighbourhoods of Jerusalem – between the old and new sections of the city. The Black Panther movement started here. Living conditions are as follows:

38 percent of the residents live in crowded conditions, with more than 3 to a room.

58 percent live more than 2 to a room.

58 percent of the dwellings are damp.

31 percent of families have more than 6 children. The family in building number 5 on Prophets Street, for instance, has 8 children living in one and a half rooms.

Out of a class of 25 pupils, only 3 have been accepted at a secondary vocational school. None of them were accepted into an academic secondary school.

19 percent of the youth (12-17 years old) neither studies nor works.

25 percent of the youth does not go into the army (i.e. they refuse to do military service).

39 percent of the men (22-30 years old) are unemployed.

65 percent of children are born to an illiterate mother or father.

25 percent of children have two illiterate parents.

50 percent of adults have had no primary schooling.

We must point out that most of these illiterates were either born or raised in 'progressive' Israel, and not in the 'primitive' Arab states.[1]

In 1982 the authorities built three air-raid shelters, but not a single residential unit.[2] A number of families therefore decided to break the law and challenge the military authorities by squatting in an air-raid shelter.

The authorities are trying to get the residents to leave this strategically important district between the old and new cities of Jerusalem, where there have been amicable contacts between Sephardim and Palestinians from the old city. This is considered to be treasonable by the settlers who want to demolish the district and built a chic Ashkenazi suburb in its place. Charlie Biton, the leader of the Black Panthers, was raised and lives here. He has been accused of holding secret meetings with Abu Jihad in Switzerland and of having a secret Swiss bank account. Thus we see that the authorities, the intelligence agencies and the secret police consider the Moroccans and Iraqis of this district a 'security risk' which must be removed from the heart of the city.

Shelly Ben 'Ami claims that her husband is in prison and that she is homeless. Moreover her son suffers from tracheitis. Many parents, children and grandchildren live together in one-room flats. Orli Idri points out that she lives with her husband and five children in a dilapidated house which they have forcibly occupied. The house is exposed to cold winds, rain and damp since its windows do not close properly. Her children have all caught tracheitis. 24 families were compelled to buy very cheap flats in Ma'aleh Adumim on the occupied West Bank, but they are fighting to return to Musrara because they support Palestinian rights and oppose the occupation and settlement of the West Bank.

In 1967 there were 6,000 residents in Musrara. By 1983 the authorities had managed to remove 3,000 of them. The remainder remain under pressure to evacuate the district completely. The mayor of Jerusalem, Teddy Kollek, said that overcrowding in Jerusalem is four times worse than that in Tel Aviv and that the construction of plush Ashkenazi suburbs could lead to disturbances in Sephardi areas, similar to the Moroccan agitation in Wadi al-Salib in Haifa in 1959.[3]

Shekhunat Ha'argazim (Slum of Boxes) in Tel Aviv: This is one of the slum districts in south Tel Aviv. (The largest slum district is the Hatikvah district, which has 5,000 flats of which 3,000 are 1.5 room flats.[4] In April 1987 there were newspaper reports that crime in these districts had become chronic and was caused by some Palestinians who lived there and worked in Tel Aviv – even though the municipality rejected these claims. Shekhunat Ha'argazim is inhabited by Sephardim who fled the transit camps, the development towns and the moshavim, and as such the municipality refuses to provide services to them. Thus they have no water and electricity and no street or sewer repairs are carried out. The unsanitary conditions are a public danger and crime is rife amongst the disaffected youth.

Ha'aretz reported on 24 October 1980 that the residents were building houses out of empty barrels, wood and tar. The whole area is overrun by armies of rats and the inhabitants are exposed to damp, rain and biting cold. The district is populated by 200 families. When the rain is heavy, the drains overflow. During the summer the drains give off an intolerable odour as well as hosting armies of pestilential insects. The people of this district originally came from the Arab world in 1950. A considerable proportion are now aged and infirm with no one to care for them.

In 1975 the municipality decided to transfer them to other residential areas, and in the framework of this decision 28 families were resettled when the programme came to a halt due to a 'lack of funds'. The municipality then decided to give an emolument to anyone who left the district though the amount offered was not enough to buy another flat.

Not too far away the municipality, in spite of its lack of funds, built the beautiful suburb of Neveh Sharett for Jews from the Soviet Union. This blatant discrimination led to much resentment and anti-Russian violence. Sephardi children took to throwing stones at these beautiful new flats. A large number of the new-arrivals then emigrated to the United States, saying that they did not want to live in a cemetery with those 'black Arabs', meaning the Sephardi Jews.[5]

District 'D' in Tiberias: A report by Gideon Elon in *Ha'aretz* on 3 April 1981 stated that this slum had 12,000 inhabitants, that is, half of the population of Tiberias. The district is noted for its ugly housing, the piles of rubbish everywhere and its remoteness from the rest of the town. Thus many of its residents have fled, leaving behind 233 empty flats. The remaining flats are overcrowded, with an average room occupancy of 2-3 people. The flats are very small, having an area of between 34 and 54m². The biggest flat has a floor area of 64m². They are beset by damp and foul odours. There are between 300-500 families living solely off welfare payments, and 200 families with more than 10 children. There are also hundreds of illiterate women since pupils leave school before the end of their compulsory education. There are scores of children who neither study nor work, and the government sends between 40-50 children every year to special centres for children without parents in Israel.

The head of the Slum Clearance Project, Hayyim Hecht, says that most of the workers in the district work in kibbutz factories in the Jordan Valley. The kibbutz members treat these workers like peasants, using them for the most menial jobs and paying them poor wages. The opportunities for vocational advancement are extremely limited. Over the last few years, the rupture between the 'socialist' bosses and the workers has become acute. He continued that many have taken to drugs and gambling. Crime and mugging are so rampant in the district that it is dangerous for girls to go out alone at night. Gady Ben Porat, Director of the Community Centre, points out the slum revival programme which started after 1979 is purely cosmetic in that it does not deal with the root problems.

In Petah Tikvah, Z. Shasha and his family were reduced to living in the streets, in front of the court building. Both of his children fell ill, and Shasha himself had kidney and respiratory problems. He had been forced to do hard and unaccustomed work as a house-painter. He had also tried to become a Muslim and a Christian and to return to Iraq in protest against Zionist injustice. After the government had put him off for 40 days, he committed suicide by setting himself alight in June 1987. Only then, after an outcry in the media, did the government grant his widow and orphans a rented apartment. Z. Shasha came from a well-known and respectable family in Baghdad – the Bet Shasha family.[6] The middle class background of Mr Shasha and others is to be stressed since Israeli agents are telling the well-off Sephardi community in Britain that all the unfortunate Sephardi Jews in Israel originated from the Baghdad slum Abu Sifen, from the 'caves of Libya', or the 'Atlas Mountains of Morocco.'

NOTES

1 *Ha'aretz*, 15 June 1979 to correspondent Akiva Eldar.
2 *Zu Haderekh*, 9 February 1983.
3 *Ha'aretz*, 6 March 1970.
4 *Ha'aretz*, 15 June 1979.
5 Ibid.
6 Weekly supplement to *Ha'aretz*, 26 June 1987.

Bibliography

Sources of Hebrew Documents mentioned in the notes:

The Minutes of the Knesset
The Archives of the State of Israel
The Archives of the Labour Party (Mapai) of Israel
Zionist Executive Council
Archives of the Defence Force of Israel
Files of the Immigration Department
Central Zionist Archives
Diary of David Ben-Gurion

Hebrew Books:

'Ahad Ha'am, *Kol Kitve 'Ahad Ha'am* (Complete Works), Dvir Publication House, Tel-Aviv, 1947; see essay 'Emeth Me-eretz Yisrael' (The Truth from the Land of Israel), 1891.

Ben-Gurion, David, *Netzah Yisrael* (The Eternity of Israel), 'Ayanot, Tel-Aviv, 1964.

Ben-Menahem, Yitzhak, *'Adam Ve-Lohem* (A Man and a Fighter), 'Ami-Hai publication, 1975.

Ben-Simhon, Gabriel, *Melekh Maroca'i* (A Moroccan King), a play, 'Edi Publications, Tel-Aviv, 1980.

Bernstein, Deborah, *Hasotziologia Kotelet et Ha-'Aliya* (The Sociology of Immigration), Mahbarot Lemehkar Ulevikoret, Booklet No. 1, Haifa, 1978.

– *Ha-ma'abarot Bishnot Ha-Hamishim* (The Transit Camps in the 1950s), Mahbarot Lemehkar Ulevikoret, Booklet No. 5, Haifa, 1980.

Biton, Erez, *Minhah Maroca'it* (A Moroccan Prayer), poetry, Traklin publication, Tel-Aviv, 1979.

Blas, Shim'on, *Ha Ma'barah* (The Transit Camp) a novel, 'Am 'Oved-Sifriyyah La'am publication, Tel-Aviv, 1964.

Chouraqui, A., *Korot Hayehudim Bitzfon Afrika* (The History of the Jews in North Africa), Tel-Aviv, 1975.

Cohen, H.Y., *Ha-pe'ilut ha-tziyonit Be-'Iraq* (Zionist Activity in Iraq), The Zionist Library, Jerusalem, 1969.

– *Ha-Gormim La'Aliya Me'Artzot Asia ve Afrika Bame'ah Ha'Esrim* (The Causes of Immigration from the Countries of Asia and Africa in the Twentieth Century), Jerusalem, 1970.

– *Mekorot Le-Toldot Ha-yehudim Be-'Artzot Ha-Mizrah Ha-Tikhon Be-yamenu* (Sources for the History of the Jews in the the Middle Eastern Countries in Our Time), Jerusalem, 1972.

Druian, Nitsa, *Tzmihatah Ve-Hitpathutah Shel Ha-'Edah Ha-Temanit Be-Eretz Yisrael Bishnot 1882-1914* (The Rise and Development of the Yemenite Community in the Land of Israel 1882-1914), Yad Ben Tzvi, 1980.

Elon, Amos, 'Shevu'ayim Be-Yisrael Ha-Sheniya (A Fortnight in the Second Israel)' in *'Olim Be-Yisrael* (Immigrants in Israel), Ha'aretz publication, Tel-Aviv, 1951.

Eliachar, Eliahu, *Lihyot 'Im Ha-Palistinim* (Life with the Palestinians), The Council of the Sephardi Community, Jerusalem, 1975.

– *Lihyot 'Im Yehudim* (Life with the Jews), Marcus & Co., Jerusalem, 1980.

Gluska, Zekharia, *Lemaan Yehudei Teman* (For the Jews of the Yemen), published by Y.B. Gluska, 1974.

Heffer, 'Aliza, *Ha'ukhlusiya ve Habniya be-Yisrael 1948-1973* (The Population and the Construction Industry in Israel from 1948-1973), Ministry of Housing, Jerusalem, 1975.

Israel, *Statistical Abstract of Israel*, Central Bureau of Statistics 1973, 1980, 1986 inter alia.

Israel, The Bank of Israel, *Changes in trade related wage rates from 1957/8 to 1963/4.*

Israel, Bureau of the Prime Minister, 1968.

Israel, *Industry Past & Future*, Ministry of Trade & Industry, Jerusalem.

Israel, *Duwah shel hava'ada ha-ben misradith leheker matzav ha-ma'barot* (Report of the inter-ministerial committee on the situation in the transit camps), The State Archives, Dept. No.95, c/6161 file no. 242105, 1954.

Jewish Agency, The, *Dappe 'Aliya* (Pages on Immigration) 1950B, Department of Immigration, 1950.

Koren, Yitzhak, *Kibbutz Hagaluyot be-hithavuto* (The Process of the Ingathering), 'Am 'Oved, 1964.

Menahem, Nahum, *Metahim ve-aflaya 'adatit be-yisrael* (Tension and Ethnic Discrimination in Israel) Rubin, Ramat-Gan, Israel, 1983.

Mikhael, Sami, *Shavim ve-shavim yoter* (Equal and More Equal), a novel, Bustan Publications. 1976.

Namir, M., *Mul Pene hama'barot* (Facing the Transit Camps), Otpaz, Tel Aviv, 1972.

Nini, Yehuda, 'Reflections on the Destruction of the Third Temple', *Shedemot* (a kibbutz publication), spring 1971.

– *Aliyot yehude teman le-eretz yisrael* (The Immigration of the Yemenite Jews to the Land of Israel) PhD thesis, University of Tel Aviv, 1976.

– *Yahasan shel hibbat Tzion ve-hatenuah hatzionit la-'aliya miteman* (The Attitude of Hibbat Zion and the Zionist Movement to the Immigration from the Yemen), Jerusalem, 1977.

– *Ole Teman 1882-1914* (Immigrants from the Yemen 1882-1914), Cathedra, October 1977.

Peres, Yohanan, *Yahase 'edot be-yisrael* (Ethnic Relations in Israel), 1977.

Swirski, Dr Shlomo, *Lo Nehshalim 'ella Menuhshalim* (They are not Backward but Made Backward), Mahbarot lemehkar ulevikoret, Haifa, 1981.

Swirski, Dr Shlomo and D. Bernstein, *Mi 'avad, bameh, 'avur mi, 'utmurat ma? Happituah hakalkali shel yisrael vehithavut hlukat ha'avodah ha'adatit* (Who worked, in what, for whom and for what wage? Economic Development in Israel and the Creation of the Ethnic Division of Labour), Mahbarot lemehkar ulevikoret, No. 4, Haifa, 1980.

Swirski, Dr Shlomo and M. Shushan, *'Ayyarot happituah likrat mahar shoneh* (Development Towns, Towards a Different Future), Yated, Haifa, 1985.

Segev, Tom, *1949 Hayisraelim harishonim* (1949 The First Israelis), Domino Press, Jerusalem, 1984.

Shtal, A, *Metahim ben 'adatiyim be-yisrael* (Ethnic Tension in Israel), Ministry of Education, Jerusalem, 1980.

Hebrew Periodicals mentioned in the notes:

Hamizrah hehadash, 1950-1981.
Megamot, No 20 (1974) and July 1957 (Dr Moshe Smilansky).
Molad, Issue no. 12.
Pe'amim, Issue no. 1 (1979) and no. 8 (1981).
Shevet va-'am, issues: 1954, 1958, 1959, 1960, 1970.

Hebrew Newspapers mentioned in the notes:

'Al-Hamishmar
Ha'aretz
Hadashot
Ha'olam Hazze
Ma'ariv
Yedi'ot Aharonot
Zu Haderekh

Arabic Books, Periodicals and Documents:

Abu Mazin, M.A., *Mulahazat hawl hijrat yahud al-'iraq* (Comments on the Emigration of the Iraqi Jews), Al-Tali'ah, Cairo, July 1976.

Al-Rawi, *'Usbat mukafahat al-sahyuniyya* (The Anti-Zionist League), Centre of Palestinian Studies, Baghdad University, 1978.

Al-A'zami, Walid Muhammad Sa'id, *Intifadat Rashid 'Ali Al-Gaylani*, Baghdad, 1986.

Al-Qashtini, Khalid, *Al-Judhr al-tarikhiyyah li-'l-'unsuriyyah al-sahyuniyyah* (The Historical Roots of Zionist Racism), Beirut, 1981.

'Abd Al-Rahmin, "Awdat al-yahud, al-mas'alah wa-'l-hulul' (The Return of the Jews – The Problem and the Solutions) in *Shu'un filastiniyyah* No. 59, 1986.

Bar Mashi, I., *Al-khuruj min al-'iraq* (The Exodus from Iraq), published by the Council of the Sephardi Community, Jerusalem, 1975.

Fahmi, *Sumum al-af'a al-sahyuniyyah* (The Poison of the Zionist Snake), Baghdad, 1952.

Hageniza of Cairo, A collection of thousands of Jewish documents, discovered in a Cairo synagogue at the end of the 19th century.

Mu'allim, 'Izzat Sasson, *'Ala Difaf al-furat* (On the Banks of the Euphrates), Dar Al-Mashriq, Shafa 'Amr, Israel, 1980.

Muhammad Ibn Ishaq, *Sirat rasul Allah* (Biography of God's Messenger) in *Sirat ibn Hisham* (8th Century).

Muharib, A., 'Al-hijrah al-yamaniyyah wa-'l-'amal al-'ibri', (The Yemenite Immigration and Hebrew Labour) in *Shu'un filastiniyyah*, August 1973.

Qujman, Y., *Al-musiqa al-fanniyyah al-mu'asira fi al-'iraq* (The Art of Contemporary Music In Iraq), Act, London, 1978.

Segev, Tom, *1949 - Al-isra'iliyyun al-awa'il* (1949 – The First Israelis), Translation from Hebrew, Institute for Palestinian Studies, Beirut, 1986.

Sa'ad, *Al-hijrah al-yamaniyyah ila filastin* (The Yemenite Emigration to Palestine). Institute for Palestine Studies, Beirut, 1969.

Sartre, Jean Paul, *Les Temps Modernes*, a special issue on Sephardi Jews in Israel, translated into Arabic by Fu'ad Jadid as *Isra'il al-thaniya* (The Second Israel), Publications of Occupied Palestine, 1981.

Tikriti, *'Usbat mukafahat al-sahyuniyya* (The Anti-Zionist League), Centre of Palestinian Studies, Baghdad University, 1978.

Yasin, *'Usbat mukafahat al-sahyuniyya* (The Anti-Zionist League), Shu'un filastiniyyah, No. 15, November 1972.

Zilkha, Y., *Al-Sahyuniyya 'aduwat al-'arab wa-'l-yahud* (Zionism is the Enemy of Arabs and Jews), Baghdad, 1946.

English Books, Periodicals and Documents:

Abd al-Muhsin, K., *The Political Career of Muhammed Ja'far*, Abu Altimman 1908-1937, SOAS, London University 1983.

Adler, Marcus, *The Itinerary of Benjamin of Tudela*, London, 1907.

Amikam, Michael, Letters, *New Statesman*, 21 March 1980 and 25 July 1980.

Baron, Salo W., *A Social and Religious History of the Jews*, New York, 1952 and 1957.

Batatu, H., *The Old Social Classes and the Revolutionary Movement in Iraq*, Princeton University Press, 1978.

Bein, Alex, *The Return to the Land. A History of Jewish Settlement in Israel*, The Youth and Hechalutz Department of the Zionist Organisation, Jerusalem, 1952.

Ben-Yoseph, A., Letter, *The Guardian*, 4 June 1979.

Berger, E., *Who Knows Better Must Say So*, American Council for Judaism, New York, 1955.

Brenner, Lenni, *Zionism in the Age of Dictators*, Croom Helm, London, 1983.

British Foreign Office Documents: included in the notes.

Chouraqui, A., *A History of the Jews of North Africa*, Philadelphia, 1968.

Cohen, A., *Israel and the Arab World*, W.H. Allen, London, 1970.

Cohen, H.J., *The Anti-Jewish Farhud in Baghdad in 1941*, Middle Eastern Studies, Vol. 3, October 1966.

Cohen, H.J., *The Jews of the Middle East, 1860-1972*, Israel University Press. Jerusalem, 1973.

Davis, Uri, *Israel: Utopia Incorporated*, Zed, London, 1977 (Chapter 3).

Eliyahu, Ezra ben-Hakham, 'Israel's Sephardic Jews', *Middle East International*, March 1978.

Eskandarany, Y.J., 'Egyptian Jewry - Why It Declined', *Khamsin* 5, 1978, Pluto Press.

Ezra, Habibah, Letter to *Outwrite*, July, 1983.

Fichel, W.J., *Jew's in the Economic and Political Life of Medieval Islam*, London, 1937.

Gaon, N., *Jerusalem Post*, 9 October 1980.

Giladi, G., Letter in *Guardian*, 5 August 1985.

Goitein, S.D., *Jews and Arabs*, Schocken Books. New York, 1976.

Hillel, Shlomo, *Operation Babylon*, Fontana, 1989.

Hirst, David, 'Disillusioned Jews Flock Back to Morocco', *Guardian*, 2 October 1979.

Hirst, David, *The Gun and The Olive Branch*, Futura, 1978.

Hoder, A., *Russian Jews, Black Jews and Non-Jewish Jews*, ISRACA No 5. January 1973. Agitprop Bookshop, London.

International Herald Tribune, 'Increasing Violence In Israeli Election Blamed on Ethnic Hostility', 19 June 1981.

Kadourie, Naim, Letters in *Tribune* (London), 21 August 1981, 14 May 1982 and 17 August 1984.

Kedourie, Elie, *The Chatham House Version and Other Middle Eastern Studies*, Weidenfeld and Nicholson. London, 1970.

Kedourie, Eli, 'The Jews of Baghdad in 1910', *Middle Eastern Studies*, Vol. 7, No. 3, October 1971.

Kimche, Jon and David, *The Secret Roads*, Hyperion Press, 1976.

Labour Review, *How the Zionists Have Fought Peace*, London, July 1982. Zionist Anti-Semitism, 1978.

Landau, M.J., *Jews in Nineteenth Century Egypt*, New York University Press, 1969.

Landshut, S., 'Jewish Communities of the Middle East', *Jewish Chronicle*, 1950. London.

Lewis, Bernard, *The Jews of Islam*, RKP, London, 1984.

Lissak, M., *Social Mobility in Israeli Society*, University Press, Jerusalem, 1969.

Noah, M., *Travels in Europe and Africa*, New York. 1819.

Quiros, F.T.B de, *The Spanish Jews*, translated from the Spanish by J.I. Palmer, Madrid, 1972.

Rejwan, N., *The Jews of Iraq*, Weidenfeld & Nicholson, London, 1985.

Roth, Cecil, *A Bird's Eye View of Jewish History*, Cincinnati, 1935.

Sassoon, David S., *A History of the Jews in Baghdad*, Letchworth, 1949.

– 'The History of the Jews of Basra', *Jewish Quarterly Review*, N.S., vol. 17, pp 407-469.

Schechtman, J.B., *On the Wings of Eagles*, New York, 1961.

Shama, A., *Immigration Without Integration*, Sohenman, Cambridge, Mass., 1977.

Shapiro, R., 'Zionism and its Oriental Subjects' *Khamsin* 5, Pluto Press, 1978.

Shemesh, K., 'The Origin and Development of Israel's Black Panther Movement' in *Israel and the Palestinians*, Ithaca, London, 1975.

– *Documents from Israel, 1967-73*, Ithaca, London, 1975.

Shiblak, Abbas, *The Lure of Zion. The Case of the Iraqi Jews*, Alsaqi Books, London, 1986.

Smooha, Sammy, *Israel, Pluralism and Conflict*, R.K.P., 1978.

Twena, A.H. ed., *Dispersion and Liberation*, Vol 5: Jewish Education in Baghdad, Geoula Synagogue Committee, Ramlai, 1975.

Walker, Christopher, *The Times*, 17 June 1980, 5 June 1981 and 22 April 1983.

Woolfson, Marion, *Prophets in Babylon*, Faber & Faber, London, 1980.

Yerubal, J. et al, Letters in *Tribune* (London) from 30 November 1979 to 17 August 1984.

Index

*Medieval Arabic personal names, and those in Hebrew, are listed under their first elements. Modern personal names of Arabs and Jews follow Western style and are arranged on the basis of the equivalents of surnames followed by forenames.